The Automatic Fetish

BEVERLEY BEST works on Marx's critique of political economy and teaches in the department of Sociology and Anthropology at Concordia University, Montreal. She is the Vice-President of the Marxist Literary Group.

The Automatic Fetish

The Law of Value in Marx's *Capital*

Beverley Best

VERSO

London • New York

First published by Verso 2024
© Beverley Best 2024

1 3 5 7 9 10 8 6 4 2

Verso
UK: 6 Meard Street, London W1F 0EG
US: 388 Atlantic Avenue, Brooklyn, NY 11217
versobooks.com

Verso is the imprint of New Left Books

ISBN-13: 978-1-80429-480-2
ISBN-13: 978-1-80429-481-9 (UK EBK)
ISBN-13: 978-1-80429-482-6 (US EBK)

British Library Cataloguing in Publication Data
A catalogue record for this book is available from the British Library

Library of Congress Cataloging-in-Publication Data

Names: Best, Beverley, author.
Title: The automatic fetish : the law of value in marx's capital / Beverley
    Best.
Description: London ; New York : Verso, 2024. | Includes bibliographical
    references and index.
Identifiers: LCCN 2023055299 (print) | LCCN 2023055300 (ebook) | ISBN
    9781804294802 (trade paperback) | ISBN 9781804294826 (ebook)
Subjects: LCSH: Marxian economics. | Capital. | Marx, Karl, 1818-1883.
    Kapital.
Classification: LCC HB97.5 .B3937 2024 (print) | LCC HB97.5 (ebook) | DDC
    335.4/12—dc23/eng/20231229
LC record available at https://lccn.loc.gov/2023055299
LC ebook record available at https://lccn.loc.gov/2023055300

Typeset in Minion by Hewer Text UK Ltd, Edinburgh
Printed and bound by CPI Group (UK) Ltd, Croydon CR0 4YY

Crisis, for us, is no longer a rare state in our movement, but the current state of our movement. Hence those theories that wish to pull us in from the storm. They are all regressive. They coax us back to minimal slopes, to historical curves that are nearly flat. But this would mean returning to the ancient reservoirs, to the general stores of weak circulations. In a word, quitting fire and water to recover air and earth: leaving industry and its energies for agriculture and its slow meta-stabilities. Sailing and tilling. The proposed choice between perpetual movement, impossible without destruction, and a perennial invariance. Materially, either fire or earth. Equilibrium or dynamism.

The new science [of the Commune] escapes the dilemma. Everything is conceived by it as a deviation from equilibrium. It is no longer archaic constancy nor the movement produced by the destruction of equilibria; it is the instance, understood as disparity. This is what life does to elude death temporarily; this is how material substances subsist in spite of degradation. Theory and practice of circumstance, space of renaissance.

Michel Serres, The Birth of Physics

For ordinary perception declares by itself that corpus exists.
Unless trust in perception is firmly founded and flourishes,
in the case of hidden things there will be nothing to which we can refer
to prove anything at all with the reasoning power of the mind
Lucretius, De Rerum Natura, 1.422–5 (trans. Thomas Nail)

Contents

Acknowledgements   ix

Introduction   Unreconstructing Marx: The Perceptual
                Physics of Capital   1

Part I
THE PHYSICS OF CAPITAL AND THE MYSTIFICATION OF
   SURPLUS-VALUE   13

1 Rate of Profit: Production   15
2 General Rate of Profit: Competition   51
3 Falling Rate of Profit: Crisis   91

Part II
SHAPESHIFTING: CAPITAL'S SOCIAL FORMS (WHERE MYSTIFICATION
   OF SURPLUS-VALUE DEEPENS AT THE SURFACE)   135

4 Transformation of Profit I: Commercial Profit   137
5 Transformation of Profit II: Interest   171

6 Transformation of Profit III: Ground-Rent   237

Conclusion   The Revenues and Their Sources:
              The Three Faces of Surplus-Value   323

Index   343

Acknowledgements

Acknowledgements are where we take account of our debts. So, let's make a list! The support and solidarity of many comrades sustained me during the writing of this book and beyond. To these friends – for the day in, day out – I am so fortunate to be indebted: The Chorus (Skye, Leanne and Jackie), Matt & Jen, Anouk & Max, Damian, Marc & Zara, JP, Océane, Homa, Magda, Jess, Sandra & Darren, the Coopers, Karin & Richard. Jen – housemate for the bulk of the writing – thanks for taking the greater share of chores so that I could carry on (and for reminding me when it was time to stop for a glass of wine). r.d., thanks for your guidance on the slow donkey trail of reading. To the darling Changlings in my life, thanks for wanting more than what's on offer so far.

Thank you to all my MLG comrades for being my teachers, now, for many years. In addition to their ideas, I have depended heavily on the solidarity of Courtney Maloney, Ericka Beckman, Bret Benjamin, Paul Stasi, Kanishka Chowdury, Barbara Foley, and Neil Larsen. Rick Gruneau has been my mentor in this work for close to three decades and counting. My wonderful graduate students and the sarcastically named Speculative Cluster keep me honest and hopeful – easily the best part of the job. I am grateful to Colleen Lye, Chris Nealon, Richard Dienst, Werner Bonefeld, Amy De'Ath, Ericka Beckman, Bret Benjamin, Joshua Clover, Nicolas Brown, and Fredric Jameson for reading all or parts of the book in its stages. Sam Chambers helped me write a better book proposal. Charlie Bond and Chelsey Ancliffe worked on the references and index. Comrade Budgen and Jeanne Tao shepherded the book through Verso, and Sam Smith did the fine-tooth combing. Once again, my friend Geoffrey Farmer let me use a photo of his astonishing artwork so that my other friend and artist, Matt Soar, could turn it into a beautiful book cover.

The book is dedicated to two people who will never read it: my mother Joan Best – the life of every party; and my comrade Kevin Floyd, who would have debated it with me at every turn – the greatest joy.

Introduction

Unreconstructing Marx: The Perceptual Physics of Capital

In the social production of their life, men enter into definite relations that are indispensable and independent of their will; these relations of production correspond to a definite stage of development of their material forces of production. The sum total of these relations of production constitutes the economic structure of society – the real foundation, on which rises a legal and political superstructure and to which correspond definite forms of social consciousness. The mode of production of material life determines the social, political and intellectual life process in general. It is not the consciousness of men that determines their being, but, on the contrary, their social being that determines their consciousness.

– Karl Marx

This passage from the preface to Marx's *Contribution to the Critique of Political Economy* is one of the most scrutinized statements in Marx's vast oeuvre. It is also often dismissed as one of Marx's most dogmatic. The opinion, therefore, that there could be nothing more to say about it is understandable, as is the wish that no one *would* say anything more about it. Marx's figure of structure and superstructure (or, more commonly, base/superstructure) has caused havoc among commentators, having been rejected by Marxist, non-, or post-Marxist thinkers alike for whom, for different reasons, the rare use of the metaphor is still one time too many. After the preface, Marx returns only rarely to the base/superstructure metaphor verbatim. However, my argument in this book is that the dynamic it seeks to capture remains at the heart of Marx's critique of political economy, in *Capital*, and in his critical theory of capitalist sociality, tout court.

This book sets out to elaborate this dynamic by following Marx's critique in *Capital* III, step by step, through the material prepared for that volume. What we find is that the question of determinacy is at the heart of the matter throughout and provides the bridge between volumes I, II, and III.[1] In fact, it is precisely what is found objectionable in the preface, namely, the so-called economic determinism of the base/superstructure metaphor that orients and coheres the analysis in *Capital* III – even if we will need to name and characterize it differently than have Marx's reconstructors.

What sort of social dynamic does Marx articulate in this passage? Its animating force, according to Marx, is the social production of material and conscious life, a collective doing and making that inadvertently invents a world – a mode of sociality that excretes an assemblage of objectivities taken to be natural and intractable. This observation begins and ends Marx's description of what is common to all modes of social reproduction, past or present.[2] From here forward, Marx's analysis will submit only one mode of social life – the capitalist assemblage, per se – to the power of abstraction. In the following passage from *Capital* III

---

1 We intentionally follow the order of Marx's draft material, assembled as such posthumously by Engels, in order to grasp the movement Marx seeks to capture in *Capital* III: each step of the analysis builds on, and moves forward from, the step that precedes it. In doing so, each step recalibrates the meaning of the preceding one, just as Marx does in *Capital* I. Engels's ordering of the material is entirely coherent and accomplishes the work that Marx requires of the exposition: Marx's theory of the movement of capital in creating a world in its image is never posited but rather always demonstrated, and the order of the exposition carries the demonstration. On the viability of Engels's assemblage of the draft material for *Capital* III (the mistaken and unfortunate change of title notwithstanding), see Fred Moseley's introduction to the recent republication of the notebook material for *Capital* III: Karl Marx, *The Economic Manuscript of 1864–1865: Capital, Book Three: Forms [Gestaltungen] of the Process as a Whole*, ed. Fred Moseley, trans. Ben Fowkes, Brill, 2015.

2 Marx refers to the activities constituting social reproduction in any formation as 'the labour process,' as described in the section on 'The Labour Process' in chapter seven of *Capital* I. It is a rare category that characterizes a necessity that transcends capital. It points back to formations before capitalist sociality, as well as to worlds that might come after. See Karl Marx, *Capital: A Critique of Political Economy*, vol. 1, trans. Ben Fowkes, Penguin, 1990.

– one that virtually restates the formulation in the preface – Marx pivots between, on the one hand, a capitalist mode of production that shares with every other mode of production (once existing or conceivable) the fact that it emerges contingently from particular historical conditions, and, on the other hand, a capitalist mode of production that represents, once standing on its feet, a departure from every other preceding mode of production. In other words, capital's one commonality with all other modes of social life is its radical historicity, which, in the case of capital, has produced a mode of sociality distinct from any other to date:

> The scientific analysis of the capitalist mode of production proves . . . that this is a mode of production of a particular kind and a specific historical determinacy; that like any other particular mode of production it assumes a given level of social productive forces and of their forms of development as its historical precondition, a condition that is itself the historical result and product of a previous process and from which the new mode of production proceeds as its given foundation; that the relations of production corresponding to this specific and historically determined mode of production – relations into which men enter in their social life-process, in the production of their social life – have a specific, historical and transitory character. (118)[3]

That capital is radically historical is a point on which most readers of Marx agree; we do not need to labour it. Instead, it is the grounds of capital's distinction from preceding modes of production that I want to underscore: according to Marx, capital constitutes a specific mode of historical determinacy. The illustration of that specific-to-capital mode of determinacy is the thrust of Marx's critique of political economy and, as we will see – spoiler alert! – the movement of value and value's social forms is at its core. Reading the preface from the hindsight of *Capital* (*Capital* III in particular, as I will show), it becomes clear that the base of the base/superstructure is the singular dynamic that Marx calls 'capital' itself – a social relation that invents a world in its image, a particular mode of sociality that we can also call 'value'. Capital is

---

3 Every page number given in text is from Karl Marx, *Capital*, vol. 3, trans. David Fernbach, Penguin, 1981. All other citations will be given in footnotes.

value-in-motion; capital is a value-machine. What makes capital unique
is that its base (concept, essence), while an objective outgrowth of its
historical conditions, is nonetheless formless: immaterial, invisible,
supra-sensible. To invoke a world, it must take form.[4] But the movement
of the capital-base taking form is also the movement of its *disappearance
into* its phenomenal forms. The social substance of a capitalist society
disappears into its worldly forms: into naturalized economic categories;
into legal and political formations; into forms of social consciousness
(thought-objects, personifications, origin and surface stories, and so
on). In other words, the capitalist base disappears into its superstructure.
Acts become objects, which now confront their makers as autonomous
forces, subjecting their makers in the double sense of the term.[5] The real
autonomy of the social forms in which capital moves in the world,
however, is precisely what Marx thinks *against* in the passage from the
preface. In *Capital* III, the through line of analysis is the illustration of
this very same dynamic. Here, Marx does not simply posit that surplus-
value disappears into profit; he demonstrates how, and why, it is that
profit must subsequently disappear into its own derivative surface-
forms. Social forms beget social forms, and in *Capital* III we learn why
they do.

The base/superstructure figure is sometimes dismissed, either as part
of or in response to the charge of economic determinism. The
formulation in the preface, cited above, is certainly emphatic and
unequivocal: 'The mode of production of material life determines the
social, political and intellectual life process in general. It is not the
consciousness of men that determines their being, but, on the contrary,
their social being that determines their consciousness.' Rather than read
this passage as an early iteration of an analysis that will become more
nuanced as it develops, more open to a model of mutual determination

---

4 This is a logical sequence, not a chronological one. As we will see, capital's forms-
in-waiting pre-exist capital itself as social substance. The movement of capital's social
forms brings into being the concept of capital as a real, invisible, determining,
gravitational force. It is a movement that turns effect into cause and calls up the
dialectical thinking required to map it.

5 'Labour becomes bound up in its object: labour has been objectified, the object
has been worked on. What on the side of the worker appeared in the form of unrest
[*Unruhe*] now appears, on the side of the product, in the form of being [*Sein*], as a fixed,
immobile characteristic. The worker has spun, and the product is a spinning' (Marx,
Capital I, 287). Acts also become infrastructure, institutions – again, superstructure.

or 'conditioning' of relative constituents (or, at least, open to reconstruction along these lines), *Capital* III is the protracted demonstration of these same social physics, just as described in the preface. In other words, Marx means exactly what he says. However, if capitalist social physics constitute a mode of determinism, it is not one of 'the economy' in the everyday understanding of that sphere and its constitutive activities.[6] Instead, the defining feature of *this* determinism is that *it appears not to be one*; its movement is value-in-motion, and value, let us recall, disappears.

The charge of economic determinism is, in fact, an overly hasty characterization of Marx's theory of value. The movement of value determines a specific, delimited range of possible expressions taken by value's forms, rather than determining, directly or mechanically, any single one – a movement that dissimulates value as the centre of gravity of capitalist sociality altogether. This mode of value determinism is endemic to 'capital full-blown'.[7] Capital is a regime of social averages and tipping points: socially average labour time constitutes value and serves

---

6   Far from being the motor of capitalist social life, it is an inverted, naturalized 'economy' that Marx's dialectical thinking puts on its feet – itself one of value's forms of expression. The term 'economic base', however, has confused things. It has been mistaken for 'the economy' in its colloquial sense. It is not that. It would be better to think of it as the base of the economic abstractions that inform the untruth of what Marx calls 'the world as it actually is'. For a discussion of the critique of economic objectivity, see Werner Bonefeld in Werner Bonefeld and Chris O'Kane, eds, *Adorno and Marx*, Bloomsbury, 2022, chapters 2 and 6. In chapter 6, Bonefeld recalls 'Adorno's characterization of negative dialectics as the critique of "the ontology of the wrong state of things" ' (104). Adorno's turn of phrase is useful here too. On the first page of chapter 2, Bonefeld characterizes the object(ive) of critical theory, and it extends to that of Marx: '[Critical theory] asks about the social constitution of the (economic) abstractions and it asks about the historically specific character of the social relations that assume the form of a relationship between seemingly natural economic things' (23).

7   Value dissimulates as it determines. That value is a dissimulation machine poses, then, a representational or, as I have construed it elsewhere, aesthetic problem. For capital as a representational problem, see Fredric Jameson, *Representing Capital: A Reading of Volume One*, Verso, 2014. In Beverley Best, *Marx and the Dynamic of the Capital Formation: An Aesthetics of Political Economy*, Palgrave Macmillan, 2010, I construe capital as a generalized mode of representation that informs what is possible to imagine, do, and make collectively as an 'aesthetic problem'. It is also a theory of experience as the individualization (and autonomization) of a set of conditions that transcend the individual: an exteriority that mediates the feeling of interiority, an affect that is always already collective, social, but that operates with the force of the immediate and embodied. It is, therefore, also a question of praxis.

as value's unit of measurement; value is measured as productivity, which is, again, a social average – the ratio of total social labour time (living labour, abstracted) to total social product (dead labour, living labour objectified). Value exerts its determining force *as* productivity because productivity determines the costs of things: it determines the range of things that can be, and are, produced; the scale of production (also a delimited range); and, finally, the range of possibilities for the distribution of the product. As we will see, the movement of value, which takes form as productivity, pre-empts any real relativism between the differentiated parts of the capital machine, even if that is the working appearance of things. The derivation of capital's forms (i.e., the function of abstraction) moves in one direction only. Social substance and its forms of expression (base and superstructure, if you like) are not mutually determining or conditioning. Since the 1970s, the configuration of capital has told a story about the dissolution of the performative boundaries that once demarcated the economy from the zones of politics, culture, science, art, and so on. This surface story is real; it is the outward, always-changing face of the particular, historical stage of development of capitalist accumulation (i.e., of global productivity, as we will see) that emerges in the second half of the twentieth century. It does not, however, signal the obsolescence of value and its determining operation. As always, in capital, 'modern economics [and the stories it tells are] the theoretical expression of the capitalist mode of production' (917):

> The specific economic form in which unpaid surplus labour is pumped out of the direct producers determines the relationship of domination and servitude, as this grows directly out of the production itself and reacts back on it in turn as a determinant. On this is based the entire configuration of the economic community arising from the actual relations of production, and hence also its specific political form. It is in each case the direct relationship of the owners of the conditions of production to the immediate producers – a relationship whose particular form naturally corresponds always to a certain level of development of the type and manner of labour, and hence to its social productive power – in which we find the innermost secret, the hidden basis of the entire social edifice, and hence also the political form of the relationship of sovereignty and dependence, in short, the specific form of state in each case. This does not prevent the same

economic basis – the same in its major conditions – from displaying endless variations and gradations in its appearance, as the result of innumerable different empirical circumstances, natural conditions, racial relations, historical influences acting from outside, etc., and these can only be understood by analyzing these empirically given conditions. (927–8)

This passage from *Capital* III elaborates what Marx, slightly earlier, calls 'economic base' as 'the direct relationship of the owners of the conditions of production to the immediate producers . . . the innermost secret, the hidden basis of the entire social edifice'. The economic base is a relationship; we can also describe it as a dynamic, or movement, that congeals into 'endless variations and gradations in its appearance' – variations that are limited only by the contingencies of the historical development of capital and, therefore, not at all random but virtually unlimited and always exceeding any accounting of them. Capital, as social content, is always other than any one of its forms of appearance, even when, taken together, as the movement of content/form, they constitute the capitalist totality.

Why insist on Marx's dialectical determinism – on situating value-in-motion as the ineluctable centre of gravity of capitalist social life? Capturing Marx's analysis matters only from the standpoint of the future anterior, for the matter of theorizing capital's transformation as a virtual but unrealized possibility. Marx's analysis of capital's drive to burst through its own constraints and turn into something else, however distant or unrealizable that possibility appears, is punctual and persistent throughout *Capital* III. To detect capital's own radical alterity, one must grasp both the distinction between capital's secret, hidden dynamic and its forms of appearance, as well as their ultimate identity as two standpoints on a singular historical process. As the direction of determination moves from value to its social forms, so the obsolescence of capital as social formation can only be a function of the abolition of the social relation at its core, whether that remains an imaginary, aspirational development or otherwise.

The Perceptual Physics of Capital

This book is an exegesis of Marx's analysis in *Capital* III. When one reads volume III consecutively in one stretch, the unswerving consistency of the book's analytical objective is abundantly clear across its significant (and unfinished!) length.[8] Particularly striking is the relentlessness of the illustration of the study's central thesis, as stated in the very first paragraph of the book:

> Our concern is . . . to discover and present the concrete forms which grow out of the *process of capital's movement considered as a whole*. In their actual movement, capitals confront one another in certain concrete forms, and, in relation to these, both the shape capital assumes in the immediate production process and its shape in the process of circulation appear merely as particular moments. The configurations of capital, as developed in this volume, thus approach step by step the form in which they appear on the surface of society, in the action of different capitals on one another, i.e. in competition, and in the everyday consciousness of the agents of production themselves. (117)

As stated, Marx's concern is to demonstrate how the movement of capital, as social relation, takes particular forms of appearance in the world as it actually is – forms that, from any individual, discrete stand-point on the capital formation, mystify the actual, essential character of capital's movement. The *narrowness* and explicit delimitations of Marx's object of analysis are often mistaken: this is not an analysis of the capitalist formation, of capitalist society in its theoretically infinite variations.

---

8 The posthumous compilation of *Capital* III as organized for publication by Engels works perfectly well for this exegetical exercise. With the exception of the unfortunate changing of the volume's title, Engels's arrangement of the material for *Capital* III does not, as some have suggested, distort the movement and meaning of Marx's analysis. Fred Moseley's study of Marx's notebooks in comparison with the published volume (serving as a new introduction to the material) confirms this understanding (Marx, *Economic Manuscript of 1864–1865*). But simply reading the book as published, front to back, puts the consistency, clarity, and logical flow of Marx's argument in unmistakable evidence. The published form is useful in mapping the fluent sequence of the volume's parts, and Engels's reworking of Marx's calculations in the ground-rent tables in part VI is also helpful, as we will see.

Rather, this is a study of capital's hidden, inner movement and the identification of its historical conditions of emergence. It is a study of the formation and determinacy of what Marx calls the *concept* of capital – of that which becomes, once capital is standing on its feet, the centre of gravity of capitalist sociality. This gravitational force generates phenomenal forms that (to be even more precise) *invert* capital's own internal movement. Capital's forms are real; they are objective incarnations that carry capital's equally objective, if immaterial and 'suprasensible', content: 'objectified labour in its general social form' (502). The exposition of this dynamic of essence-appearance constitutes the through line of *Capital* III; it is the trunk that articulates each of the book's extended analytical branches.

In this exegesis of Marx's analysis, I characterize this dynamic as a 'perceptual physics'.[9] The term is meant to capture a theory of value and its disappearance into its social forms as a theory of motion. As such, this is a dynamic specific to the capitalist mode of production and its particular excrescences. Capital is unique in its dissimulating movement: it excretes naturalized economic objectivities – and a zone conventionalized as 'the economy' – that congeal into a social world of inverted and mystifying appearances. This dynamic can also be characterized as a function of abstraction that moves to the core of capitalist sociality; it is a movement that carries the question of mediation to every aspect of the capitalist formation, without exception, for the length of capital's zombie-span.[10] However strange it may sound to

---

9 After playing around with different terms to capture the dynamic that forms the core of Marx's study, reading Michel Serres's meditation on Lucretius in *The Birth of Physics* caused the penny to drop, and the decision to characterize Marx's theory of value as a perceptual *physics* was made under the influence of that book: 'Everything is projected onto kinematics. Ontology conceals itself behind the theory of movement. This is an outdated thesis: all of physics reduces to mechanics. It is called mechanism. Ontology is the motive force of mechanism.' Michel Serres, *The Birth of Physics*, Rowman & Littlefield, 2018, 82.

10 Sohn-Rethel's category of 'real abstraction' addresses similar concerns as the movement I tend to call 'the function of abstraction' in *Marx and the Dynamic of the Capital Formation*. Unfortunately, Sohn-Rethel's formulation was not on my radar in 2003 when I carried out that study of *Capital* I, and the benefits of learning from Sohn-Rethel were lost to me for that project. I stick with my own reading and formulation of Marx nonetheless because, for better or worse, I know what I intend to capture and say with it, and my formulation and Sohn-Rethel's are not fully flush. See Alfred Sohn-Rethel, *Intellectual and Manual Labour: A Critique of Epistemology*, Brill, 2020.

contemporary ears, for Marx, value's dissimulating movement (i.e., capital's concept) can be mapped with scientific and even mathematical precision. Today, the idea of a science of social forms sounds outmoded and anachronistic. One of the objectives of this book is to explore what the scientific analysis (in Marx's terms) of the movement of capital's forms involves, and to demonstrate its ongoing relevance and necessity, whatever we call it. Capital's forms of appearance are not produced in people's heads as faulty ideas; they are produced in the world and confront the everyday consciousness of capital's bearers – the very same agents whose activity creates them in the first place – challenging, and setting the terms for, their very survival.[11]

The perceptual physics of capital captures the processes that Marx calls, on the one hand, mystification and, on the other, the fetish character of value's social forms. In Marx's analysis, the process of mystification and its kin, the movement of the capital fetish, pertain to the two aspects of capitalist accumulation: the production of surplus-value and its distribution. The systematic process of obscuring, in the immediate appearance of things, the means by which value expands – that is, the means by which value becomes capital – is inherent to capitalist accumulation, as we will see. A gravitational pull on capital's bearers towards a certain way of seeing, categorizing, and understanding the world is an objective dimension of the movement of capital. Capital generates a pantheon of self-representations that inform by both betraying and confirming (on different registers) our experiences in the world. At the same time, people are constantly challenging, analysing, and disassembling these surface stories. The capacity to do so is universal; the time and space to undertake the work is limited and rare.

Both mystification and fetishization involve the perceptual delinking of the phenomenon of profit from its social substance, surplus-value. Throughout *Capital* III, Marx articulates this formulation in a number of ways, using a number of terms, stabilizing the point through a combination of repetition and expositional variation. In each variation

---

11   Even though what I am invoking with the concept of a perceptual physics comes from, and moves towards, a different place from that of Paolo Virno, there is a kinship with his formulation of perception as a combination of sense faculties that, like a language, does not belong to the individual but rather precedes the individual, a 'pre-individual reality which is at the foundation of individuation'. Paolo Virno, *A Grammar of the Multitude*, Semiotext(e), 2003, 76–7.

– historical or hypothetical case study, scenario, series of tables of calculations, and so on – the point remains consistent: in the world as it actually is, surplus-value appears (and disappears) in the form of profit. The mystification of surplus-value as profit – where profit simultaneously is, and is not, surplus-value – is the perceptual movement that stabilizes capital as a mode of domination; it facilitates the perceptual delinking of profit and surplus-value in everyday life, in the quotidian semblance of things. The significance of this perceptual delinking is central to the critical analysis of capital where surplus-value is the link between abstract wealth (value) and living human labour in cooperation as the singular generating source of that wealth, without exception.

The means by which surplus-value is created and becomes profit – that is, the property of owners of the means of production – are well understood by readers of *Capital* I: surplus-value is the abstraction/socialization of surplus labour. Abstract labour is the social form taken by living, cooperative labour, objectified in the commodity, in the goods and services produced under conditions of capitalist production – goods destined for exchange. In the continuous process of capitalist production-circulation, a series of content-form derivations unfurl in capital's reproduction: an unpaid portion of living, human cooperative labour takes the form of surplus abstract/socialized labour, which takes the form of surplus-value, which takes the form of profit. In the course of its distribution, profit takes the form of revenues: profit of enterprise, interest, rent, wages. In this book, we follow the movement of each one of these derivations in closer detail. What we find is that, despite appearances to the contrary, the gravitational force of value *holds* at every moment of capitalist accumulation. Every theoretical excursion Marx takes in *Capital* III, throughout each one of the book's seven parts, serves to illustrate this point. At the same time, the book lays out a singular, sustained analysis, step by step, each step incorporating and building on the one before.

For this reason, in order to grasp the holism of the analysis, it is important to maintain the sequence of the exposition in *Capital* III. Therefore, in our reconstruction of Marx's full theory of the movement of value, we follow the analysis step by step, in its organic sequence. Each chapter of this book takes up the material in one of the seven parts of *Capital* III and, in turn, works through it. To illustrate the internal consistency of Marx's analysis in *Capital* III, I have limited the discussion to this text only; however, I have quoted the text extensively in order to demonstrate that everything I attribute to it is there – indeed, it is *all* there. What readers will find surprising is just how much *is* there, and how much of the analysis speaks to contemporary debates and problematics in the wide field of critical social theory. Because this book focuses almost exclusively on *Capital* III, and intends to be of service to groups of people reading the book together, all in-text page references are to the easily accessible 1981 Penguin edition. Any references to other texts are cited in the footnotes.

PART I

The Physics of Capital and the Mystification of Surplus-Value

1

Rate of Profit: Production

Cost Price – Fixed Capital and Circulating Capital – The Social Factory and So-Called 'Free Labour' – Conclusion: The Physics of Perception, Conception, Consciousness

Marx undertakes a deceptively substantial amount of groundwork in elaborating capital's perceptual physics in the seemingly slight and inconsequential opening two chapters of *Capital* III, 'Cost Price and Profit' and 'The Rate of Profit'. In these two chapters, the observation that becomes the book's refrain is articulated early on: On the one hand, profit and surplus-value are identical in substance and magnitude; both are constituted by unpaid surplus labour congealed in the social form of money. On the other hand, profit and surplus-value, 'in the world as it actually is' (117; 134), will never appear as what they are, two expressions of the same social substance; rather, surplus-value will systematically *disappear* into the empirical form of profit. The dissimilation of profit and surplus-value, in the world and therefore in the mind, thwarts the potentially subversive comprehension that the living labour of the proletariat is the singular source of capitalist wealth – wealth that is surreptitiously (but also legally and 'transparently') appropriated by the capitalist class. Further, this dissimilation conceals an even more potentially subversive understanding: if the human activity of producing goods, when that activity is carried out in the form of wage labour, is the *only* activity that produces value and consequently *all* wealth in a capitalist society, that means that a great portion, even a majority, of human and non-human activity – creative, innovative, nurturing, cultivating, life-producing and sustaining, inventive, entrepreneurial, and so on – falls outside of the conditions required for it to take the form of social wealth altogether.[1] In other words, in a capitalist mode of production, when human activity is not mobilized directly by capital, it does not – *cannot* – count as wealth (as *value*) in the narrow and increasingly exclusionary conditions of capitalist accumulation. The 'how' and 'why' of this dynamic cannot be read directly from the experience of it, even though experiential accounts illustrate the complexities of its lived realities. Nonetheless, Marx argues, 'it is completely wrong-headed to seek directly to present the laws of the profit rate as laws of the rate of surplus-value, or vice versa' (136). Rather, theoretical analysis (specifically, what Marx calls science, or the power of abstraction) is needed in order to arrive at the totalizing point of view that can hold capital's contradictory, individual standpoints – its numerous possible narrative and analytical entrées – in the head (and in the body, as an aesthetic experience) simultaneously.

The nature and means of capitalist extortion may be hidden (even as their social consequences are blatant and ubiquitous), but they can be revealed through analysis. This is the political subtext of an analysis that is, prima facie, an 'economic' one and, even, as Marx states, a mathematical one. The mathematical comportment of the analysis returns us to the question of the significance of the category of cost price in the exposition in chapters 1 and 2 and elaborated in the remaining five chapters of part I of *Capital* III.

Cost Price

At this early stage of the analysis, we bring to the table what we know from *Capital* I: commodities are forms of value constituted in the continuity of their production and circulation, as goods produced for

---

1 The goods in question can be material or immaterial; their physical properties are inconsequential for determining if they take the value form. The distinction between material and immaterial labour is meaningless within the terms of Marx's theory of value.

the purpose of sale and consumption as both means of subsistence and means of further production. 'Cost price' refers to the value sum of the elements that the capitalist must procure and consume in order to produce a certain commodity – elements such as machinery, raw and ancillary materials, and labour-power. The value composition of a manufacturer's product remains the same whether we speak of a single commodity, the aggregate product of a 'batch' or production cycle, or a manufacturer's product for a year. With this in mind, we can say that the cost price of a commodity is the sum of the value of those elements that represent the capitalist's investment in both constant and variable capital, that is, the sum of capital laid out for both means of production and labour-power. We also recall from *Capital* I the importance of the distinction between constant capital (c) and variable capital (v) as categories that facilitate a 'totalizing analysis' of the means of value's expansion in the 'hidden abode of production'. We return to this important analytical distinction shortly. From the standpoint of the capitalist owner of the means of production, however, there is no distinction between constant and variable capital, between capital invested in raw material and capital invested in labour-power. From the point of view of the capitalist manufacturer, there are simply the various costs associated with production. In chapter 1 of *Capital* III, then, Marx designates cost price as k, where $c + v = k$, to represent the appearance of the costs of production from the standpoint of the capitalist (the purchaser of the means of production), and which corresponds to a more generalized appearance of how the business of manufacturing goods or services is carried out.

Whatever cost price (k, or undifferentiated productive capital) is perceived to be by the capitalist – capital investment, production costs, and so on – it is an imposing figure: cost price is the 'minimum limit to the sale price of a commodity' (128); it marks the borderline between a profitable and an unprofitable production cycle. If the value that returns to the capitalist after circulation is greater than the cost price of production, the capitalist appropriates that surplus of value above cost price as profit. If the value that returns to the capitalist is less than the cost price of production, then the capitalist has lost that diminished portion of capital from the initial investment. Cost price represents the minimum magnitude of value that must return from circulation in order to repeat the production cycle at its present scale: 'If [the commodity] is sold beneath this cost price, the components of productive capital that were expended cannot be fully replaced from the price of sale' (128). Cost price is, therefore, a disciplining objective appearance of capitalist production; as we will see, it is a deceptive appearance from the vantage of the totality of the capital dynamic, but it is a material appearance nonetheless. It consequently assumes what Marx calls an 'independence' as a category of production: decisions are made and production is organized around the need to generate returns on capital that surpass cost price. Further, cost price as objective appearance achieves its independence, or 'autonomy', more widely in capitalist society as a figure of common sense. The understanding that private enterprise must make a profit – that returns from doing business must exceed the costs of doing business, else the venture is pointless and unviable – is 'common knowledge' for employers and employees alike. As Marx states with respect to the materiality of cost price:

> The independence that this portion of value acquires makes itself constantly felt in practice in the actual production of the commodity, as it must constantly be transformed back again into the form of productive capital by way of the circulation process, i.e. the cost price of the commodity must continuously buy back the elements of production consumed in its production. (118–19)

Throughout *Capital* III, Marx reiterates this formulation like a refrain: value's social forms (in this case cost price) move with an abstracted, yet material, independence. In variations of Marx's articulation of the process, he describes this independence as a process of externalization or, more often, as a process of autonomization. The repetitive and slightly varied characterizations of the process reinforce a singularity of move-ment: value's appearances are disarticulated from the social dynamics/relations that generate them, allowing the appearances – the categories, the forms – to achieve a quasi-autonomy, a provisional, self-referential logic that informs practice and perception in a capitalist mode of produc-tion. The effect of the movement, which Marx unfurls step by step, is the perceptual (and conceptual) delinking of profit and surplus-value:

> In this Part, the rate of profit is taken as numerically different from the rate of surplus-value; profit and surplus-value on the other hand are

treated as numerically identical magnitudes, different only in form. In the following Part we shall observe *the further development of the externalization by which profit presents itself as a magnitude distinct from surplus-value* in a numerical respect as well. (139–40, my emphasis)

The question is, then, what essential mediation is concealed by the disarticulated category of cost price? We know from *Capital* I that the value of a commodity is not simply the sum of the value of the constant capital (means of production) and the variable capital (labour-power) mobilized in its production. In purchasing labour-power, the capitalist instead receives the value of the product of living labour expended in production. In Marx's words, 'In place of the value of the labour-power, which is what figures in the capital advance, we have the living, value-creating labour-power that actually *functions* as productive capital' (120). Living, value-creating labour produces a greater magnitude of value than the value of labour-power itself; it can be represented as the value of labour-power, plus a portion of that value in surplus, say, 50 percent, or 100 percent, and so on. The actual value of the commodity (C) is therefore the sum of the constant capital (c) and variable capital (v) *plus* the surplus-value (s) generated on variable capital, or, $C = c + v + s$. Since we have established that $c + v =$ cost price (k), we can also say that a commodity's value is the sum of the commodity's cost price and the surplus-value generated in its production, or, $C = k + s$.

Again, as we know from *Capital* I, surplus-value generated in production, through the application of living labour, is not paid for by the capitalist; it is the workers' 'free gift' to the capitalist and, as we will see, more precisely, to the capitalist class. The commodity's cost price refers to the 'cost' to *the capitalist* to produce it; cost price measures an expenditure of capital. The commodity's value, on the other hand, refers to the cost of producing a commodity from the totalized standpoint of the system; it measures, as Marx states, an expenditure of labour and, in this way, the cost of the commodity to its direct producers:

What the commodity costs the capitalist, and what it actually does cost to produce it, are two completely different quantities. The portion of the commodity's value that consists of surplus-value costs the capital-ist nothing, for the very reason that it costs the worker his unpaid

labour . . . The capitalist cost of the commodity [its cost price] is measured by the expenditure of *capital*, whereas the actual cost of the
commodity [its value] is measured by the expenditure of *labour*. (118)

The immediate significance of cost price to the capitalist initiates a
series of subsequent appearances that present an inverted picture of the
inner movement of the process (121). Marx states, 'Cost price . . . in the
economy of capital, present[s] the false semblance of an actual category
of value production' (119). Cost price appears to have a determining
role in the amount of profit that returns to the capitalist as an outcome
of the production-circulation cycle: a commodity can be sold on the
market for a certain price; given this fact, it appears as though the more
aggressively the manufacturer can reduce the capital advanced for the
production of that commodity, the greater their profit on its sale. Two
distorted appearances are at work here, each undermining the perception
of the continuity between the value identified as profit and the surplus-
value created by living labour in production: 'From the standpoint of
capitalist production, however, this actual state of affairs necessarily
appears upside down' (121).

    First, it appears as though the rationalization of cost price to the
greatest extent possible has a direct impact on the amount of profit
generated in enterprise, when, in fact, cost price has no bearing on the
magnitude of value generated in production and realized in circulation.
As we know from *Capital* I, the value of the means of production
(constant capital) is transferred to the finished commodity without a
change in magnitude; it is what Marx calls 'reappearing value' (119). If
the value of constant capital invested is lowered in one way or another,
then a lesser amount of value will reappear in the finished commodity,
whose total value will be relatively lower accordingly. The magnitude of
surplus-value generated in production, however, remains unchanged
whether the value of constant capital increases or decreases.[2] Second,

---

2 The magnitude of surplus-value remains unchanged, but the capitalist's profit
may be increased if this lowered price of *c* puts the capitalist at an, albeit temporary,
advantage with respect to their competitors. That advantage is temporary because the
decreased value of *c* is either contingent on advantageous but non-reproducible
circumstances, or, those circumstances can be systematized and generalized throughout
the sphere of production (more efficient means of resource extraction that cheapens raw
material, for instance). In the second case, the provisional lower value of the commodity

the immediate appearance of the determining significance of cost price for the capitalist creates the impression that profit is generated in circulation rather than where it is actually generated, in production:

> The excess of value or surplus-value realized with the sale of the commodity thus appears to the capitalist as an excess of its sale price over its value, instead of an excess of its value over its cost price, so that the surplus-value concealed in the commodity is not simply realized by its sale, but actually derives from the sale itself. (128)

It appears as though profit is the result of selling the commodity for more than it cost to produce, that profit is the result of the 'sales effort' involved in selling the commodity above its value. If cost price is the cost to the capitalist of producing the commodity, then the higher the selling price above cost price, the greater is the amount of profit that falls to the seller. However, we know from *Capital* I that this is not the case: commodities are not sold at their cost prices but, rather, at their values, and surplus-value is already a portion of the commodity's total value.[3] Surplus-value may be realized in circulation when the commodity is sold, but it is congealed as a portion of the commodity's value in the production process. So long as the commodity is sold above its cost price, it can be sold *below* its value and still return a profit to the seller. Competition, in fact, will drive capitalists to do exactly that, to

---

eventually becomes the commodity's new market value as these advantageous conditions are generalized and nullified through competition. If the commodity does shake out at a new, lower market value, and if it is a commodity in the basket of goods and services that constitutes the value of labour-power, it reduces the value of labour-power and consequently augments the system's relative surplus-value-generating capacity, in turn increasing the general rate of profit: 'Assuming a constant level of exploitation of labour, the profit rate can only change here, with the mass of surplus-value remaining the same, in three cases: if the value of the constant capital changes, if the value of the variable capital changes, or if both change. All these result in a change in C, thereby changing s/C, the general rate of profit. In each case, therefore, a change in the general rate of profit assumes a change in the value of the commodities which enter as formative elements into the constant capital, the variable capital, or both simultaneously' (266). We are getting ahead of the exposition, however, and will return to the dynamics of the general rate of profit in the next chapter.

3   We will see in chapter 2 that values take the form of prices in the upside-down world of competition; we do not need to address this transformation of form at this point.

undersell competitors while still selling above cost price: 'The basic law of capitalist competition . . . depends . . . on this difference between the value and the cost price of commodities and the possibility deriving from this of selling commodities below their value at a profit' (128). Under favourable circumstances (that, for structural reasons, are only ever provisional), it is also possible to sell commodities *above* their values, which inflates profit above the amount of surplus-value congealed in the commodity. Nonetheless, for any individual production cycle, regardless of the circumstances in which it proceeds, returning profit will be a portion of the surplus-value already congealed in the commodity. That portion could be 90 percent, 100 percent, or 110 percent – in other words, profit will be a portion of surplus-value that constitutes a lesser, equal, or greater magnitude of the commodity's surplus-value.

To understand how this can be the case, and why it is an index of the perceptual movement of capital more generally, we look beyond the frame of the individual enterprise and individual production cycle to the wider frame of capitalist competition in general – one investment of capital confronting other capital investments in the marketplace.[4] If the profit that a commodity realizes in the marketplace can be either greater or lesser than its surplus-value (and this is almost always the case; it is a coincidence when commodities are sold at their real values), the question is, how do we account for that greater or lesser portion of value that falls to the seller? In the case of a commodity sold for less than its value, a portion of its surplus-value ends up in the pocket of the purchaser, taking the form of money *not* spent. In the case of a commodity sold for more than its value, the entirety of the commodity's surplus-value ends up in the pocket of the seller, plus an extra portion of already-existing value from the purchaser's pocket. This extra portion from the purchaser's pocket is not newly created surplus-value but, rather, a portion of value that already exists, either as another capitalist's

---

4 The sphere of capitalist competition is the frame of reference that Marx introduces in part II, and the analysis remains thus oriented for the rest of *Capital* III. This frame of reference is the upside-down world of capitalist competition (134), the battle of capital against capital, where the only real agents at play (the actual bearers of capital) are the collective capitalist and the collective worker, or, the capitalist class and the working class, and where class struggle drives the movement of the whole as effectively as it is concealed from immediate observation.

capital advanced to buy the means of production or as a portion of a worker's wages used to buy the means of subsistence.

The significant point is that the only newly created value in the circuit of capital is the surplus-value created in production. The fact that a capitalist's profit may be greater or lesser than the amount of surplus-value contained in the commodity merely obfuscates the reality that surplus-value is generated solely in production and never in circulation. This reality also conceals the fact that surplus-value, and therefore the entirety of capitalist wealth, is produced by workers:

> The immediate process of production is itself simply an evanescent moment which is constantly passing over into the process of circulation, and vice versa, so that any inkling of the source of his profit, i.e. of the nature of surplus-value, which dawns more or less clearly on the capitalist in the production process itself, appears at the most as an equally valid moment alongside the notion that the excess that is realized stems from a movement that is independent of the production process itself and derives from the sphere of circulation, a movement therefore that capital possesses independently of its relation to labour. These phenomena of circulation are even adduced by modern economists such as Ramsay, Malthus, Senior, Torrens, etc. as direct proofs that capital in its mere material existence, independently of its social relation to labour (which is precisely how it comes to be capital), is an autonomous source of surplus-value alongside labour and independent of it. (135–6)

In Marx's analysis of the perceptual physics of capital, cost price is the initial category from which all others will derive, not unlike the expositional function of 'the commodity' in *Capital* I. We will discover, for instance, that cost price is the foundational category on which Marx builds an analysis of the rate of profit in the rest of part I, the general rate of profit in part II, and the falling rate of profit in part III.

As we have established, cost price represents the capital advanced in production and therefore the minimum magnitude of value that must return to the capitalist to buy back the means of production and reinitiate the cycle. To illustrate the way this objective requirement for the capitalist operates a 'sleight of hand' for capital, we follow Marx in the assumption that commodities are sold at their values, and that profit and surplus-value will therefore coincide as magnitudes at each stage of the analysis and/or of capital's circuit of reproduction. The surplus-value that is generated in production over and above cost price constitutes the capitalist's profit; the ratio of this surplus-value (s) to cost price ($c + v$) is, therefore, the rate of profit, or, $\frac{s}{c+v}$. For the capitalist, the rate of profit is the mathematical translation of the singular purpose of enterprise. However, from the point of view of capital's movement as a whole, the magnitude of surplus-value generated in production is unaffected by the magnitude of constant capital (c); constant capital is simply reappearing value that is transferred by productive labour to the commodity unaltered in magnitude and can therefore be removed from the equation. The magnitude of surplus-value, rather, is determined entirely by the magnitude of variable capital (v); the rate of surplus-value is therefore surplus-value in relation to variable capital, or, $\frac{s}{v}$: 'We have already seen how . . . s, the surplus-value, derives only from a change in the value of v, the variable capital, and is therefore originally simply an increment to the variable capital' (124).

Therefore, despite profit and surplus-value being identical in substance and magnitude from the vantage of capital's circuitry, the rate of profit and the rate of surplus-value will be systematically different. Rate of profit and rate of surplus-value will always depart as numerical figures. The only apparent exception is where the value invested as constant capital (c) is zero – which is not a genuine exception because, while rate of profit and rate of surplus-value will converge numerically, they will depart in concept and configuration. Meanwhile, even though it is the rate of surplus-value that determines the magnitude of profit generated in production, for the capitalist the category of the rate of surplus-value has no meaning or reality; for the capitalist there is only the magnitude of capital invested and the rate of return on that investment. Therefore, the capitalist approaches cost price as k, rather than as $c + v$, eliminating any distinction between means of production and labour-power with respect to the roles they play in production and, along with that distinction, the concept for understanding the real nature of valorization:

> [For the capitalist,] the portion of capital laid out on labour is distinguished from that laid out on means of production such as cotton or coal only by the fact that it serves as payment for a materially

different element of production and in no way by the fact that it plays a functionally different role in the process of forming commodity value, and therefore also in the valorization process of capital . . . What we see here [on the surface of things] are only finished and existing values – the value portions of the capital advanced which enter the formation of the product's value – and not an element that creates new value. The distinction between constant and variable capital has disappeared. (122)

The disappearance of the functional distinction between constant and variable capital generates the surface appearance that the additional value that falls to the capitalist at the end of the cycle is the justified outcome of their own enterprising activity – of simply the possession of (or access to) capital in the first place, but also an outcome of effective management decisions, a creative sales effort, and so on:

It is clear enough to the capitalist that this additional value derives from the productive activities which he undertakes with his capital, i.e. that it derives from the capital itself . . . As far as the capital actually used up in the course of production is concerned . . . surplus-value appears to derive equally from the different value elements of this capital, both means of production and labour. For these elements are both equally involved in the formation of the cost price. They both add their values, present as capital advances, to the value of the product and are not distinguished as constant and variable magnitudes. (125)

The collapse of variable and constant capital into cost price, according to Marx, causes great 'confusion . . . in the minds of economists' and 'the valorization process of capital [to be] completely mystified' (124). Here, we arrive at the first of many characterizations of the process of mystification. The different characterizations capture different aspects of the process, yet each reveals something consistent about the movement and the appearances it generates, namely, the obfuscation of the identity of profit and surplus-value, and the subsequent obfuscation of the source of all capitalist wealth in the cooperative labour of workers. Concealing the identity of profit and surplus-value also mystifies the *location* of the production of wealth. While the creation of value takes place exclusively in production, the everyday appearance of things suggests it is generated in circulation, in the course of buying and selling, as a function of an effective 'sales effort'.[5]

Fixed Capital and Circulating Capital

Cost price designates the sum of value invested in production that reappears in the value of the finished commodity; it includes, as a portion of c (constant capital), the value lost by the instruments of labour – the wear and tear on machinery, for example – which congeals as a component of the commodity's social substance. The commodity represents 'circulating capital'; however, its production requires an advance of capital that comprises both circulating and fixed capital. The categories of fixed and circulating capital make it possible to name, and thus theorize, a distinction that serves to further mystify the source of surplus-value in living labour.[6] In the course of production, fixed capital – buildings or machinery – is applied in its entirety, all at once; even when the entirety of its value is not transferred, the whole of any machine is engaged in the production of each commodity:

> In its material capacity, the entire capital serves to form the product, the means of labour as much as the production materials and labour

---

5   This appearance reaches its mystifying apogee in contemporary analyses of finance capital and so-called financialization, or 'circulatory capitalism', that proliferated after the 2008 global financial crisis. Before the crisis, as well as in an explosion of critical work after, many argued that financialization, emerging in the 1970s, is a regime of accumulation characterized by a new modality of value creation driven by financial industries and operating in the sphere of circulation. The theorization of money and finance capital is a central part of any analysis of the movement of capital, as much today as it has always been, and we will do so, extensively, in chapter 5. We will see that Marx's argument still stands – that the fetishism of circulation is a typical perceptual habit of political economists (Marx's principal targets were Robert Torrens and Thomas Malthus) who move the stage of self-valorizing value to circulation, making it appear plausible that 'something . . . [can] come out of nothing': 'Torrens manages to evade this creation from nothing only by shifting it from the sphere of commodity production to the sphere of commodity circulation' (129).

6   Capitalist 'business as usual' proceeds as 'the world as it actually is' (117; 134). This phrase is repeated many times in *Capital* III and identifies the play of capital's social forms.

itself. The entire capital is materially involved in the labour process, even if only a part of it is involved in the process of valorization. (126)

While all surplus-value consists of appropriated surplus labour, the process cannot proceed without the application of the entire capital advanced. Labour-power in the form of variable capital does not generate surplus-value simply as a consequence of its consumption in production; the process is facilitated by the *means* of labour, represented by an investment in fixed capital. Fixed capital may contribute only a small portion of its overall value to the cost price of any single commodity, but it is applied as a whole to the production of every commodity and to the formation of surplus-value (126; 132). Marx quotes English economist Thomas Malthus to capture the practical assumption of the capitalist and economist, that 'surplus-value springs simultaneously from all parts of the capital applied': 'The capitalist . . . expects an equal profit upon all the parts of the capital which he advances.' In analysis, we can see that surplus-value is factored on variable capital; however, in the upside-down world of capitalist competition in practice, profit is factored on a sum of value that demands a different category of production: 'applied capital in general' (126). 'Applied capital in general' captures the material appearance – described by Malthus above – that capital, in and of itself, has the capacity to generate profit simply by virtue of its being put into motion. Once again, we arrive at the central thesis of *Capital* III: profit is the mystified form – the 'transformed form' – of surplus-value, and the particular capacity of living labour to produce surplus-value is mistaken for the capacity of the automatic subject of capital itself:

As this supposed derivative of the total capital advanced, the surplus-value takes on the transformed form of *profit* . . . Profit, as we are originally faced with it, is thus the same thing as surplus-value, save in a mystified form, though one that necessarily arises from the capitalist mode of production. Because no distinction between constant and variable capital can be recognized in the apparent formation of the cost price, the origin of the change in value that occurs in the course of the production process is shifted from the variable capital to the capital as a whole. Because the price of labour-power appears at one pole in the transformed form of wages, surplus-value appears at the other pole in the transformed form of profit. (126–7)

Machinery, in the form of fixed capital, enacts the subject–object inversion that characterizes the movement of capitalist development more generally. Marx unfurls this formulation most explicitly in the *Grundrisse*: machinery as the 'accumulation of knowledge and of skill, of the general productive forces of the social brain', is 'absorbed into capital, as opposed to labour, and hence appears as an attribute of capital.'[7] The phrase 'as opposed to labour' has two meanings. First, the force of accumulated knowledge and skill – the force of the social brain – appears as an attribute of capital rather than as an outcome of human beings building knowledge in collaboration, directly or indirectly, over time. In *Capital* III, Marx refers to the collaborative building of knowledge – an evanescent, utopian spin on what collective human activity is at its core despite its truncated expression in a capitalist mode of production – as 'universal labour' and distinguishes it from 'communal labour' or directly cooperative engagement:

> Universal labour is all scientific work, all discovery and invention. It is brought about partly by the cooperation of men now living, but partly also by building on earlier work. Communal labour, however, simply involves the direct cooperation of individuals. (199)

The second meaning is that accumulated knowledge and skill, objectified in machinery, in its capitalist integument, stands in opposition to the workers, who become appendages to the means of production in the workplace, but also more widely in the formation of a surplus population made redundant to the production process in the course of its progressive mechanization. In this image, machinery is the objectification of social, subjective capacities and agencies that, when organized by capitalist production relations, can be mobilized only by capital, administered by its collective proprietor, the capitalist class. As such, machinery – the objectification of 'society's science' – appears as a force brought to bear on the world and its creative enterprise by

---

7   Karl Marx, *Grundrisse: Foundations of the Critique of Political Economy*, trans. Martin Nicolaus, Penguin, 1993, 694.

capital itself, a force antagonistic to the embodied source of human ingenuity that created it.[8]

Here, we can invoke Marx's formulation of the fetish, in this case, the fetish character of fixed capital: fixed capital, 'whose physical presence or use value is machinery', generates the 'semblance of validity' around the objective illusion that fixed capital itself 'creates value and hence also surplus-value' for its proprietor.[9] Marx characterizes fetishization as the process whereby capital's social forms accrue to themselves, in the general consciousness of capital's bearers, the value-creating capacity that is, in reality, an attribute of living labour alone. The fetish is a dynamic that emerges with 'the full development of capital', the achievement of a sufficient degree of systemic maturity whereby

> the entire production process appears as not subsumed under the direct skilfulness of the worker, but rather as the technological application of science. [It is] hence, the tendency of capital to give production a scientific character; direct labour [is] reduced to a mere moment of this process.[10]

In part II of *Capital* III, we will see that the fetish character of the category of 'applied capital in general', where value appears to be created by capital in any particular form simply by virtue of its being *applied* as capital, expresses 'the basic law of capitalist competition . . . the law that governs the general rate of profit and the so-called prices of production determined by it' (127–8). More specifically, the category of 'applied capital in general' facilitates the appearance that the world of capitalist competition is a struggle between capitalists – a heroic battle of entrepreneurial wits and ingenuity undertaken by individual enterprises against the field of all other competing enterprises – rather than what it actually is: a struggle between capital and labour, between the collective capitalist (or capitalist class) and the collective worker (or working class).[11]

---

8   Ibid., 694.
9   Ibid., 703.
10   Ibid., 699.
11   'Collective capitalist' and 'collective worker' refer to structural agencies of purchaser of labour power and producer of surplus-value, respectively. These 'bearers' of capital do not refer to a collective or uniform consciousness, but they can stand for a set of material interests (or social needs) that are expressed by those who carry these subject positions – interests that are systematically either met or thwarted by the process in question.

Rate of Profit

In chapter 1 of *Capital* III, Marx theorizes the identity/nonidentity of surplus-value and profit; using Marx's typical dialectical formulation, we could say that profit both is and is not surplus-value:[12] identical as objectified social labour time, surplus-value and profit are mutually repelled as objective thought forms. Profit is the transformed form of surplus-value, as well as its mystification, such that surplus-value's potential for unlocking the secret that the source of wealth is living labour is obliterated along with the category itself. The category of profit, meanwhile, points to the opposite conclusion, that the source of wealth is capital, in any form, applied in general: 'Since all sections of capital equally appear as sources of the excess value (profit), the capital relation is mystified' (136). The dynamic of the capital formation itself generates this unresolvable contradiction between profit and surplus-value; suspending the contradiction in analysis is therefore adequate to its object, as the grasping of irreducible vantage points on the process as a whole. The dialectic is a method of theorizing that is both generated by capital and required by it, in order to grasp capital's movement in concept. It is a mode of thinking through abstraction – itself an expression of capital's mediation of object of analysis and method of analysis.

However, in chapter 2 of *Capital* III, we learn that the dialectical relationship between surplus-value and profit is derived from another essence-appearance dynamic that is presupposed by – or logically prior to – the transformation of surplus-value into profit, namely, the transformation of *rate of surplus-value* into *rate of profit*:

> It is the transformation of surplus-value into profit that is derived from the transformation of the rate of surplus-value into the profit

---

12   Holloway also describes this formulation as a dialectical one: something that both is and is not an expression of irreducible movement. Entities, conditions, and so on are never static in the capitalist configuration but rather always coming into being, always transforming into something else. Another way of saying this is that capital, as value in motion, exists by constantly changing form; it is a shapeshifter. See John Holloway, 'Change the World without Taking Power', *Capital and Class* 29(1), 2005, 39–42. See also Werner Bonefeld, 'Capital Par Excellence: On Money as an Obscure Thing', *Estudios de Filosofía* (62), 2020, 33–56.

rate, not the other way round. In actual fact, the rate of profit is the historical starting point. Surplus-value and the rate of surplus-value are, relative to this, the invisible essence to be investigated, whereas the rate of profit and hence the form of surplus-value as profit are visible surface phenomena. (134)

Marx's famous instructions for materialist analysis, as minimal as they are, tell us to begin where bourgeois thinkers typically end up: with the chaotic conception of the imagined concrete, that is, with visible surface phenomena.[13] In this case, we begin with the interests of individual capitalists as they, themselves, perceive them to be, according to the terms of competitive private enterprise. From the vantage of the capitalist, the value that returns over and above cost price is profit. This ratio, the ratio of the cost of doing business against the revenues from doing business – the difference representing profit – is a code, a hieroglyph, that contains the hidden source of capital's perceptual distortions. This ratio, rate of profit, is 'ground zero', the movement from which the capitalist's inverted thought-forms derive. These perceptual physics – objective abstractions and their subsequent autonomization – are systemic to capitalist accumulation. They bludgeon their way into a form of 'common sense' and inform how capital's bearers perceive their own material interests, collapsing world-making, and life-making, into profit-making. On its face, determination of the rate of profit is a 'purely mathematical' question (141). Behind its mask, however, it is political; it is the mathematical expression of class struggle:

> As far as the individual capitalist is concerned, it is evident enough that the only thing that interests him is the ratio of the surplus-value, the excess value which he receives from selling his commodities, to the total capital advanced for the production of these commodities, whereas not only do the specific ratios of this excess value to the particular components of his capital, and its inner connections with them, not interest him, but it is actually in his interest to disguise these particular ratios and inner connections.

---

13   I am referring to Marx's sparse discussion of 'Method in Political Economy' in the *Grundrisse*, 100–8.

Even though the excess value of the commodity over its cost price arises in the immediate process of production, it is only in the circulation process in as much as in the world as it actually is, the world of competition, i.e. on the market, it depends on market conditions whether or not this excess is realized and to what extent. It needs no further elaboration here that, if a commodity is sold above or below its value, there is simply a different distribution of the surplus-value, and that this distribution, the altered ratio in which various individuals partake of the surplus-value, in no way affects either the magnitude or the character of the surplus-value itself. Not only is the circulation process, for its part, the scene of those transformations that were considered in Volume 2, but these also coincide with actual competition, the purchase and sale of commodities above or below their value, so that as far as the individual capitalist is concerned, the surplus-value that he realizes depends just as much on this mutual cheating as on the direct exploitation of labour. (134)

One of capital's advantages in class struggle is consolidated in the disjunction of production and circulation, in the way that capitalist production both *is and is not* circulation. Exploitation – the extraction of surplus-value – without exception (and to this day), takes place in production, but its process is realized, animated, and given social form in the sphere of circulation, the sphere of competition – the sphere of 'mutual swindling and cheating among the capitalists' – where the battle between capital's representatives conceals the antagonism between capital and labour (235).

Let us look more closely at the mathematical configuration of this fundamental antagonism. The all-important ratio from the vantage point of the capitalist is surplus-value over total capital advanced: $\frac{s}{c+v}$, or the rate of profit. However, the all-important ratio from the dialectical vantage point of the capitalist system is surplus-value over variable capital: $\frac{s}{v}$, or the rate of surplus-value. As we know from *Capital* I, the rate of surplus-value is the ratio of unpaid (extorted) labour time over paid labour time – the ratio that congeals into the material form of every commodity as an exchange-value, and the process of congealing and concealing that constitutes the commodity's fetish character. This ratio, the logical, mathematical expression of class struggle, expresses the

value-generating capacity of the total social capital and the distribution
of that total social capital – the portion that falls to the capitalist class
over the portion that falls to the working class at any historical
conjuncture of the system.

The core argument in *Capital* III is that the movement of capital as a
whole throws up barriers to its undistorted perception and
comprehension that inhibit generalized consciousness of living labour
as the source of capitalist wealth and, therefore, of the legitimate claim
of the working class (including those who 'produce' workers!) – not just
on the surplus-value generated in production but on *the whole kit and
caboodle*![14] The point made in chapter 2 is that this impediment to
comprehension stems logically from the systematic difference between
the two ratios in question, the rate of profit and the rate of surplus-value.
Despite the fact that s, as the excess value that returns to the capitalist in
the culmination of production-circulation, is identical in substance and
magnitude in the case of each ratio (rate of profit as $\frac{s}{c+v}$ and rate of
surplus-value as $\frac{s}{v}$), the ratios themselves will always depart as both
figures and percentages. In other words, as a result of their structural
composition, rate of profit and rate of surplus-value will always be different mathematical values. Even if the value of c in the rate of profit is zero,
and the numerical values in the case of the two percentages are thus
contingently aligned, the compositional distinction between the two
figures persists:

> Thus even if the rate of profit is numerically different from the rate of
> surplus-value, while surplus-value and profit are in fact the same and
> even numerically identical, profit is still for all that a transformed
> form of surplus-value, a form in which its origins and the secret of its
> existence are veiled and obliterated. In point of fact, profit is the form
> of appearance of surplus-value, and the latter can be sifted out from
> the former only by analysis. In surplus-value, the relationship
> between capital and labour is laid bare. In the relationship between
> capital and profit, i.e. between capital and surplus-value as it appears

---

14   Making such a claim is revolutionary in orientation, as opposed to merely a
matter of redistribution, in that it could only be realized in an associated mode of
production and through the abolition of the value form, the condition of which is the
separation of producers from the means of production.

on the one hand as an excess over the cost price of the commodity realized in the circulation process and on the other hand as an excess determined more precisely by its relationship to the total capital, *capital appears as a relationship to itself*, a relationship in which it is distinguished, as an original sum of value, from another new value that it posits. It appears to consciousness as if capital creates this new value in the course of its movement through the production and circulation processes. But how this happens is now mystified, and appears to derive from hidden qualities that are inherent in capital itself.

The further we trace out the valorization process of capital, the more is the capital relationship mystified and the less are the secrets of its internal organization laid bare. (139)

As a mathematical figure, the rate of profit is inherently different from the rate of surplus-value; they represent 'two different standards for measuring the same quantity' (134). In other words, without the concept of the *difference* between c and v, one cannot arrive at the concept of the *identity* of surplus-value and profit, nor at the concept of surplus-value as the value-expression of the capacity belonging solely to living labour to create more value than the value objectified in its own commodified form as labour-power. This comprehension is precisely what is obscured in the category of the rate of profit, the only working category for the capitalist – the ruling class – and consequently the 'ruling idea' about the purpose of commodity production altogether. With the category of rate of profit, the excess value that returns to the capitalist appears to be as much a consequence of the investment in c (means of production) as v (labour-power), undermining the crucial distinction between these two capital investments: only one – labour-power – will become a spring of fresh surplus-value in its productive consumption. The distinctiveness of labour-power from the other means of production, which only transfer their value to the value of the product, is mystified when these two capital investments are collapsed into the undifferentiated expenses that form the capitalist's cost price of production.

In chapters 3 through 7, which make up the bulk of part I, Marx illustrates the theoretical postulates introduced in chapters 1 and 2. These chapters consist of case studies, both hypothetical and historical, that illustrate the changes to the rate of profit when there is a change in any of its constituent variables: a rise or fall in the cost of raw material, ancillary material, and/or machinery (constant capital); a rise or fall in the cost of labour (wages); a change in the intensity of labour (a change in the rate of surplus-value by means other than a rise or fall in wages); and so on. In each of these case studies, Marx demonstrates the guiding argument of part I: at this stage of the analysis, where the substance and magnitude of surplus-value and profit are identical, rate of surplus-value and rate of profit as ratios/percentages will systematically depart numerically:[15]

> We have dealt with all possible cases of variation of v, c and C in our equation. We have seen how the profit rate can fall, rise, or remain the same, with the rate of surplus-value constant throughout, in so far as the slightest alteration in the ratio between v and c or C is sufficient to alter the profit rate as well. (155)

While the rate of surplus-value is determined by the value and productivity of the combined worker (the collective worker), the rate of profit is determined by the rate of surplus-value and the value composition of the capital – the ratio and sum of c and v (161). Case by case, Marx isolates each of the equation variables while altering one or both of the remaining variables in order to demonstrate the impact of every possible modification. What becomes apparent is that the identity of surplus-value and profit cannot be rendered empirically. Every possible variation in the rate of surplus-value (rising, falling, or constant) may correspond to any possible variation of the rate of profit (rising, falling, or constant):

> It results from all these . . . cases, therefore, that a rising profit rate can correspond to a falling or a rising rate of surplus-value, a falling profit rate can correspond to a rising or a falling rate of surplus-value, and a rate of profit that remains the same can also correspond to a rising or a falling rate of surplus-value. We have already shown . . . that a rising,

---

15 'At this stage of the analysis', meaning, before we examine the dynamic that generates a *general* rate of profit as a result of the effects of competition and credit across the system in part I.

falling or unchanged rate of profit can also correspond to a rate of
surplus-value that remains the same. (161)

The situation consolidates the deep mystification of the source of
capitalist profit in living labour:

> But if we start from this rate of profit, we can never establish any
> specific relationship between the excess [s] and the part of capital laid
> out on wages [v] . . . What the rate of profit as such shows is rather a
> uniform relationship of the excess to equally important parts of the
> capital [means of production and labour], which from this point of
> view exhibits no internal distinctions apart from that between fixed
> and circulating. (138)

From the standpoint of the capitalist, the only calculation of
concern (the only calculation that exists!) is rate of profit – the immediate form of appearance that today dictates global production and
commerce across the world market. While the value of constant capital has no bearing on the rate or magnitude of surplus-value, it does
have a direct impact on the rate of profit: a decrease in the cost of c
relative to the other variables increases rate of profit. For this reason,
the first priority of the capitalist, in both consciousness and practice,
is to diminish the cost of raw material and machinery, or the cost of
the use of raw material and machinery. Marx explores the various
means by which the capitalist attacks this objective (and its attending
consequences on the production process and labour conditions) in
chapter 5, 'Economy in the Use of Constant Capital', documenting
strategies ranging from methods of utilizing raw materials more
rationally in production and thereby cheapening their cost (good-
quality raw material tends to absorb labour more rationally and effectively, thereby augmenting the rate of profit), to the development of
economies of scale, to inventing new uses for (as well as selling) waste
materials, to methods for reducing the depreciation of machinery, to
the dogged pursuit of free trade agreements that lower duties on
imported raw materials. The training and disciplining of workers,
apart from having a potential impact on the productivity of labour,
also serves the rationalized use of raw material, thereby potentially
increasing the rate of profit:

The fanaticism that the capitalist shows for economizing on means of production is now comprehensible. If nothing is to be lost or wasted, if the means of production are to be used only in the manner required by production itself, then this depends partly on the workers' training and skill and partly on the discipline that the capitalist exerts over the combined workers, which would become superfluous in a state of society where the workers worked on their own account . . . The same fanaticism is also expressed inversely in the form of skimping on elements of production, which is a major way of lowering the value of the constant capital in relation to the variable and thus of increasing the rate of profit. (176)

For the capitalist, reducing the cost of the means of production augments the relative profit that returns at the end of the produc-tion-circulation cycle; once again, it appears as though this fact has nothing at all to do with labour and is, rather, a power inherent to capital itself:

> Yet the economical use of constant capital still appears to the capi-talist as a requirement completely alien to the worker and absolutely independent of him, a requirement which does not concern the worker in the least . . . To a still higher level than is the case with other powers intrinsic to labour, this economy in the use of means of production, this method of attaining a certain result with the least possible expense, appears as a power inherent in capital and a method specific to and characteristic of the capitalist mode of production. (177–8)

The attribution of social power to capital constitutes capital's perceptual physics – its real appearance as self-valorizing value, as the 'automatic subject'.[16] Meanwhile, if increasing the rate of profit through the econom-ical use of constant capital can appear as though it has nothing to do with labour, the consequences for labour of such economization cannot be hidden. Economizing strategies have an impact on working condi-tions that is brutal and direct, and section 2 of chapter 5 ('Savings on the

---

16 Marx characterizes capital as the automatic subject of a capitalist mode of production in *Capital* I.

Conditions of Work at the Workers' Expense') is dedicated to this illustration:

> Just as the capitalist mode of production promotes on the one hand the development of the productive forces of social labour, so on the other hand does it promote economy in the use of constant capital.
> Yet there is more to this than the alienation and indifference that the worker, as the bearer of living labour, has towards the economical, i.e. rational and frugal use of his conditions of labour. The contradictory and antithetical character of the capitalist mode of production leads it to count the squandering of the life and health of the worker, and the depression of his conditions of existence, as itself an economy in the use of constant capital, and hence a means for raising the rate of profit. (179)

In this section, Marx reproduces reports that were made throughout England on working conditions and worker health in mines, factories, and other enclosed workspaces, documenting the 'destruction of life, limb and health' that resulted from inadequate drainage and ventilation, ill-constructed shafts and roadways, overcrowding of workers in cramped spaces, the suppression of precautionary safety measures, and the 'profitable use of children'. Marx contrasts the extreme frugality in the use of dead labour objectified in means of production with the equally extreme squandering of living labour, of flesh and blood, of brains and muscles, that typifies capitalist production to this day: 'It is only through the most tremendous waste of individual development that the development of humanity in general is secured and pursued, in that epoch of history that directly precedes the conscious reconstruction of human society' (182). This ongoing and yet unimaginable inversion – the sacrifice of living labour for the sake of securing dead labour – is an expression of the ineluctable need to increase the rate of profit of enterprise.

The Social Factory and So-Called Free Labour

There is a partial (or immediate) verity in the practice of calculating profit on capital investment in both c and v: labour, as 'applied' labour-power, only creates value in the course of transferring the value of c to the finished product: 'In order that a definite quantity of labour may be realized in commodities, and therefore form value, a definite quantity of materials and means of labour is required' (137). In other words, labour creates value solely through the process of working with and on means of production, in working up raw material into commodities:

> Even though it is only the variable part of capital that creates surplus-value, it does so only under the condition that the other parts are advanced as well, i.e. the conditions of production for labour. Since the capitalist can exploit labour only by advancing constant capital, and since he can valorize the constant capital only by advancing the variable, these are both one and the same in his eyes, and this is all the more so in that the actual degree of his profit is determined in relation not to his variable capital but to his total capital; not by the rate of surplus-value but by the rate of profit, which as we shall see, may remain the same while expressing different rates of surplus-value. (133)

An analysis of the necessary, if indirect, role played by constant capital in the formation of value can be brought to current theories of so-called free labour: everyday activities performed voluntarily – usually involving digital platforms, including social media – that provide companies with media content, data, and ears/eyes on advertising, all of which become a basis for privatized profit-making. Some commentators use the term 'prosumer' to characterize the consumer-become-producer – the unpaid digital labourer who 'works' through consuming, and whose voluntary labour is exploited by capitalist enterprise under the aegis of leisure-time and/or the administration of everyday life.[17] Some commentators, including the critical communications theorist Christian Fuchs, argue that this 'unpaid digital labour' produces surplus-value for the capitalist and is therefore subject to Marx's critique of productive labour – a crucial category in the analysis of the value form:

---

17   The term 'prosumer' was introduced by Alvin Toffler in *The Third Wave*, William Morrow, 1980, 267.

Users spend time on corporate Internet platforms that are funded by targeted advertising capital accumulation models. The time spent on corporate platforms is the value created by their unpaid digital labour. Their digital labour creates social relations, profile data, user-generated content and transaction data (browsing behavior) – a data commodity that is offered for sale by Internet corporations to advertising clients that can select certain user groups they want to target. The act of exploitation is already created by the circumstance that users create a data commodity, in which their online work time is objectified, and that they do not own this data themselves, but rather corporate Internet platforms with the help of terms of use and privacy policies acquire ownership of this data. Corporate Internet platforms offer the data commodity that is the result of Internet prosumption activity for sale to advertisers. The value realization process, the transformation of value into profit, takes place when targeted users view the advertisement (pay per view) or click on it (pay per click). Not all data commodities are sold all of the time and specific groups of data commodities are more popular than others, but exploitation always takes place at the point of the production and appropriation of the commodity and prior to a commodity's sale.[18]

With the good intention of critically reframing the (often empirical or positivist) conception of 'prosumption', Fuchs, in this passage, rightly points out that many of the activities now 'outsourced' to consumers, as unpaid digital labourers, were once performed by waged employees. According to Fuchs, since that activity is now unwaged, it represents an especially high rate of exploitation, and the large profits generated by the companies that benefit from this activity index a new mode of value production and appropriation: 'If Internet users become productive prosumers, then in terms of Marxian class theory this means that they become productive labourers who produce surplus value and are exploited by capital, because for Marx productive labour generates surplus value.'[19]

---

18 Christian Fuchs, *Digital Labour and Karl Marx*, 2014, 95–6.
19 Ibid., 107. Fuchs presents an elaborate argument as to how and why unpaid online user activity should be analysed as value-generating productive labour – a process that, for Fuchs, involves the 'sublation' of 'the contradiction between superfluous and necessary labour' and the subsequent transfer of the function of value creation to unpaid

Fuchs's theory, however, is a significant departure from that of Marx. As we know from *Capital* I, value-producing labour is always (because it must be) coincident with wage labour (which is to say, it must take the form of private property), the legal form of socialized (abstract) labour in its capitalist integument. Without exception, it is labour performed *on the clock.*[20] The activity of digital media users does not meet the conditions under which labour produces surplus-value. However, that does not mean that surplus-value is not generated in the process of mining the traces of digital activity: waged workers who carry out the gathering, coordination, compilation, and analysis of these traces and turn them into 'data', and into sellable data commodities, indeed generate surplus-value in the context of the private enterprises that sell these data commodities. As with any other commodity, tangible or intangible, when it goes to market surplus socialized labour is congealed as a portion of the commodity as value-quantum – a portion that is realized as profit if and when the commodity is sold.

In the analysis of the movement of capital, determining which activities constitute productive labour and which do not – that is, the identification of which activities, literally, cannot 'count' as capital, because they are not exchanged as private property – is not simply an academic exercise.[21] A return to the question of cost price will demonstrate the significance of the distinction between productive and unproductive labour. Digital media users *do* provide capital with an important 'free gift' that comes not in the form of free labour but rather in that of abundant, readily accessible (and consequently relatively

---

labour (108). Fuchs produces a scheme through which one can calculate how much value was appropriated from free labour by a company in a given year, based on the profits generated by the company in that year. However, in *Capital* III, Marx demonstrates that rate and magnitude of profit are not manifested company by company but are, rather, the function of a general rate of profit where a certain amount of surplus-value and hence profit will fall to each aliquot part of the total social capital advanced in production. From the point of view of Marx's analysis, then, we must come to a different conclusion about the contribution of so-called free labour for capital. We look at Marx's theory of the general rate of profit in the next chapter.

20   This aspect of Marx's analysis is central and fundamental to *Capital* I. I will not rehearse the analysis here but rather move forward from it, as stipulated, and articulate it with the analysis in *Capital* III.

21   As we know, some waged labour is also unproductive of surplus-value, even while being necessary to advance the circuit of capital and realize surplus-value. Marx explains this dynamic in *Capital* I and explores it more extensively in *Capital* II.

cheap) *raw material*: namely, the digital traces of online activity, mined and assembled into data commodities whose use-value is to provide companies with insight into the who, what, when, where, and how of consumer behaviour.[22] Accessible, abundant, and cheap raw material maintains the value of c, means of production, relatively low. A low investment in constant capital lowers the cost price $(c + v)$ of production and increases the rate of profit for industries that can instrumentalize this material. In our hypothetical case, if the value of all other inputs remains the same, rate of surplus-value will also be unchanged and, as we will explore in the next chapter, this advantageous ratio between rate of profit and rate of surplus-value provides a temporary and provisional boost to the value-generating capacity of the system as a whole. For now, we can point out that the activity of participating in our own digital surveillance – generating the raw material of 'big data' commodities – is no more free labour for capital than is the chemical process that creates gold in ore.

However, generalized participation in online activity also augments the profitability of industry as well as the production of surplus-value system wide, indirectly, over time, by putting a downward pressure on the value of labour-power. The technical and communicational skills acquired by a population when so much of everyday life is carried out online increasingly become skills that workers are expected to possess as competitively 'hireable' employees.[23] This is the case not only for that growing segment of the workforce called the cybertariat but also for the workforce in general, in parts of the world where such a development is feasible given the virtually mandatory engagement with the digital.[24] This historically evolving inventory of skill, capacity, and know-how embodied by the average worker is what Marx calls, in the *Grundrisse*, 'the general intellect'. The more conventional the possession of certain

---

22   Mining and extraction is, rather, the best analogy for the procurement of this raw material on the part of digital media and platform industries, or any company that collects and sells our digital trace material.

23   I am thinking of technical and communicational skills such as knowledge of computers and a wide range of digital devices; user knowledge of digital software, applications, and platforms; research; sleuthing; the navigation of social media as networking, distributional, and promotional tools; and so on. I am sure this list is much longer and includes 'anti-social' capacities as well.

24   Ursula Huws, *Labour in the Global Digital Economy: The Cybertariat Comes of Age*, Monthly Review Press, 2014.

skills and knowledge becomes, the less these capacities register as the outcome of formal training and specialization. Gradually, in capital's regime of social averages, labour, highly trained in all modes digital, no longer counts as complex labour, that is, as a multiple of a unit of simple labour. In its capitalist straitjacket, once-specialized labour comes to represent the new baseline of *un*skilled labour, a unit of simple labour-power, and its value diminishes accordingly. In its capitalist integument, therefore, the development of the general intellect is a means to reduce the value of labour-power – generalized skilling as a method of deskilling labour that takes the form of a magnitude of value – thereby increasing the ratio of surplus labour time to socially necessary labour time as portions of the labour time objectified in the social product.

In this indirect way, therefore, the nigh-universal participation in online activity *does* facilitate a greater production of surplus-value. But, rather than representing free labour for the capitalist, online participation represents free worker training, the benefits of which fall to the capitalist class in the diminished cost of the variable capital (v) investment, that is, in cost price.[25] In the upside-down world of capitalist forms, an intensification of exploitation takes the surface appearance of a highly technically skilled pool of social labour – sold at bargain prices! Later in *Capital* III (part V, chapter 23), Marx makes this same point with reference to the growing generalization of 'special training' in supervision and management in capitalist enterprise. With the bulking up of the management layer of the labour hierarchy that attends the expansion of capitalist enterprise, the wider accumulation of this specialized training forces down the value of what earlier counted as more highly skilled labour-power: 'With the formation of a numerous class of industrial and commercial managers', wages fall, 'just like wages for skilled labour in general, with the general development that reduces the costs of production of labour-power with special training' (513). In a rare moment of agreement, Marx quotes English philosopher John Stuart Mill on this point: 'The general relaxation of conventional barriers, the increased facilities of education tend to bring down the wages of skilled labour instead of raising those of the unskilled' (513n79). The more that (potential) workers expand their repertoire of capacities useful to

---

25   Or, in other words, in the growth of surplus-value as a portion of the commodity's total value.

(potential) employers on their own time, as opposed to their employer's time, the more is the value of labour-power diminished by lowering the direct cost of its production. With capitalist development, an expanding general intellect reduces of the portion of the total social surplus-value that returns to the worker in the form of the wage, along with the generalized reduction of the cost price of production for the capitalist class.

The theorization of which activities produce new value for the capital machine (and under what circumstances) is not simply an obsession of Marxologists, as is sometimes claimed.[26] The fact that unwaged online activity does not – because it *cannot* – count as value-creating labour is the outward expression of capital's inner movement. A society's configuration around productive and unproductive labour (always historical, always changing) mediates its surface characteristics and developmental range of possibility, just as it directly determines capital's own reproduction, its social averages, and its tipping-points. Value is an accounting category. Its content is socialized labour time. At any given moment, value is an objective, if non-empirical, magnitude. As a quantum, value is absolute and determinant; as a dynamic, it is a moving contradiction: the surface laws of competition compel the capitalist to reduce production costs in order to increase profit. The capitalist does this by reducing the investment in labour as a ratio of the overall capital investment – that is, by increasing productivity. The consequences of increasing productivity, in human terms, is the expulsion of workers

---

26 Marx captures the distinction between value-generating and non-value-generating activity with the categories of productive and unproductive labour. Theorized in *Capital* I but explored in detail in *Capital* II and *Theories of Surplus-Value*, all labour performed outside of the wage relation is unproductive, while only labour that is waged can be productive of value. Waged labour is also unproductive if it is not involved in the direct production of commodities but is nonetheless labour required to realize surplus-value in circulation. Unproductive waged labour does not produce value; instead, it absorbs a portion of the total social surplus-value in its function as merchant's or finance capital (i.e., what is sometimes called circulatory capital). As capital, therefore, its movement is redistributive rather than productive. I undertake a fuller value-critique of the redistributive function of finance capital in chapter 5 below, and in 'Political Economy through the Looking Glass: Imagining Six Impossible Things about Finance before Breakfast,' *Historical Materialism* 25(3), 2017, 76–100. I undertake a value critique of waged and unwaged social reproductive labour in 'Wages for Housework Redux: The Utopian Dialectic of the Value Form,' *Theory and Event* 24(4), 2021, 896–921.

from the production process.[27] The consequence for capital is the destruction of the only generative source of surplus-value system wide: living human labour. Capital carries on by breaking down. This contradictory movement does not register in the consciousness of the collective capitalist; it operates behind their back. The historical character of the social formation – whether it is manifesting the characteristics of boom times or stagnation times, fierce or quieted class struggle, and so on – is a global index of the system's value-producing capacity in the course of its eventual necessary, progressive breakdown. In analysis, we look to square the state of capital's internal breakdown with its surface appearances, its manifested characteristics, its empirical forms. Today, however, symptoms of deep and chronic stagnation cannot be squared with the theory of a social-world-turned-social-factory that proliferates ever-new modes of value creation. If this were the case, value would be pumping into the system at a historically high degree; it would be manifesting high general rates of profit, falling rates of unemployment, increasing wages, capital migrating towards productive industry, higher corporate tax rates, and so on. On the contrary, chronic stagnation suggests something very different: value's self-cannibalization of its capacity to generate new value, the ongoing shrinking ratio of new value to the total social product, and the concomitant instability and degeneration of the system (a dynamic we will explore in detail in chapter 3).[28]

We return to this chapter's central line of inquiry: the mystifications generated in the movement of capital as revealed by the categories cost price and rate of profit. From the standpoint of the capitalist or capitalist enterprise, cost price is the aggregate cost of undifferentiated means of production, or simply the cost of doing business. However, from the standpoint of the movement of capital as a whole,[29] we must differentiate between the two components of cost price, constant capital (*c*) and variable capital (*v*) – one an investment in dead labour, the other in

---

27 This is the consequence of increasing productivity *in a capitalist mode of production only*.

28 The character of current stagnation is what Endnotes calls capital's 'holding pattern with declining altitude'. *Endnotes*, 'The Holding Pattern,' September 2013, endnotes.org.uk.

29 That is also to say, from the standpoint of the capital–labour antagonism, or the capitalist totality.

living labour – in order to analyse how a shift in the ratio between them generates systematic consequences – which are, in their human terms, largely dire.[30]

Capital has not surreptitiously turned everything we do into exploitable (value-generating) labour. A more apt critique of the social-world-turned-social-factory is that capital *can only fail* to turn most of what we do into exploitable labour, and this is increasingly the case when capital, in its personification *as capitalist*, strives to remove living labour from productive enterprise in order to reduce the costs of doing business. It is important to register that in this movement, the interests (or standpoints) of capital and the capitalist depart. The immediate interests of the capitalist in increasing the rate of profit (by reducing investment in labour) contradicts the historical interests of capital in expanding the system-wide pool of waged labour as productive resource. Instead, this resource is diminished, and from the standpoint of capital, more and more of what people *do* day in, day out – the varied, creative, generative, reproductive, and sustaining practice of everyday life, the quotidian poetry of survival, as well as heroic disruptions to the status quo – does not *count*. *Capital* is capital's own obstacle. The real subsumption of labour by capital increasingly takes the form of the redundancy of labour and its expulsion from the value circuit – an understated scandal captured by Fredric Jameson in the observation that *Capital* is simply a book about unemployment.[31] Marx's method throughout *Capital* is a dialectic of cool and warm: cool, technical abstractions – cost price, constant and variable capital, rate of profit – accumulate to build a picture of the disastrous consequences for the warm, vibrant matter of sociality.[32]

---

30   The wider historical consequences of capital's shifting organic composition is explored in Joshua Clover's *Riot. Strike. Riot: The New Era of Uprisings*, Verso, 2016; and in Aaron Benanav and Joshua Clover, 'Can Dialectics Break BRICS?', *South Atlantic Quarterly* 113(4), Fall 2014, 743–59.

31   Fredric Jameson, *Representing Capital: A Reading of Volume One*, Verso, 2014, 2.

32   I am thinking of Ernst Bloch's warm and cool streams of Marxist theory as elaborated in the three-volume *The Principle of Hope*, MIT Press, 1986.

Conclusion: The Physics of Perception, Conception, Consciousness

The seemingly inconsequential collapsing of c and v – that mundane business as usual and concomitant everyday appearance of things – transforms 'surplus-value . . . into the form of profit, *by way of the rate of profit.*' The process carries out the 'extension of that inversion of subject and object which already occurs in the course of the production process itself' (136, my emphasis). For Marx, the peculiarities of capitalist production – socialized production trussed up in the straitjacket of private property – amounts to an inversion of subject and object that further gives rise to inverted perceptions, and conceptions, of the situation and the stakes involved:

> All the subjective productive forces of labour present themselves as productive forces of capital.[33] On the one hand, value, i.e. the past labour that dominates living labour is personified into the capitalist; on the other hand, the worker conversely appears as mere objectified labour-power, as a commodity. *This inverted relationship necessarily gives rise, even in the simple relation of production itself, to a correspondingly inverted conception of the situation, a transposed consciousness*, which is further developed by the transformations and modifications of the circulation process proper. (136, my emphasis)

In part I of *Capital* III, Marx begins the analysis of this process, which he describes as a 'purely social' dynamic,[34] and which I will refer to throughout as capital's perceptual physics. As we will see, its consistent and systematic elaboration is the through line of the entire volume, from the first paragraph to the unfinished chapter on 'Classes'. In the passage above, Marx argues that the process of accumulation, operating 'behind the backs' of us all, produces inverted images of itself, perceptions that settle into the generalized understanding of 'how things are' and 'how things work' – perceptions that inform the collective sense we make of

---

33 Here, Marx is referencing *Grundrisse*, 694; Karl Marx, *Capital: A Critique of Political Economy*, vol. 1, trans. Ben Fowkes, Penguin, 1990, 450–53.

34 'Purely social' is Marx's refrain-like description of value throughout the early chapters of *Capital* I.

'the world of phenomena' (138). A capitalist mode of production is the production of a perverted and topsy-turvy world of appearances; appearances are the taking-form of an invisible social content.

Marx narrativizes capital's perceptual physics through the concept of the fetish. Marx's deployment of the concept of the fetish in *Capital* III is consistent with that of *Capital* I and II, although in III there is both a broadening and a focusing of the concept.[35] Here, the fetish articulates the systematic severing of the conceptual link between profit and surplus-value, a delinking that consequently obfuscates the subject/object identity of profit and living human labour. The fetish is a form of appearance (the capital fetish, the money fetish, the profit fetish, and so on) that mystifies the singular source of capitalist profit in living human labour; it obliterates from immediate perception the missing link: surplus-value.

In his supplementary remarks at the end of part I, Marx makes a short catalogue of appearances generated through the fetish character of the category 'rate of profit'. Earlier in this chapter, we noted that the simple perceptual collapsing of constant and variable capital in the category of cost price prepares the ground for capital to assume the role of automatic subject, the intrinsic power of value to self-valorize. However, rate of profit is an empirical category, and whether it increases or decreases in any particular case depends on the price of the means of production that have been secured by the owner/manager of enterprise. The category rate of profit, therefore, allows the capitalist, as the owner of the social power of capital, to imagine themselves to be the driving agent of this power. Marx writes, 'Rates of profits can be very different according to whether raw materials are purchased cheaply or less cheaply, [or] with more or less specialist knowledge.' Profit rates can be different

> according to whether the machinery employed is productive, suitable or cheap; according to whether the overall arrangement of the production process in its various stages is more or less satisfactory, with wastage of material avoided, [and with] management and supervision [that is] simple and effective . . .
>
> In short, given the surplus-value that accrues to a certain variable capital, it still depends very much on the business acumen of the

---

35 Marx refers to the movement of the fetish only once in *Capital* II.

individual, either the capitalist himself or his managers and salespeople, whether this same surplus-value is expressed in a higher or lower rate of profit and therefore whether it delivers a greater or lesser amount of profit . . . This variation in the way the same mass of surplus-value is expressed . . . may also stem from other sources; it can even arise purely and simply from the variation in the business skill with which . . . enterprises are conducted. *And this circumstance misleads the capitalist by convincing him that his profit is due not to the exploitation of labour, but at least in part also to other circumstances independent of this, and in particular his own individual action.* (235–6, my emphasis)

In the transposed consciousness of the capitalist, shrewdness in the affairs of business manifests in advantageous profit margins. The mythologized persona of the capitalist – the embodiment of initiative, pioneering self-sacrifice, fearlessness, heroic resourcefulness and vision, the motor of progress – is one of the ruling ideas which underwrites the interests of the ruling class, and which continues to make it possible (so far) for the capitalist class to weather such extensive and relentless evidence to the contrary. To this day, the notion that profitable business serves the wider common good is a ruling idea. We will explore other automatic appearances generated by capital's movement in the chapters that follow. For now, let us stipulate that a full-spectrum analysis of the movement of value obliges us to keep on standby the questions of perception and consciousness, representation and mediation, ideology and affect, narrative and cognitive mapping.[36]

Rate of profit is the crucial concern from the standpoint of the capitalist. However, for the analysis of the movement of capital considered as a whole, the crucial concern is, rather, the *relationship between* the rate of profit and the rate of surplus-value – an index of (what Marx refers to more often in *Capital* I as) the organic composition of capital. This relationship is expressed in the magnitude and distribution of the total social product system-wide; it determines the size of the pool of value generated by the system and distributed among

---

36 I am invoking Fredric Jameson's widely cited concept of cognitive mapping. See his essay 'Cognitive Mapping', in *Marxism and the Interpretation of Culture*, University of Illinois Press, 1988, 347–57.

the parties who have a legal claim to a portion of that value in whatever form it may take (profit, revenue, interest, rent, wages, taxes, 'social wage', etc.) across the world market. The world market is not the scaling up of capitalist production but, rather, the ground-zero of the system – 'the very basis and living atmosphere of the capitalist mode of production' – and therefore the base (or totalized) standpoint of analysis (205). The deeper significance of the relationship between the rate of profit and the rate of surplus-value is therefore not prima facie – that is, not found in its mathematical terms. As with the organic composition of capital, its elaboration reveals the impact that such 'blindly asserted [global] social averages' and their forms of appearance have on the lives of the human beings who are the makers and bearers of the system, and the producers of capitalist wealth as alien property:

> We have to make a certain distinction, in connection with this economy in the use of constant capital. If the mass of the capital applied grows, and with it also the sum of capital value, this first involves simply the concentration of more capital in a single hand. However, it is precisely this greater mass employed by one capital (which generally corresponds also to an absolutely greater, if relatively smaller number of workers) that permits economies in constant capital. If we take the individual capitalist, we see a growth in the size of his necessary capital outlay, and particularly in the fixed capital; but in relation to the mass of material to be worked up and the labour to be exploited, its value relatively declines. (180–1)

The organic composition of capital is the mathematical expression of the historical development of productivity, which, in its capitalist guise, expresses the systemic need to expel living labour from the production process and, therefore, the systematic proliferation of human need itself, unmet and denied.

2

General Rate of Profit: Competition

Capital's Centre of Gravity – General Rate of Profit – The Fetish Character of Supply and Demand – Conclusion: Class Struggle and the Freemasonry of the Capitalist Class

In competition, everything appears upside down (311). The immanent laws of capitalist production, from the standpoint of market competition (829), present not simply a false appearance, but rather an inverted one (338). Consequently, says Marx, it is 'one of the tasks of science to reduce the visible and merely apparent movement [of capitalist economic relations] to the actual inner movement' (429). Marx begins this work in part II and continues it throughout the rest of the volume. In *Capital* I and II, Marx theorizes the dialectical relationship between production and circulation: production and circulation are simultaneously identical and distinct. They are identical in that they are continuous and form a unified process: each moment presupposes the other. Yet, they are distinct: production and circulation are distinct temporally, spatially, as activities, enterprises, and actors. More fundamentally, they are logically distinct moments of the reproduction process. The movement of capital, such as it is, is reproduced as a function of the logical separation of the two spheres of activity. Wealth, in its capitalist form, is created and extorted exclusively through the activities that constitute the sphere (and category) of production. On the other hand, wealth is realized and distributed, and its original extortion mystified and concealed, by means of the activities constituting the sphere (and category) of circulation. The relationship between production and circulation produces and generalizes a certain way of knowing and understanding the world, at the same time that it conceals alternative ones.

When Marx speaks of circulation in *Capital* III, unlike in I and II, he does so predominantly through the image of market competition. The stage for the analysis of *Capital* III is the pursuit of profit in the marketplace, capitalists alienating accumulated wealth in order to produce more, as compelled by the imperatives of competition. In this context, the depoliticized matter-of-fact of buying and selling conceals the reciprocal cheating and swindling that takes place between the representatives of capital investments. Whether the commodities are purchased/consumed as means of production or subsistence makes no difference at this stage of the analysis. The crucial dynamic is a perceptual one: the market, as the arena of the pursuit of profit – enhanced by 'cheating, cunning, expertise, talent and a thousand and one market conjunctures' (966) – is the world of capital's phenomenal appearances where everything is presented distortedly and, in fact, standing on its head (829). This is the world, as Marx often refers to it, 'as it *actually* is'.

In part II of *Capital* III, Marx looks at how inter-capitalist competition, or the surface movement of economic relations, conceals its internal logic as the antagonism between labour and capital, or 'class struggle' as structural presupposition. Competition constitutes a process that Marx calls *equalization*, or the approximate balancing out of the amount of profit that falls to each aliquot part of the total social capital invested, regardless of its composition, across all spheres of production during a given period of time (258). The significance of competition, for Marx's analysis, is that it *is* the movement of equalization (488). Equalization precipitates the perceptual inversion that is characterized by two fundamental formal derivations. First, rate of profit transforms into 'general rate of profit'. Second, cost price transforms into 'production price'. As we will see, with the categories general rate of profit and production price we are one logical step further removed from the identity of profit and surplus-value. Consequently, these derivations – these transformations of form – represent a deepening of the fetish character that mystifies the source of all capitalist wealth in living labour.

Capital's Centre of Gravity

Part II opens with a reminder and a caution for the reader. Chapter 8 begins with a sketch of the analysis to follow. As we shift focus to the activity constituting the world of competition – the world of appearances – Marx reminds the reader that the objective is to identify the essence-appearance dynamic (or dialectic) that generates certain specific phenomenal (and material, in their effects) appearances, and to anchor the analysis in the essential, inner movement of capital – the 'inner connections of economic relations' (485). To do so entails distinguishing between what *is* essential to the movement of capital and what is not. As we will illustrate throughout, at the inner, essential core of capital is *value*, a commodity/market-mediated (i.e., 'thing-like') social relationship identified in the earliest pages of *Capital* I and taking centre-stage across three volumes of exposition. However, value – objectified social labour, capital's singular social content – becomes increasingly more mediated and obscure as we move through the surface stories of the marketplace. Here, essence and appearance systematically depart, and Marx cautions the reader against reifying the operating illusions that conceal what is essential versus what is accidental to the movement of capital. Price, for instance, derives from value, and never the other way around; price is always fundamentally determined and never determining. We will explore below why this is the case.

Marx issues this caution by invoking, for the first of many times in *Capital* III, what he calls 'the concept of capital' in a formulation he has already rehearsed in *Capital* I and the *Grundrisse*:

> In a general analysis of the present kind, it is assumed throughout that actual conditions correspond to their *concept*, or, and this amounts to the same thing, actual conditions are depicted only in so far as they express their own general type. (242, my emphasis)

Capital's concept, Marx says, refers to the prevailing conditions of a capitalist society that have congealed into a general type. But if 'the law of value' is a condition of production-circulation in capitalist society, what exactly does it mean to say that value expresses its own general type, and how does this situation come to be the case? What is the historical process that generates value as an essential dimension of the movement of capital while the rising and falling of wages, or the pressures of supply and demand, do not have this status?

In the historical process that produces capital's concept, that which Marx calls 'conditions' could also be called 'social relations'. For example, a collectivity organized by its means of subsistence (farm, family, clan, etc.) interacts with another collectivity as mutual traders of their surplus product, each group of producers meeting the other's need for this or that good or service. The relationship of exchangers-of-surplus stabilizes when the practice is repeated again and again over time and conventionalized. At first, the practice – an exchange or cooperation to mutual advantage – is contingent and accidental, carried out with only immediate intention or design to meet relatively discrete needs and desires of whatever kind. With the conventionalization of the arrangement, the outcomes it facilitates become predictable and dependable. The social relationships constituted by the practice, at first ad hoc, stabilize around it and become formalized, institutionalized – that is, objective relations. Consequently (and the directionality of the development is crucial: the concept of capital is an *outcome*, not an origin), these social relationships become the conditions for, and are presupposed by, other collective practices, patterns of consumption, subsistence needs, and so on that derive therefrom. The once-accidental practice becomes the ground that determines the range of possible expressions and configurations of sociality going forward. For instance, the trade of qualitatively dissimilar goods between two groups for the purpose of meeting reciprocal needs emerges through repetition as the objective condition for other practices that derive from it and depend on predictable access to the original good or service. Here, readers will recognize Marx's description of the historical emergence of capital as a system of private and anonymous, mutual dependency – as a set of social relationships mediated by the goods and services that come to circulate as if they drag their producers to market instead of the other way around.

The historical emergence of value as an objective condition of capitalist production-circulation points to another aspect of this process of a new world emerging from the old. The increasingly systematic exchange of certain quantities of goods between parties posits a necessary equivalence between irreducibly distinct goods that must nonetheless be an expression of a common quality. Establishment of an equivalence between goods is accidental *but necessary* in order to depoliticize exchange – that is, to dress it in the costume of 'transparency', in the guise of mutual advantage, as opposed to it being a matter of one party taking advantage of another.[1] With qualitatively different goods, there is only one commonality between them: the quality of being the products of human labour in general. Human labour in general, or abstract labour, quantified as units of production time, emerges as the singular commensurable quality between goods that are now, in the context of formalized patterns of exchange, *commodities*: goods produced for the purpose of exchange rather than for the purpose of subsistence. Subsistence is consequently mediated by the exchange of needed goods.

In this process, abstract labour – quantified units of collective production time – can, *logically*, only refer to *social* labour (as opposed to concrete labour) as that which congeals as the social substance of the commodity. The commodity, as a magnitude of value, must represent a social average of required production time rather than an individual, historically discrete expenditure of labour time. If the latter were the case, then goods would remain incommensurable and exchange would remain ad hoc and accidental; capital cannot emerge in this scenario. Rather, for capital to emerge, goods must become equal magnitudes of value (and therefore must be magnitudes of social, abstract labour, i.e., social abstractions) *because* people and their capacities cannot be made equal. The fundamental, irreducible inequality of human beings and their capacities must be concealed behind, submerged within, the commodities that step into their places as agents. The systematization of exchange, and the consolidation of a mode of social reproduction where the needs of a society's members are met through the increasingly collective but impersonal and uncoordinated productive activity of private units of producers, precipitates *socially necessary labour time* – an average labour time required for the production of any particular good or service – as the social content of commodities. Goods, at first produced as accidental surpluses of subsistence goods, when produced for the purpose of exchange, must be produced in a quantity that past experience has demonstrated can be absorbed by the market, i.e., by demand. Socially necessary labour time therefore congeals as the social

---

1   The capitalist state becomes the guardian of market-exchange transparency and depoliticization.

substance of value, as the now-established condition of exchange, as the material form of the social relation between anonymous exchangers of commodities.

Value emerges as a historically produced objectivity and confronts its agents as such, informing ongoing practice, determining its range of motion as well as what can be produced, how much, under what circumstances, to meet which needs, and so on. As an objective condition, value is nonetheless invisible and formless – 'immaterial and objective,' as Marx says in *Capital* I. As such, value must take a phenomenal form; the commodity is the phenomenal body of value. With respect to capital's concept (capital's essential movement), it makes no difference whatsoever whether the commodity, as value's bodily form, is 'material' or 'immaterial'.[2] As the body of value, one commodity is singled out, by practicality and convention, as the universal equivalent in order to function as the mediator of exchange – that is, to step into the role of money. The value of a commodity, which can only be expressed in the form of another commodity with which it always already exists in a relation of exchange-equivalence, takes the form of a certain amount of money, that is, an equivalent magnitude of objectified abstract labour in the form of money: the commodity's exchange-value. In turn, in the marketplace, exchange-values step into their final 'actual world' forms as prices.

However, in the actual world of competition and real upside-down appearances, a commodity's price (one empirical money-expression) will always logically depart from its exchange-value (as a different, ideal, 'non-expressed' money-expression). A multitude of market circum-stances – a demand or inadequate supply that favours the seller, a glut that favours the buyer, a particularly effective sales strategy, a swell of popular identification with a product, and so on – will push and pull a commodity's price above or below its value. Empirically, a commodity's price will only ever coincide with its value accidently. Only in exceptional cases, where the push and pull of market forces balance one another out such that their combined effect on price is to hold it in one place, will capital's empirical representation align with

---

2 It will make a difference in the sphere of the machinations of competition for profit, but it will not determine the essential movement of capital as a form of value. The movement of determination moves in one direction, and it is non-reversible.

its concept. Nonetheless, value determines the range of the potential fluctuations of price, while price does not – *cannot* – exert a reciprocal force on value. Price fluctuations represent recently past, ongoing, or anticipated market pressures on the expression of value. What must logically be the case in a capitalist mode of production is that *value tethers price*.[3] Despite the fact that a commodity's price will rise above or fall below its value, its orbit is determined by value as its *centre of gravity*:

> If the prices at which commodities exchange for one another are to correspond approximately to their values, nothing more is needed than (1) that the exchange of different commodities ceases to be purely accidental or merely occasional; (2) that, in so far as we are dealing with the direct exchange of commodities, these commodities are produced on both sides in relative quantities that approximately correspond to mutual need, something that is learned from the reciprocal experience of trading and which therefore arises precisely as a result of the continuing exchange; and (3) that, as far as selling is concerned, no natural or artificial monopolies enable one of the contracting parties to sell above value, or force them to sell cheap, below value. By accidental monopoly, we mean the monopoly that accrues to buyer or seller as a result of the accidental state of supply and demand.
>
> The assumption that commodities from different spheres of production are sold at their values naturally means no more than that *this value is the centre of gravity around which price turns and at which its constant rise and fall is balanced out.* (278–9, my emphasis)

The empirical manifestations of capital, its surface appearances, will therefore systematically depart from capital's concept, despite the latter's determining, if invisible, objectivity. Marx refers to this process as *abstraction*. The social function of abstraction is the historical production of objectivity, the sedimentation and materialization of once-contingent social relations into the conditions that must prevail for capital to

---

3 Contrary to what some commentators have recently suggested, we have not seen the obsolescence of the 'law of value', only its misunderstanding here and there.

reproduce itself *as* capital from a certain stage of development onwards.[4] It also captures the process of the historical constitution of what Marx refers to as capital's 'general laws' or 'tendencies'. When a social relation or practice (value) becomes objectified/abstracted as capital's general law, it asserts itself as a 'social power' against any individual or incidental relation or practice: 'As capitalist production advances, so also do its requirements become more extensive, and it subjects all the social preconditions that frame the production process to its specific character and immanent laws' (297–8). Capital's general law of value asserts itself as a centre of gravity keeping every individual act of commodity exchange in orbit. In other words, capital's general laws can be flouted occasionally, as exception; however, to cleave from capital's general laws systematically is to subvert capitalist reproduction tout court. It is for this reason that Marx emphasizes the importance of accurately distinguishing between the dimensions that constitute the concept of capital from those that are contingent and accidental – not only, of course, for the sake of an accurate analysis of the capitalist system, but, more significantly, for the sake of a clear understanding of what is required to render the system obsolete.

In analysis, therefore, we distinguish between those conditions that were present and instrumental in capital's emergence – capital's historical preconditions – and those that the developing formation generates as its own concept, its own posited presuppositions. The latter are produced by the developing system and asserted as requirements of its own reproduction. What emerges as essential to the movement of capital does not exist as a precondition for the development of capital. That which is essential to capital's movement, value for instance, is posited *by* the development of capital itself. In generating and positing its own presuppositions, capital represents a kind of evolutionary movement in *reverse* – the inverse of a teleological movement. As an expression of the same process, conditions that were historically necessary for capital's emergence and development (mercantile carry trade, usury, pre-capitalist markets, pre-capitalist forms of money, enslaved labour in the colonial territories) are succeeded by the new necessary conditions of what Marx

---

4   Sohn-Rethel's term for this process, configured somewhat differently from my own reading, is real abstraction. See Alfred Sohn-Rethel, *Intellectual and Manual Labour: A Critique of Epistemology*, Brill, 2020.

often calls capital 'full blown', even as the previous conditions may continue to exist.[5] The concept of capital, capital in its 'pure form', emerges only at a relatively mature stage of the development of capitalist society itself, the stage of capital full blown; and when it does, it forces all that came before to dance to a new tune – infuses all that came before with the new soul of capital, as Marx says in *Capital* I.

When analysis shifts to the sphere of competition, capital's core connections are more highly mediated and therefore even more deeply obscured than they are in the sphere of production. To isolate how the inner movement of capital compels its surface forms, further theoretical detective work is necessary. In part II, Marx continues the analysis of the mystifying appearance-essence dynamic of profit and surplus-value and their perceptual delinking, although now as it plays out in the sphere of competition. In part I, Marx examined the systematic deviation between the *rates* of surplus-value and profit yielded by the same production cycle, while the magnitudes of surplus-value and profit remained identical. In part II, Marx examines a further perceptual divergence derived from the initial one: the systematic discrepancy between *magnitudes* of surplus-value and profit yielded by the same production cycle, a perceptual effect of the competition between capitals for market share. As we will see, competition generates an empirical world of (approximately) equalized *rates* of profit – and, consequently, equalized *magnitudes* of profit – that fall to every aliquot portion of the total social capital investment. This empirical process of equalization of rates *and* magnitudes of profit among competing capitals (a balancing out over time that preserves the impression that one capitalist can skilfully outmanoeuvre their competitors) produces the upside-down appearance that profit is yielded by capital in general, regardless of whether it is capital invested in labour, machinery, raw material, promotion, transportation, or rent. However, in a capitalist

---

5 According to Marx, slavery in the Americas and Caribbean was historically necessary in the transition to a global capitalist system in one way that is still not widely observed, in that the value form required the scale of production it facilitated and which fed a growing world market. We explore this dynamic in chapter 6 (on part VI of *Capital* III). See Nick Nesbitt, *The Price of Slavery: Capitalism and Revolution in the Caribbean*, University of Virginia Press, 2022; Peter Linebaugh's review of Robin Blackburn's *The Making of New World Slavery: From the Baroque to the Modern*, in *Historical Materialism* 1(1), 1997, 185–95; Beverley Best, 'Marx's Critical Theory of Slavery', *Historical Materialism*, forthcoming.

economy, the empirical stage is an inversion of the essential character of things.

Marx's objective in part II is to demonstrate the way in which rates of profit – and thereby magnitudes of profit per aliquot share of capital invested – are equalized among enterprises that make up a singular field of production (auto manufacturing, for example) as well as *across* fields of production that constitute a national 'economy'.[6] As the process of equalization expresses the surface-appearances of economic relations, Marx recalls capital's inner movement: different spheres of production – today, the multitude of enterprises that constitute the world market and produce an inestimable number of qualitatively incommensurable goods and services – will generate different rates of profit and different magnitudes of surplus-value (and hence different magnitudes of surplus-value's identical substance, profit). In other words, from the totalized vantage point of the capital system, different productive enterprises contribute vastly different amounts of surplus-value to the overall system – surplus-value that is then distributed, in various ways (as we will see), between the parties with a legal claim to a portion of it as revenue, in the form of wages, interest, rent, or profit of enterprise. Building on the formulation in part I, the reason for this vastly differing multitude of rates and magnitudes of surplus-value/profit among capitals is clear: (1) different production processes are characterized by vastly different technical compositions, a varying number of labour

6   Once trade has developed between nation-states to the extent where there is little distinction between national rates of surplus-value, as is generally the case in the era of 'globalization,' equalization proceeds to organize the global market in the same way. The dynamics of the global market are not yet observed in part II; however, as Marx points out, we could look at them in a similar way as we do national dynamics. In fact, eventually, in the analysis, we will need to think of 'national economies' as abstractions of the total global social product: 'The distinctions between rates of surplus-value in different countries and hence between the different national levels of exploitation of labour are completely outside the scope of our present investigation. The object of this Part is simply to present the way in which a general rate of profit is arrived at within one particular country. It is clear for all, however, that in comparing different national rates of profit one need only combine what has been developed earlier with the arguments to be developed here. One would first consider the variation between national rates of surplus-value and then compare, on the basis of these given rates of surplus-value, how national rates of profit differ. In so far as their variation is not the result of variation in the national rates of surplus-value, it must be due to circumstances in which, as in this chapter, surplus-value is assumed to be everywhere the same, to be constant' (242).

hours required to carry out production, varying degrees of automation, differing character and quantity of raw material consumed, different transportation requirements, and so on; (2) different production processes will therefore express different organic compositions of capital; and, finally, (3) different organic compositions of capital – capitals constituted by different ratios of variable to constant components – yield varying rates of profit and magnitudes of surplus-value.

For instance, we know that if the rate of surplus-value is constant (which can indeed be assumed and therefore set aside as a variable) and if the value of variable capital (wages) remains constant, rate of profit will fluctuate in inverse proportion to fluctuations in the value of constant capital and to the length of turnover time (242; 243):

> We showed in the previous chapter that, if the rate of surplus-value is taken as constant, the rate of profit yielded by a particular capital can rise or fall as a result of circumstances that increase or decrease the value of one or other portion of the constant capital, and thereby affect the ratio between the constant and variable components of capital as a whole. We also noted that circumstances which lengthen or shorten a capital's turn-over time may affect the rate of profit in a similar way. (242)

However, we have also established that the magnitude of surplus-value/ profit is *not* affected by fluctuations in the value of constant capital but rather only by fluctuations in the value of variable capital, the latter being an index of productivity, or, the number of labour hours required to transfer the value of the constant capital to the product, while adding its own value plus surplus to the product's total value. Therefore, capitals that set different quantities of labour in motion, as they will inevitably do in production processes of varied technical composition, will generate very different amounts of surplus-value/profit:

> Capitals of the same size, or capitals of different magnitudes reduced to percentages, operating with the same working day and the same degree of exploitation of labour, thus produce very different amounts of surplus-value and therefore profit, and this is because their variable portions differ according to the differing organic composition of capital in different spheres of production, which means that different quantities of living labour are set in motion, and hence also different

quantities of surplus labour, of the substance of surplus-value and therefore of profit, are appropriated. (248)

Marx proceeds to illustrate these logical conditions with several examples of each case; his simplest example will suffice to make the point here: taking the rate of surplus-value as 100 percent, a capital of 100 with a composition of $90c + 10v$ yields a surplus-value of 10 and a rate of profit of 10 percent. On the other hand, a capital of 100 with a composition of $10c + 90v$ yields a surplus-value of 90 and a rate of profit of 90 percent (249). Here, two equal capitals yield different rates of profit *and* magnitudes of surplus-value/profit when their value compositions diverge. Different types of production will inevitably require varying organic compositions of capital investment that reflect its technical composition: again, some industries will require more or fewer labour hours to carry out production, raw material of varying species and quantities, more or less costly machinery, complex infrastructure, and so on. Marx expounds:

> From this it follows naturally that the rates of profit [and magnitudes of profit] in different spheres of production that exist simultaneously alongside one another will differ if, other things remaining equal, either the turnover times of the capitals invested differ, or the value relations between the organic components of these capitals [i.e., the ratio of passive to active capital] in different branches of production [differ]. (243)

Furthermore, Marx points out, if this were *not* the case – if the magnitude of capital invested determined the rate and magnitude of profit generated regardless of its ratio of constant to variable components – then *'value and surplus-value would have to [consist of] something other than objectified labour'* (248, my emphasis).

That capitals of equal size (or capitals of unequal size taken by percentage) in different branches of industry that are characterized by differing organic compositions necessarily yield unequal rates and magnitudes of profit *is an assertion of the law of value*: under these circumstances, unequal profit rates must prevail (249; 252). Why, then, is this not the case in the 'world as it actually is'? Why does the empirical state of things contradict the law of value and present an average rate of profit across branches of industry on equal portions of capital invested, regardless of their value composition? Why, for instance, 'is [it] only within the same sphere of production, where the organic composition of capital is therefore given, or between different spheres of production with the same organic composition of capital, that the mass of profit stands in exact proportion to the mass of capital employed' (249)? As Marx points out,

> There is no doubt . . . that in actual fact, ignoring inessential, accidental circumstances that cancel each other out, no such variation in the average rate of profit exists . . . The theory of value thus appears incompatible with the actual movement, incompatible with the actual phenomena of production, and it might seem that we must abandon all hope of understanding these phenomena. (252)

The explanation is contained in the fragment excised from the preceding quotation: in a capitalist society, the empirical state of things – the world of immediate appearances – cannot coincide with capital's inner movement 'without abolishing the entire system of capitalist production' (252, my emphasis). The system's core characteristics, enumerated below, form a totality that requires the divergence of essence and appearance as a means of its own continuation: (1) it is a system of predominantly privately owned and managed and, therefore, uncoordinated (i.e., competitive) productive enterprises; (2) the production of goods and services for the satisfaction of human needs and desires is not an end in itself but, rather, a means to the end-pursuit of realizing profit for private enterprise; and (3) viability of private enterprise is contingent on realizing more profit than one's competitors over a sustained period of time. Under these conditions of operation, if some branches of industry were routinely more profitable than others, private investment would not gravitate to less profitable spheres of production, as doing so would contradict the only motive for engaging in private enterprise in the first place. As capitalist production relies on inter-capitalist trade, with each capitalist entirely dependent on their brethren for means of production, and on finding a ready-made army of workers who must also turn to the market for means of survival, the possibility for all necessary branches of production to attract capital, where each branch of industry represents at least a potential for profit that is comparable to others, is an inherent requirement of the system. As such, inherently unequal profit-generating capacities among industries would have made it impossible for a capitalist mode of production to emerge at all, never mind reproduce itself. Here, again, we are confronted with Marx's central thesis in *Capital* III: a capitalist mode of production, as a condition of its reproduction, generates, and then posits as its own presupposition, a set of appearances that inverts its inner movement.

General Rate of Profit

Cost price is the phenomenal form in which constant and variable (passive and active) capital are conflated from the standpoint of the capitalist. An equality between two or more capital investments, expressed as cost prices, conceals the inherent inequality of the amounts of surplus-value those investments contribute to the pool of total social capital under non-exceptional circumstances. For capitalists, as the personifications of individual capitals, cost price is the baseline of competition; competition is animated by the drive to lower cost price with respect to the magnitude of profit anticipated to return to the capitalist at the end of the production-circulation cycle. The collective, if uncoordinated, activity of competition between capitals inadvertently carries out the process of equalization that generates the phenomenon of an average rate of profit across branches of production: 'This equality in the cost prices forms the basis for the competition between capital investments by means of which an average profit is produced' (253). Competition therefore presupposes the phenomenon of an average rate of profit at the same time as it produces and posits it.

The process of equalization is also the process that Marx calls the transformation of cost price into production price, but from a different standpoint on the system. It is unfortunate that the meaning of 'transformation' in Marx's analysis has been misconstrued, as illustrated by certain contributions to the debate on 'the transformation problem', or, by the fact that this debate ensued at all.[7] 'Transformation' does not

---

7   On the so-called transformation problem, see Fred Moseley, *Money and Totality: A Macro-Monetary Interpretation of Marx's Logic and the End of the 'Transformation Problem'*, Haymarket Books, 2017; Fred Moseley, 'Money Has No Price: Marx's Theory of Money and the Transformation Problem', in *Marx's Theory of Money: Modern Appraisals*, Palgrave Macmillan, 2005, 192–206; *Guglielmo* Carchedi, *Behind the Crisis:*

signify a change from one thing or state to another, in a sequential or progressive sense, where A becomes B and is therefore no longer A. Cost price does not undergo a quantitative change to become production price, as if a price, representing a certain amount of money, becomes a different price and a different amount of money. The latter is a model of two empirical phenomena – one phenomenon becoming another as a sequence or event in time. Rather, Marx is articulating a logical distinction, two different standpoints on the totality of the process, where one standpoint derives from another and yet each exists simultaneously – a difference that is also an identity. Marx endeavours to capture a dialectical movement with these terms, cost price and production price: a singular substance or *content*, value, that expresses itself simultaneously in the forms of cost price and production price, each form expressing a different but synchronic moment of the process. On the one hand, from the standpoint of productive consumption, that is, from the standpoint of acquiring the means of production – or, buying in order to sell – a certain quantity of value will express itself as cost price. On the other hand, from the standpoint of alienating the product that results from production in order to secure a profit – or, selling in order to buy – that same quantity of value will express itself as production price. One capitalist's cost price is simultaneously another capitalist's production price, and vice versa.

The internal distinction between cost price and production price is not expressed empirically; from the immediate (non-totalized) perspective of the capitalist, as either buyer *or* seller, there is only *the price at which the means of production are procured* and *the price at which the product is sold*, with the difference representing profit – the latter being the consequence of a savvy sales effort that pushes the selling price above the procuring price. The inner connections that differentiate cost price from production price can only be represented in analysis,

Marx's Dialectics of Value and Knowledge, Haymarket Books, 2011; Alfred Saad-Filho, *The Value of Marx: Political Economy for Contemporary Capitalism*, Routledge, 2002; Ben Fine, Costas Lapavitsas, and Alfred Saad-Filho, 'Transforming the Transformation Problem: Why the "New Interpretation" Is a Wrong Turning', *Review of Radical Political Economics* 36(1), 2004, 3–19; Anwar Shaikh, *Capitalism: Competition, Conflict, Crises*, Oxford University Press, 2016; Gérard Duménil and Duncan Foley, 'The Marxian Transformation Problem', in S. Durlauf and L. E. Blume (eds), *The New Palgrave Dictionary of Economics*, 2nd ed., Palgrave Macmillan, 2008.

that is, from the standpoint of the totality of the system (from the point of view of abstraction); as such, they are categories necessary to capture capital's inner movement. From the point of view of analysis, that which represents production price to the seller – a portion of which is profit (representing, as we will see, an *average* return on the magnitude of capital invested) – simultaneously represents cost price to the buyer (simply the cost of doing business) and the means and promise of future profit. The seller sells a product whose value (the basis of its price) comprises a certain amount of surplus-value that is materialized as profit; the buyer finds a product on the market of a certain value (the basis of *its* price) where the portion of the product's value that was surplus-value is hidden in the price of the means of production:

> The elements of productive capital are generally bought on the market in capitalist production, so that their prices include an already realized profit and accordingly include the production price of one branch of industry together with the profit contained in it, so that the profit in one branch of industry goes into the cost price of another. (259–60)

As we can now see, the meaning of transformation, with respect to the idea of the 'transformation of cost price into production price', is the meaning that Marx invokes when he speaks of a 'transformation of form'. As with the transformation of surplus-value into profit that we examined in chapter 1, profit, from the standpoint of the capitalist class, is the phenomenal form taken by surplus-value in the sphere of competition; surplus-value expresses itself, in the world of appearances, *as* profit. In the movement Marx exposits in part II, the same quantity of value expresses itself from the point of view of one enterprise as cost price, and from the point of view of another enterprise as production price:

> In Volumes 1 and 2 we were only concerned with the *values* of commodities. Now a part of this value has split away as the *cost price*, on the one hand, while on the other, the *production price* of the commodity has also developed, as a transformed form of value. (263)

To invoke the dialectical formulation that recurs throughout the three volumes of *Capital*, cost price both is and is not production price. This dynamic will become increasingly clear as we examine the process of equalization.

To form a general rate of profit, profit rates in each individual branch of industry must undergo an averaging out based on a cost price that is typical for that branch given the scale of production. As we know from *Capital* I, in order for an enterprise to remain viable over time, it must carry out production at a rate of productivity that does not generally fall below a socially average amount of necessary labour time. This requirement entails participation at a standard level of technical capacity for that particular sphere of production. The imperative to achieve a typical level of productivity in turn standardizes the technical composition of production and, consequently, the organic composition of capital in any given branch of industry, such that we can speak of an average rate of profit for each given branch. This is the dynamic of 'levelling out' – of technical composition, of organic composition, and of profit rate – in each individual sphere of production that is presupposed by a general rate of profit across spheres of production: 'In the absence of such a development [of average rates of profit in each sphere of production], the general rate of profit (and hence also the production price of the commodity) remains a meaningless and irrational conception' (257).

The true value of commodities comprises their cost price (the combined value of constant and variable capital) plus the surplus-value generated in the process of mobilizing variable capital in the absorption of constant capital (i.e., in the course of the production). However, commodities are not sold at their values; they are sold at their production prices, and values and production prices only converge accidently. As established above, if commodities were sold at their values, the system of capitalist production would collapse. Production price, then, is an index of the dynamic of a wider 'levelling out' of the profit that falls to individual capitals, relative to their size, across the entire sphere of production – a process necessary for the reproduction of the system as a whole. Production price consists of a commodity's cost price plus an amount of value that represents the general rate of profit as a percentage of the cost price: 'The production price of a commodity equals its cost price plus the percentage profit added to it in accordance with the general rate of profit, its cost price plus the average profit' (257).

Production price, therefore, presupposes a general rate of profit. The general rate of profit is the average of the profit rates across all branches of industry that constitute a national (and today global) market. However, for the profit rates between spheres of production to undergo an averaging out in the formation of a general rate of profit, commodities must be sold at their production prices. The ongoing collective practice of selling commodities at their production prices – that is, some above and some below their true values – is the means by which the general rate of profit is formed. It appears, therefore, that production price and a general rate of profit are tautological, each presupposing the other as its condition of formation: 'The really difficult question here is this: how does this equalization lead to a general rate of profit, since this is evidently a result and cannot be a point of departure?' (274). Rather than a relation of cause and effect, it is, more precisely, a dialectical relation of mutual causality: as capital develops as a mode of production, the outcome of this uncoordinated and largely unintentional collective doing is that production price and a general rate of profit emerge together as two moments (expressions) of the same process. Their dialectical (symbiotic) relationship is posited in the course of capital's development as a presupposition of the reproduction of the more developed system itself. Equalization is, therefore, a characteristic of the system at a relatively mature stage of development:

> In theory, we assume that the laws of the capitalist mode of production develop in their pure form. In reality, this is only an approximation; but the approximation is all the more exact, the more the capitalist mode of production is developed and the less it is adulterated by survivals of earlier economic conditions with which it is amalgamated. (275)

> The exchange of commodities at their values, or at approximately these values, thus corresponds to a much lower stage of development than the exchange at prices of production, for which a definite degree of capitalist development is needed . . . Apart from the way in which the law of value governs prices and their movement, it is also quite apposite to view the values of commodities not only as theoretically prior to the prices of production, but also as historically prior to them. This applies to those conditions in which the means of production belong to the worker, and this condition is to be found, in both the

ancient and the modern world, among peasant proprietors and handicraftsmen who work for themselves. (277–8)

The levelling out that is both cause and effect of the formation of production price and general rate of profit occurs when some commodities are sold above their values and others below. In order for a particular branch of industry to remain viable, it must attract a sufficient amount of productive investment. Commodities that are the product of industries with low individual profit rates, which express a standardized value composition of the capital investment typical for that industry, will conventionally be sold above their values, while the reverse will be the case for commodities produced in industries with consistently low organic value composition and which therefore express a typically higher individual rate of profit. This balancing process happens indirectly, in the course of capital chasing higher profit levels in one branch of production at the expense of other branches less promising (at least at the time). Made possible by the fluidity of the money form of value, capital, at least in its money form, is always potentially mobile (and must be). Capital's mobility allows investment to be redirected from one sphere of production to another:

If commodities were sold at their values ... this would mean very different rates of profit in the different spheres of production, as we have already explained, according to the differing organic composition of the masses of capital applied. Capital withdraws from a sphere with a low rate of profit and wends its way to others that yield higher profit. This constant migration, the distribution of capital between the different spheres according to where the profit rate is rising and where it is falling, is what produces a relationship between supply and demand such that the average profit is the same in various different spheres, and values are therefore transformed into prices of production. (297)

The need to give priority to competitive profit rates entails that, when rates are low, one can either hold back investment or redirect capital towards a different sphere of production.[8] In the above passage, Marx

---

8 The former situation is colloquially referred to in mainstream economic discourse as an investment strike on the part of the capitalist class; it is both cause and effect of capitalist economic stagnation.

describes the way in which the promise of future profit attracts further investment to spheres of production with relatively high or rising rates of profit. The increasing concentration of capital in that sphere of production will eventually lead to a saturation of the market, its levelling out and subsequent dropping off. The reverse movement occurs in the case of overly concentrated spheres of production where the rate of profit is consequently declining; lower rates of profit cause capital to flee that branch of industry. In turn, the evacuation of that branch of industry has a balancing effect such that profit rates are eventually restored once again. In this way, rates of profit are balanced out as commodity prices are pushed and pulled against their true values in a kind of feedback loop.

These prices will tend to settle into a pattern that is relatively consistent if levels of productivity – an index of the value of the product – in relation to other spheres of production remain stable over time. If productivity levels change in any branch of industry, this will be expressed in a change of the value of the product, and prices will adjust to level out the profit that falls to this branch of industry in relation to other branches once again:

> Whatever may be the ways in which the prices of different commodities are first established or fixed in relation to one another, the law of value governs their movement. When the labour-time required for their production falls, prices fall; and where it rises, prices rise, as long as other circumstances remain equal. (277)

Again, for some commodities, prices will be relatively stable – and consistently above or below the value of the product – when the amount of profit that falls to those branches of industry with consistently low labour investment in relation to raw material and technical means (i.e., capitals of high organic composition), or those with consistently higher than average investment requirements in raw material and technical means in relation to labour, will consistently produce commodities that express a rate of profit that is above or below average. In order to precipitate the equalling out that is required by the reproduction of the system, those commodities that express a true rate of profit that is consistently lower than average (which are in a position to command a higher price that is then conventionalized) will settle into a production price that is above the commodity's value and vice versa. This pushing of the price above value reflects the competitive orientation of the market; the commodity is simply in a competitive position to command a price higher than its value – a situation that continues if the demand for the commodity exerts such pressure. If not, the commodity's production price will sink closer to its value.

The equalization process is an ongoing balancing between the totality of commodities that make up a national (and today global) productive sphere; a change in the price of one commodity can be balanced out by a change in the price of another, cancelling the general effect of either change. Further, because production prices are not a *direct* expression of the commodity's value (i.e., they consist not of cost price plus the surplus-value contained in the commodity but, rather, of the combination of cost price plus average profit), a change in the value of the commodity does not necessarily produce a change in the commodity's production price:

> All changes in the price of production of a commodity can be ultimately reduced to a change in value, but not all changes in the value of a commodity need find expression in a change in the price of production, since this is not determined simply by the value of the particular commodity in question, but rather by the total value of all commodities. A change in commodity A, therefore, may be balanced by an opposite change in commodity B, so that the general proportion remains the same. (308)

Marx illustrates this movement in mathematical terms by taking five capitals equal in magnitude (all cost prices of 100, for the sake of example) and stabilizing the rate of surplus-value at 100 percent, in order to neutralize the effects of this latter variable (254–7). To represent the diversity of different spheres of production, each capital has a different value composition and therefore generates a different magnitude of surplus-value and a different rate of profit. Following Marx's example, if we posit the five magnitudes of surplus-value generated (100 percent of each of the five variable portions of capital) as 20, 30, 40, 15, and 5, we have five rates of profit of 20 percent, 30 percent, 40 percent, 15 percent, and 5 percent. To illustrate the dynamic of equalization between capitals, Marx then shifts the frame of reference and asks the reader to conceive of each of the five individual capitals as representing a different portion of a single capital, as in the case of one enterprise comprising five different departments, each department expressing a different value composition. From within this new frame of reference, we can posit a single capital of 500 (the sum of the five departments) and observe our former varying magnitudes of surplus-value and profit rates as those representing each distinct department. In this newly framed example, the magnitude of surplus-value generated by the enterprise as a single capital would be the sum of each of the magnitudes of the five departments ($110 = 20 + 30 + 40 + 15 + 5$), while the *rate of profit for the enterprise as a whole* would be the average of each of the rates of profit for the individual departments (22 percent).

At this point in the illustration, Marx shifts the frame of reference once again and asks the reader to conceive the single enterprise as a total social capital of 500, and a general rate of profit of 22 percent. We recall that the cost price for each individual capital is 100; at a general rate of profit of 22 percent, the total social capital yields five individual products, each with a production price of 122. The equalized rate of profit – and, in this case, magnitude of profit, since the capitals are equal in size – that falls to each branch of industry, regardless of its value composition, is 22. Here, then, a total social capital of 500 produces a total value product of 5 x 122, or 610. While the total surplus-value generated is 110, an equalized portion of 22 falls to each individual capital (or each branch of industry):

> Thus although the capitalists in the different spheres of production get back on the sale of their commodities the capital values consumed to produce them [i.e., the value expressed in the cost price], they do not secure the surplus-value and hence profit that is produced in their own sphere in connection with the production of these commodities. What they secure is only the surplus-value and hence profit that falls to the share of each aliquot part of the total social capital, when evenly distributed, from the total social surplus-value or profit produced in a given time by the social capital in all spheres of production.
> ... While this portion, the cost price, is completely governed by the outlay within each respective sphere of production, the other component of commodity price, the profit that is added to this cost price, is governed not by the mass of profit that is produced by this

specific capital in its specific sphere of production, but by the mass of profit that falls on average to each capital invested, as an aliquot part of the total social capital invested in the total production, during a given period of time. (258)

If equalization were not to take place (impossible in a capitalist mode of production, but illustrative as a thought experiment), each individual capital that produces at a different rate of profit would receive a different magnitude of profit, as in our example, 20, 30, 40, 15, and 5. The total surplus-value remains, in this scenario, as it must, a sum of 110. The process of equalization therefore represents a *redistribution* of surplus-value, and not in any way a change in the magnitude of social value produced.

In this illustration, cost prices are equal in magnitude; however, if cost prices were different magnitudes, this would not change the outcome. The amount of profit that falls to any capital investment will be the percentage of that cost price expressed by the general rate of profit, or, an equal portion for every 100 units: 22 on 100; 44 on 200; 33 on 150; and so on. However, despite how the surplus-value generated by the total social capital is distributed – and, in the world of capitalist forms, this is by average profit on cost price – its magnitude is determined, as it ever was, by the productivity of labour, that is, by the magnitude of variable capital and the rate of surplus-value. This entails, logically, that total commodity value must be equal to the sum of all prices of production:

> The total price of commodities I–V [our earlier five capitals] would thus be the same as their total value, i.e. the sum of the cost prices I–V plus the sum of the surplus-value or profit produced; in point of fact, therefore, the monetary expression for the total quantity of labour, both past and newly added, contained in the commodities I–V. And in the same manner, the sum of prices of production for the commodities produced in society as a whole – taking the totality of all branches of production – is equal to the sum of their values. (259)

Of course, there is never a cessation of the system of production-circulation to carry out such a calculation; the 'transformation' of commodity value into production price is a logical condition of the movement of capital rather than an empirically demonstrable one. Marx points out that the quantitative equality between total social value and the totality of production prices – an equality that is an index of their essential identity and therefore a conceptual bridge from price to value, and from value (as dead labour) to living labour – is, on the surface of things, 'contradicted by the fact that . . . prices include an already real-ized profit . . . so that the profit in one branch of industry goes into the cost price of another [and thus concealed]' (259–60). Prices will always be a fluctuation around an ideal average; they cannot be otherwise except under accidental circumstances. Since variable capital, taking the form of wages, is equal to the 'value product of the number of hours that the worker must work in order to produce [their] necessary means of subsistence', it too will depart from its true value as the production prices of those commodities that form the means of subsistence will also depart from their values. It is evident, logically, however, that whenever the price of one commodity is pulled above its value, it must be pushed below its value in the price of another commodity. It is also evident that this movement is constant and cannot be 'measured' empirically despite its mathematical orientation: 'With the whole of capitalist production, it is always only in a very intricate and approximate way, as an average of perpetual fluctuations which can never be firmly fixed, that the general law prevails as the dominant tendency' (261). The necessary delay in correspondence between *cause* – 'a change in the total sum of labour-time needed to produce the commodities', for instance (266) – and *effect* further prohibits the 'measuring' of the general rate of profit and its expression in production price:

> For all the great changes that constantly occur in the actual rates of profit in particular spheres of production . . . a genuine change in the general rate of profit, one not simply brought about by exceptional economic events, is the final outcome of a whole series of protracted oscillations, which require a good deal of time before they are consolidated and balanced out to produce a change in the general rate. (266)

Marx's analysis illustrates the transformation of commodity value into production price as a *logical* movement that generates a particular self-explanation; it is neither a quantitative change nor a change in substance.

The general rate of profit is determined by two factors, one of which we have already looked at, and one we have yet to: the first is '(1) the organic composition of the capitals in the various spheres of production, i.e. the different rates of profit in the particular spheres'. The general rate of profit is the average of the rates of profit in each individual sphere of production; each individual rate of profit, therefore, will factor into the general rate. The second determining factor is '(2) the distribution of the total social capital between these different spheres, i.e. the relative magnitudes of the capitals invested in each particular sphere of the total social capital swallowed up by each particular sphere of production' (263). If a sphere of production with a relatively higher rate of profit absorbs the lion's share of total social capital, this will be reflected in a higher general rate of profit, and vice versa. This bestows a significance on the nature of the industries that dominate in scale the productive landscape in any given historical conjuncture.

The mobility of capital is a requisite for the balancing-out process that forms the general rate of profit; the more mobile capital is, the more efficient the process (298). All mechanisms that enhance the ease and speed of the mobility of capital are, therefore, internally rational to the system. The credit system, the dynamics of both commercial and finance capital (as we will see in chapter 4), and free trade are the principal mechanisms facilitating the movement of capital from one sphere of investment to another. As Marx points out, the credit system 'concentrates together the inorganic mass of available social capital vis-à-vis the individual capitalist' and allows for large scale competitive investments by a single enterprise that would not otherwise be possible. However, the credit system also facilitates the concentration of capital in the hands of individual capitalists or enterprises by allowing social capital to be used to buy or bankrupt competing interests. While the concentration of capital is required for large investment in fixed capital, the greater the amount of fixed capital involved in production, the more the mobility of capital is impeded: 'In every sphere of actual production ... industry, agriculture, mining, etc., the transfer of capital from one sector to another presents significant difficulties, particularly on account of the fixed capital involved' (310–11). In this way, the credit system, by making it possible to build up large and less flexible entities – in extreme cases, creating monopolies or oligopolies – also serves to arrest the flow of capital and expresses a counter tendency to capital's mobility, a contradictory movement inherent to the movement of finance capital itself. In addition to the mobility of capital in the money form, the mobility of capital in the form of labour-power is also a requisite for the equalization process. As Marx further expounds, the 'constant equalization of ever-renewed inequalities is accomplished more quickly ... the more rapidly labour-power can be moved from one sphere to another and from one local point of production to another'. He continues,

> [This condition] presupposes the abolition of all laws that prevent workers from moving from one sphere of production to another or from one local seat of production to any other. Indifference of the worker to the content of his work. Greatest possible reduction of work in all spheres of production to simple labour. Disappearance of all prejudices of trade and craft among the workers. Finally and especially, the subjection of the worker to the capitalist mode of production. Further details on this belong in the special study of competition. (298)[9]

Competition between capitals and the pursuit of higher profit rates necessitate the mobility of capital and labour. The expression of the competition between capitals, and between workers on the job market, is the 'tendency to equalization': the creation of a gravitational orbit of profit around an 'ideal mean position' that does not exist as an empirical phenomenon (except accidentally) but that is entirely, if invisibly, determined by the value of (the objectified labour in) commodities. The material effect of this process is the equalization of the portions of profit that fall to every 100 units of capital (273). This 'balancing out' entails that every 'competitive advantage' achieved by an individual capital is ultimately temporary. Competition, in the upside-down world of capitalist forms, amounts to the neutralization of competition. The immediate or surface reality of competition, the concrete form that represents the perspective of the individual capitalist and worker, is an inverted appearance of the process of capital's movement considered as

---

9   Marx never undertook the special study on competition, which he refers to several times throughout *Capital* III. We have not seen the disappearance of prejudice surrounding trade and craft among workers; if anything, we have witnessed the opposite.

a whole (117). In lieu of the heroic capitalist besting their competitors, we have, in essence, a situation where

> the various different capitals . . . are in the position of shareholders in a joint-stock company, in which the dividends are evenly distributed for each 100 units, and hence are distinguished, as far as the individual capitalists are concerned, only according to the size of the capital that each of them has put into the common enterprise, according to his relative participation in this common enterprise, according to the number of his shares. (258)

Capitalists, the personifications of capital, can only raise their individual profit margins by raising the general rate of profit for all capitalists. Locked into this united effort, capitalists are competitors only in the surface appearance of things. Marx refers to this moving contradiction as 'the freemasonry of the capitalist class': 'We thus have a mathematically exact demonstration of why the capitalists, no matter how little love is lost among them in their mutual competition, are nevertheless united by a real freemasonry vis-à-vis the working class as a whole' (300). We will return to elaborate this fundamental perceptual inversion and its implications in the concluding section of the chapter. First, though, we will look more closely at the surface dynamics of competition that are the conditions for the emergence of a general rate of profit but that also produce the false appearance of supply and demand as the determination of price – an enduring surface story of capital.

The Fetish Character of Supply and Demand

Marx is particularly concerned to demonstrate (and takes much of chapter 10 to do so) that the common knowledge among capitalists and vulgar economists alike – that price is determined by the tension between supply and demand – is an erroneous, inverted perception. To illustrate the point, Marx examines two value forms: market value and market price. We have established that the formation of a general rate of profit requires the equalization of profit rates in individual spheres of production. This entails the averaging out of the individual values of commodities of a particular species and quality in each of those spheres – that is, the formation of *market values* – and the trans-formation of these market values into their monetary expressions, *market prices*. As we will see, market prices fluctuate around their centre of gravity, market value (279). Changes in supply and/or demand will push or pull market prices above or below their market value, creating the surface appearance that supply and demand deter-mine market price. As such, the concept of value appears superfluous to the determination of market prices.

The law of value entails that there will always be variation in the indi-vidual values of commodities (of the same genre and quality) produced by different enterprises because there will be individual variation in the compositions of capital investment (281). Market value is the average of the various individual commodity values that constitute a particular sphere of production in a given period of time. Market value is, there-fore, an 'ideal average', and, in ordinary circumstances, individual commodity values will stand either above or below their market values. Market value is, therefore, the value magnitude of commodities 'produced under average conditions in the sphere in question, and forming the great mass of its commodities' (279). If, in extraordinary circumstances, the bulk of commodities in a particular sphere of production are produced under worse-than-average conditions, market value will rise to express the greater amount of labour expended in their production. When the bulk of commodities are produced under better than average conditions, the situation is the reverse: market value will drop to express the lesser amount of labour expended in their production. This situation entails that

> if the supply of commodities at the average value, i.e. the mean value of the mass that lies between the two extremes, satisfies the customary demand, the commodities whose individual value stands below the market price will realize an extra surplus-value or surplus profit, while those whose individual value stands above the market price will be unable to realize a part of the surplus-value which they contain. (279)

Market prices, as the monetary expression of market values, will align with market values only when the bulk of those commodities (again, commodities of the same genre and quality, produced by the competing enterprises in a particular sphere of production) are produced at average levels of socially necessary labour time. Here, again, we can think of commodity value as the 'centre of gravity around which price turns and at which its constant rise and fall is balanced out' (279):

> This movement of capitals is always brought about in the first place by the state of market prices, which raise profits above the general average level in one place, and reduce it below the average in another. We are still leaving commercial capital out of consideration for the time being, as we have yet to introduce it, but as is shown by the paroxysms of speculation in certain favoured articles that suddenly break out, this can withdraw masses of capital from one line of business with extraordinary rapidity and fling them just as suddenly into another. (310)

Marx's invocation of 'customary demand' is a critique of economic orthodoxy that conflates it with the idea of social need as an objective and pre-existing quantity of goods and services required to sustain and reproduce the social formation at its current state of development (or standardized 'civilizational' expectations). In vulgar economics, demand is a relatively inflexible social need that pulls price upwards when demand exceeds supply and pushes price downwards when demand falls short of supply. For Marx, however, market demand is objective in the dialectical and historical sense; it is social need that 'has money to back it up' (282). 'Demand', in other words, is plastic and endogenous to market dynamics; it does not reflect a set of human and social needs and desires that develop externally to, or transcend, the needs of the capitalist mode of production itself.

> If a commodity is to be sold at its market value, i.e. in proportion to the socially necessary labour contained in it, the total quantity of social labour which is applied to produce the overall amount of this kind of commodity must correspond to the quantity of the social need for it, i.e. to the social need with money to back it up. Competition, and the fluctuations in market price which correspond to fluctuations in the relationship of demand and supply, constantly seek to reduce the total quantity of labour applied to each kind of commodity to this level. (294)

It is more accurate to say, therefore, that price determines supply. If demand is social need with money to back it up, 'if the price were higher than the mean market value . . . the demand would be less' (279). In the case of demand for means of production, the price of those means will inform the scale of production and not the other way around; 'cotton prices determine the supply of cotton goods' (292). Demand for the means of subsistence, on the other hand, is informed by the relation of wages to the total surplus-value; working-class 'demand' cannot expand without a larger portion of total surplus-value distributed in the form of wages (281). As Marx points out, the market can only absorb a definite mass of a certain commodity at a particular price. If the mass of commodities on the market oversteps social need (demand with money to back it up), commodities must be sold at a market price that is below their market value. If the reverse is the case and demand is not satisfied by the available product, then the market value will adjust to express the greater amount of necessary labour required to produce the mass of commodities absorbed. The movement illustrates that supply and demand have an impact on market price; the relationship between market price and supply and demand is mutually informing. However, in this dance, both are determined by market value. Therefore,

> if the market value changes, the conditions at which the whole mass
> of commodities can be sold will also change. If the market value falls,
> the social need is on average expanded (this always means here the
> need which has money to back it up), and within certain limits the
> society can absorb larger quantities of commodities. If the market
> value rises, the social need for the commodities contracts and smaller
> quantities are absorbed. Thus if supply and demand regulate market
> price, or rather the departures of market price from market value, the
> market value in turn regulates the relationship between demand and
> supply, or the centre around which fluctuations of demand and supply
> make the market price oscillate. (282)

Consequently, Marx argues, 'absolutely nothing can be explained by the relationship of demand and supply, before explaining the basis on which this relationship functions' (282). If the quantity of a certain commodity is too large and cannot be absorbed, or too small and readily absorbed without satisfying social need, market prices will diverge from market value accordingly, deflated against market value in the first case and inflated in the second (286; 289). We know from chapter 1 that the value of the capitalist's product is equivalent to the value of cost price plus a certain amount of surplus-value. Inflation or deflation against its value entails that the capitalist receives, after circulation, a greater or lesser portion of the surplus-value already congealed in the commodity. In unfavourable market circumstances, the price of the commodity might even fall below the cost price. But when the value of a commodity produced by one enterprise is deflated against its value, another commodity produced by a different enterprise is inflated against *its* value. These distortions of value occur constantly, and they balance each other out over a period of time, producing the generalized appearance that supply and demand actually do coincide. They coincide, however, 'only as the average of the movement' – the average that becomes market value (291). Therefore, to theorize from the fluctuations produced by supply and demand, in themselves, explains nothing (289). As Marx argues, it is simple to understand the divergences of market prices from market values; however,

> the real difficulty lies in determining what is involved when demand and supply are said to coincide ... [because if] demand and supply cancel one another out, they cease to explain anything, have no effect on market value and leave us completely in the dark as to why this market value is expressed in precisely such a sum of money and no other. (290–1)

Commodities sold at their values express 'the rational, natural law of equilibrium between them', and *this* law is what needs to be explained; *this* is the invisible but law-like tendency that is the 'basis on which divergences have to be explained, and not the converse' (289).

Herein lies the purpose of an analysis of capital as a movement of 'pure form', as concept. Market value does not exist as phenomenon; 'in actual fact demand and supply never coincide', or if they do, it is only by chance. Market value is, rather, a 'law-like form' that moves 'independently of the appearance produced by the movement of demand and supply'. It is the objective condition (social relationship) generated by capital's own development and posited as its own presupposition; it is 'theoretical' with more than 'theoretical significance': 'This average figure [market value] is by no means of merely theoretical significance. It is, rather, practically important for capital whose investment is calculated over the fluctuations and compensations of a more or less fixed period of time' (291).

We set market value – theoretical and determining – against the empirical fetishes of market price and supply/demand, whose tautological relationship amounts to nothing more than a balancing out around their mean values, neutralizing the impact of the fluctuation of prices altogether. In aggregate, the constant fluctuation of prices is an expression of *stasis*. Marx states,

> The relationship between demand and supply thus explains on the one hand simply the divergences of market price from market value, while on the other hand it explains the tendency for these divergences to be removed, i.e. for the effect of the demand and supply relationship to be cancelled. (292)

The fetish character of the appearance of market dynamism, of the frenetic push and pull between entrepreneurial disrupters battling it out for market-share, conceals the opposite: paralysis.

The dynamic between market value and market price is presupposed by the development of prices of production and a general rate of profit. For prices of production to exist as phenomena, the dynamics of market value/price must be the historical foundation for that movement. Prices of production come to take the place of market value/price in the course of capital's development:

> What we have said here of market values holds also for the price of production, as soon as this takes the place of market value. The price of production is regulated in each sphere, and regulated too according to particular circumstances. But it is again the centre around which the daily market prices revolve, and at which they are balanced out in definite periods. (280)

According to Marx, we can think of the relationship between market value/price and production price as a historical development as well as a conceptual or logical one:

What competition brings about, first of all in one sphere, is the establishment of a uniform market value and market price out of the various individual values of commodities. But it is only the competition of capitals in *different* spheres that brings forth the production price that equalizes the rates of profit between those spheres. The latter process requires a higher development of the capitalist mode of production than the former. (281)

Further, the resulting stasis in individual spheres of production as an effect of the balancing out of price fluctuations around market values is reproduced *across* spheres of production to produce a relatively stable general rate of profit over a period of time. In the way that the fluctuation of market prices comes to balance out around an 'ideal average', the daily ups and downs of profit rates in individual spheres of production are neutralized in the general rate of profit (269). For any individual profit rate to have an impact on the general rate of profit, that pressure must be consolidated and sustained for a sufficient length of time (270). The latter does take place, as we will see in the next chapter, while the day-to-day expression of the process is, again, one of paralysis:

Changes take place within each particular sphere of production, departures from the general rate of profit, which on the one hand balance each other out over a certain period of time and hence do not react back on the general rate, while on the other hand they do not react back on it because they are cancelled out by other simultaneous local fluctuations. Since the general rate of profit is determined not only by the average rate of profit in each sphere, but also by the distribution of the total capital between the various particular spheres, and since this distribution is constantly changing, *we have again a constant source of change in the general rate of profit – but a source of change that also becomes paralysed, for the most part, given the uninterrupted and all-round character of this movement.* (269, my emphasis)

Conclusion: Class Struggle and the Freemasonry of the Capitalist Class

While surplus-value and profit are identical in substance and magnitude, each of these forms represents a different way of calculating masses of objectified labour: profit as a magnitude of value sits in ratio to the value of cost price, and surplus-value as the same magnitude sits in ratio to the value of variable capital. Consequently, the *rates* of profit and surplus-value systematically diverge as numerical figures, even while their magnitudes remain the same. Their numerical divergence, signalling the collapse of the distinction between constant-passive and variable-active capital, dissimulates surplus-value as profit, thereby concealing the true source of profit in living labour. This is the dynamic that Marx refers to as mystification:

> Given . . . that the rate of profit can rise or fall, with the rate of surplus-value remaining the same, and that all that interests the capitalist in practice is his rate of profit, this circumstance also completely obscures and mystifies the real origin of surplus-value from the very beginning . . . the organic distinction between constant and variable capital is obliterated in the concept of profit. In actual fact, therefore, surplus-value denies its own origin in this, its transformed form, which is profit; it loses its character and becomes unrecognizable. (267)

For Marx, capital, in its reproduction as both a system of exploitation and a mode of domination, is a dynamic of social content and social form that is also a mode of representation – the production of particular distorted appearances that stabilize into a generalized 'common sense'. We might have once called this process ideology, and we might still,[10] so long as we recognize the objectivity of the inner connections of the 'economic' (that are, in fact, social) relations that constitute the ground of subjectivity – our subjective and embodied comportments, 'performances', identifications, and so on.

---

10 We *might*, but perhaps we should not. Fredric Jameson once suggested that it is a shame not to have a different word for the movement I am both characterizing and positing as the central theme of *Capital* III. In agreement, 'capital's perceptual physics' is the resulting mouthful.

In part II, where the analysis moves to the sphere of market competition, the process of mystification deepens. If in part I we examine the transformation of surplus-value into profit, a change of form that leaves their equality as magnitudes intact, in part II we see profit diverge from surplus-value in magnitude with the emergence of the form (and category) of production price. In the actual world of capitalist forms, the magnitude of profit that falls to every one hundred units of capital is an expression, not of the rate of surplus-value generated by the particular enterprise, but rather of the general rate of profit, an average formed on the value produced by the total social capital set in motion. In this configuration, we see the vestigial perceptual link between profit and surplus-value obliterated:

> [With the formation of the general rate of profit,] it is now purely accidental if the surplus-value actually produced in a particular sphere of production, and therefore the profit, coincides with the profit contained in the commodity's sale price. In the case now under consideration, profit and surplus-value themselves, and not just their rates will as a rule be genuinely different magnitudes. (267–8)

Despite Marx's caveat that an understanding of these mechanics is available to any observer who undertakes the work of their analysis, this process goes on behind the back of the capitalist, the worker, and the economist alike. The immediate material interests of the capitalist in their own reproduction as such, however, are served by the process of mystification that stabilizes the system. Meanwhile, the interests of the worker, structurally aligned with those of species and planet, are subverted by the mystification that conceals the fact that it is *their* creative life force that is objectified as alienated wealth and contorted into the drive to produce for production's sake:

> The actual difference in magnitude between profit and surplus-value in the various spheres of production (and not merely between rate of profit and rate of surplus-value) now completely conceals the true nature and origin of profit, not only for the capitalist, who has here a particular interest in deceiving himself, but also for the worker. With the transformation of values into prices of production, the very basis for determining value is now removed from view . . . profit appears . . .

as something standing outside the immanent value of the commodity. But what happens now [with the establishment of a general rate of profit] is that this idea is completely confirmed, reinforced and hardened by the fact that the profit added to the cost price is not actually determined, if the particular spheres of production are taken separately, by the value formation that proceeds within these branches, but on the contrary established quite externally to them. (268)

As a category, production price signals a deepening of capital's mystification and a further obscuration of the source of profit in living labour. Its dynamic is that of the fetish: 'The practical capitalist, imprisoned in the competitive struggle and in no way penetrating the phenomena it exhibits, cannot but be completely incapable of recognizing, behind the semblance, the inner essence and the inner form of this process' (269). Production price is what the capitalist *anticipates* they will receive on the market for their commodity and, in the end, is an approximation of what they *do* receive. The rationale for calling this value-derived form 'production price' is that it is the value magnitude that represents the necessary means of production that must be procured on the market in order to carry out production; in other words, it is the value magnitude that will become the capitalist's *cost price* of production: 'We call it the price of production because in the long term it is the condition of supply, the condition for the reproduction of commodities, in each particular sphere of production' (300).

Individual capitalists are conscious of, and internalize, a standardized range of production prices that they must realize on the market in order to compensate themselves accordingly and to carry out production once again; this means 'they take these [prices] into account in their calculations among themselves' (312). Production prices become the baseline for compensation of enterprise more generally: production that proves to be more risky than average, that turns over more slowly than average, that presents more complicated shipping logistics, and so on, will be compensated with the tacit authorization to increase prices to a degree that is conventional. The stabilization of production price as a baseline of compensation functions as a kind of insurance system for the collective capitalist, mitigating the risk of investment by compensating those branches that must absorb a greater amount. The capitalist's internalization of the category of production price is, at the same time, the process of the category's *externalization* (as described in chapter 1) or, alternatively, the *autonomization* of the category as a material and objective social force. As Marx expounds,

> The price of production is . . . a completely externalized and *prima facie* irrational form of commodity value, a form that appears in competition and is therefore present in the consciousness of the vulgar capitalist and consequently also in that of the vulgar economist. (300)

In the end, all these dynamics forge the appearance, in the consciousness of the capitalist and therefore more widely, that profit is the outcome of astute management within the traditional conventions of business practice rather than the extortion of surplus labour. This inversion of appearance is precisely what Marx calls the fetish movement of capital:

> All these grounds for compensation that make themselves mutually felt in the reciprocal calculation of commodity prices by the capitalists in different branches of production are simply related to the fact that they all have an equal claim on the common booty, the total surplus-value, in proportion to their capital. It *appears* to them, rather, that the profit which they pocket is something different from the surplus-value they extort; that the grounds for compensation do not simply equalize their participation in the total surplus-value, but that they actually *create profit itself.* (313)

Despite this, what the capitalist receives with production price is not the surplus-value/profit generated by their own workers' living labour but, rather, the average profit on their capital investment as an aliquot portion of the total social capital. Each individual capital functions as only a 'fragment of the total [social] capital' and each capitalist as a 'shareholder in the whole social enterprise, partaking in the overall profit in proportion to the size of his share of capital' (312). Marx states,

> At a given level of exploitation of labour, the mass of surplus-value that is created in a particular sphere of production is now more important for the overall average profit of the social capital, and thus

for the capitalist class in general, than it is directly for the capitalist within each particular branch of production. (268)

Capitalists, imagining that they are locked in battle, in fact work for each other; Marx refers to their operational unity as the freemasonry of the capitalist class (300):

> From what has been said so far, we can see that each individual capitalist, just like the totality of all capitalists in each particular sphere of production, participates in the exploitation of the entire working class by capital as a whole, and in the level of this exploitation; not just in terms of general class sympathy, but in a direct economic sense, since, taking all other circumstances as given, including the value of the total constant capital advanced, the average rate of profit depends on the level of exploitation of labour by capital as a whole. (298–9)

If the magnitude of profit that falls to each capitalist is their share of the total surplus-value produced on the total social capital, then each capitalist has a stake in the deepening exploitation of labour as a class regardless of their individual investment in variable capital. A capitalist who does not employ any workers has as much interest in raising the general rate of surplus-value (i.e., raising the overall productivity of workers, the intensity of exploitation) as does a capitalist who invests only variable capital and no constant (299). While impossible in practice, these examples illustrate the way in which individual capitalists are, in essence, merely representatives of capital as a *social power*. They also illustrate a corresponding perceptual inversion: a capitalist's choice to employ fewer workers in order to reduce their investment in variable capital has both the appearance and partial, immediate reality of a means to increase profit. However, with respect to capital's core movement, the capitalist's choice actually produces the opposite result: the diminishment of the total magnitude of surplus-value generated by the system, the pool of abstract wealth from which each individual enterprise takes its share. Marx articulates the objectivity of this inverted appearance by framing it as a question that capital's surface story of profit compels:

How therefore can living labour be the exclusive source of profit, since a reduction in the quantity of labour needed for production not only seems not to affect the profit, but rather to be the immediate source of increasing profit, in certain circumstances, at least for the individual capitalist? (270)

On the one hand, the individual capitalist, from the point of view of the process as a whole, is insignificant and a pretence of competitive agency; that which the capitalist appropriates is an always already determined, if approximate, portion of what is appropriated collectively, as a collective subject. On the other hand, what each individual representative of the capitalist class receives is a share of the surplus-value generated not by individual workers, or workers grouped by enterprise, or even by a particular sphere of production, but by the working class as a whole, across spheres of production – that is, by the worker as collective subject. At the concept of capital, the only agency in play is the agency of collective subjects, of the working class and the capitalist class, locked in a structural antagonism that is mystified by the fetish categories of capital's world of phenomena and appearances. The capitalist exploits as a class and divides up the spoils while believing in their own heroic battles, victories, and defeats. At the same time, workers are exploited as a class, individualize their survival and their succumbing, and imagine wrongly that to get ahead means leaving their fellow worker-competitors behind.

3

Falling Rate of Profit: Crisis

Productivity's Progress (from This World, to That Which Is to Come) – Countertendencies – Contradiction and Crisis – Conclusion: Mathematics and Class Struggle

Part III of *Capital* III theorizes capital's contradictory internal movement and the phenomenal forms of appearance thrown off by that movement. As we will see, capital's internal contradictions do not simply pose a problem for the management, regulation, or governance of the system. Rather, capital's movement manifests the systemic crisis of the mode of production itself. Marx's analysis of the dynamics of capitalist crisis is theoretical, mathematical, and advances by way of abstraction, while the political subtext of the analysis is consistent and emphatic: the expressions of capitalist crisis subvert the material interests – widely construed – of all of the system's bearers, while they heap ever more misery on those who constitute the collective subject of the working class and, more again, on those rendered surplus to the production of surplus-value altogether – a growing portion of the working class.

In *Capital* III, the category of the working class is itself an abstraction. It conceptualizes in one category those subjected to the wage contract directly, those who have been thrown out of employment (temporarily or permanently), the 'underemployed', informalized workers, and, finally, the growing population of people made entirely surplus to any kind of employment whatsoever. Surplus populations play a significant role in the viability of capitalist accumulation in several respects: by absorbing those who are permanently expelled from the wage relation into extra-capitalist survival formations and configurations of social reproduction; by forming a standby (if never actualized) labour force that, because of intensified competition for employment, provides the necessary downward pressure on the level of wages and ensures the employer's ability to secure workers despite worsening labour conditions and stagnating wages; and by forming the base of a necessarily stratified collective subject – a working-class hierarchy – that creates a comportment of competition between workers.[1]

However, despite the deep fragmentation and stratification of the working class 'in the world as it actually is', from the point of view of capital's inner movement, the process of exploitation is unifying and simplifying: labour produces surplus-value for capital, and it does so in full cooperation across spheres of production like differentiated components of the same machine – 'simple labour' in cooperation with complex, relatively secure labour in cooperation with transient or precarious, each 'strata' indistinguishable at its concept in its commodified form as labour-power, and in its functional form as living labour mobilized. The weight of capital's contradictions is thrust more heavily, and brutally, on some workers than on others.[2] Exploitation, however, requires that workers collectively bear the category of labour,

---

1   The stratification of the working class sets workers against each other, the unemployed against the employed, the low-waged against the more highly waged, those with pensions against those without such benefits, gendered and racialized workers against those 'non-differentiated' with respect to these technologies of group-differentiation, and so on. This development of ongoing stratification generates the appearance that the structured interests of the members of the working class are fundamentally fragmented and antagonistic. That appearance has real and material consequences for the entirety of capital's history.

2   For a theoretical account of the relationship between the processes of exploitation and subalternization, and the need for Marxist critique to play better attention to the latter, see Sourayan Mookerjea, 'Accumulated Violence, or, the Wars of Exploitation: Notes Toward a Post-Western Marxism', *Mediations* 32(1), Fall 2018, 95–114; Bret Benjamin, 'Developmental Aspiration at the End of Accumulation: The New International Economic Order and the Antinomies of the Bandung Era', *Mediations* 32(1), Fall 2018, 37–70; Kanishka Chowdury, *Border Rules: An Abolitionist Refusal*, Palgrave Macmillan, 2023; Jairus Banaji, *Theory as History: Essays on Modes of Production*, Brill, 2010; Himani Bannerji, *Thinking through: Essays on Feminism, Marxism and Anti-Racism*, Women's Press, 1995.

and are thereby rendered identical as logical functions; that, in their separation from the means of production, they are indistinguishable as producers of capitalist wealth; and that their claim to a portion of this wealth grows relatively smaller as accumulation proceeds.

Marx's exposition of capital's system-crisis in *Capital* III foregoes an analysis of its effects and consequences in human terms for a focus on its logical movement. Rather than a political critique of human suffering, Marx demonstrates that the 'material substratum' of human suffering is mystified in its mediation by objective conditions rendered in mathematical terms (375). On the rare occasion that Marx lauds the classical economic analysis of David Ricardo, it is for taking a similarly totalizing approach, namely in offering a 'non-humanized' representation of capital's productive forces in their historical development, according to their own immanent compulsions:

> It is the rate of profit that is the driving force in capitalist production, and nothing is produced save what can be produced at a profit. Hence the concern of the English economists over the decline in the profit rate. If Ricardo is disquieted even by the very possibility of this, that precisely shows his deep understanding of the conditions of capitalist production. What other people reproach him for, i.e. that he is unconcerned with 'human beings' and concentrates exclusively on the development of the productive forces when considering capitalist production – whatever sacrifices of human beings and capital *values* this is bought with – is precisely his significant contribution. The development of the productive forces of social labour is capital's historic mission and justification. For that very reason, it unwittingly creates the material conditions for a higher form of production. (368)

We will return later to the idea that the historical development of capitalist production is also the development of a potential, if not-yet-realized, portal to a 'higher' (non-capitalist, associated, intentionally organized, etc.) mode of production. It is an example of the radical – utopian, even – comportment of Marx's dialectical method. The purpose of invoking Ricardo, however, is to show that Ricardo recognized, even if he could not fully explain, the fundamental contradiction animating capital's movement: that the development and growth of capitalist production, driven by the pursuit of profit, is, at the same time, the internal breakdown of the system itself, that is, the progressive negation of the conditions of capitalist production: 'What disturbs Ricardo is the way that the rate of profit, which is the stimulus of capitalist production and both the condition for and the driving force in accumulation, is endangered by the development of production itself' (368).

The contradictory movement we will explore in this chapter is as such: accumulation is the defining and immanent movement – the historical mission – of the automatic subject, capital. Meanwhile, for capital's representative, the capitalist class, the defining motivation and purpose – accumulation's surface story – is the pursuit of profit. Since capitalists must compete with each other to secure the profit they chase, *rate* of profit, as the expression of their success or failure, defines the viability of enterprise; securing a favourable rate of profit is the endgame of the 'competitive struggle' between capitals (365). The contradiction, or dialectical movement, of the process lies here: on the one hand, the competitive struggle to increase profit rates drives accumulation forward; on the other hand, the competitive struggle to increase profit rates causes the rate of profit to fall across all spheres of production and, in doing so, jeopardizes further accumulation. Capitalist accumulation is compelled forward in a way that is bound to its self-hindrance. This contradictory movement takes the phenomenal form of periodic crises, localized breakdowns in the system (in various forms), or, less frequently, a system-wide stagnation or crash, as we saw with the global financial crisis of 2008. As we will see, from the point of view of capital, system crisis represents a temporary *solution* to an encountered barrier to accumulation, to a contradiction that can no longer be managed by capital's current configuration, and with respect to which capital must reconfigure in order to carry out its historical mission.

In part III, Marx theorizes the law of the tendential fall in the rate of profit and examines the structural conditions for crisis immanent to the movement of capitalist accumulation. This dimension of Marx's analysis, for self-evident reasons, has received much attention since the economic crash of 2008. We will follow Marx's analysis across part III and locate the invisible thread that connects capitalist crisis and its dire consequences to the dynamics of the falling rate of profit.

Productivity's Progress (from This World, to That Which Is to Come)

Capital I builds an analysis of the capitalist mode of production as a system of expanding wealth, where accumulation is capital's driving force and sine qua non: for capital to live on, it must expand. Marx's critique of value is that of the specific form and substance of capitalist wealth. It is also the critique of a specific movement and its mytholo-gization: the movement of value as it creates more value, and the appearance that it can do so on its own steam. This is capital's defini-tion and mythos. The process of accumulation takes the phenomenal form, in the world of appearances, of the competitive struggle between capitals to secure profit. Of course, securing profit is not sufficient in itself. If the actions taken to meet this goal increase the costs of production more than the returning profit, then the effort is in vain. The objective of the individual capitalist is, therefore, to secure an advantageous *rate* of profit – a favourable ratio of profit to production costs. From the perspective of the individual enterprise, i.e., 'from the standpoint of capitalist production itself' (368), the goal is to increase the mass of profit in relation to the cost of doing business. Again, from the standpoint of capitalist production, if the length of the work-ing day remains constant, the only way to increase the mass of profit is to increase the mass of *product* – the mass of commodities – produced in a day (in an hour, or in a production cycle), relative to the competition.

For the capitalist, the inverted appearance of things that generates the intuitive and practical necessity of augmenting productivity is this: the commodity produced for market is a value equal to its cost price; the capitalist then inflates the commodity's cost price to sell it at its production price; the difference between cost price (what it costs the capitalist to produce the commodity) and production price (the price at which the capitalist will sell the commodity) is the portion of the commodity's value that represents the capitalist's profit. The capitalist imagines that if they can produce more commodities per hour (per day, per production cycle) than their competitors, they can then offer their comparable commodity at a lower price and capture a larger share of the market. In the perception of the capitalist, what they lose in profit per commodity by lowering the commodity's price, they are compensated for by selling a greater number of commodities – underselling the competition in order to outsell them:

> This phenomenon *simply appears on the surface* as a fall in the amount of profit on the individual commodity, a fall in its price, and a growth in the mass of profit on the increased total number of commodities produced by the total social capital or the total capital of the individual capitalist. *The matter is then conceived* as if the capitalist voluntarily made less profit on the individual commodity, but compensated himself by the greater number of commodities which he now produces. (337, my emphasis)

In favourable circumstances, the mass of profit yielded by the greater mass of product increases more than what is lost by cheapening the individual commodity. This greater mass of profit, in appearance, is achieved through *multiplication*, through setting the price of the individual commodity and multiplying (and realizing) that price as many times as possible, and at ever-increasing numbers (338). This is one dimension of the way in which, in a capitalist mode of production, growth is by necessity endless; the imperative of competition demands it.

This surface story (and corresponding practice of the capitalist) presupposes the progressive development of the social productivity of labour. But if this is the surface story, what is actually going on below the surface? If the capitalist responds to competitive struggle with other capitals by exploiting what human ingenuity makes possible – greater productivity through technical means – in order to sell a larger quantity of a cheaper commodity, what dynamics are in motion at the level of capital's concept? The historically compelled growth of labour productivity is the material pivot that articulates the inverted appearance from the standpoint of capitalist production described above, with the inner relations of capital's movement considered as a whole. Part III of *Capital* III explores how, at this deeper level, increased productivity in its capitalist expression entails a 'gradual fall in the general rate of profit' of enterprise system-wide (318).[3]

---

3   We will explore the consequences of the fall in the rate of profit in human terms in the final section.

To illustrate the dynamic of the falling rate of profit, Marx stabilizes wages, the length of the working day, and the rate of surplus-value (i.e., presumes an unchanged level of exploitation of labour). As we know, variable capital (v) represents a certain amount of wages paid out by the capitalist, which in turn represents a 'definite number of workers set in motion' (317). A definite number of workers, working at a certain level of productivity, absorbs a definite amount of value in the form of the means of production (raw material, depreciation of machinery), transferring the value of these means of production – or, the value of the constant capital (c) – to the value of the product. The expression of the definite amount of c that can be absorbed and transferred by v is another way of describing the organic composition of a capital investment. To conceive of the definite quantity of raw material that can be worked up by a certain number of workers is simply to posit the organic composition of a certain capital investment as a ratio of c to v. A rise in productivity entails increasing the quantity of commodities produced per day (hour, cycle, year) without increasing the number of workers required to produce them – that is, without increasing the investment in wages, or, v. Even better, from the standpoint of capitalist production, would be to increase the output of product while *reducing* the wage obligation. To either stabilize or reduce investment in v (reducing the number of labour hours per commodity), some kind of technical development of the labour process itself is required, whether through the introduction of new production methods, new modes of organizing either the process or the cooperation of workers, new machines, or other technologies that streamline or rationalize some aspect of the process. The deep contradictions involved in the introduction of new productive technologies and methods in the specific context of capitalist production are the subject of analysis, famously, in chapter 15 of *Capital* I.

Here, however, Marx explores the implications of new productive capacities for the general rate of profit, per se. The production of a greater quantity of product necessarily requires the consumption of a greater quantity of means of production – more raw material and, in some cases, a more rapid depreciation of tools and machinery.[4] In other words, greater output requires an increased investment in constant

---

4   In the case of so-called immaterial goods, this may not be the case. This scenario will be explored in the next section on countertendencies to the falling rate of profit.

capital, c. Supposing a stable rate of surplus-value, if the magnitude of v remains the same (or falls; however, for the moment, we will ignore this scenario as there is no difference in formulation between a stable or falling investment in v), and the magnitude of c increases, rate of profit must logically fall. The mathematical expression of this dynamic is very clear, as Marx illustrates:

$c = 100$ and $v = 100$, then rate of profit is the surplus-value over total capital, $\frac{100}{200}$, or 50%

$c = 200$ and $v = 100$, then rate of profit is $\frac{100}{300}$, or $33\frac{1}{3}$%

$c = 400$ and $v = 100$, then rate of profit is $\frac{100}{400}$, or 25%

$c = 1,000$ and $v = 100$, then rate of profit is $\frac{100}{1000}$, or 10%

And so on.

As shown, if investment in constant capital rises and investment in variable capital remains the same, rate of profit falls. If, as investment in c rises, the investment in v were to decrease, as opposed to remain stable – which we can imagine might be the case in production processes introducing 'labour-saving technologies' and increasing levels of automation – the fall in the rate of profit would be steeper. In either case,

the same rate of surplus-value . . . and an unchanged level of exploita-tion of labour, is expressed in a falling rate of profit, as the value of the constant capital and hence the total capital grows with the constant capital's material volume. (317)

As the output of an enterprise, compelled by the necessity of competi-tion, grows, the value portion of the product that represents constant capital grows *faster* in relation to the value portion that represents vari-able capital; that is, investment in raw material grows faster as a portion of the total capital in proportion to investment in labour-power. In *Capital* I, Marx refers to this dynamic – the increasing ratio of c to v in the course of the historical development of the production process – as the growing organic composition of capital. Because increasing produc-tivity compels all capitalist industry generally speaking, the growing organic composition of capital will occur in all spheres of production, or, as Marx says, 'at least the decisive ones'. Some enterprises will be exceptional, but these will not affect the general law. The growing organic composition of individual enterprises, of individual capitals,

> therefore involves changes in the average organic composition of the total capital belonging to a given society, [and] this gradual growth in the constant capital, in relation to the variable, must necessarily result in a *gradual fall in the general rate of profit* . . . This simply means that the same number of workers or the same quantity of labour-power that is made available by a variable capital of a given value, as a result of the specific methods of production that develop within capitalist production, sets in motion, works up, and productively consumes, within the same period, an ever-growing mass of means of labour, machinery and fixed capital of all kinds, and raw and ancillary materials – in other words, the same number of workers operate with a constant capital of ever-growing scale. This progressive decline in the variable capital in relation to the constant capital, and hence in relation to the total capital as well, is identical with the progressively rising organic composition, on average, of the social capital as a whole. It is just another expression for the progressive development of the social productivity of labour. (318)

In this dynamic, total social capital grows – capital that takes the form of a growing magnitude of individual exchange values needing to be realized. As the magnitude of exchange values grows – and, therefore, the mass of use-values in circulation – each product contains less value (and its price is thereby cheapened): each product 'contains a smaller sum of labour than at a lower stage of development of production' (318). Even if the rate of surplus-value were to increase, expressed in a higher ratio of unpaid to paid labour constituting each commodity, the absolute greater mass of surplus-value, or unpaid living labour, would continue to be expressed in a proportionally greater portion of objectified labour applied in production. Therefore, the rate of profit falls not only if the rate of surplus-value stays the same but even if it increases (327): 'It is a self-evident necessity, deriving from the nature of the capitalist mode of production itself, that as it advances the general average rate of surplus-value must be expressed in a falling general rate of profit' (319).

Marx emphasizes the need to consider the dynamics of the general law of the falling rate of profit *before* analysing profit's decomposition into its constituent forms: industrial profit, commercial profit, interest, and ground-rent. As we will see, profit, as a universal and unified category, does not have an empirical expression but rather takes these phenomenal subcategories or forms that represent the different portions of the total profit that accrue to the different representative claims on it – claims made by the industrialist or manufacturer, financier/banker/creditor, property holder or landlord, speculator, shareholder, patent or copyright holder, marketer, retailer, distributor, and so on. With respect to capital's perceptual physics, the way in which the subcategories of profit 'attain an autonomous position towards each other' is significant (319; 320). When profit decomposes into its constituent portions, each portion takes on the appearance of profit that was achieved independently of the other forms; the retailer, marketer, or copyright holder imagines that their profit is come by independently, as the outcome of their own individual capital investments on the one hand, and their own enterprising skill and acuity on the other. They do not assume what is in fact the case: that their profit is a slice of the surplus-value generated by productive labour and therefore a share of what the industrialist has appropriated, after dividing it up and apportioning the respective shares as the costs of doing business. These forms of profit, therefore, assume not only the appearance but also, consequently, the objectivity in practice of mutually autonomous value-expressions and mutually autonomous 'achievements' of the various claimholders. Marx describes this process, alternatively, as externalization: categories that are internal derivatives of the system take on the inverted appearance of categories that are external and ahistorical. The industrial capitalist's profit is what is left over after the other various claims to a portion of it have received their shares. The industrial capitalist's profit is come by, therefore, as a matter of *division* and not a matter of multiplication, as they imagine:

> Since everything presents a false appearance in competition, in fact an upside down one, it is possible for the individual capitalist to imagine: (1) that he reduces his profit on the individual commodity by cutting his price, but makes a bigger profit on account of the greater quantity of commodities that he sells; (2) that he fixes the price of the individual commodity and then determines the price of the total

product by multiplication, *whereas the original process is one of division* . . . In actual fact, the fall in commodity prices and the rise in the mass of profit on the increased mass of cheapened commodities is simply another expression of the law of the falling profit rate in the context of a simultaneously rising mass of profit. (338, my emphasis)

Profit-in-general, equivalent in substance and quantity to surplus-value, is subject to the law of the falling rate of profit *before* its division into its constituent forms – a process that we will begin to consider in the following chapter. Therefore, the exposition of the law must precede that of the decomposition of profit since the law, operating at the level of capital's concept, determines the magnitude of the profit available in the first place to be divided up among its mutually dependent (and only apparently competing) stakeholders.

The law of the progressive fall in the rate of profit expresses the historical compulsion of the productive capacity of social labour to grow and, therefore, the progressive growth in the total social capital set in motion in a given society over time. Here, we arrive at the contradiction that animates the law and its development as a barrier to capital's own continuing reproduction. Increased productivity entails the absorption of a greater mass of means of production in the production process, growing the total mass of capital in motion. As growth continues, a greater amount of labour-power is also required to absorb the means of production, even if this greater investment in variable capital grows more slowly in relation to the growth in constant capital. Therefore, 'the absolute mass of labour set in motion and exploited by the social capital [grows], and with it the absolute mass of surplus labour it appropriates' (322–3). This situation entails that the falling rate of profit is accompanied by the concomitant growth in the absolute mass of profit generated on the expanded social capital. The decline in the rate of profit therefore signals a *relative* decline in the surplus labour that is expressed in surplus-value, and not an absolute decline. For example, if the growing mass of total capital demands that the amount paid out in wages (the investment in variable capital) grows from 2 to 3 million, the amount paid out in means of production may grow, at the same time, from 4 to 15 million. Here, as in this example, assuming a stable working day and level of exploitation, we would have an absolute growth in surplus labour and, hence, surplus-value, even though it would be expressed in a falling rate of profit (323). Marx refers to this contradictory movement as the 'double-edged law of a decline in the profit *rate* coupled with a simultaneous increase in the absolute *mass* of profit, arising from the same reasons' (326):

> The number of workers employed by capital, i.e. the absolute mass of surplus labour it sets in motion, and hence the absolute mass of surplus labour it absorbs, the mass of surplus-value it produces, and the absolute of profit if produces, *can* therefore grow, and progressively so, despite the progressive fall in the rate of profit. This not only *can* but *must* be the case – discounting transient fluctuations – on the basis of capitalist production. (324)

As an expression of the growth of productivity of social labour, as the absolute mass of surplus-value/profit grows from the standpoint of the total social capital as a variable magnitude, every fixed magnitude of capital – say, every capital of 100 – will contain less absolute surplus-value/profit than before (327–8). As Marx expounds,

> The same reasons that produce an absolute decline in surplus-value and hence profit of a given capital, thus also in the rate of profit as reckoned as a percentage, bring about a growth in the absolute mass of the surplus-value and profit appropriated by the social capital (i.e. by the totality of capitalists). (327)

To look at the matter from a slightly different angle, 'a greater amount of total capital is required in order to set the same quantity of labour-power in motion and to absorb the same amount of surplus labour [as before]' (328). As the rate of profit falls with the increased absorption of means of production, to yield the same quantity of profit as before, the mass of capital must grow in the same proportion that the rate of profit falls. Marx's numerical illustration is as such:

> If the rate of profit falls from 40 percent to 20 percent, the total capital must rise in the ration of 20:40 if the result is to remain the same. If the profit rate had fallen from 40 percent to 8 percent, the capital would have to grow in the ratio 8:40, i.e. by five times. (329)

This illustration speaks to the growth in total capital required to *maintain* a certain magnitude of profit in the context of the competitive pressure and thus necessity to increase productivity (i.e., in the context of a higher organic composition of capital). However, this is not the capitalist's objective; the objective, rather, is to increase the mass of profit generated in enterprise. For the magnitude of profit to grow in absolute terms, total capital 'must grow in a *higher* ratio than that in which the profit rate falls' (329, my emphasis); capital must grow to the extent that it requires a greater investment in variable capital than it did before the fall: 'If the variable part of a capital of 100 falls from 40 to 20, the total capital must rise to more than 200 if it is to deploy a variable capital of more than 40.' In summary,

> thus the same development in the social productivity of labour is expressed, with the advance of the capitalist mode of production, on the one hand in a progressive tendency for the rate of profit to fall and on the other in a constant growth in the absolute mass of the surplus-value or profit appropriated; so that, by and large, the relative decline in the variable capital and profit goes together with an absolute increase in both. (329)

The consequence, in human terms, of this double-edged law, which we will explore in more detail later on, is the production of a surplus population of workers – the production of *potential* workers, separated from the means of production, a reserve army of the never- or no-longer-employed – that is entirely immanent to the contradictory movement of capital. Again, under the conditions of stable wages and rate of exploitation, an increase in the wage obligation (variable capital) from 2 to 3 million signifies a growth in the number of workers employed – a growth, for example, from 2 to 3 million workers. In this case, an absolute growth in the number of workers corresponds with an ongoing, routine expulsion of workers from the production process, as relatively fewer workers are needed to absorb every 100 units of means of production as the productivity of social labour develops. On the one hand, therefore, capital calls a growing workforce into existence as it develops. On the other hand, capital creates a relative surplus population of workers whose claim to a portion of the social surplus-value is precarious or prevented altogether:

In the same proportion as capitalist production develops, therefore, there also develops the possibility of a relative surplus working population, not because the productivity of social labour *declines* but rather because it *increases*, i.e. not from an absolute disproportion between labour and the means of subsistence, or the means of producing these means of subsistence, but rather from a disproportion arising from the capitalist exploitation of labour, the disproportion between the progressive growth of capital and the relative decline in its need for a growing population. (328–9)

The creation of 'massive armies of workers' representing the 'progressive increase in the total labour-power applied' also reflects the greater magnitude of product put into circulation (326). A growing absolute number of workers, absorbing a growing magnitude of means of production, entails a greater mass of use-values produced – commodities taking the form of both new means of production and means of subsistence, exchange values that must be realized. A relatively lower ratio of employed workers to the value of the social product in circulation, this social product demanding to be valorized, expresses the tendency to systemic crisis endemic to the dynamic of the falling rate of profit. The inverted spiral of growth (towards crisis) continues as 'additional labour [must then] be appropriated in order for this additional wealth to be transformed back into capital', concentrating this augmented wealth in the hands of the larger capitalists (i.e., carrying out the process of accumulation) and providing the 'material means for increasing productivity' (324), once again, in the form of new techniques and technologies of production. A surplus working population and surplus capital walk hand in hand:

> Growth in the means of production entails a growth in the working population, the creation of a surplus population that corresponds to the surplus capital or even exceeds its overall requirements, thus leading to an over-population of workers. A momentary excess of surplus capital over the working population it commands has a double effect. On the one hand it will gradually increase the working population by raising wages . . . while on the other hand, by using methods that create relative surplus-value (introduction and improvement of machinery), it produces far more quickly an artificial

and relative over-population, which in turn is the forcing house for a really rapid increase in the number of people – since, under capitalist production, misery produces population. (324–5)

In the upside-down world of capitalist production, *misery produces population* rather than depleting it. In the perceptual physics of capital, the internal relations that generate this dynamic – the simultaneous and contradictory (or tautological) generation of mutually existing surplus labour-power and surplus capital – are submerged, hidden from the surface appearance of things: 'Just as everything is expressed upside down in competition, and hence in the consciousness of its agents, so too is this law – I mean this inner and necessary connection between two apparently contradictory phenomena' (331). A falling general rate of profit, on the one hand, and growth in the absolute mass of surplus labour (surplus-value, profit), on the other, form a structurally necessary double-reality of capitalist production in motion.

Countertendencies

Marx introduces the movement of counteracting influences on the law of the falling rate of profit by pointing out that given 'the enormous development in the productive powers of social labour' in the nineteenth century, what demands explanation is not why and how the rate of profit falls under these conditions but, rather, why the rate of profit has not fallen more dramatically. Given the vast increase in fixed capital and machinery that came to characterize production from 1835 to 1865, as well as what must have been almost unimaginably large quantities of raw material now routinely absorbed by these productive technologies, one would have expected the general rate of profit over this period of time to have fallen more steeply than it did. We must, then, take account of the factors that work against the law, cancelling and delaying its effects, at least provisionally or temporarily. Despite countertendencies that restore or increase profit rates here and there, the rate of profit will fall in the long run; the imperatives of productivity and competition cannot ultimately be eradicated (337).

Profit rates will be restored, temporarily, under circumstances that increase the value of variable capital in relation to constant capital – that is, under circumstances that lower the average composition of capital. For instance, as we examined earlier, any force, or collective practice on the part of the capitalist class, that reduces the value of constant capital (such as free trade) will have the effect of lowering capital's organic composition. If this lowering of composition is to be generalized, it must be a force or practice in play across spheres of production or, alternatively, at least in those spheres of production that are particularly dominant and absorb the greater amount of social capital such that the average composition of capital in these industries affects the average composition of capital more widely.

Such counterforces are, in fact, always in play, and this is one of the reasons why Marx argues that the law of the falling rate of profit operates as a 'tendency'. A tendency is a law delayed or weakened by counteracting factors (341); it cannot be observed empirically, discretely, in its pure movement. Hence, Marx refers to the general law as 'the *tendential* fall in the rate of profit'. Nonetheless, just because the general law is never expressed empirically in its pure or ideal form – just because it is always in the process of being acted on by counterforces – does not mean that the general law is not a determining movement in capital's trajectory. The double-edged law of the falling rate of profit and the simultaneous increase in the absolute mass of profit operates on the level of capital's concept, like a force of gravity, determining the extent to which counteracting forces succeed, or not, in delaying the next impending barrier to accumulation, or whether capital manifests in crisis. Marx identifies five counteracting factors to the general law of the falling rate of profit and deals briefly with each in turn.[5] We can recognize each factor as a force in operation today, even when their contemporary empirical expressions would be unrecognizable (unimaginable!) to the bearers of the process in earlier conjunctures.

---

5   Paul Mattick points out that Henryk Grossman claims to have been the first reader of Marx to recognize that Marx's list of factors counteracting the falling rate of profit is taken quite directly from J. S. Mill, and unattributed as such. Grossman suggests that this is not necessarily surprising, given Marx's rather scathing criticism of Mill's analysis. Paul Mattick, 'Henryk Grossman: Theory of Accumulation and Breakdown', in Beverley Best, Werner Bonefeld, and Chris O'Kane (eds), *The Sage Handbook of Frankfurt School Critical Theory*, Sage, 2018, 86n28.

1. Increase in the production of relative and absolute surplus-value

The first counteracting factor discussed by Marx is the increase in the production of relative and absolute surplus-value. The production of relative surplus-value increases when the exploitation of labour is intensified, while the production of absolute surplus-value increases when the working day is lengthened (augmenting the amount of time the worker is producing value for the employer). From *Capital* I, we are familiar with Marx's extensive historical illustration of how each of these methods was carried out from capital's early stages to the mid-nineteenth century. In some cases, methods for intensifying the extraction of both relative and absolute surplus-value have changed little since then. In other cases, at least in their surface expressions, the circumstances and modalities of production could not appear more transformed. At the level of capital's concept, however, even these dramatic transformations express particular continuities of internal dynamic.

The development of any type of production process is a particular historical trajectory; each case must be examined individually. The only thing we can establish in abstraction, when that development coincides with capitalist production relations, are the general tendencies in motion in the production of both relative and absolute surplus-value that inform the process in each case. In this regard, we could think of the historical constellation of transformations in production-distribution invoked by the term 'globalization' as a dense field of tendency and countertendency. For instance, the relocation of production to places where the value of labour-power is low increases the product's constitutive ratio of unpaid to paid labour, thereby increasing the rate of surplus-value if and when the value in the product is realized. In this moment, the relocation of production represents a countertendency to falling profitability system-wide. This outcome, however, may meet its own contradiction: if (and only if) the capital that the capitalist saves on the wage obligation is absorbed by large fixed capital investments in the form of highly technologized and automated production infrastructure that facilitates a high level of productivity and absorbs large quantities of means of production, the movement of countertendency turns into its opposite and becomes a force of declining profit rate – or, more precisely, represents two opposing forces operating at once. The same historical development – the relocation of production to global production zones where the value of labour-power is low – manifests both relatively high levels of labour exploitation *and* high productivity, and is therefore a double force that simultaneously augments *and* depresses the rate of profit:

> It has already been shown, moreover, and this forms the real secret of the tendential fall in the rate of profit, that the procedures for producing relative surplus-value are based, by and large, either on transforming as much as possible of a given amount of labour into surplus-value or on spending as little as possible [on] labour in general in relation to the capital advanced; so that the same reasons that permit the level of exploitation of labour to increase make it impossible to exploit as much labour as before with the same total capital. These are the counteracting tendencies which, while they act to bring about a rise in the rate of surplus-value, simultaneously lead to a fall in the mass of surplus-value produced by a given capital, hence a fall in the rate of profit. (340)

In the field of tendency and countertendency that characterizes the complex process of globalization, low-wage production zones – China, beginning in the 1980s, often serves as the programmatic case – illustrate the trajectory that Marx describes here: massive armies of workers are created, a portion of which are subsequently made surplus when increasingly less labour-power is required to sustain historically elevated and rising levels of productivity in newly industrialized regions.[6] At the same time, a countertendency is in motion: the low value of labour-power and concomitant high rates of exploitation will delay falling rates of profit, even if temporarily, and 'this effect can be greater or lesser, depending on the specific proportions in which the antithetical movement takes place' (341). Because of the historically lower value of the labour-power of women and children, their greater numbers in the global workforce also represent a countertendency to falling profitability, and one that characterizes both low- and higher-wage production zones. While the history that genders industrial workforces in context-specific

---

6   A recent theorization and historical illustration of this dynamic is Aaron Benanav and Joshua Clover, 'Can Dialectics Break BRICS?', *South Atlantic Quarterly* 113(4), Fall 2014, 743–59.

ways is not subject to generalization, the internal dynamic that compels the gendering of labour as a means to lower the price of labour continues to this day:

> The introduction of female and child labour on a mass scale should be mentioned here too, in so far as the family as a whole has now to supply capital with a greater quantity of surplus labour than before, even if the sum of their wages increases, which is by no means always the case. (340)[7]

Low-value labour-power reduces the value of commodities that serve as the means of subsistence for workers in higher-wage production zones as well, depressing the value of labour-power and increasing the contribution of relative surplus-value made in higher-wage zones, again, acting as a counterforce to the falling rate of profit system-wide. The overall viability of global capital as value-producing machine will be an averaging out of the individual value contributions that feed into it, a totalized balancing out as a global rate of profit – a push and pull around an average technical composition of productive enterprise globally, against the deeper downward pull of the tendency of the rate of profit to fall. So-called globalization signals a historical period of the dramatic acceleration of this balancing process as a function of the greater and more rapid circulation of capital itself, in all its forms.

When we turn to the production of absolute surplus-value as a countertendency to the general law of falling profitability, we are considering all means and methods, past and present, of lengthening the working day. Again, all cases will be specific to historical situation and will look radically different from one to the next; they include the ongoing use of coercion and brute force, the overturn of labour regulation and protections (or their avoidance altogether – often the

---

7   In 'Wages for Housework Redux: The Utopian Dialectic of the Value Form' (*Theory and Event* 24[4], 2021, 896–921), I theorize the difference between informalized gendered labour and gendered labour that coincides with the wage relation from the standpoint of the value form. Informalized labour does not add new value to the pool of social wealth system-wide, but it does allow the owner of capital to draw more value from that pool as a ratio of their investment, and to an even greater extent if that informal labour is gendered – that is, price depressed. Informalized labour therefore contributes to the tendency for falling profitability. Gendered labour that is waged, on the other hand, represents a countertendency.

work of free trade agreements), technologized means of 'flexibilizing' the location and time of work so that more of the worker's day can be captured by the labour process, and intensified labour market competition.[8] One worker who holds two or three different jobs, representing multiple part-time shifts carried out in the course of one day, is another means of extending the average single working day, and the generalization of this situation – a method of capturing more absolute surplus-value system-wide.

2. Depression of wages below the value of labour-power

The second counteracting factor, the reduction of wages below the value of labour-power, is discussed only briefly by Marx since it does not impact on the general analysis of capital. Nonetheless, as Marx points out, it is one of 'the most important factors in stemming the tendency for the rate of profit to fall' (342). The depression of wages can be an outcome of intensified labour market competition, high unemployment, and similar pressures that would temporarily (even if for extended periods of time) allow the capitalist to purchase labour-power more cheaply than they could under different circumstances. It is important to distinguish the reduction of wages from an actual fall in the value of labour-power; the latter has an internal connection to the tendential fall in the rate of profit in a way that the depression of wages does not.[9] The value of labour-power can remain stable, or even rise, while external pressures and circumstances can force wages below the value of labour-power and function as a counteracting force to falling profitability.

---

8   Sociologist Juliet Schor has extensively researched the lengthening of the average working day and work hours per year, per worker, in North America beginning in the 1970s. See Juliet Schor, *The Overworked American: The Unexpected Decline of Leisure*, Basic Books, 1993.

9   To review this connection in summary: the value of labour-power is reduced when increased productivity lowers the value of the staple goods and services that go into labour-power's reproduction. Falling profitability and the falling value of labour-power are, therefore, two expressions of the same historical process of increasing the productivity of social labour in its capitalist form as property. On these grounds, Marx instructs us to dismiss the common cry of the collective capitalist that falling profit rates are due to rising wages: 'The tendential fall in the rate of profit is linked with a tendential rise in the rate of surplus-value, i.e. in the level of exploitation of labour. Nothing is more absurd, then, than to explain the fall in the rate of profit in terms of a rise in wage rates' (347).

For example, in circumstances that are today both extreme and banal, people fleeing dire living conditions in one region (because of war, climate catastrophe, persecution, or other circumstances that tax the means of reproduction) will form a portion of the casual or low-wage working population of another region. For the sake of survival, these migrant workers may be willing to work for wages that are below the value of the means of subsistence. We must add to this cost of survival, which exerts a downward pressure on wages more generally, the misdirected resentment (sometimes culminating in violence) of resident populations who perceive the competition of migrant or 'foreign' workers as the source of their worsening material conditions of life and livelihood. The resentment of so-called domestic workers might be compounded by expectations informed by the memory or myth of once-upon-a-time working conditions that accommodated better lives and livelihoods for themselves and their families.[10]

As we know from *Capital* I, the capitalist class cannot permanently depress wages below the value of labour-power without risking the depletion of the working population itself (even if the current almost-unimaginable swelling of surplus populations around the world suggests otherwise). For those compelled to work for wages below the value of their labour-power, the reproduction of the household may be shared among extended family members (who may or may not be wage labourers themselves) as a means to survive under conditions of extreme or extended wage depression. When this arrangement becomes generalized – more permanent than provisional – it also exerts a double (contradictory) pressure on the value of labour-power. On the one hand, the value of labour-power is reduced as fewer commodified goods and services go into the basket of basic requirements for its reproduction. On the other hand, the value of labour-power rises when it must *account for* (in the mathematical sense) the reproduction of an extended number of household members. The resulting, if provisional, value of labour-power – whether ultimately increasing or decreasing under these

---

10 A Canadian government policy called the Temporary Foreign Workers Program allows Canadian employers to hire so-called foreign workers on a temporary basis at pay below the legal minimum wage for resident or citizen workers. The policy is a force that contributes to the depression of the price of labour of both 'temporary' *and* 'domestic' workers, reinforcing the distinct misery of each (specifically, the subalternization of temporary workers).

pressures – will reflect the greater force in the balance between the two if the balance is sustained over a significant period of time.

It is sometimes suggested that the unwaged labour involved in reproducing a household – the myriad domestic, caregiving, and organizational activities involved in the work of social reproduction, widely construed – should be considered as value-generating labour in that it 'produces' workers and, consequently, labour-power, and thereby the means of capitalist accumulation altogether. According to this argument, since reproductive labour is performed unwaged, it represents the highest degree possible of exploitation and value extraction, unrecognized as such by orthodox Marxian analyses of the process. While it is not the case that activities undertaken outside of the wage contract contribute value directly to the pool of social surplus-value – in other words, those activities are not 'productive' in the mathematical terms of capitalist accumulation – the deeper, critical importance of what is now widely referred to as 'social reproduction theory' is in theorizing the relationship between *the whole of social life* (the often-neglected 'work' of making communal life and well-being, or simply surviving) to the exigencies of capitalist accumulation.[11] If not value-generating per se, social

---

11 Foundational texts on social reproduction theory include, Mariarosa Dalla Costa and Selma James, *The Power of Women and the Subversion of the Community*, Falling Wall Press, 1975; Silvia Federici, 'Wages Against Housework', The Power of Women Collective and Falling Wall Press, 1975; Maria Mies, *Patriarchy and Accumulation on a World Scale*, Zed, 1986; Leopoldina Fortunati, *The Arcane of Production: Housework, Prostitution, Labour and Capital*, Autonomedia, 1989; Silvia Federici, *Caliban and the Witch: Women, the Body and Primitive Accumulation*, Autonomedia, 2004; Lise Vogel's *Marxism and the Oppression of Women* (introduction by Susan Ferguson and David McNally), Brill, 2013; Kathi Weeks's *The Problem with Work*, Duke, 2011; Tithi Bhattacharya (ed.), *Social Reproduction Theory*, Pluto, 2017; Kate Bezanson and Meg Luxton (eds), *Social Reproduction*, McGill-Queens, 2006; Silvia Federici, *Revolution at Point Zero: Housework, Reproduction and Feminist Struggle*, PM Press, 2012. Texts that take up the question of social reproduction and the value form more directly include, Endnotes (Maya Gonzalez and Jeanne Neton), 'The Logic of Gender: On the Separation of Spheres and the Process of Abjection', *Endnotes 3: Gender, Race, Class and Other Misfortunes*, 2013; Roswitha Scholz, 'Patriarchy and Commodity Society', in Neil Larsen et al. (eds), *Marxism and the Critique of Value*, MCM´ Publishing, 2014; Kevin Floyd, 'Automatic Subjects: Gendered Labour and Abstract Life', *Historical Materialism* 24(2), 2016; Marth E. Gimenez, *Marx, Women, and Capitalist Social Reproduction*, Brill, 2019; Amy De'Ath, 'Hidden Abodes and Inner Bonds: Literary Study and Marxism-Feminism', in Colleen Lye and Chris Nealon, eds., *After Marx: Literature, Theory, and Value in the Twenty-First Century*, Cambridge University Press, 2022; Amy De'Ath, 'Gender and Social Reproduction', in Beverley Best, Werner Bonefeld and Chris O'Kane (eds), *The*

reproductive 'labour' *does* represent an indispensable 'free gift' (again, a *vital* gift, literally) to capital, and one of which the collective capitalist takes immediate advantage. However, what the collective capitalist neither sees nor understands (nor cares about, with respect to their immediate interests) is that the 'advantage of the free gift' from the standpoint of capital's totalized, systemic (and narrower!) terms represents a force of falling profitability down the road.

As we know from *Capital* I, labour that produces surplus-value – labour that 'counts for' and can be 'counted by' capital – coincides with the wage relation, in the context of which it transports socialized labour, abstract labour – the substance of capitalist wealth – into the form of private property. Only labour that coincides with the wage relation moves as socialized, abstracted labour; only in this movement does labour acquire the capacity to *valorize value* and thereby participate in the formation of the general rate of profit. It is in this way that labour is 'productive' in the very narrow terms of this fundamental category; it does not refer to a human capacity but, rather, to a mode of mathematical imbrication that is specific to capital. Activity undertaken outside of the wage relation does not enter directly into the formation of the general rate of profit in terms of augmenting or diminishing the system's capacity to form value. The body of work now widely referred to as social reproduction theory, emerging in the 1970s and energized again since the early 2000s, has concentrated, with historical and theoretical insight, on the relationship between capitalist social forms/relations and the

---

Sage Handbook of Frankfurt School Critical Theory, Volume 3, Sage, 2018; Marina Vishmidt, 'Counter (Re-)Productive Labour', *Auto Italia*, 2012, autoitaliasoutheast.org; Beverley Best, 'Wages for Housework Redux: Social Reproduction and the Utopian Dialectic of the Value Form', *Theory and Event*, 24(4), 2021, 896–921. The 'debate' on social reproductive labour as productive labour continues in several journal special issues: *Viewpoint Magazine* special dossier on 'Gender and Capitalism', 2015; *Historical Materialism* 24(2), 2016; *Radical Philosophy* 2(04), 2019. Finally, key texts in theorizing the whole social, aesthetic form of life as the double movement of strategy of capitalist accumulation, on the one hand, and utopia, on the other, see, Kay Gabriel, 'Gender as Accumulation Strategy', *Invert*, May 2020; Jordy Rosenberg and Kay Gabriel, 'Pleasure and Provocation: Kay Gabriel Interview with Jordy Rosenberg', *Salvage*, April 18, 2018; Sophie Lewis, *Full Surrogacy Now: Feminism Against Family*, Verso, 2019; Sophie Lewis, *Abolish the Family: A Manifesto for Care and Liberation*, Verso, 2022; M. E. O'Brien, 'Communizing Care', *Pinko*, 15 October 2019; M. E. O'Brien and Eman Abdelhadi, *Everything for Everyone: An Oral History of the New York Commune 2052–2072*, Common Notions, 2022.

quasi-infinite forms of life-making that cannot *not* be impacted by the movement of capital but which are not directly subsumed by it either. Capital's profound precarity is that it cannot capture these forms of life-making unless it can somehow turn them into abstract labour. Labour, in its capitalist form, is the *inverse* of creative, life-giving, life-sustaining, community-building activity that is meaningful and valuable in and for itself, on its own terms – whatever those may be and however a collectivity may choose to define them. *This* is the salient critique of social reproduction that is embedded in a Marxian theory of value: that if we could graph the irreducible variety of forms of life-making on a pie chart, only a very thin wedge of that chart would constitute the activity that capital is able to turn into productive labour – that is, that capital is able to harness for the production of value. With respect to the question of the falling rate of profit, this already-thin wedge *grows thinner* as the productivity of social labour increases.

3. Reducing the cost of means of production

The third countertendency against the falling rate of profit is the cheapening of the elements of constant capital (i.e., means of production; raw materials and machinery). We can consider this factor summarily, as does Marx, since we have already examined, in the first chapter, the impact that a change in the value of constant capital has on the rate of profit, and the significance of this change from the standpoint of the capitalist. Reduction of the price of raw materials and other means of production is a priority of the capitalist as a means of augmenting their rate of profit – which is indeed the effect. What the capitalist does not perceive, generally speaking, is that their profit has increased not by the reduction of the cost of raw material but, rather, by a reduction in the value of c and a corresponding increase in the ratio of surplus-value to the value of the total capital invested. If an individual capitalist is able to reduce the cost of the means of production by some method that their competition has yet to employ – that is, 'before the method is universally applied' (341) – then they are in a position to extract extra profit without adjustment to the general rate. However, once the method is universally applied, the generalized reduction in constant capital investment will have the effect of increasing the general rate of profit – a countertendency to its immanent, progressive fall.

We can draw an example from chapter 1, where we looked at a relatively new source of raw material in the form of users' digital traces generated in the course of online activity. These traces are abundant and cheap raw material for industries that collect and turn them into data commodities. We established that the activity that generates these traces – our voluntary and/or obliged daily online life – is not so much 'free labour' that creates value for industry directly as it is a 'free gift' to the capitalist class in its production of a resource that takes the form of constant capital in the production process. It is, rather, in the context of production that value-generating labour is performed by the waged labour involved in harvesting these digital traces, of aggregating them into 'big data', of undertaking the analysis of this data, and of compiling the results into information commodities. Since those entities involved today in the mining and selling of digital trace material are large companies (such as Alphabet/Google, Amazon, and Facebook) that absorb a substantial portion of the total social capital investment, their participation in the formation of the general rate of profit *does* represent a current countertendency to its decline. In fact, from the point of view of capital-as-value-machine, any time the capitalist class succeeds at lowering the cost of some raw material – or the price of the earth's or atmosphere's resources more generally – it represents a counterforce to falling profitability and, by lowering the value of staple goods, a means of lowering the value of labour-power as well.[12]

---

12 A similar argument appears in Jason Moore, *Capitalism in the Web of Life*, Verso, 2015. Moore argues that capitalist civilization over the past five centuries has relied on the appropriation of what he calls 'cheap nature'; colonialism, imperial war, and other forms of ongoing political coercion have made it possible for capitalist industry to maintain low production costs by relying on the exploitation of artificially cheap food, energy, land, forests, water, air, and, of course, labour. Moore does not take up the movement of value in his analysis, nor, therefore, the internal dynamics of the capital-machine itself. If Moore's analysis is correct that capital's terminal crisis will be ecological, and that capital, if unchallenged, will render the earth's environment uninhabitable for humans and other species, then a critique of capitalist value as life-subverting social technology is in any case superfluous for being too late. However, what the critique of value would bring to Moore's analysis would be to displace its terms altogether and show how fundamentally the movement of capital distorts the perception of that same movement: capital's terminal ecological crisis is not brought by 'cheap nature' per se but, rather, by nature commodified tout court. For instance, if the resources Moore calls cheap nature had been made, over the past five centuries, 'expensive' for capital to procure, nothing whatsoever would be different with respect to how quickly or wantonly industry would burn through them. Value critique shows us that the distinction

4. The production of a surplus population

The fourth countertendency to falling profitability is capital's systemic production of a relative surplus population. As we have established, 'the creation of such a surplus population is inseparable from the development of labour productivity and is accelerated by it' (343). At the same time that the development of labour productivity expresses itself in the creation of a surplus population, it also expresses itself in a falling rate of profit; these are two internally connected moments of the same historical process. Separated from the means of production yet reliant on waged labour to secure the means of subsistence, the surplus population finds itself unable to enter into a wage contract for lack of viable employment, as capital requires decreasing labour-power for every one hundred units of constant capital set in motion. Capital generates an army of available workers – workers in reserve – waiting to step into any vacated or newly opened contract. The larger the surplus, the greater the downward pressure on the wage as the price of labour-power, as the exigencies of survival compel workers in reserve to undercut their competitors on the job market – now a 'globalized' market – and comply with wages often lower than the value of labour-power. The result is an increasing quantity of price-depressed available labour.

The quantity of available labour can become sufficiently large, and consequently sufficiently cheap, that it becomes more cost efficient in

---

between 'cheap' and 'expensive' is meaningless when the problem is a system of internally dysfunctional *ratios* of socialized labour. If nature were 'expensive', prices of goods would be higher (although, relative to what?), and corresponding to these 'higher' prices, profits would be higher, the value of labour-power would be higher, and so on. But the ratio between these things would be unaltered, as would the crisis situation of late capital more generally, as would be the world in which we find ourselves today. The category 'cheap nature' is merely the standpoint of the system approaching a crisis where an imperative of infinite growth comes up against the obstacle of the planet's organic, finite limits. It is a crisis of nature contorted *into the form of exchange-value*. Industry could despoil 'expensive' nature and labour as quickly as it can 'cheap' nature and labour, because profits would be 'higher' as well – irreversibly altering the climate and destroying its dependent life forms at the same pace, just at a higher price point! Marx's objective in *Capital* III is to show that it's all relative. The distinction between a low/cheap exchange-value or high/costly exchange-value is meaningless from the standpoint of value critique – the latter would displace these terms altogether. 'Cheap nature' is a false category from the perspective of Marx's critique; cheap nature or expensive nature makes no difference with respect to the movement of capital. It is commodified nature (its *form*) that brings us to where we are today.

some branches of production to mobilize this cheap labour-power rather than to invest in the technical automation of the functions performed by that labour. According to Marx, 'It is in turn a reason why the more or less incomplete subordination of labour to capital persists in several branches of production, and longer indeed than would seem to correspond at first sight to the general level of development' (343). Giovanni Arrighi, in his study *Adam Smith in Beijing*, observes this dynamic in the process of the industrialization of China beginning roughly in the 1980s.[13] The displacement of subsistence farmers and large portions of the peasantry from rural areas undergoing state-led conversion to profit-organized, industrial agricultural and manufacturing production generated not only the largest human migration in history but also one of the largest surplus populations in history. A vast available workforce and some of the cheapest labour in the world led both Chinese and foreign industrialists to organize industry in China around more labour-intensive production processes – delaying but ultimately not preventing the reorganization towards productivity and automation that competition would eventually, if gradually, compel. Arrighi's analysis of the industrialization of production in China illustrates Marx's explanation of this dynamic: that the production of a large surplus population forces down the price of labour to the extent that it comes to delay the immanent forces of automation and compulsions of labour productivity itself. In these cases, the investment in variable capital remains high in proportion to constant capital, even if wages are below average, arresting, if only temporarily, the falling rate of profit.

Marx concludes the discussion of surplus population by drawing attention, again, to the double movement that simultaneously produces both tendency and countertendency and, consequently, a surface expression of paralysis: '[We see] once again how the same factors that produce the tendency for the rate of profit to fall also moderate the realization of this tendency' (343); 'the same reasons that produce the tendential fall in the rate of profit also produce a counterweight to this tendency, which paralyzes its effect to a greater or lesser extent' (344).

---

13   Giovanni Arrighi, *Adam Smith in Beijing*, Verso, 2007.

5. Foreign trade

The fifth counteracting factor is foreign trade. Trade between the private industries of nation-states is compelled by two structural requirements of capitalist industry: (1) the need to reduce production costs; and (2) the concomitant need to access new markets that will absorb a growing product. Communication and transportation capacities built over the course of the twentieth century have transformed the surface modalities (scale, speed, degree of coordination) of production-distribution beyond imagination, past or present. Nonetheless, these two requirements assert themselves, in essence, across all stages of capitalist development, and meeting them requires the superstructural form of the capitalist state in establishing the necessary legal framework, infrastructure, and institutional arrangements, including the means of sanctioned coercion (a military and a police force) to carry them out. Competition between 'national capitals' obfuscates what is, in essence, a collaborative 'freemasonry' of the global capitalist class.[14] States seeking to secure the interests of their own national industries do so, where possible, by controlling and exploiting the resources of other nation-states, whether in the form of military occupation, expansionist violence, foreign investment, or the diplomatic cosmopolitanism of international relations and free trade agreements. However, free trade agreements that serve as vehicles for global corporations to circumvent the laws of any individual nation-state that hinders profit-making, along with the enthusiasm of the political leaders who court these agreements, expose the alignment of the interests of capital and the capitalist state for what it is: a dynamic of content and form.

On the one hand, foreign trade constitutes a countertendency to the falling rate of profit: it gives industry access to the cheapest means of production anywhere in the world, thereby forcing down the cost of constant capital more generally. The cheapening of constant capital also lowers the value of the means of subsistence, of the commodities that constitute the value of labour-power, which increases the rate of surplus-value and the rate of profit. On the other hand, capitalist production is compelled to expand, and reduction of the cost of means of production facilitates this by 'permit[ting] the scale of production to be expanded . . .

---

14   As discussed in chapter 2 above.

accelerat[ing] accumulation ... accelerat[ing] the fall in the variable capital as against the constant, and hence [accelerating] the fall in the rate of profit' (344). Once again, foreign trade enacts a double movement of tendency and countertendency. The simultaneous push and pull against the profit rate may arrest the effect of either force to a greater or lesser extent.

Meanwhile, over time, the development of the productivity of social labour carries on apace, ramping up the system's value metabolism and hailing wider markets to absorb a growing social product. As Marx points out, foreign trade may have been

> the basis of capitalist production in its infancy, [but] it becomes the *specific product* of the capitalist mode of production as this progresses, through the inner necessity of this mode of production and its need for an ever extended market. (344, my emphasis)

Globalization and the proliferation of free trade agreements between blocks of trading states do not emerge from the development of foreign trade in general but, rather, from the development of capitalist foreign trade per se – a historical process that precipitates foreign trade newly informed, as an expression of a particular social relation, and posits it (and its more mature forms, 'globalization' and the legal frameworks of 'free trade') as its own precondition.

Marx considers the effect of foreign and colonial trade on the general rate of profit, asking: 'Is the general rate of profit raised by the higher profit made by capital invested in foreign trade, and colonial trade in particular?' (344). The context that informs Marx's question is the level of industrialization characterizing production in England, western Europe, and, increasingly, the United States in the mid-nineteenth century, which was significantly greater than in the colonized territories, such as India or China – the colonial 'trading competitors' in question. Different degrees of industrialization entail different levels of productivity and yield different rates of surplus-value and different average rates of profit. Profit rates will generally be higher in the colonized territory, owing to a lower degree of industrialization and, therefore, lower capital composition of investment. Commodities exported from England to India, for example, produced at a higher level of productivity, would contain less objectified labour than a comparable commodity produced in India and could, therefore, be sold in that market above their values while at prices lower than the comparable Indian-made product: 'The more [industrially] advanced country sells its goods above their value, even though still more cheaply than it competitors' (345), owing to its higher degree of productivity. In this scenario, the competition in trade between empire and colony reproduces the dynamic between local competitors, where one competitor achieves greater productivity ahead of the competition and, consequently, yields a surplus profit until the time that this new, higher level of productivity – and its respective value composition – has become universalized, and all surplus profit equalized.

Nonetheless, Marx's answer to his own question is yes:

> There is no reason why the higher rates of profit that capital invested in certain branches yields in this way, and brings home to its country of origin, should not enter into the equalization of the general rate of profit and hence raise this in due proportion, unless monopolies stand in the way. (345)

Marx's suggestion is that the level of integration characterizing the world market was already sufficient in the second half of the nineteenth century to carry out the equalization of surplus profits that would otherwise have fallen to more highly productive/industrialized producers. Today, the question itself is redundant. A global division of labour nigh complete has standardized technical compositions of production planet-wide; the equalization process proceeds at the same scale. The comparatively lower value of labour-power in former colonial territories, expressed in higher rates of surplus-value, offers prospects for higher rates of profit and draws investment away from former industrial centres of empire in the now-colloquial process of so-called deindustrialization. An eye to the dynamics of the value form in the context of globalization reveals how and why the long global march of capitalist industrialization must eventually be expressed in (1) the de-industrialization of high-wage regions; (2) a 'race to the bottom' with respect to the cheapening of labour in all regions (i.e., in the global South *and* North); and (3) the highly stratified but increasingly elusive prospects for material security and well-being for the populations of both hemispheres.

Contradiction and Crisis

As we know, a falling rate of profit coincides with a rise in the mass of profit, entailing that, as the annual product of labour expands, 'a greater part of [that product] is appropriated by the capitalist under the heading of capital (as replacement for the capital used up) and a relatively smaller part is appropriated under the heading of profit'. As greater amounts of objectified labour (in the form of means of production) are absorbed in production, a smaller portion of living labour is applied to the transfer of value from raw material to finished product. To make the same quantity of profit as before, the overall quantity of capital mobilized in production must increase. This situation

> brings about a simultaneous concentration of capital, since the condi-tions of production now require the use of capital on a massive scale. It also leads to the centralization of this capital, i.e. the swallowing up of small capitalists by big and their decapitalization. (354)

As small capitalists succumb, they are thrown into the pool of available labour, now reliant on a wage to procure the means of subsistence. This situation amounts to the ongoing separation of producers from the means of production, the historical process that forms the concept of capital itself, 'raised to a higher power' as 'the centralization of capitals already existing in a few hands, and the decapitalization of many' (354–5). If countertendencies to the falling rate of profit – forces of decentrali-zation – 'were not constantly at work alongside this centripetal force' of centralization, capital would be unable to displace its own internal contradictions. In other words, the system would collapse where it otherwise hobbles along.

'The *true barrier* to capitalist production is *capital itself*' (358). Marx's observation resonates as loudly today as ever. As a falling rate of profit is expressed in a growing centralization of capital, it

> slows down the formation of new, independent capitals and thus appears as a threat to the development of the capitalist produc-tion process; it promotes overproduction, speculation and crises, and leads to the existence of excess capital alongside a surplus population. (350)

These symptomatic expressions of capital's internal antagonism are, at this late stage, a matter of such routine that they disappear into the landscape, into the everyday business-as-usual of capitalist society. Even so, falling profit rates, and the 'investment strikes' they provoke on the part of capital, typified nineteenth century capital as well and were, likewise, conventionally (and unknowingly) explained as contingencies external to the system. Capital's first barriers, however, are internal – including the barrier that we will shortly call 'class struggle' – dynamics we can also call capital's tendency to crisis. From the standpoint of the movement of capital as a whole, distinct from the immediate standpoint of individual capitals, crisis does not represent itself as a malfunction of the system but, rather, as the system's diversion from pending collapse; crisis is capital's *inverted solution* to the barriers it generates as it develops.

The production and realization of surplus-value is capital's singular, if two-part, objective; as the inversion of the 'common good', capitalist society elevates the production and realization of surplus-value above all other objectives:

> It should never be forgotten that the production of this surplus-value – and the transformation of a portion of it back into capital, or accumulation, forms an integral part of surplus-value production – is the immediate purpose and the determining motive of capital production. Capitalist production, therefore, should never be depicted as something that it is not, i.e. as production whose immediate purpose is consumption, or the production of means of enjoyment for the capitalist. This would be to ignore completely its specific character, as this is expressed in its basic inner pattern. (351–2)

The law of the falling rate of profit refers to capital's internal movement towards arresting its own capacity to realize surplus-value. The effects of the law are mitigated and delayed by its twin movement in countertendencies, dynamics that enhance the system's capacity to produce surplus-value at the same time:

> These various influences sometimes tend to exhibit themselves side by side, spatially; at other times one after the other, temporally; and at

certain points the conflict of contending agencies breaks through in crises. Crises are never more than momentary, violent solutions for the existing contradictions, violent eruptions that re-establish the disturbed balance for the time being. (357)

Crisis is one of the means by which capital displaces the obstacles it erects between itself and its singular objective. Capital's crisis tendency is the fault-line that runs between the production and realization of surplus-value – the systemic vulnerability introduced by the fact that the production and realization of surplus-value are two distinct moments of capital's circuit. Living labour set in motion in the immediate production of commodities destined for the market may be the singular location, and means, of producing surplus-value. But surplus-value produced is not yet surplus-value realized.

As capital develops, the mass of social product, and the mass of surplus-value congealed therein, 'swells to monstrous proportions'. For that surplus-value to be realized, the social product must be sold. But the development of productivity lowers the ratio of variable to constant capital, which is to say that a diminishing amount of labour-power is engaged in the production of an expanding social product. As relatively fewer workers enter the wage contract, the disproportion between the mass of product and the consumptive capacity that it meets in the marketplace – itself a magnitude of value –thwarts the realization of the surplus-value congealed in the total social product:

> The conditions for immediate exploitation and for the realization of
> that exploitation are not identical. Not only are they separate in time
> and space, they are also separate in theory. The former is restricted
> only by the society's productive forces, the latter by the proportionality
> between the different branches of production and by the society's
> power of consumption. (352)

The restriction on consumption imposed by capital's drive to accumulate is generalized and 'absolute': it is the negation of a society's capacity to satisfy the full breadth (and, in many cases, even the bare minimum) of human needs (352–3). It is the systematic denial of the human capacity to create and partake in abundance:

[Society's power of consumption] is determined neither by the absolute power of production nor by the absolute power of consumption but rather by the power of consumption within a given framework of antagonistic conditions of distribution, which reduce the consumption of the vast majority of society to a minimum level, only capable of varying within more or less narrow limits. (352)

This functional contradiction could not be sharper than in the image of a society that with one hand invests monumental human effort, creativity, resources, and social infrastructure on the promotion, advertising, and selling of goods and services while, with the other hand, systematically restricts the consumptive capacity of the majority.

Capital's functioning contradictions stack up faster than unsaleable product: (1) the forces that increase the working population simultaneously create a relative surplus population (357); (2) falling profits rates that exist side by side with the growing mass of capital compel the devaluation of existing capital that, in turn, delays the fall in profit rate and accelerates accumulation (357); (3) with the development of productivity, the organic composition of capital rises and labour is expelled from the production process, threatening the system's capacity to generate the surplus-value that is its sine qua non:

The profit rate does not fall because labour becomes less productive but rather because it becomes more productive. The rise in the rate of surplus-value and the fall in the rate of profit are simply particular forms that express the growing productivity of labour in capitalist terms. (347, my emphasis)

(4) capital, as a process whose singular orientation is the creation of surplus-value, to this end, drives 'towards an absolute development of the productive forces *irrespective* of value' and at the expense of the surplus-value contained therein (357, my emphasis). This contradictory movement forces a tectonic shift along the fault-line separating the two parts of the process: exploitation/production on one side and realization of surplus-value on the other. The fault-line cracks open; value cannot be valorized, surplus-value cannot be realized, and the devaluation of existing capital allows capital to pursue its historical mission another day – concentrated in fewer hands – and to carry out its singular purpose

of valorizing existing capital to the greatest extent possible. That which is a crisis from the standpoint of certain individual capitals (as well as newly redundant workers, their dependents, the state and local governments who rely on tax revenue, and so on) is a solution from the standpoint of the movement of capital as a whole:

> The periodic devaluation of the existing capital, which is a means, immanent to the capitalist mode of production, for delaying the fall in the profit rate and accelerating the accumulation of capital value by the formation of new capital, disturbs the given conditions in which the circulation and reproduction process of capital takes place, and is therefore accompanied by sudden stoppages and crises in the production process. (358)

Capital overcomes its immanent barriers by summoning new barriers further down the path of its own development; it generates the conditions that will precipitate new obstacles, but on a wider and 'more powerful scale' (358). The central contradiction is this: the means which capital applies to its purpose constantly come into conflict with that purpose; the unrestricted development of the forces of social production come into conflict with the restricted end – the valorization of existing capital. Another way of designating this same contradictory movement is 'overaccumulation'. As we have seen, overaccumulation is expressed by a falling rate of profit; it produces a relative surplus population at one pole and a growing total social capital – what Marx calls a 'plethora of capital' – at the other: 'unoccupied capital on the one hand and an unemployed working population on the other' (359). Immobilized capital side by side with immobilized workers is the double expression of the singular process of overaccumulation.

The process of overaccumulation can advance to the point where the mass of profit produced no longer compensates for the profit lost due to the fall in its rate of production. Marx refers to this situation as the absolute overproduction of capital. In this scenario, total social capital grows in proportion to the workforce to the extent where neither the relative nor absolute surplus labour-time of the workforce can be extended, and the portion of profit reinvested in production (the portion representing the total capital's growing magnitude) produces no more surplus-value, or even less surplus-value, than did the original capital investment before its augmentation (360). Crisis, in the form of the devaluation of objectified labour, is the only response in capital's repertoire to absolute overproduction, the moment when the movement of overaccumulation reaches an insurmountable barrier with respect to the ongoing valorization of capital in its existing configuration. Crisis represents the necessary sacrifice of portions of the total social capital carried out through competitive struggle between capital's representatives. For the sake of lowering the value-metabolism, portions of the total social capital must stand idle, unoccupied, or be destroyed altogether.

The characteristics of competitive struggle between capitals will be particular, case by case: large enterprises (representing large concentrations of capital) swallow up or make redundant smaller enterprises – whether older established ones or younger, upstart ones. New 'innovative' enterprises replace older ones; larger enterprises that are able to function temporarily at a loss do so in order to ruin more vulnerable enterprises; portions of profit are withheld from reinvestment and become idle 'so as to not devalue [the] original capital' (361); unoccupied capital is redirected towards mechanisms of redistribution of the total social profit, as we will explore in forthcoming chapters on finance and the credit system. Whatever the particular circumstances, portions of the total social capital are forced to relinquish the property of functioning as capital and fail to be valorized (361; 362). When the general rate of profit is stable and advantageous, even in the early stages of decline, there is enough profit generated for reinvestment to proceed, and competition expresses a 'practical freemasonry of the capitalist class', consolidating its interests against labour. However, when a *loss* of profit must be absorbed, the interests of the capitalist class splinter into 'a struggle of enemy brothers':

> As long as everything goes well, competition acts, as is always the case when the general rate of profit is settled, as a practical freemasonry of the capitalist class, so that they all share in the common booty in proportion to the size of the portion that each puts in. But as soon as it is no longer a question of division of profit, but rather of loss, each seeks as far as he can to restrict his own share of this loss and pass it on to someone else. For the class as a whole, the loss is unavoidable. But how much each individual member has to bear, the extent to which he has to participate in it, now becomes a question of

strength and cunning, and competition now becomes a struggle of enemy brothers. The opposition between the interest of each individual capitalist and that of the capitalist class as a whole now comes into its own, in the same way as competition was previously the instrument through which the identity of the capitalists' interests was asserted. (361–2)

But capital that stands idle in the context of its overproduction does so side by side with a growing surplus population that grows in size as stagnation and crisis unfold:

> The same causes that have raised the productivity of labour, increased the mass of commodity products, extended markets, accelerated the accumulation of capital, in terms of both mass and value, and lowered the rate of profit, these same causes have produced and continue to produce, a relative surplus population, a surplus population of workers who are not employed by this excess capital on account of the low level of exploitation of labour at which they would have to be employed, or at least on account of the low rate of profit they would yield at the given rate of exploitation. (364)

In the colonial-era context of Marx's writing, surplus capital was routinely sent to colonial territories in search of labour that could be exploited at higher rates than in the industrializing empire, with the objective of generating higher rates of profit. A century and a half on, from the place of former industrial empire, capital continues to be sent abroad for the same reasons, and the scenario of so-called post-industrialism captures the culmination of the process. The now-perfunctory lament on the part of certain sections of the working class 'set free' in the former industrial core when capital flees – 'They are taking our jobs!' – signals the anger and confusion of a shrinking industrial working class confronting desperate prospects – an anger which is obfuscated and leveraged for political gain but which expresses an inverted perception of a deeper reality. As Marx points out, surplus capital *could*, of course, be employed 'at home' (in this instance, in the post-industrial core economies); the conditions which compel it to search for cheaper labour-power in the already 'post-industrializing' imperial peripheral economies are particular to capitalist production alone (364–5). Only the historical logic of capitalist production limits where and how surplus wealth can be mobilized.

Of course, the very notion of 'surplus wealth' is nonsensical in any social formation save a capitalist one. Like the idea of 'too much of a good thing', an overabundance of social wealth is meaningless in absolute terms. Too much of a good thing is only possible, never mind a vulnerability, with respect to a system whose compulsion towards the absolute development of productive forces comes into 'continuous conflict with the specific *conditions* of production', the *only* conditions that are able to set that system in motion (366). Overproduction, as the phenomenal form of the process of overaccumulation, is only overproduction in capitalist terms; there is no such phenomenon in absolute or general terms (364). Majority portions of humanity (which continue to expand as the surplus population grows) have always lived under absolute conditions of underproduction and under-consumption. In no other set of historical conditions could a crisis of need, experienced by so many – for food, clean running water, energy, medicine, housing, tools, health care, education, leisure time, communication technologies, public transportation, childcare, eldercare, rest and relaxation, and so on – take the inverted appearance of an insufficient demand for goods and services, where 'demand must [then] be sought in distant markets in order to pay workers back home the average measure of the necessary means of subsistence' (366). Topsy-turvy world, indeed!

Conclusion: Mathematics and Class Struggle

The contradictions of capitalist accumulation produce an upside-down world of actualities that cannot be oriented to the most simple and intuitive premise: that the expansion or contraction of production and consumption be determined by the 'needs of socially developed human beings'. Rather, for the purposes of social need, capitalist production 'appears completely inadequate'. The reason for its inadequacy, as Marx points out repeatedly, is that production and consumption in capitalist society are not ends in themselves but rather subordinated as means to a historically relative end, the growth and concentration of capitalist wealth as the private property of a minority of interests that masquerade as the common good: 'Production comes to a standstill not at the point where needs are satisfied, but rather where the production and realization of profit impose this' (367). The autonomization of profit as tautology – as its own rationale and justification – is an outcome of capital's growth and concentration. The latter obfuscate capital's parochial orientations and objectify capital as a social power – as an automatic subject that places the collective capitalist in the role of functionary, on the one hand, and confronts the producers of social wealth as an alien and oppressive force, on the other:

> We have seen how the growing accumulation of capital involves its growing concentration. Thus the power of capital grows, in other words the autonomy of the social conditions of production, as personified by the capitalist, is asserted more and more as against the actual producers. Capital shows itself more and more to be a social power, with the capitalist as its functionary – a power that no longer stands in any possible kind of relationship to what the work of one particular individual can create, but an alienated social power which has gained an autonomous position and confronts society as a thing, and as the power that the capitalist has through this thing. The contradiction between the general social power into which capital has developed and the private power of the individual capitalists over these social conditions of production develops ever more blatantly, *while this development also contains the solution to this situation, in that it simultaneously raises the conditions of production into general, communal, social conditions.* This transformation is brought about by the development of the productive forces under capitalist production and by the manner and form in which this development is accomplished. (373, my emphasis)

Throughout *Capital* III, Marx scatters speculative deductions (like the one emphasized above) that depict the necessary movement of capital's social content as driving straight through capital's formation of private power, and out the other side. These signals, that an associated mode of production is a bona fide historical possibility, punctuate Marx's critique, as does the reminder that the proletariat will need to fight for the opportunity to realize it and will confront a violent counter-revolutionary challenge at every step of the way, as history had, and has since, demonstrated. But the image of Marx's speculative deductions is consistent: the transition from capital to post-capital will not be a matter of replacing a capitalist mode of production with an alternative associated mode of production but, rather, of activating the virtual, if not-yet-actualized, dimensions of capital itself; it will be a matter of developing *through*, as opposed to against, capital's inbuilt portals to another 'non-existent but non-fictional', higher because intentional, form of social modality: 'The development of the productive forces of social labour is capital's historic mission and justification. *For that very reason, it unwittingly creates the material conditions for a higher form of production*' (368). However, even as capital's volatility intensifies across the twentieth century, and continues apace in the twenty-first, its internal contradictions appear to be inversely proportional to its stability as a social power, which has increased as a function of its ongoing expansion and integration. Capital throws up obstacles to the producers of social wealth's perception and experience of themselves as the makers of this world, and of a different one to come – as builders of an associated mode of production lying dormant as a virtuality within capital itself.

If, from the standpoint of the general movement of capital, crisis represents a temporary solution to endemic stagnation, from the standpoint of the proletariat, crisis entails precarity, unemployment, poverty, illness, gendered and racialized violence, and social exclusion: 'Stagnation in production makes part of the working class idle and hence places the employed workers in conditions where they have to accept a fall in wages, even beneath the average' (363). Accumulation takes place via the 'dispossession and impoverishment of the great mass of the producers' of surplus-value (358). Marx suggests that the diminishing ratio of living labour to objectified labour in the production process will eventually reach a revolutionary tipping point:

> A development in the productive forces that would reduce the absolute number of workers, and actually enable the whole nation to accomplish its entire production in a shorter period of time, would produce a revolution, since it would put the majority of the population out of action. (372)

But what appeared inevitable for Marx challenges today's imagination. One of the present obstacles with respect to conceptualizing an exit from a capitalist mode of production is a proletariat deeply stratified around degrees of social vulnerability and exposure to risk, deprivation, and death – a subalternization of access to a portion of social wealth, expressed in wage hierarchies (including the absolute expulsion from the wage) that index long histories of technologies of power and subjugation that we capture in the categories of race, Indigeneity, gender, sexuality, ability, age, property, citizenship, and so on.

Capital negates the actualization of abundance in the prohibition of the absolute development of production and consumption. However, as we know, austerity towards the means of life-making is not carried out uniformly. By hierarchizing the capacity to consume – from survival-threatening exclusion to a superfluity of spending power – capital creates real schisms among those who produce wealth for others. These divisions it exploits to hobble any efforts towards alliance, across differentiated groups, against capital. But this fragmentation of the proletariat is capital's surface story, the movement of capital 'in the world as it actually is'. There is another story: the inversion of this one, equally objective, if the immaterial mirror of the first. The negation of abundance implies not only the imposition of limits on the means of capitalist forms of consumption – on access to goods and services supplied by capitalist markets. The negation of abundance also refers to the stricture on non-capitalist consumption – on the production of needs, and the means to satisfy them, that can only be undertaken outside of the purview of capital, in non-capitalist configurations. Capital denies *associated* modes of social reproduction, as well as *associated* modes of production-distribution of goods and services.[15] This deeper negation of abundance, *operating at the level of*

---

15 Even so, non-capitalist life-making is never completely subsumed in a capitalist society; extra-capitalist modes of social reproduction incubate in its interstices, under the radar of, and in inherent opposition to, the value/market nexus. John Holloway makes this point in 'Change the World without Taking Power', *Capital and Class* 29(1), 2005, 39–42. 'Value-market nexus' is Joshua Clover's phrase in *Riot. Strike. Riot: The New Era of Uprisings*, Verso, 2016. I would make this whole analysis a footnote to Rebecca Solnit's work on hope (*A Paradise Built in Hell: The Extraordinary Communities that Arise in Disaster*, Penguin, 2010; *Hope in the Dark: Untold Histories, Wild Possibilities*, Haymarket Books, 2016), and to the vast and growing body of work on abolition, revolutionary envisioning, and the communizing of care; see, for example, Ruth Wilson Gilmore, *Abolition Geography: Essays Towards Liberation*, Verso, 2022; Kanishka Chowdury, *Border Rules: An Abolitionist Refusal*, Palgrave Macmillan, 2023; Ruth Wilson Gilmore and Naomi Murakawa (eds), *Change Everything: Racial Capitalism and the Case for Abolition*, Haymarket Books, 2024; Robyn Maynard and Leanne

capital's concept, is imposed equally on capital's bearers despite the deep stratification and subalternization of the way it structures them in the world as it actually is. Rather than fragmentation and irreducible difference, this negation of non-capitalist abundance expresses a fundamental universality of the separated – because capital can only separate absolutely. The negation of non-capitalist abundance therefore signals an irreducible unity of interest in the overcoming of separation.

The idea that capital posits a negative universality – a spectral equality – between each bearer of the collective subject of the proletariat, in their essential separation from the means of production, immediately appears as an outrageous and negligent suggestion. Surely the specific histories of oppression and the extreme material disparity that actualize the proletariat – ranging from relative privilege, to brutal exclusion and violence – refute it outright.[16] There is no question that class struggle is carried out in the world as it actually is, and that it advances only with the necessary attention to the mediations that produce group-differentiations as technologies of power. However, the idea that capital posits a fundamental (if negative) immaterial (but objective) equality between its bearers is to use theory to reveal what is concealed by 'the chaotic concrete' – by the 'dazzling power of false immediacy' – in order to conceptualize across difference and stratification, and to locate the real possibility introduced by capital as spectral equality in abstraction whose negative presence it is the work of the dialectic to assert.[17] If dialectical analysis has a practical application in this context, it is to provide the means to imagine the unimaginable articulation of contemporary struggles in their historical and material specificity as a unified anti-capitalist mobilization. Capital's ineluctable movement grounds the apparently unlikely proposal that capital itself generates (and then posits as its presupposition) a conceptual equality between those it separates as an objective virtuality to be exploited. In fact, the

---

Betasamosake Simpson, *Rehearsals for Living*, Vintage Canada, 2023; as well as the work of Sophie Lewis and M. E. O'Brien cited above.

16   Again, I point to the work of Sourayan Mookerjea in 'Accumulated Violence, or, the Wars of Exploitation'.

17   The 'chaotic concrete' is Marx's term in the *Grundrisse*; the 'dazzling power of false immediacy' is Theodor Adorno and Max Horkheimer's term in *The Dialectic of Enlightenment*, Continuum, 1994.

dialectical analysis of capital's movement arrives at an idea that sounds even less intuitive: that the systemic negation of abundance, and the restriction of non-capitalist forms of life-making, is the social content of class struggle. Capital's negation of non-capitalist abundance chokes social reproduction for both classes of the great simplification, that is, for both collective subjects who bear the categories labour *and* capital. From this more totalized standpoint, class struggle not only unifies those separated from the means of production (and, therefore, from the means of life) but is waged on behalf of the collective worker and collective capitalist alike. This is the historical universality of proletarian struggle, unified and planetary at the level of its concept.[18]

---

18   And what is revealed by Lukács's proletarian standpoint, in my opinion. See Georg Lukács, *History and Class Consciousness: Studies in Marxist Dialectics*, MIT Press, 1972.

PART II

Shapeshifting: Capital's Social Forms (Where Mystification of Surplus-Value Deepens at the Surface)

4

Transformation of Profit I: Commercial Profit

The Autonomization of Merchant's Capital (or, The Decomposition of Capital into Industrial and Merchant's Capital) – The Perceptual Physics of Merchant's Profit – Conclusion: The Historical Production of the Value Form (Is the Historical Production of Its Method of Analysis)

In part I of this book (chapters 1–3), we followed Marx's exposition of the movement through which surplus-value takes the concrete form of *profit*. This movement – the inversion of the essence of surplus-value in its appearance – severs the perception of surplus-value from its conceptual origin in living labour engaged in production. Now, in part II (chapters 4–6), we follow Marx's exposition of the decomposition of profit into the surface forms of industrial profit, commercial profit, interest, and ground-rent. These derivatives of profit-in-general posit their corresponding 'origins' in the phenomenal world of capitalist competition: industrial capital, merchant's capital, interest-bearing capital, and landed property. Profit's social forms deepen the mystification of surplus-value; they operate as fetishes to the second power.

The social forms of capital and their corresponding forms of profit emerge co-constitutively; as historical formations, they are specific to a capitalist mode of production. Like capital-in-general, capital's social forms are the accidental outgrowths of developing traditional modes of production and trade: the commodity (and the global formation that it indexes) emerges from small-scale, localized production of means of subsistence and luxury goods and the exchange of the surplus product of that activity between communities and regional markets. Early modern mercantile trade routes and associated patterns of activity eventually come to dominate and subsume traditional social relations and their corresponding modes of social reproduction.[1] However, the logical relationship between capital and its social forms is also a historical outgrowth. As we will see, merchant's capital, interest-bearing capital, and (modern) landownership all have pre-capitalist forms – mercantilism, money-lending for profit (usury), and aristocratic land entitlements, respectively – that are the traditional social material out of which capitalist forms emerge. The gradual transformation of these pre-capitalist modalities through the emptying out of their social substance and their reconstitution as forms of capital is the process of the development of the capitalist mode of production itself, as well as the historical emergence of capital as a logical movement; it is a historical development that posits capital in its 'pure form' (i.e., in its concept) as the logical presupposition of its phenomenal expressions, as their invisible centre of gravity. What Marx calls the concept of capital emerges both as product of capitalist development – the outcome of capitalism 'full blown' – *and* as the logical presupposition of capital's phenomenal forms. The logical emergence of capital in its concept, as social substance, moves forward in reverse; it is a process that posits its own conditions of possibility.

In part IV of *Capital* III, as throughout, Marx's object of analysis is the movement of capital as organizational logic, that is, 'capital in its basic inner structure' (379). Capital as logic is an immaterial objectivity; it has no immediate empirical form. Therefore, its exposition must map the dynamic between capital as social content and its phenomenal forms of appearance – the phenomenal expressions of that content, as Marx says, in 'the world as it actually is'. Since it is this material dynamic that is the object of the study, Marx gives minimal attention to the forms themselves, providing only the basic description required to unfurl the central analysis. Accounts of market trends, sales strategy and

---

1   In the final chapter of part IV of *Capital* III (chapter 20), Marx looks at the historical emergence of merchant's capital, in particular, from pre-capitalist modes of production and commerce. We will look at Marx's historical narrative of the emergence of merchant's capital at the end of this chapter.

inter-capitalist competition, advertising and public relations, commercial or distributional logistics, and ongoing forms of class struggle and labour mobilization are largely absent unless they impact on the general analysis of capital's inner connections. Technological developments in production and distribution, or the reorganization of work and workplaces as aesthetic and affective environments, in *Capital's* narrow terms of analysis, are germane only in their impact on productivity, speed of circulation, intensity of labour exploitation, and the resulting general rate of surplus-value.[2]

The historical development of capital as social formation, as a mode of politics (macro and micro), as formations of resistance and struggle, as histories/technologies of group differentiation and oppression, as developing configurations of social reproduction, as aesthetics and cultural formations, as interlocking ideologies, subjectivities, and/or affective comportments – all these concrete forms are peripheral to Marx's analysis, not because they are peripheral in significance; the matter is the reverse. The need for a comprehensive analysis of capital's social forms is stressed many times throughout *Capital* III. According to the early (but abandoned) plan for *Capital*, Marx initially intended to dedicate separate volumes to the credit system, the world market, the state, and the character of capitalist competition.[3] For instance, he refers many times to the elaboration of this or that point in a forthcoming study on 'Competition among Capitals' (e.g., on 205, 298, and 426) – a project he would never undertake (426). However, in what would become the unfinished three-part study in its existing form, the scope of analysis is intentionally narrowly defined. For example, in chapter 6 Marx states,

The phenomena under investigation in this chapter assume for their full development the credit system and competition on the world

---

2   In other words, the vast majority of the dimensions of capitalist society and capitalist reproduction are absent from the analysis across the three volumes of *Capital*.

3   Ernest Mandel argues that there is no evidence that this initial plan was abandoned. I would argue that the organic structure and coherency of the division of *Capital's* material between the three volumes as they now exist (even unfinished) suggests that the initial plan *was* abandoned. See Mandel's 'Introduction to Volume 3 of *Capital*,' in *Capital* III; for Mandel's discussion of Marx's plan for *Capital*, see 'The Plan of *Capital*' in his introduction to Karl Marx, *Capital: A Critique of Political Economy*, vol. 1, trans. Ben Fowkes, Penguin, 1990, 27–8.

market, the latter being the very basis and living atmosphere of the capitalist mode of production. *These concrete forms of capitalist production, however, can be comprehensively depicted only after the general nature of capital is understood; it is therefore outside the scope of this work to present them* – they belong to a possible continuation. (205, my emphasis)

If the effort to define the object in question were only an academic exercise, the stakes would be low.[4] However, Marx's wager is more substantial: once capital is established as a dominant organizing social logic, its 'basic inner structure' (379) must be reproduced for accumulation to proceed *at any subsequent historical stage of development, despite what transformations may occur at the level of capital's formal expressions.* One of *Capital's* subtexts, therefore, is the idea that grasping the (perceptual) physics of capitalist accumulation is one dimension of its dismantling. As a revolutionary text (if we accept that proposition), *Capital's* comportment is pedagogical. Of course, struggles against capital's everyday forms of barbarism do not wait on scientific analysis. Nevertheless, the generalized abolition of the value form, of a dominant mode of abstraction and equalization, will be intentional, an assertion of collective will – a movement with a provisional plan, even if, inevitably, a plan destined to be scrapped. An idea of what such a programme will entail, and of what an associated mode of production might look like, orients Marx's sustained focus on the conditions for the reproduction of the value form – that is, its inner structure – which is also to say, the conditions for its abolition. Here, in part II, we will continue to follow Marx in observing only 'such detail as is needed in order to analyse capital in its basic inner structure' (379).

---

4   The object of Marx's analysis is different from the object of Marx's critique, but they are related. If theorists have rightly pointed out that *Capital* is a *critique of political economy* (the study's title being a compelling clue) where political economy is understood as emerging discipline and body of knowledge, as discourse, as set of inverted presuppositions, a world and point of view comported as the disavowal of the negative, the theoretical expression of capital itself, and so on, then that critique itself presupposes Marx's wider and sustained analysis of the movement of capital. The two things are not separate.

The Autonomization of Merchant's Capital (or, The Decomposition of Capital into Industrial and Merchant's Capital)

Capital I and II explore the buying and selling of commodities as the serial metamorphosis of the form of value; value moves through circuits of exchange as the ongoing transformation of money into commodities, and commodities into money. In circulation, C (commodities) and M (money) are continuously taking each other's place; this is the case for both simple commodity circulation (C–M–C), as well as for its inversion/ suspension in capitalist circulation, or M–C–M. We learn in *Capital* I that value's constant transformation of form between C and M is the shape-shifting capacity that makes capitalist accumulation possible; it is the capacity through which value conceals a crucial change in its own magnitude, a quantitative change famously annotated as M–C–M′. This circuit is the metamorphosis of value in motion, or, value's modality as capital. Capital is expanding value: a quantitative transformation of value that is facilitated by a qualitative transformation of value.

In *Capital* I and II, the analysis of the movement of value through circuits of exchange operates on the register of core-abstraction where the categories, commodity and money – first-order derivatives of the value form – are sufficient to carry the analysis. In *Capital* III, the analysis moves on from this initial abstraction to consider the sphere of circulation as a more concrete combination of determinants; the mise en scène shifts to the sphere of market activity 'in the world as it actually is'. Now, on the register of surface-concretion, commodity and money undergo a further transformation of form and assume the stations of either industrial capital or merchant's capital (or, as interest or ground rent, as we will explore in the next two chapters).

In discussing the material in part IV, we continue to use Marx's term 'merchant's capital', even though it may sound anachronistic to contemporary readers. To replace the term with something more contemporary, like 'commercial capital', 'retail capital', or 'circulatory capital', is feasible and would have the benefit of underscoring the ongoing currency of Marx's analysis; however, it could also introduce confusion for those cross-checking Marx's analysis directly. To add further potential confusion, Marx already uses the term 'commercial capital', along with the term 'money-dealing capital', to designate two subspecies of merchant's capital. As we will see, 'merchant's capital' is a wider term that designates capital that functions strictly in the arena of circulation to facilitate the purchase and sale of commodities. It decomposes into two further subspecies of capital that facilitate circulation: commercial capital (or commodity-dealing capital) and money-dealing capital. We will define these two modalities of capital as we go. A couple of times, Marx uses the term 'trading capital' interchangeably with 'merchant's capital'. Again, to avoid confusion, we will refer to merchant's capital only when designating capital that operates exclusively in the sphere of circulation and which decomposes into commercial and money-dealing capital. One advantage of the term 'merchant's capital' is that it resonates with its pre-capitalist origins in mercantilism, suggesting both a continuity of form and the fundamental transformation of social content to which the term makes reference.

As we know from *Capital* I, value is created (or valorized) in the sphere of production and yet realized in the sphere of circulation. Capitalist accumulation is the process whereby capital moves from production to circulation and, upon returning to the money form in the course of circulation, returns to the sphere of production to be once again set in motion. Capitalist accumulation is a quantitative movement as much as it is a qualitative metamorphosis of form: from the point of view of the total social capital, the production and realization of surplus-value is a singular, two-stage cycle of augmenting value. To successfully fulfil its mission of accumulation, each cycle augments the magnitude of value that was thrown into the initial process. The realization of surplus-value in circulation is, therefore, one necessary moment of a complete and viable accumulation cycle operating in combination with, but logically – and, typically, spatially and temporally – separate from, the moment of production. One portion, therefore, of the total capital set in motion to carry out a cycle of accumulation will be mobilized in the service of realizing surplus-value in the sphere of circulation. This portion of the total capital investment will be engaged in carrying out those activities that facilitate the buying and selling of commodities: wholesaling, retailing, marketing, advertising, accounting, related administrative services, and the conversion of currencies to facilitate trade across legal jurisdictions (i.e., currency conversion to facilitate trade on the world market). Capital set in motion to fulfil these services assumes the social form that Marx designates as merchant's capital. The movement of merchant's capital, as a social form of capital-in-general, has the effect of creating a generalized perception of the location and modality of value's augmentation that inverts what is actually the case.

To carry out a single accumulation cycle, one portion of the total capital investment must be applied to the functions of production, and another portion to the functions of circulation. Capital's personifier in circulation, the merchant capitalist, functions as an agent of accumulation as a whole, and their activities, as the extension of the production process in the sphere of circulation. The merchant capitalist performs the functions that the industrial capitalist could feasibly undertake themselves, and which they would need to undertake in the absence of such a division of labour:

> The operations of the merchant are nothing more than those operations that must always be performed to transform the producer's commodity capital into money, operations which accomplish the functions of commodity capital in the circulation and reproduction process. If selling were the exclusive business of a mere agent of the producer, instead of being performed by an independent merchant, and purchase likewise, this connection would not be obscured for one moment.
>
> Commercial capital [as one subspecies of merchant's capital], therefore, is absolutely nothing more than the commodity capital of the producer which has to go through the process of transformation into money, to perform its function as commodity capital on the market; only instead of being an incidental operation carried out by the producer himself, this function now appears as the exclusive operation of a particular species of capitalist, the merchant, and acquires independence as the business of a particular capital investment. (382)

The formation of merchant's capital is, therefore, the process of the dissociation of the functions that facilitate the circulation of commodities from those involved directly in their production. In this historical division of labour, capital-in-general, as the moment of internal cohesiveness of the accumulation process, moves, in the course of its expansion, from the sphere of production to the sphere of circulation and back again. Merchant's capital, on the other hand, as empirical social form, remains exclusively in the sphere of circulation, generating the appearance of its fundamental separation and merely external relationship to production. The dissociation of the functions of the industrial and merchant capitalist is also, consequently, the dissociation of the capital investments that propel these activities. The emergence of merchant's capital is the internal dissociation of productive capital from itself:

> In as much as this function [of circulation, buying and selling, warehousing, etc.] acquires independent life as a special function of a special capital and is fixed by the division of labour as a function that falls to a particular species of capitalists (*sic*), commodity capital becomes commodity-dealing capital or commercial capital . . . in this function as circulation capital, it is distinguished from its own existence as productive capital. These are two separate and distinct forms of existence of the same capital . . . Commercial capital, then, is nothing but the transformed form of a portion of this circulation capital which is always to be found on the market, in the course of its metamorphosis, and perpetually confined to the circulation sphere. (379–80)

In other words, merchant's capital simultaneously *is and is not* industrial capital. At the same time, a commodity is not simply a commodity: it takes the form of industrial capital in the hands of the manufacturer, and merchant's capital in the hands of the merchant.

The conditional possibility for the dissociation of merchant's capital and industrial capital is the serial nature (the spatial and temporal separation) of the moments of value's production and realization. Accumulation can only proceed by way of the separation of these moments and, at the same time, is served by it in the way that the specialization of capitalist functions shortens turnover times and entails that less value in the money form is required for the circulation of value in the commodity form. While production and circulation, with their corresponding functions and capital investments, co-constitute the accumulation process, their seriality and spatial-temporal divergence generate the appearance of being distinct spheres of enterprise that are mediated only externally and accidentally by the market. This inverted appearance, or phenomenal dissociation, of the movement of industrial and merchant's capital, mystifies their internal dependence – their identity – and is the basis for their autonomization (384). The achievement of an 'external autonomy in combination with an inner connection' (419) is the way that Marx describes the movement of externalization, or separation in appearance, of capital's social forms from their internal connection, *as* capital-in-general, and the subsequent objectification of these forms as economic realities that organize and compel the decisions, practices, behaviour, ideologies, and institutional arrangements of the bearers of capitalist economies and capitalist society more widely. The autonomization of merchant's capital entails, therefore, the sedimentation of both the social forms of industrial and merchant's capital as objective formations compelling the surface dynamics of capitalist society, including their expression in forms of consciousness:

> As the reader will have recognized in dismay, the analysis of the real, inner connections of the capitalist production process is a very intricate thing and a work of great detail; it is one of the tasks of science to reduce the visible and merely apparent movement to the actual inner movement. Accordingly, it will be completely self-evident that, in the heads of the agents of capitalist production and circulation, ideas must necessarily form about the laws of production that diverge completely from these laws and are merely the expression in consciousness of the apparent movement. The ideas of a merchant, a stock-jobber or a banker are necessarily quite upside-down. The ideas of the manufacturers are vitiated by the acts of circulation to which their capital is subjected and by the equalization of the general rate of profit. (428)

Marx observes a further decomposition of merchant's capital into two subspecies: commercial capital (or commodity-dealing capital) and money-dealing capital. The proliferation of capital's surface-forms indexes the developing specialization of the activities required by the accumulation process. The specialization of activities multiplies capital's personifiers and corresponding new categories of capital investments. 'Commercial capital' refers to capital engaged in activities dealing directly with commodities: wholesaling, retailing, marketing, and all related accounting and administrative labour. According to the explanation in *Capital* II, Marx does not include transportation, distribution, and storage services in the category of industries that fall under the purview of commercial capital; we can put consumer data collection and analysis services together with transportation in this category. The provision of these services, according to Marx, is carried out only nominally in the sphere of circulation and constitutes productive (i.e., value-generating) industries, often continuous with the functions that absorb commercial capital but are not to be confused with commercial capital investments as such. On the productive industries of transportation and storage, Marx states,

> We have already explained (Volume 2, Chapter 6, 'The Costs of Circulation', 2 and 3) the extent to which the transport industry, storage and the dispersal of goods in a distributable form should be viewed as production processes that continue within the process of circulation. These incidents in the circulation of the commodity capital are sometimes confused with functions peculiar to commodity capital; they are sometimes linked in practice with the specific functions peculiar to this capital, although as the social division of labour develops, so the function of commercial capital also evolves in pure form, i.e. separately from these real functions and independent of them . . . We only have this *pure form* [of commercial capital] once those functions [of transportation and storage] are discarded and removed. (379–80, my emphasis)

In Marx's analysis, the product-services of transportation and storage industries are consumed as means of production by industrial and commercial capitalists and therefore represent, for the latter, production costs and constant capital investments (388). What distinguishes transportation and storage industries from those enterprises mobilizing commercial capital is that the latter do not generate new surplus-value but are, rather, involved exclusively in realizing surplus-value produced elsewhere. As we will explore in the next section, this situation entails that the profit made on commercial capital represents a redistribution of a portion of surplus-value generated elsewhere, in productive industry. Once the activities that absorb commercial capital have developed to the point where they function autonomously as enterprises, and where the capital they engage need never exit the sphere of circulation, Marx refers (as in the above passage) to commercial capital as having achieved the status of 'pure form'. At this stage, we might also call commercial capital 'pure fetish', a value form that not only mystifies the genuine source of value in living labour, but also represents a capital investment that no longer must come into contact with living labour whatsoever in its capacity to draw a profit for its owner – a perceptual mystification of an even higher degree than capital engaged directly in production, or, a fetish derived from (or, one that presupposes) a logically prior fetish.

Money-dealing capital is a second subspecies of merchant's capital. Like commercial capital, money-dealing capital is 'the evolution of a specific kind of capital' (383), internally identical with capital-in-general and externally – phenomenally – operating exclusively in the sphere of circulation. 'Money-dealing capital' refers to capital employed in the service of converting money from one currency into another to facilitate trade between parties operating in different local currencies; the money-dealer is the 'cashier for merchants and industrial capitalists' (435). Like commercial capital, money-dealing capital is a 'definite part of the total capital [that] now separates off and becomes autonomous in the form of money capital . . . [and performs this function of currency conversion] for the entire class of industrial and commercial capitalists' (431). Money-dealing capital emerges with capitalist production itself in the same way that the world market is the very basis and presupposition of capitalist production and not simply an index of a later stage of its development (451). The function of converting money from one currency to another is a necessary dimension of the reproduction of capital at all stages of development:

> As world money, national money discards its local character; one national money is expressed in another, and in this way they are all reduced to their gold and silver content. Since both these commodities circulate as world money, they have to be reduced in turn to their mutual value ratio, which is constantly changing. The money-dealer makes it his own special business to carry on this intermediary function. Money-changing and the bullion trade are thus the original forms of the money business and arise from the double function of money: as national coin and as world money. (434–5)

As Marx states, 'The movements of this money capital are thus again simply movements of a now independent part of the industrial capital in the course of its reproduction process' (431). In other words, money is not simply money; it assumes the form of industrial capital in the hands of the industrialist, and that of money-dealing capital in the hands of the money-converting merchant. Nonetheless, a perceptual inversion is set in motion by money's decomposition into its specialized functions: from the standpoint of the total social capital, the money capital that is the stock and trade of the money merchant is simply a portion of the money capital set in motion by industrialists and merchants, and the functions performed by the money-dealers, simply the necessary tasks of the industrialists and merchants, now carried out (i.e., mediated) by these specialized capitalists (438).

At all stages of capitalist production, it is typical for enterprises that perform the function of converting currencies to also perform an array of other money-related services, most of which involve some configuration of lending and borrowing (investment management, securities trading, preparing and vending derivatives and other financial products for speculating, hedging, and so on). These other services, all aspects of the credit system, generate revenue (primarily but not exclusively) either in the form of service fees or interest. Money lent as credit assumes the social form of interest-bearing capital and is distinct from the form of money-dealing capital as a subspecies of merchant's capital; we will elaborate interest-bearing capital as social form and the dynamic of the credit system in the next chapter, when we look at the analysis in part V. For now, Marx's point is to recognize money-dealing capital and interest-bearing capital as distinct forms while often being grouped together as services in the social division of labour and corresponding specializations characteristic of a capitalist system: 'Money-dealing is fully developed, even if still in its first beginnings, as soon as the functions of lending and borrowing, and trade on credit, are combined with its other functions' (436). The grouping together of money-dealing and credit as money-related services is a surface-form; the two services, however, are configured differently in their mode of claiming a portion of surplus-value generated in production, even if both forms represent modes of redistributing surplus-value, specifically, from the agents of productive capital to other factions of the capitalist class:

> Money-dealing in the pure form in which we are considering it here,
> i.e. separate from the credit system, thus only bears on the technical

side of one aspect of commodity circulation, i.e. monetary circulation and the various functions of money that arise from it. (438)

The merchant, or commodity dealer, steps in to represent the commodity in the sphere of circulation, replacing the commodity manufacturer in undertaking the functions that animate the marketplace (387). The appearance of the merchant's independence in these functions – the perceptual inversion of an internal structural dependence – and the merchant's evolution as a specialized capitalist in the social division of labour is built on, as well as deepens and objectifies in turn, the appearance of the specialization of capitals and the corresponding perception that all capitals are self-valorizing regardless of how they are mobilized. The perceptual delinking, or autonomization, of merchant's capital and productive capital is carried out when the merchant advances their 'own' money capital that is then, in the course of enterprise (and apparently independently), valorized. For the services of buying and selling commodities, the merchant 'makes a profit', and, as with any circuit of capital by definition, the metamorphosis of capital is expressed in an augmentation of value: M–C–M′ (386). We will look at the source of merchant's profit in the next section.

Capital's decomposition into industrial and merchant's capital is compelled by the advantages it presents for accumulation: when certain functions become their own 'special business', they can assemble economies of scale that could otherwise not be achieved if that function were carried out as one department of productive enterprise: '[A service like converting currency, for example,] becomes a special business, and because it is performed as a special business for the monetary mechanism of the entire class, it is concentrated and undertaken on a large scale' (433). To intensify accumulation, the capitalist increases the scale of production and shortens the turnover time of the capital investment, both of which can be better achieved with the intervention of an independent merchant's capital. In the division of labour between producer and retailer, the producer is able to alienate their product rapidly and en masse to the retailer, expediting the movement of C–M that allows the producer to convert M back into the means of production (M–C) (387). In this way, the producer is not required to halt production until the product of the previous cycle is consumed. Without the intervention of the merchant, the producer would need to hold back a portion of their productive capital in the form of a money reserve that could be used to procure new means of production while the product from the previous cycle completed its endgame. To hold a portion of the total social productive capital in reserve diminishes the size of the total social capital set in motion productively at any one time and compromises the scale of accumulation for the sake of increasing its speed. The intervention of the merchant may not abolish altogether the need to divide capital up in this way . However, it does allow money capital held in reserve to be reduced to a much-smaller portion of the capital mobilized in production. Without the merchant's intervention, the money reserve of the manufacturer would need to be greater than the portion of capital invested in production in order to account for the necessarily expanded value locked up in the subsequent production cycle (387).

The division of labour between producer and merchant therefore enables productive 'capital to operate on a bigger scale' (393) as well as to shorten its circulation time (392). However, merchant's capital is also functionally rationalized in this division of labour. The turnover time of one commercial capital is not restricted by the turnover time of one corresponding industrial capital, as it would be if the industrialist were required to retail their own product (388). After the investment of a particular commercial capital, once the merchant has converted C back into M, their subsequent investment is not attendant on the next batch of commodities produced by the original industrial capital. Rather, the same commercial capital, once it is turned over, can purchase the product of numerous other industrial capitals; it can turn over several times, and purchase the product of several different capitalists, in the course of a single turnover of any one industrial capital:

> The turnover of one commercial capital is not identical with the turn-over or the reproduction, once only, of an equally large industrial capital; it is equal, rather, to the sum of the turnovers of a number of such capitals, whether in the same sphere of production or in different ones. (389)

Thus, the ratio between commercial capital and industrial capital is not one to one; the more developed the capitalist mode of production, 'the more quickly the commercial capital turns over, the smaller is the part of the total money capital that figures as commercial capital, and vice versa' (389).

From the point of view of the total social capital, we can think of the capital that, 'in the hands of the merchant', facilitates the work of buying and selling commodities as that portion of the industrialist's productive capital that must be held in reserve to advance the ongoing metamorphosis of commodities into money and money into commodities (391). It is as if the industrialist outsources the management of the circulatory aspects of the reproduction cycle and, for undertaking this management, as we will see, the merchant appropriates a portion of the surplus-value generated. In absolute terms, the magnitude of surplus-value to be distributed among the capitalist class is increased through the division of the functions between specialized capitals (392–3). In this way, the decomposition of capital into its social forms enacts the double movement with respect to accumulation that we have come to expect: on the one hand, 'in so far as it cuts down the turnover time, it increases the ratio of surplus-value to the capital advanced, i.e. the rate of profit [is increased]'; on the other hand, in so far as it enables 'capital to operate on a bigger scale, its functioning promotes the productivity of industrial capital and its accumulation', and this enhances the tendency for the rate of profit to fall (393).

The Perceptual Physics of Merchant's Profit

What impact does the formation of merchant's capital have on the production of surplus-value, on the transformation of surplus-value into profit, and on the general rate of profit and its distribution? Further, what role does merchant's capital play in the inverted surface appearance of all these related processes? To illustrate these dynamics, we will follow Marx in focusing on commercial capital, the subspecies of merchant's capital that is directly involved in the sale and purchase of commodities. We proceed from the standpoint of the total social capital and the two phases of capital's reproduction – value's production and realization – and the understanding that while value is realized in the sphere of circulation, no value whatsoever is produced in the course of buying and selling. This fact does not change just because commercial capital is an autonomized portion of productive capital operating in the marketplace:

> Commercial capital is nothing more than capital functioning within the circulation sphere. The circulation process is one phase in the reproduction process as a whole. But in the process of circulation, no value is produced, and thus also no surplus-value. The same value simply undergoes changes of form. Nothing at all happens except the metamorphosis of commodities, which by its very nature has nothing to do with the creation or alteration of value. If a surplus-value is realized on the sale of a commodity produced, this is because it already existed in the commodity . . . Commercial capital thus creates neither value nor surplus-value, at least not directly. (392)

> If these operations [buying in order to sell] are not such as to create any value or surplus-value for the industrial capitalists themselves, they cannot possibly do so when they are performed by other persons instead. (394)

Like industrial capital, commercial capital yields the average profit (395). But, if commercial capital does not create surplus-value, from where does the profit that falls to the merchant derive? In the world of capital's social forms, the appearance of the source of commercial profit informs common sense: the merchant purchases the product of the manufacturer at a certain price and resells the product at a higher price; the difference between the purchase price and the sale price represents the merchant's profit – a profit that must absorb the costs of doing business (395). However, as we know, for Marx, this common sense is 'mere semblance' (395; 396; 397). Up to this point in the analysis, we have assumed that producers sell their commodities at their prices of production and that these are the prices that commodities take to market. Now, in light of the intervention of the merchant, and the mediation of merchant's capital, we must adjust this assumption.

We continue to posit that commodities are sold at their prices of production; however, now it is the merchant, rather than the producer, who sells at this price. Value cannot be created out of thin air, by will or wishing. Since merchants do not subject the commodities they purchase to 'any intervening process in which they might absorb new surplus-value' (396), we must suppose that it is the merchant who sells the commodity at its approximate value, and the producer who sells below this value magnitude. Marx calls the merchant's sale price the commercial price, or 'real price' (399). We must now assume that the producers' production price (the price at which they sell to the merchant) is lower than the commodity's value and that the merchant appropriates as profit the difference between the commodity's production price and its real, commercial price. In this way, the industrial capitalist does not appropriate the full magnitude of surplus-value generated in production. Rather, the industrial capitalist *shares* (without intention or awareness of doing so) a portion of this surplus-value with the merchant capitalist, who pockets their share as profit. This sharing of surplus-value entails that the intervention of merchant's capital in the process of capital's reproduction bears on the formation of the general rate of profit and therefore, indirectly, on every capital investment (398).

Marx exposits the process in mathematical terms; we work on the register of the concept, that is, not with individual capitals but rather with the total social capital. We can simplify Marx's already-simple calculations, while still demonstrating the same logical premise.[5] In chapter 2, we calculated the general rate of profit: supposing a total social capital investment of 90, with a composition of $70c$ and $20v$, and a rate of surplus-value of 100 percent, the surplus-value generated is 20 and the value of the total product, C ($70c + 20v + 20s$), is 110. The general rate of profit would be 20 (surplus-value) over 90 (productive capital, or cost price), or 22.22 percent. Now we adjust the calculation to account for the division of labour between manufacturer and merchant. If the merchant invests 10 (i.e., purchases a portion of the producer's product at a price of 10), they have purchased a portion of the product that represents one-ninth of the producer's cost price, leaving the other portions to be purchased by other merchants in order to realize the value contained in the total product. With this additional investment of commercial capital, the total capital investment, *industrial + commercial capital*, is now 100. With this new total capital investment of 100, the commercial portion of 10 over the total 100 represents a share of, and claim on, one-tenth of the surplus-value generated by the total capital,

---

5   We will recreate Marx's calculation, step by step, from page 398 of *Capital* III.

which remains at 20, since the commercial capital portion generates no new value. The commercial capital investment therefore appropriates one-tenth of 20, or, 2. The new rate of profit for the merchant (and the industrialist, as we will see) after the division of labour is, therefore, 2 over the commercial capital investment of 10, or 20 percent. The intervention of commercial capital has adjusted the rate of profit from 22.22 percent to 20 percent. The surplus-value (profit) to be divided among the remaining nine-tenths is now 20 percent of the remaining 90, or 18. That is, even though the rate of surplus-value is 100 percent, the producer's investment of 90 ($70c + 20v$) yields 18 in profit (expressing the new rate of profit of 20 percent) instead of 20 (or the original rate of 22.22 percent). Under these new circumstances, the price at which C is sold to the merchants by the producer, after the latter has set their investment of 90 in motion, is their new production price, or $70c + 20v + 18s = 108$. The merchants, collectively, will purchase C, the product of an investment of 90, at the new production price of 108 and sell it at the real, commercial price (the price that approximates the real value of C) of 110. In this way, as we have determined, a commercial investment of 10 will yield a profit of 2 (for a rate of profit of 20 percent), and a productive investment of 90 will yield a profit of 18 (for a rate of profit of 20 percent).

In this calculation, the merchant makes a profit of 2, but not because they sell the commodity above its value. Rather, the merchant sells the commodity *at* its value and pockets a portion of the surplus-value already contained in the commodity – surplus-value that is now divided between the merchant and the industrialist, according to the size of their capital investments. Both merchant and industrialist 'make' the general rate of profit on their respective investments. The industrialist invests 90 for a profit of 18, while the merchant invests 10 at a profit of 2. Both the merchant's investment and profit are one-ninth that of the industrialist. Meanwhile, the general rate of profit is adjusted downwards from 22.22 percent to 20 percent to account for the division of labour between the enterprises of the merchant and industrialist. In this way, 'commercial capital thus contributes to the formation of the general rate of profit according to the proportion it forms in the total capital' (398).

We now have a more developed formulation of the price of production. The industrialist's price of production continues to be cost price plus general rate of profit, the price at which they sell to the merchant – in our calculation, 108. This new production price, however, is calculated as the ratio of surplus-value to the *sum* of productive and commercial capital; it is a magnitude that no longer represents the commodity's real value. The commodity's real value, unaltered by the intervention of merchant capital, now includes the merchant's profit of 2, for a real, commercial price of 110 (399). The commodity's real value is the selling price for the merchant; it is the centre of gravity around which the commodity's empirical price will orbit:

> The merchant's sale price is higher than his purchase price not because it is above the total value, but rather because his purchase price is below this total value . . . The general rate of profit thus already takes account of the deduction from the surplus-value which falls to commercial capital, i.e. a deduction from the profit of industrial capital. (400)

The decrease in the general rate of profit that is the result of the dissociation of industrial and merchant's capital is more than compensated for by the increase in the rate of profit that is the result of the reduction in turnover times and the smaller amounts of reserve capital required by producers, who can now throw this capital into production without directing it towards circulation. These are the immediate advantages that push and pull against the long-term structural contradictions of the movement of developing capital; they correspond with the appearance that capital can operate exclusively in one domain or the other:

> Instead of the industrial capitalist spending more time on the circulation process, the merchant now spends this time; instead of being forced to advance additional capital for circulation, the merchant advances it; or, what comes to the same thing, whereas previously a substantial portion of the industrial capital was constantly entering and leaving the circulation process, now the merchant's capital is cooped up there permanently. And whereas previously the industrial capitalist made a smaller profit now he has to abandon a part of his [albeit, augmented] profit completely to the merchant. (404–5)

Commercial capital enters into the equalization process of the general rate of profit with a double, contradictory movement: (1) it lowers the rate by dividing profit between manufacturer and merchant; (2) it increases the rate by augmenting the scale of the process (406). It is a movement that expresses both tendency and countertendency.

Since the function of merchant's capital is to carry out the realization of value contained in commodities by taking over these functions from productive capital, no part of the profit that falls to merchant's capital comes from setting variable capital in motion.[6] Rather, merchant's capital takes a share of the value generated in production. If the commercial enterprise is very small, it is conceivable (if unlikely) that the merchant need not mobilize any variable capital to secure the profit that their commercial investment yields; the merchant may perform the labour involved themselves. Such a small enterprise would yield a small profit, a profit that might constitute no more income for the merchant than would the average wage, or even less (404). If the enterprise succeeds and expands, however, our merchant will need to engage workers to undertake the increased labour involved and thereby set variable capital in motion. While this mobilized variable capital generates no new value, it is nonetheless capital mobilized 'for the purpose of valorizing the capital advanced' – *all* capital, constant and variable. The new investment of variable capital will also yield the average rate of profit, and it will do so with the same consequences that we observed with the merchant's constant capital: the increased ratio of merchant's capital (*constant + variable*) to industrial capital constituting the total social capital pushes the general rate of profit downward while, at the same time, the process of accumulation expands with the increased scale of the production-circulation facilitated by the growth of circulation-directed enterprise.

Even though variable capital invested in commercial enterprise does not generate new value for the system, there is still a sense in which the merchant exploits the unpaid labour of commercial workers. As we know, the value of labour-power is determined by the value of the goods and services necessary for its reproduction: 'the value of [the commercial worker's] labour-power, and therefore his wage, is determined, like that

---

6   The logical function of merchant's capital is unknown to the merchant and differentiated from their intention.

of all other wage-labourers, by the production and reproduction costs of this particular labour-power and not by the product of his labour' (406). The engagement of commercial workers facilitates the expansion of commercial enterprise, thereby making it possible for the merchant to appropriate a greater share of the surplus-value generated in production. The greater amount of value (in the form of higher profits) that the merchant can now appropriate in a day exceeds the value of the worker's labour-power for that day. This discrepancy between the magnitude of value exchanged for labour-power and the magnitude of value by which the merchant's profit is augmented as a result of engaging the worker is *the form that unpaid commercial labour takes in the sphere of circulation*. It is the modality of exploitation of commercial workers in the sphere of circulation, the manner in which workers 'directly produce profit for their employers, even though they do not directly produce surplus-value (of which profit is simply a transformed form)' (407):

> For the individual merchant, the amount of his profit depends on the amount of capital that he can employ in this process, and he can employ all the more capital in buying and selling, the greater the unpaid labour of his clerks. The very function by virtue of which the commercial capitalist's money is capital is performed in large measure by his employees, on his instructions. Their unpaid labour, even though it does not create surplus-value, does create his ability to appropriate surplus-value, which, as far as this capital is concerned, gives exactly the same result; i.e. it is its source of profit. Otherwise the business of commerce could never be conducted in the capitalist manner, or on a large scale.
>
> Just as the unpaid labour of the worker creates surplus-value for productive capital directly, so also does the unpaid labour of the commercial employee create a share in that surplus-value for commercial capital. (407–8)

In other words, commercial workers perform the service of transferring value to commercial capital that would otherwise fall to industrial capital:

> Commercial capital's relationship to surplus-value is different from that of industrial capital. The latter produces surplus-value by directly

appropriating the unpaid labour of others. The former appropriates a portion of this surplus-value by getting it transferred from industrial capital to itself. (407)

Commercial workers also facilitate a greater scale of production and, therefore, the production of value that would not otherwise be possible. As a capitalist mode of production develops from an emergent to a dominant formation, traditional relations between producers and merchants are gradually subsumed by capitalist production relations that come to invert the balance of power that previously fell to the merchant over the producers of goods. The modality and imperatives of capitalist production come to determine the scale and organization of commerce – of the circulation of commodities. The scale and speed at which commercial capital is able to realize the surplus-value in commodities is contingent on the scale and speed at which commodities objectifying surplus-value are produced:

> [The scope of commercial labour] depends on the magnitude of values produced and to be realized . . . A labour of this kind functions not as the cause of the respective magnitudes and amounts of these valued, as does directly productive labour, but is rather a consequence of them. It is similar with the other costs of circulation. If there is much to be weighed, measured, packed and transported, there must be plenty there in the first place. The amount of packing and transport work, etc. depends on the mass of the commodities that are objects of this activity and not the other way round. (414)

Today more than ever, the tremendous concentration of capital in enterprises involved in the circulation of commodities creates a very different appearance. The power of retailers such as Walmart to consolidate consumer demand, and thereby to largely dictate the terms and scale of production down the value chain – obliging producers to force down production costs and shorten delivery times – led commentators in the 1990s to baptize these developments as the 'Walmartization' of capitalism. The developments are unthinkable outside of the context of the logistics revolution, and the application of the information, communication, transportation, and computational technologies that animate it. The observation that circulatory capital has gained the upper hand on productive capital in the battle over control and profit is accurate with respect to the surface movement of capitalist forms: enormous economies of scale do allow massive retailers to wield power over producers. With respect to capital's inner movement, however, the same development signals a continuity rather than a transformation in modality: the expansion of commercial enterprises is a *consequence* of technological and organizational enhancements in capitalist productivity. The commercial sphere expands because developments in productive capacity make it possible and, therefore, compel it.

From the vantage of mid-nineteenth-century London, the 'commercial worker proper belong[ed] to the better-paid class of wage-labourer'; commercial labour required certain skills that situated it as 'above-average labour' with respect to the cost of its reproduction. However, Marx points out that the average commercial wage 'has a tendency to fall as the capitalist mode of production advances' as a function of the increasing division of labour within commercial enterprise, where the range of tasks performed by each worker becomes narrower and the skill set of the worker less costly to reproduce (414). Today, this downward pressure on commercial wages is accelerated by another development: the particular historical character of that which Marx refers to in the *Grundrisse* as 'the general intellect', and which he refers to in *Capital* III as 'the general extension of popular education' (415). Already, for Marx, a social world characterized by a growing commercial sphere entailed that the generalization of the 'basic skills, knowledge of commerce and languages, etc., [were] reproduced ever more quickly, easily, generally, and cheaply, the more the capitalist mode of production adapt[ed] teaching methods, etc. to practical purposes' (414–5). Marx observes that the development of the general intellect entails that skilled labour can eventually be recruited from the lower strata of the working class, from among workers 'accustomed to a lower standard of living'. This process continues to advance, and currently, as then, a growing pool of sufficiently (often, overly) skilled workers, as Marx says, 'increases supply, and with it competition. With a few exceptions, therefore, the labour-power of these people is devalued with the advance of capitalist production; their wages fall, whereas their working ability increases' (415).

This last point is crucial. The resulting situation is, in Marx's famous words, perverted and topsy turvy: as a capitalist mode of production develops, labour becomes more skilled as labour-power becomes less valuable – worth *less*, in the mathematical calculation of capitalist exploitation. If we think of the general intellect as the diffusion of a certain set of skills, technical and scientific capacity – historically defined, both practical and abstract knowledge – throughout a population, in the present 'post-industrial' conjuncture, the process has excelled in diffusing skills that are particularly instrumental for commercial enterprise: communications and 'networking'; a naturalized facility for the languages of buying and selling; information dissemination; researching goods and services; promotional skills such as marketing, branding, 'spinning', and selling ideas, opinions, ventures, or 'oneself'; and image/narrative production and management – in particular, an aestheticized comportment towards the object world and an ability to arrange, capture, and archive one's surroundings and 'experiences' in images and quasi-promotional narratives with the objective of soliciting feedback from audiences. We could not imagine the development of these skills outside of the generalized adoption of digital technologies, networks, applications, and platforms that form the constellation of social media. The outcome of this combination is the production of the layperson as highly skilled commercial practitioner – expert buyer, seller, marketer, brander, image-maker – and the consequent devaluation of these skills in the course of their diffusion, that is, in the calculation of the value of commercial labour-power.

Commercial labour once represented a high degree of specialization. Today, it is typical to be versed in an even more specialized set of commercial skills: the manoeuvres of everyday life. In the accounting process of the value abstraction, above-average labour is turned into average labour, which increases the profitability of commercial capital since a greater portion of the surplus-value it captures can be turned into profits when a smaller portion goes to the worker in the form of wages. As we observed above, and especially in the extreme case of giant retailers, this increasing concentration of capital in the sphere of circulation dispenses a greater power and influence to commercial entities over the terms and circumstances of production, deepening the appearance of the autonomy of circulation and its constituent functions from those of production.

The dynamics that constitute merchant's capital generate a series of inverted appearances that contribute to the wider perceptual physics of capital, a process that mystifies the source of all surplus-value in living labour – in people doing and making, collectively. We observed that a portion of productive capital must be applied to the business of selling the product in order to realize the surplus-value congealed in it. The division of productive capital into one portion that facilitates the functions of production and another portion that facilitates the functions of circulation – where each portion comes to operate exclusively in one sphere or the other, and under the purview of its respective capitalist agent – expands capital's capacity for accumulation. The drive to expand the scale of accumulation thereby compels the decomposition of capital into its social forms of industrial capital and merchant's capital. This decomposition is, at the same time, a perceptual dynamic; we have referred to it as autonomization. The internal identity of industrial and merchant's capital – from the point of view of the totality of the reproduction process, one productive capital investment – assumes its phenomenal appearance as two separate, autonomous capitals that meet in the marketplace, coincidentally, as competing investments that have no internal connection.

The surface autonomy of capital's social forms bestows on them an objectivity that organizes political economy accordingly. Independent in appearance while being one station of a concatenation in essence, capital's social forms obfuscate their animating contradictions on the one hand, and their symptomatic expressions on the other, rendering both thoroughly inexplicable from the fragmented and partial view of things that inform a general, operating knowledge of the world. The fact that merchant's capital yields the general rate of profit, apparently without any reference to or collaboration with the industrial sector (outside of adhering to the anarchic formal equality of market exchange), generates, as a tendency, the general perception that profit-making is an attribute of capital in itself, regardless of where or how it is invested, so long as it is done with the requisite amount of entrepreneurial know-how. The singular location and means of the creation of surplus-value is thus mystified.

The autonomy/dependence contradiction inherent to capital's social forms, merchant's capital included, drives towards systemic crisis. For example, commercial capital's quasi-autonomy allows it to function, provisionally, as a means of pushing accumulation beyond its immediate barriers. The intervention of commercial capital eliminates the need for the industrial capitalist to reserve a portion of capital to cover the costs of circulation, thereby facilitating the expansion of production and, consequently, consumer demand. At some point, equally inevitable and impossible to foresee, accumulation tips over into overaccumulation, demand falls short of supply, 'stocks become too high', value created cannot be realized, and 'the inner connection' between commercial capital and its ultimately determining productive counterpart 'is forcibly re-established by way of a crisis' (419), marking an 'end to the apparent prosperity' (420). That capital is, in its surface modality, fragmented into a social division of quasi-autonomous investments and operations that, under the surface, are inextricably interconnected entails that the sphere of production or industry in which crises erupt – the industry which signals the arrival of the tipping point – will not have played *the* causal role in its arrival:

> This explains the phenomenon that crises do not first break out and are not first apparent in the retail trade, which bears on immediate consumption, but rather in the sphere of wholesale trade, as well as banking, which places the money capital of the entire society at the wholesalers' disposal. (419)

Crisis momentarily breaks through capital's surface narratives; once again, distorted perceptions prevail. It appears as though the commercial price of commodities is determined by the merchant as the one who decides whether 'to sell many commodities at a low profit on the individual commodity, or a few commodities at a high profit' (421). The reality is that hidden limits determine that the commodity's commercial price will fall somewhere between the commodity's production price (the industrialist's cost price plus their portion of profit) and its actual value (production price plus the merchant's portion of profit), at least for any sustained amount of time without jeopardizing the viability of the enterprise. It is not the merchant but, rather, the overall development of the capitalist mode of production that determines both production price and general rate of profit; the merchant can sustain the illusion of independence only when price hovers inside its existential limits. With rare, historically contingent exceptions – such as a monopoly in either the production or circulation of a good or service – any sustained transgression of the limits on price shatters the illusion of the merchant's independence either by subverting the viability of the enterprise altogether or, if it's not too late, by forcing price back within its systemic boundaries.

Marx enumerates circumstances that 'foster the popular prejudice' that the merchant determines the sale price of their commodity and, consequently, determines the magnitude of profit they reap. First, in the battle of the marketplace, merchants will strategically lower prices in an effort to outsell competing merchants – fellow 'shareholders in the total commercial capital' – and eject them from the battle permanently, if possible. Second, public policy may set the market price of certain goods and services; it may lower the price of staples or life-saving drugs, or raise the minimum price of labour. State regulation of prices is necessary to ameliorate the most predatory practices encouraged by the system, but it also fosters the illusion that prices can be set arbitrarily, as opposed to being ultimately determined by the system. Third, an increase in productivity across an industry lowers the production price of the commodity in question and, consequently, lowers its commercial price. As a result, demand will sometimes grow faster than supply, and this will pull the commodity's market price above its value. As we already explored, this situation can only be temporary; however, it represents a window of time in which the merchant is able to appropriate a greater-than-average return on their investment. Fourth, 'a merchant may reduce sale price . . . in order to turn over a larger capital more quickly' (422).

This last point brings us to another of commercial capital's legerdemain, in the movement of its autonomization: the turnover time of commercial capital appears to determine price, and to do so independently of the circumstances of production. As we know, the faster an industrial capital turns over, the greater the number of production cycles resolved in a year – circulation permitting.[7] The greater the number of production cycles per year, the greater the magnitude of surplus-value produced, and the greater the upward pressure – 'other circumstances remaining equal' – on the general rate of profit. Commercial capital, we also know, does not create surplus-value nor, therefore, profit; as such, it does not have a determining influence on the general rate of profit, other

---

7   As Marx points out, circulation capacity and active demand assert, in this way, a negative limit on surplus-value creation, as opposed to representing a positive determinant on the general rate of profit.

than to take its annual share of the profit that industrial capital produces according to its portion of the total social capital (424). For commercial capital, therefore, rate of profit is an externally determined percentage of its own magnitude; in Marx's illustration (426–7), a commercial capital of 100 at a rate of profit of 15 percent will yield a profit of 15 annually. In other words, if a merchant purchases commodities from a producer at a production price of 100, the merchant will sell the commodities at a commercial price of 115, or, we could say, has a margin of 100 to 115 in which to appropriate all or some portion of the surplus-value congealed in the product that they have purchased from the producer. To sell above the commodity's value of 115 requires exceptional, and ultimately temporary, circumstances that favour the merchant over their competitors such that they are in a position to appropriate an extra portion of the total social surplus-value that would have otherwise ended up in another party's pocket. The pertinent fact, with respect to the perceptual inversion in question, is that a commercial investment of 100 per annum will yield a profit of 15 regardless of the number of times that capital turns over in the course of the year. If the capital turns over once per annum, the commercial price of the product will be 115. If the turnover time of the same commercial capital is twice per annum, the sale price of each product will represent a division of the annual profit by two, or 107.5; a turnover of five times per annum will yield a commercial price of 103 per product, or one-fifth of the annual profit per cycle; and so on.

By choosing to sell their product at a lower price, the merchant sells more quickly, increasing the number of times a single capital can be turned over in a year. The annual profit, as just illustrated, is spread over the annual number of cycles, making it appear as though the merchant determines the sale price of the product, strategically, and thereby 'earns' the profit that falls to them as a result. In reality, the commodity's price can only fluctuate within a narrow range established by the general law of value formation and distribution – a law that, in reality, cannot be outmanoeuvred by capital's agents. The illusion produced by this sleight of hand flips the direction of determination between industrial capital and merchant's capital: even though the turnover time of industrial capital does not affect the value of the individual commodity, 'it does affect the mass of the values and surplus-values that a given capital produces in a given time, via the mass of labour exploited' (427–8); the turnover time of commercial capital, on the other hand, appears to determine the price of commodities while not, ultimately, having the power to do so:

> From the standpoint of commercial capital, therefore, turnover itself seems to determine price. On the other hand, while the speed of industrial capital's turnover, in so far as it enables a given capital to exploit more or less labour, has a determining and delimiting effect on the mass of profit, and hence on the general rate of profit as well, commercial capital is faced with the rate of profit as something external to it, and this rate's inner connection with the formation of surplus-value is completely obliterated. (429)

> Thus, while a closer consideration of the influence of turnover time on value formation in the case of the individual capital leads back to the general law and the basis of political economy, viz. that commodity values are determined by the labour-time they contain, the influence of the turnover of commercial capital on commercial prices exhibits phenomena which, in the absence of a very far-reaching analysis of the intermediate stages of the process, seem to presuppose a purely arbitrary determination of prices, i.e. a determination simply by the fact that capital happens to have made up its mind to make a certain amount of profit per year. It seems in particular, through this influence of the turnover, as if the circulation process as such determines the prices of commodities, and that this is within certain limits independent of the process of production. (428)

Commercial capital performs the function of realizing the value that industrial capital has valorized, and a single commercial capital can do this many times over; the more often it does, the more surplus-value is realized. Shortening the turnover time of commercial capital therefore has an impact on the general rate of profit *indirectly*, freeing commercial capital up faster to perform for industrial capital once again. At the same time, the quicker the turnover time of a commercial capital, the smaller its magnitude may be relative to the industrial capital it valorizes: 'Velocity of circulation substitutes for the quantity of money in circulation.' Velocity, meanwhile, is enhanced with the development of the credit system, and here we arrive at the second crucial intervention into the accumulation process: namely, that of finance capital, a social form of capital whose movement we will exposit in the following chapter. For now, we can point out the function that commercial capital and finance capital share with respect to capitalist reproduction: neither value form participates in producing new value; both are mechanisms for *redistributing* value socially produced. Each time commercial capital turns over, 'it withdraws more money from circulation than it puts in'; 'this is what characterizes its turnover as a turnover of capital' (418).

Conclusion: The Historical Production of the Value Form (Is the Historical Production of Its Method of Analysis)

In a society in which the capitalist mode of production prevails, merchant's capital is one moment of the movement of capital-in-general, of the wider process of capitalist reproduction: 'Once capital takes command of production itself and gives it a completely altered and specific form[,] commercial capital [a subspecies of merchant's capital] appears simply as capital in a *particular* function.' However, if we shift focus from the synchronic to the diachronic – from the internal dynamics of capital 'full blown' to the historical emergence of capital as mode of production and prevailing social logic – commercial capital shifts to play a singular and foundational part in the story: 'In all earlier modes of production ... commercial capital rather appears as the function of capital *par excellence*' (444). As the 'oldest historical mode in which capital has an independent existence' (442), commercial capital, without collective design or intention, becomes the historical precondition for the formation of capital-in-general. In its pre-capitalist guise, commercial capital is wealth accumulating in the hands of merchant traders, facilitating the proliferating circulation of commodities and money – the accidental groundwork for a revolutionary transformation in social modality to come.

Commercial capital, older than capital-in-general, indexes consolidating networks of trade (often both serving and served by the ends of war-making and imperial expansion)[8] – commodities and money trading places, over and over again, in increasingly reproducible

---

8   See David McNally, *Blood and Money: War, Slavery, Finance, and Empire*, Haymarket, 2020.

patterns (442). But if the immediate function of commercial capital is to facilitate the exchange of commodities, its drive is to function as capital per se – money wealth employed for the purpose of expansion. As distinguished from C–M–C (the exchange of use-values), commercial capital's circuit of metamorphosis is M–C–M′; 'money, the independent form of exchange-value, is the starting point, and the increase of exchange-value[,] the independent purpose' (443). At first, merchants buy the product of small producers in one region, carry it to distant markets, and thereby mediate the exchange of the accidental surplus of subsistence-oriented agricultural and domestic industries. The circulation of surplus product between distant markets, and the profits accumulated through this activity, gradually reorient subsistence production towards production for exchange: 'It is trade that shapes the products into commodities; not the produced commodities whose movement constitutes trade' (445). The prospect of profit (for the merchant) and revenue (for the producers) subsumes the accidental character of the production of a surplus product (443). The transformation of production-for-subsistence into production-for-exchange is also the transformation of the accidental character of price into a conventionalized commensurability between otherwise-incommensurable goods. The outcome of this transformation posits the commodity, a historically novel formation: universal equality as potential. Of course, another description this novel historical outgrowth is the phantom-like objectivity of value, the specifically capitalist form of wealth – a 'social "mediation" that arises from a specific social form of production – precisely *because* it is a mediation' (441n45). As Marx says, 'Capital as capital, therefore, appears first of all in the circulation process' (445), and its unintended outcome is the production of a social logic of equivalence, the domination of a social function of abstraction:

> The quantitative relationship in which products exchange is at first completely accidental. They assume the commodity form in so far as they are in some way exchangeable, i.e. are expressions of some third thing. Continued exchange, and regular reproduction for exchange, gradually abolishes this accidental character. At the outset, however, this does not occur for the producers or consumers but rather for the mediator between the two, the merchant, who compares money

prices and pockets the difference. It is through his movement that the equivalence is established. (447)

In the period of late-stage feudalism characterized by mercantilist and colonial forms of trade, war, and plunder (448) – and a burgeoning world market – commercial capital dominates production; the distribution of profit that is accumulated through price-setting favours the merchant at the expense of producers. This period is characterized by production processes in their early stages of development and the concomitant concentration of monetary wealth in the hands of merchant traders (444). As production develops, becomes more productive, and is reorganized in ways that allow it to expand in response to both the pressures and opportunities introduced by the widening commercial sphere, productive industry eventually comes to challenge the dominance of trade and commercial industry. In a dialectical reversal, the growth of commerce produces the outcome of subordinating commerce to production, and the circulation of commodities becomes simply one aspect of the greater process of capitalist reproduction:

> In the course of scientific analysis, the formation of the general rate of profit appears to proceed from industrial capitals and the competition between them, being only later rectified, supplemented and modified by the intervention of commercial capital. *In the course of historical development, the situation is exactly the reverse.* It is commercial capital which first fixes the prices of commodities more or less according to their values, and it is the sphere of circulation that mediates the reproduction process in which a general rate of profit is first formed. Commercial profit originally determines industrial profit. It is only when the capitalist mode of production has come to prevail, and the producer has himself become a merchant, that commercial profit is reduced to the aliquot share of the total surplus-value that accrues to commercial capital as an aliquot part of the total capital concerned in the process of social reproduction. (400–1, my emphasis)

Marx calls this historical process the *solvent effect* of trade (448). Trade increasingly subjects production to the emerging social law of exchange-value; it makes 'consumption and existence more dependent on sale than on the direct use of the product'; 'it dissolves the old [customary] relationships' and erects markets in their place; it 'increases monetary circulation' and by doing so turns money into world money; 'it no longer just takes hold of surplus production, but gradually gobbles up production itself and makes entire branches of production dependent on it' (448–9). The 'sudden expansion of trade [in the sixteenth and early seventeenth centuries] and the creation of a new world market [exerts] an overwhelming influence on the defeat of the old mode of production and the rise of the capitalist mode'. Production's growing dependence on trade in the mercantile period is the motive force of its own reorientation towards growth and productivity. An emerging capitalist mode of production's 'immanent need . . . to produce on an ever greater scale drives . . . the constant expansion of the world market, so that now it is not trade that revolutionizes industry, but rather industry that constantly revolutionizes trade.' As production expands to mirror an expanding commercial sphere, and as 'commercial supremacy is now linked with the greater or lesser prevalence of the conditions for large-scale industry' (451), in a dialectical reversal of cause and effect, commerce is demoted to the 'servant of industrial production' and subordinated to production as a revolutionary force of social transformation (454).

As the power of merchant traders and bankers reaches its apogee, it is impossible to forecast the ascendancy of a capitalist mode of production and the subsumption of the commercial activity that participates in its consolidation. In these early stages of feudalism's dissolution, and the transformations compelled by enslaved labour in the form of plantation production in the colonized territories, the inner movement that drives the growing world market towards a social formation of impersonal interdependence unfolds as a historical accident, without design or inevitability. As such, the internal connections that characterize the wider transformation are discernible only in retrospect; the 'theoretical treatment' of the changing social landscape 'necessarily proceeded from the superficial phenomena of the circulation process . . . [and] hence only grasped the semblance of things'.[9] For this reason, Marx argues,

---

9   Marx insists, in argument but largely through demonstration, that a capitalist mode of production is not the telos of feudalism or colonialism but, rather, an evitable outcome that nonetheless stamps the world in its image at an indiscernible tipping point of development. With exceptions, the insistence will fall on deaf ears for many years to come.

'the genuine science of modern economics begins only when theoretical discussion moves from the circulation process to the production process' (455), which it can only do from the standpoint of capitalist production 'full blown'.

In this historical process, the theoretical approach adequate for the task of making scrutable capital's phantom-like objectivity takes form as a dimension of the object itself. As the eventual precipitate of a social formation in embryo, the emerging mode of production produces its own mode of theoretical exposition. Whatever we designate it – a dialectical hermeneutic, a power of abstraction, a mode of categorial thought, 'science', totalizing analysis – it is itself an expression of a mode of production where capital has 'taken command of the latter and given it a completely altered and specific form' (444).[10] Its movement is to reconcile in analysis what cannot be reconciled through immediate observation, measurement, or first-hand account: the relationship between capital as social content/essence and its inverted forms of appearance. In the case of merchant's capital, this theoretical treatment allows us to grasp why the demotion of commercial capital to one social form of capital-in-general does not imply its demotion in appearance. Merchant's capital's sustained appearance of independence in the sphere of circulation constitutes its fetish character; its fetishized movement mystifies the true means of its augmentation in living labour.

We move on now to look at interest-bearing capital – capital's fetish par excellence, according to Marx. Whereas commercial capital assumes its fetish character by appearing to be the origin of commercial profit, we will see that interest-bearing capital assumes its fetish character in its identity as the antagonist of commercial capital.

---

10   I argue, and attempt to illustrate, that dialectical analysis is an expression of the same mode of sociality it stages for exposition in Beverley Best, *Marx and the Dynamic of the Capital Formation: An Aesthetics of Political Economy*, Palgrave Macmillan, 2010.

5

Transformation of Profit II: Interest

Capital as Commodity – Interest-Bearing Capital as the Automatic Fetish – The Credit System as Abolition of Capital Ownership (and Post-capitalist Portal) – The Credit System – So-Called Financialization and the Dynamics of Fictitious Capital – 'The Mother of Every Insane Form' – The Beautiful Theoretical Dualism (or, The Material Idealism of Gold Convertibility) – Conclusion: From Usury to a New Sociality

As we carry on looking at the decomposition of surplus-value into its social forms, into its 'actual world' forms of profit that carry out its redistribution among competing capitalists, we turn to Marx's categories of interest and interest-bearing capital elaborated in part V of *Capital* III. Today, we are more likely to call interest-bearing capital 'finance capital', and it would be feasible to make this substitution – and tempting to do so – since it would indicate that the inner movement of capital in question continues to be determinant despite dramatic transformations in its surface appearances and empirical expressions. For instance, despite the vastly increased scale of the credit system, the proliferation of its instruments and services, the changing roles and character of financial players (including industries and their state enablers), and the ongoing invention of new methods for appropriating/expropriating social wealth through the 'democratization' of debt, the role of finance in the reproduction of a capitalist mode of production has been a history of *continuity* as much as transformation. Nonetheless, we will continue to refer to interest-bearing capital (as we did merchant's capital), so as to follow Marx's analysis step by step, with clarity, through the material in part V.

Capital as Commodity

In capitalist production, living labour sets value in motion in the form of objectified labour, or means of production. Labour (carried out under the wage contract) transfers the value of means of production (c), the value of its own labour-power (v), and an additional determined amount of surplus-value (s) (as the value form of labour's unpaid working time) to the (social) product. The appearance of things is that money, 'the independent expression of value', is the instigator and facilitator of the whole process. In other words, money, rather than living labour, appears to have the innate capacity to create more money, to magically proliferate – a partial if inadequate truth. Money's *use-value* is, therefore, as *potential capital* (459). Money as potential capital becomes a commodity when the owner of money alienates it – exchanges the use of money for a price – so that a different party can employ it *as* capital, exploiting its capacity to produce a profit:

> Money receives, besides the use-value which it possesses as money, an additional use-value, namely its ability to function as capital. Its use-value here consists precisely in the profit that it produces when transformed into capital. In this capacity of potential capital, as a means to the production of profit, it becomes a commodity, but a commodity of a special kind. Or what comes to the same thing, capital becomes a commodity. (459–60)

The use-value of money is that it can function as capital; it can 'produce in its movement a definite surplus-value, the average profit . . . besides conserving its original value' (473; 477). The capital-commodity is distinct from other commodities in that 'the consumption of its use-value not only maintains its value and use-value but in fact increases it' (473). Capital as commodity presupposes that the owner of money, as the owner of potential capital, is able to alienate that money without any alteration in its capacity to function as capital for whoever purchases its use temporarily; money's capacity as potential capital can be realized by any functioning capitalist, not strictly by its proprietor. Owners of money need never set it in motion themselves but, rather, can rely exclusively on productive capitalists to do so. That money can be alienated and then mobilized as capital by a party other than its owner is the condition for a particular personification of capital, or genre of capitalist: the money capitalist (the financier or finance capitalist). In this scenario, money is a source of income for its proprietor, the money capitalist, and a source of profit for the productive capitalist (industrial or commercial), who borrows it for a determined period of time in order to exploit its use-value as capital on terms established between the contracting parties (i.e., at a certain rate of interest).[1] There exists, therefore, an internal mutual dependency between the money capitalist and the industrial and/or commercial capitalist (475).

Capital's personification in the money capitalist presupposes the decomposition of capital-in-general into the social form of interest-bearing capital. Interest-bearing capital is value that is alienated by its owner as potential capital. The iconic form of interest-bearing capital is money – money loaned out for a designated period of time and for a price. However, value can operate as interest-bearing capital in any form: fixed or circulating capital, individually or collectively (privately or publicly) owned capital, money, tools, machinery, intellectual property (patents and copyright), vehicles and other technologies, and so on (465).[2] As a category, interest-bearing capital animates the standpoint of the money capitalist, capital's proprietor; interest is the category of revenue received in exchange for the service of loaning potential capital to the functioning capitalist. From the standpoint of the functioning capitalist (industrial or commercial), capital is simply capital; it is set in motion in production and produces a profit that legally belongs to the functioning capitalist. However, if the capital employed is

---

1 As we established in chapter 4, commercial capital is not directly productive in the sense of creating new value as is the case with industrial capital. Nonetheless, commercial capital yields the average rate of profit, and this profit – a redistributed portion of industrial profit – can function as a source of interest, or financial profit, as well as can industrial profit, even while the latter is the source of both commercial and financial profit. We will elaborate this redistributive dynamic below.

2 We will look at land as income-generating property in the analysis of ground-rent in the next chapter. Going forward, we will continue to take the money form of interest-bearing capital as the illustrative case.

the property of another, a price is paid for the service of using it. In this case, interest is the name of the price paid for the capital-commodity, for the privilege of borrowing potential capital (whether it is employed as capital or not). Therefore, from the standpoint of the money capitalist, interest is revenue on alienation of the capital-commodity; from the standpoint of the functioning capitalist, interest is the price paid for the capital-commodity. It is routine today to refer to interest as 'rent' in some circumstances, as in private property that is 'rent-seeking' when it is alienated as capital for a decided-on period of time, for a certain price, rather than being alienated outright. We will stick to the category of interest in order to differentiate it from the category of rent that we will examine in chapter 6.

Having established what interest is, we look for its source and find only one: it is a portion of the profit that is generated by the capital-commodity when it is set in motion. The functioning capitalist employs capital, which yields profit. A portion of this profit is redistributed back to the money capitalist as the price paid for the use-value of the capital-commodity. The social form of this price, this magnitude of value in the money-form, is interest:

> If the [functioning capitalist] pays the proprietor of the £100 a sum of £5, say, at the end of the year, i.e., a portion of the [say, £20] profit produced, what he pays for with this is the use-value of the £100, the use-value of its capital function, the function of producing a £20 profit. The part of the profit paid in this way is called interest, which is thus nothing but a particular name, a special title, for a part of the profit which the actually functioning capitalist has to pay to the capital's proprietor, instead of pocketing it himself. (460)

Despite appearances, as we will see, there is no form or amount of interest that is not a portion of the profit generated in productive enterprise. Since there is no way for value to be valorized outside of the production process, money cannot expand simply by being lent to another party. The revenue that the money capitalist receives for lending is a magnitude of value that must be produced somewhere and somehow, apart from this transaction. Even if the immediate source of interest for the money capitalist is the pocket of a second (or third, or fourth) money capitalist, the pocket of the functioning capitalist is the initial location for subsequent distribution of this surplus-value. In a capitalist economy, more than ever before, it is an everyday affair for money capitalists to lend and borrow between themselves, for a price, the capital-commodity: bankers lend to other bankers, speculators purchase investment instruments from hedge fund managers, and so on. Nonetheless, however many bankers, speculators, or financiers step in to mediate the accumulation process and redistribute value (in various ways) among themselves, value is only ever created anew in the production process. Moreover, at each moment, the movement of interest-bearing capital serves to mystify this fact.

Interest is the price of the use-value of the capital-commodity, but it expresses something fundamentally different than does the price of regular commodities: 'If interest is spoken of as the price of money capital, this is an irrational form of price, in complete contradiction with the concept of the price of a commodity.' Interest is an expression of a legal contract, a legal title to a portion of profit made elsewhere, the size of which is the direct outcome of capitalist competition (unlike the price of commodities) but ultimately limited by the magnitude of profit itself. With interest, then, 'price is reduced to its purely abstract form, completely lacking in content' (475). As derivatives of the function of lending and borrowing, finance and the credit system are essentially the legal expressions – abstractions – of their content, the particular social relations of capitalist production. They operate on the legal edifice of private property and the power of the state to enforce property law. The inverted appearance that the state, as the administer of a system of 'law and order' imposing a rational and stabilizing framework on the anarchic activity of market exchange, actually reverses the form–content dynamic at play. It is not the state and property law that 'govern' the character of market exchange. Rather, a capitalist system of market exchange is the determining social content that takes the form of private property (a legal expression) with the state as its enforcer and enabler. Marx emphasizes this point in refuting the notion that it is a 'natural' and state-sanctioned justice that property should yield profit, as articulated by the English banker James Gilbart in 1834: 'That a man who borrows money with a view of making a profit by it, should give some portion of this profit to the lender, is a self-evident principle of natural justice' (460n55). Marx's response is as follows:

The justice of the transactions between agents of production consists
in the fact that these transactions arise from the relations of production
as their natural consequence. The legal forms in which these economic
transactions appear as voluntary actions of the participants, as the
expression of their common will and as contracts that can be enforced
on the parties concerned by the power of the state, are mere forms
that cannot themselves determine this content. They simply express
it. (460–1)

Finance and the credit system are the organic operations of private
property – of capital ownership – and, as such, rely entirely on the power
of the state to sanction and enforce the terms of borrowing and lending
contracts. There is a common refrain today among some theorists of
finance that the growth and dominance of financial industries witness a
concomitant diminishing of the role and power of states in contemporary
global capitalism. This calculation overlooks the way in which finance
and the state are two sides of the same coin – a singular, if multivalent,
formal expression of the production relations that it presupposes.

The legal basis of the credit system, and the decomposition of capital
into its interest-bearing form, is the proprietorship of money as potential
capital. The proprietor of money advances it as capital to the functioning
capitalist (M–M). The latter transforms this money into capital (M–C–
M'). The original sum of money advanced returns to its proprietor
along with a portion of the realized capital (M'–M'). 'The [total]
movement is thus: M–M–C–M'–M'' (461); this is the circuit of interest-
bearing capital. In the process of the production and circulation of
commodities, wherein value is produced and realized (valorized) – that
is, in the circuit M–C–M' – at no individual moment in the circuit does
value, either in the form of money or commodities, assume the character
of capital (463). For instance, money is exchanged for commodities,
and, after their productive consumption, a resulting product that
represents an augmented quantity of value is exchanged for an equivalent
magnitude of value in the money-form. However, from no individual
standpoint do money and commodities assume the character of capital
per se. Money is exchanged for commodities *as* money, and commodities
are purchased and consumed *as* commodities. It is only from the
concrete, if invisible, totalized standpoint of the process as a whole – 'at
the moment where the point of departure appears as simultaneously the

point of return, in M–M´ or C–C´´ (464) – that value reveals its character as capital.

With the circuit of interest-bearing capital, the situation is different: the money capitalist alienates money *as* capital; money's destiny as capital is what circumscribes it as a commodity in the first place (464). This difference holds for the functioning capitalist, who borrows money *as* capital. Even when money is borrowed in order to consume the means of subsistence rather than to consume productively, the obligation to pay interest on the loan informs the nature of what is being exchanged, money's use-value as potential capital, whether the borrower exploits this use-value or not. What defines the commodity of the money capitalist is that money is alienated as capital. But the character of the capital-commodity is constructed on the original fetish-character of capital itself. Capital appears to expand on its own steam, while, in fact, it expands as a function of the productive capacity of living labour. The function of concealing the role of living labour in value's 'self'-valorization constitutes the movement of the capital fetish. The movement of interest-bearing capital is the extrapolation of this original fetish: what is hidden is not simply the role of living labour in production but, rather, the mediation by the entire production process itself in capital's expansion. What disappears in the circuit of interest-bearing capital is the role of mediation itself – 'the intervening mediating movement':

> Money that is lent as capital is hired out precisely as a sum of money that is maintained and increased, a sum which returns with an addition after a certain period and can go through the same process once again. It is not given out as money or as a commodity, i.e. neither exchanged for a commodity when it is advanced as money nor sold for money when it is advanced as a commodity. It is rather given out as capital. The reflexive relationship in which capital presents itself when we view the capitalist production process as a whole and a unity, and in which capital appears as money breeding money, is here simply embodied in it as its character, its capacity, without the intervening mediating movement. And it is in this capacity that it is alienated, when it is lent out as money capital. (466)

Therefore, if we were to figure the full circuit of interest-bearing capital, bringing to the surface its concealed mediations, it would look

like this: M–M–C(mp/lp) ... P ... C′–M′–M′.[3] In this visualization of
the circuit, the money owner lends capital to the producer (M–M); the
producer's investment (C) comprises means of production (mp) and
labour-power (lp) set in motion in the production process (... P ...); in
the course of production, the product expands as a magnitude of value
(C′); the entirety of which, including its surplus portion, is realized in
circulation (M′). The second M′ in this circuit represents the reflux of
the initial capital advanced, plus interest. The interest is a portion of the
total profit yielded by the initial capital, that is, a portion of the
augmented value represented by the first M′. Since the portion that
represents interest is a portion of the overall profit generated, the
magnitude of the first M′ must be greater than the magnitude of the
second M′. This logical limit on the magnitude of the portion of interest
ultimately determined by the magnitude of profit, where the latter is the
outcome of the inner dynamics of the movement of capital in general
and across all branches of production, is obfuscated by the fact that the
rate of interest is a surface phenomenon, determined nominally through
competition and enforced by legal contract. In Marx's words, in the case
of interest-bearing capital, 'all that we see is the giving-out and the
repayment. Everything that happens in between is obliterated' (471).
The perceptual obliteration of the source of interest in production, and
ultimately in the activity of living labour, as we have argued all along, is
the core argument of *Capital* III.

Interest-Bearing Capital as the Automatic Fetish

With the movement of interest-bearing capital, 'capital has become a
commodity, buying has been transformed into lending, and price [has
been transformed] into a share in the profit' (468). As was the case with
merchant's capital (chapter 4), the decomposition of capital-in-general
into interest-bearing capital is facilitated by its 'separation from the
mediating circuit' of production and reinforced by the legal technologies

---

3 For a further expansion of this circuit, see John Milios, 'Marx's Monetary
Theory of Value, Fictitious Capital and Finance,' paper presented at the second
international seminar on the 150th anniversary of *Capital*, November 3–6, 2015,
Universidad Distrital Francisco José de Caldas, Bogotá, Colombia, available at http://
users.ntua.gr/jmilios/Milios_El%20Capital_150_aniversario_Fin.pdf.

that initiate capital's movement and its reflux to the pocket of the money capitalist:

> The initial act which transfers the capital from the lender to the borrower is a legal transaction which has nothing to do with the actual reproduction process of capital, but simply introduces it. The repayment which transfers the capital that has flowed back from the borrower to the lender again is a second legal transaction, the complement of the first . . . The point of departure and the point of return, the lending-out of the capital and its recovery, thus appear as arbitrary movements mediated by legal transactions, which take place before and after the real movement of capital and have nothing to do with it as such. (469)

In the circuit of interest-bearing capital, both its lending (M–M) and its reflux (M′–M′) define the circuit and are redundant to it with respect to the process of capital's actual expansion. That the moments of lending and reflux are simple legal arrangements obliterates the two determining movements of the circuit: (1) the inner production relations with respect to which the singular source of interest is new value generated in the production process; and (2) the limitation, ultimately, of the magnitude of the interest-portion of profit by the magnitude of this new value created (i.e., by the rate and, hence, magnitude of profit [482]). Therefore, from the standpoint of the money capitalist, the circuit of interest-bearing capital is truncated as M–M′, obscuring the movement that determines interest-bearing capital *as* capital-in-general. Marx's elaboration of this dynamic is especially clear and worth quoting in full:

> The giving-out or lending of money for a certain time, and the repayment of this with interest (surplus-value), is the entire form of the movement attributable to interest-bearing capital as such. The real movement of the money lent out as capital is an operation lying beyond the transactions between lenders and borrowers. In these transactions, taken by themselves, this mediation is obliterated, invisible and not directly involved. Capital as a special kind of commodity also has a kind of alienation peculiar to it. Here therefore the return does not appear as a consequence and result of a definite series of economic processes, but rather as a consequence of a special

legal contract between buyer and seller. The period of the reflux depends on the course of the reproduction process; in the case of interest-bearing capital, its return as capital *seems* to depend simply on the contract between lender and borrower. And so the reflux of capital, in connection with this transaction no longer appears as a result determined by the production process, but rather as if the capital lent out had never lost the form of money. Of course these transactions are actually determined by the real refluxes. But this is not apparent in the transaction itself. (470)

What mystifies the movement further is that the reflux of value to the pocket of the money capitalist, in practice, has no immediate dependency on the trajectory of the capital advanced, nor on the time frame of its reproduction. The interest on a loan must be paid according to the contracted terms: at a predetermined rate, on a specified date, regardless of the duration or viability of the production cycle that sets the capital in motion, and regardless of whether the capital advanced is used as capital at all. As is the case with merchant's capital, the decomposition of capital into its social form of interest-bearing capital is also the movement of its *autonomization* (498; 499; 506): the material, if abstracted, surface phenomenon of M–M′, money that appears to breed money innately. And, as with capital's social forms more generally, interest-bearing capital expresses a dialectical movement where 'the quantitative division [of profit of enterprise between functioning capitalist and money capitalist] becomes a qualitative one' in the autonomization of a discrete form of capital (482n62; 495; 497). Today, it is a challenge simply to catalogue the myriad types of financial instruments (stocks, bonds, securities, and derivatives, such as forwards, futures, options, credit default swaps, collateralized debt obligations, and so on) that facilitate the surface movement of 'money breeding money', novel signs of continuity as 'the irrational form[s] of the real capital movement' (470).

The process of the autonomization of interest-bearing capital indexes both the irreducible presence of class struggle in the movement of capital as well as its perceptual submersion: on the one hand, interest-bearing capital presupposes wage labour at the level of its concept, as its 'complementary antithesis, the thing that makes [it] capital' (477). That is, interest signals the ownership of capital and, as such, the 'means of appropriating the product of other people's labour' (506; 505). On the other hand, the role of wage labour in the creation of new value is precisely the 'in between' moment of the production process that the circuit of interest-bearing capital submerges in its perceptual physics. The phenomenal forms of the movement of capital, and (to an even greater extent) of interest-bearing capital, submerge in perception what they simultaneously presuppose:

> This one moment, then [the reflux of value after value is lent out as capital], separated from the capitalist production process itself, whose constant result it is, and as whose constant result it is also its constant presupposition, is expressed in this way: that money, and likewise commodities, are in themselves latent, potential capital, i.e. can be sold as capital; in this form they give control of the labour of others, give a claim to the appropriation of others' labour, and are therefore self-valorizing value. (477)

Because the division of profit-in-general into profit of enterprise and interest is a function of competition, the rate of interest has no necessary connection to the inner movement of capital itself but is, rather, 'inherently accidental, purely empirical' (485):

> It is in fact only the division of capitalists into money capitalists and industrial capitalists that transforms a part of the profit into interest and creates the category of interest at all; and it is only the competition between these two kinds of capitalist that creates the rate of interest. (493)

In this regard, there is no 'natural rate of interest' (484); with the exception of its limit by the rate of profit in the last instance, it is subject to pure politics, determined by the battle between capitals and a concomitant degree of state intervention. Interest-bearing capital is, therefore, the most superficial of capital's forms, at the same time as the fetish character of its movement is the most deeply mediated: 'In the case of interest-bearing capital, everything appears in a superficial manner' (478; 515).

The purely superficial (or political) inter-capitalist competition that establishes the rate of interest is of a different nature than the competition that determines the general rate of profit (482). The general rate of profit is not an empirical phenomenon. It 'does not appear as a directly given fact' (490); rather, it is precipitated by competing enterprises, each seeking to increase their own individual rates of profit, which, by doing so, inadvertently equalize the rate of profit across branches of production. Most significantly, the general rate of profit is the outcome of this competitive push and pull *against an invisible objectivity*: the combination of all individual rates of profit that form the gravitation force (determined by the historical productivity of capital) around which the individual, empirical rates orbit but from which they cannot ultimately break. 'With the interest rate it is different' (490): the rate of interest is a locally established (even if that 'locality' is global), empirical fact, 'fixed every day' and, as such, 'presupposed in the operating calculations' of functioning capitalists (490). As an entirely irrational form, its identity is both without substance and 'sharply defined' in its empirical character, unlike the rate of profit, whose substance is capitalist production relations per se, and whose identity is thus 'blurred and hazy' (491). The 'ossification and autonomization' of interest as a value formation qualitatively distinct from profit of enterprise (498; 499) entails that the capacity to generate interest comes to be considered simply 'a general property of any sum [of money,] that it will yield 2, 3, 4, 5 percent', and that this is the case for all 'loan capital to be found on the money market' at any one time (490).

According to Marx, the socialization of loan capital on the money market is a signal moment in the development of the concept of capital; in this context, capital emerges, historically, in its pure form as concept because it emerges as 'the common capital of the class' (490). In the money market, instead of the meeting of buyers and sellers, lenders meet borrowers, and in their transactions money keeps its form, while value's necessary change of form 'is obliterated' (490; 497; 500). Rather than the differentiated competitive power of individual capitalists, money on the money market is an undifferentiated mass, 'the common capital of the class', social capital under the stewardship of bankers (490–1); 'this mutual ossification and autonomization of the two parts of the gross profit, as if they derived from two essentially separate sources, must now be fixed for the entire capitalist class and the total capital' (498):

On the money market it is only lenders and borrowers who face one another. The commodity has the same form, money. All particular forms of capital, arising from its investment in particular spheres of production or circulation, are obliterated here. It exists in the undifferentiated, self-identical form of independent value, money. Competition between particular spheres now ceases; they are all thrown together as borrowers of money, and capital confronts them all in a form still indifferent to the specific manner and mode of its application. Here capital really does emerge, in the pressure of its demand and supply, as *the common capital of the class*, whereas industrial capital appears like this only in the movement and competition between the particular spheres . . . On top of this, with the development of large-scale industry money capital emerges more and more, in so far as it appears on the market, as not represented by the original capitalist, the proprietor of this or that fraction of the mass of capital on the market, but rather as a concentrated and organized mass, placed under the control of the bankers as representatives of the social capital in quite different manner to real production. The result is that, as far as the form of demand goes, capital for loan is faced with the entire weight of a class, while, as far as supply goes, it itself appears *en masse* as loan capital. (490–1)

If the concept of capital is sutured in its socialization on the money market, the process of its formation begins with pre-capitalist practices of money-lending and usury. In its pre-capitalist form, profit from lending money represents a pure redistribution of wealth: at the conclusion of the transaction, wealth from the borrower's pocket has shifted to the pocket of the money-lender. Interest, in this case, does not represent a portion of expanding value, as it will come to do in the case of interest-bearing capital in a capitalist mode of production. However, the money-lender's profit introduces the idea of the capacity of money as inherently profit-yielding. The idea of money breeding more money crystalizes, Marx argues, 'in the popular mind', the image of 'capital par excellence', even before the capitalist mode of production is full blown (499). In the course of capital's development, interest-bearing capital steps into the world already stamped with its identity as pure capital, a fetish to the second power in its perfect disavowal of any reference to production, to living labour, or to the surplus-value that the latter creates

(500–1) – not even to the enterprise of the functioning capitalist. Marx refers to interest-bearing capital, in its disguise of transparency and self-evidentiality, as the 'automatic fetish': 'In interest-bearing capital, therefore, this automatic fetish is elaborated into its pure form, self-valorizing value, money breeding money, and in this form it no longer bears any marks of its origin' (516). The perceptual physics of interest-bearing capital represent the culminating distortion inherent to the movement of capital:

> While interest is simply one part of the profit, i.e. the surplus-value, extorted from the worker by the functioning capitalist, it now appears conversely as if interest is the specific fruit of capital, the original thing, while profit, now transformed into the form of profit of enterprise, appears as a mere accessory and trimming added in the reproduction process. The fetish character of capital and the representation of this capital fetish is now complete. In M–M′ we have the irrational form of capital, the misrepresentation and objectification of the relations of production, in its highest power: the interest-bearing form, the simple form of capital, in which it is taken as logically anterior to its own reproduction process; the ability of money or a commodity to valorize its own value independent of reproduction – the capital mystification in the most flagrant form. (516)

Interest-bearing capital, the automatic fetish, stands in the crime scene of its initial extortion, the constitutive negative presence of class struggle that haunts every phenomenal aspect of capital's circuitry. With interest-bearing capital, the mediations of exploitation are more convoluted and more invisible than with capital's other social forms: instead of confronting labour directly, money capital confronts functioning capital as its antithesis. In the upside-down world of market competition, the only apparent struggle is between the money capitalist and the functioning capitalist battling for a greater share of the spoils of enterprise, 'capital *as property* as against capital *as function*' (503). Labour appears to play no part whatsoever in this battle (504). That capital is the collective workers' own creation that confronts them as their antithesis, as alien private property and as 'the means of appropriating [more] unpaid labour', is entirely concealed, as is the means of operational confusion and gymnastic apologetics (502–3):

It is utter nonsense to suggest that all capital could be transformed into money capital without the presence of people to buy and valorize the means of production, i.e. the form in which the entire capital exists, apart from the relatively small part existing in money. Concealed in this idea, moreover, is the still greater nonsense that capital could yield interest on the basis of the capitalist mode of production without functioning as productive capital, i.e. without creating surplus-value, of which interest is simply one part; that the capitalist mode of production could proceed on its course without capitalist production. (501)[4]

The Credit System as Abolition of Capital Ownership (and Post-capitalist Portal)

The money capitalist instrumentalizes the practical illusion that the mere ownership of capital furnishes entitlement to a portion of social wealth. The directness of this cause/effect narrative also prepares the ground for the functioning capitalist to imagine that profit of enterprise rewards the ingenuity with which capital is set in motion. The functioning capitalist imagines themself an especially skilled, and therefore highly paid, *worker* (503) – a worker who earns the 'wages of the superintendence of labour', of the marshalling of profit, and of acuity in the battle of the marketplace (504; 505; 506). The functioning capitalist appears to appropriate profit as the equivalent of highly skilled labour performed alongside the lesser skilled, lesser demanding labour of the other workers. This appearance informs the consciousness of the capitalist and, in turn, the wider perceptual landscape: 'These grounds of compensation which go to determine the division of surplus-value are turned, in the capitalist's way of conceiving things, into grounds for the existence and (subjective) justification of profit as such' (506–7). The empirical separating off of a portion of the profit of enterprise as wages of superintendence that go either to the owner of enterprise – or, in the

---

4   And yet, this kind of nonsense is more current than ever. A great deal of analysis of financialization mistakes notional sums of legal claims to future value *as value itself*, instead of what they actually represent: novel means and channels of expropriating value from labour and redistributing it among representatives of the capitalist class. We will analyse this movement further on.

case of a publicly traded (shareholder-owned) company, to the managers of enterprise – reinforces the appearance.

However, this real appearance also makes way for the most remarkable dialectical reversal of categories in Marx's exposition. Interest-bearing capital, and its expression in the credit system, not only introduces the means of expanding production, and thereby of deepening the system's contradictions and further destabilizing its crisis fault-lines; it also introduces the objective means by which to push through and beyond the capital relation itself, at least 'as one element in connection with other large-scale organic revolutions in the mode of production' (743). For Marx, the social form of interest-bearing capital and its socialization in the credit system signal, on an immediate level, nothing less than the real (but unrealized) abolition of the capitalist and, on a deeper level, that of the capitalist mode of production itself, as well as its succession by an associated mode of production. As Marx states, 'There can be no doubt that the credit system will serve as a powerful lever in the course of the transition from the capitalist mode of production to the mode of production of associated labour' (743). Let us follow this utopian, which is to say dialectical, derivation of forms.

The appearance of the functioning capitalist's profit as the wages of supervision and management of capital and labour generates what it presupposes: the phenomenon of the 'specialized work' of supervision and management. As Marx expounds, the role of supervision and management may arise from the domination of labour by capital, but it also emerges as a necessary dimension of large-scale, socialized production and a concomitant division of labour per se. Socialized production, capitalist or otherwise, necessarily assigns differentiated 'productive functions . . . to particular individuals as their special work' – equally as much in the case of non-capitalist combined labour, where people might cycle through differentiated functions of the production process. The work of supervising and coordinating the differentiated productive functions of enterprise is itself one such function (510). Just as capitalist production introduces the possibility that the work of supervision can be undertaken independently of the ownership of capital, so does it 'therefore become superfluous for this work of supervision to be performed by the capitalist'. The development of capitalist production itself reveals that the work of supervision can be performed by any functionary, whether they are hired by an individual capitalist owner – or, in the case of a publicly traded (joint-stock) company, the 'collective capitalist' of shareholders – or by the workers, in the case of a cooperative or associated firm. Of course, the work of supervision may just as well be undertaken by the workers themselves, cycling through the function of supervisor as they would any of the other functions that constitute the production process: 'Cooperative factories provide the proof that the capitalist has become . . . superfluous as a functionary in production' (511).

Marx asks the reader to consider both the publicly traded ('joint-stock') company and the credit system as potential transitional forms towards an associated mode of production. The publicly traded company challenges the perception that the work of supervision is naturally the work of the capitalist or of the manager who represents them. The socialization of capital in the credit system challenges the perception that the creation of wealth begins with the ownership of capital. For Marx, these forms point to alternative modes of production that exist, in embryo, in the capitalist mode, as objective possibilities:

> In so far as the work of the capitalist does not arise from the produc-
> tion process simply as a capitalist process, i.e. does not come to an
> end with capital itself; in so far as it is not confined to the function of
> exploiting the labour of others; in so far therefore as it arises from the
> form of labour as social labour, from the combination and coopera-
> tion of many to a common result, it is just as independent of capital
> as is this form itself, once it has burst its capitalist shell. To say that
> this labour, as capitalist labour, is necessarily the function of the capi-
> talist means nothing more than that the *vulgus* cannot conceive that
> forms developed in the womb of the capitalist mode of production
> may be separated and liberated from their antithetical capitalist
> character. (511)

In contrast with the publicly traded company, in the case of the coop-
erative firm, when management or supervision becomes simply one function among a range of functions, carried out (on a permanent or rotating basis) by one or more members of the collective, 'the antithetical character of the supervisory work disappears' (512). The supervisor or manager ceases to represent capital as a dominating force confront-
ing labour as its antithesis and negation. Marx is not suggesting that the

worker-controlled cooperative firm can stand as the overcoming of the capitalist mode of production as a singular or atomized entity; indeed, he recognizes that while cooperative firms, or even associations of firms, when they exist as exceptional cases within the context of a dominant capitalist system, must 'naturally reproduce ... all the defects of the existing system' (571). Nonetheless, even with a single worker-controlled cooperative firm, *'the opposition between capital and labour is abolished here,* even if at first only in the form that the workers in association become their own capitalist, i.e. they use the means of production to valorize their own labour' (571, my emphasis). Be this as it may, the portal that opens to something other than capital is an ineradicable moment of capital itself.

Even today, as the work of management and supervision, performed either by the enterprise-owning capitalist or a hired executive of functionaries, consolidates as firmly as ever into the common working knowledge of a capitalist social division of labour, for Marx, what has been developing all along are the conditions – the real possibility (in Ernst Bloch's terms) – for the redundancy of the capitalist, and for management to be absorbed into cooperative enterprise – the conditions where the capitalist 'vanishes from the production process as someone superfluous' (512). The superfluity of the capitalist in production creates the situation where 'profit [comes] to appear in practice as what it undeniably [is] in theory, mere surplus-value, value for which no equivalent is paid' (514). The dissociation, in practice, of ownership of capital and the legal right to appropriate profit of enterprise entails that the appearance of the modality of capital moves closer to its actual inner connections; that is, profit comes to appear as what it actually is: extorted surplus-value produced by other people's labour:

> [When the right to appropriate profit from capital employed is separated from ownership of capital,] profit thus appears (and no longer just the interest ...) as simply the appropriation of other people's surplus labour, arising from the transformation of the means of production into capital; i.e. from their estrangement vis-à-vis the actual producer. (568)

However, in its bourgeois form, the publicly traded company – a form of collective-capitalist ownership made possible by the socialization of interest-bearing capital in the credit system – sustains the capital–labour relation. New instruments emerge that reinforce it, which also serve competing factions of the capitalist class by allowing them to absorb portions of profit. Industries that produce and sell derivatives and other financial instruments – the machinations of what Marx calls fictitious capital, as we will see in the next section – are one glaring example. A second example is the malignant growth of management consultancy industries since the 1980s. Marx's example is the emergence of company directory boards (corporate governing and supervisory boards), which skim off a portion of profits that would otherwise fall to shareholders:

> A new swindle with the wages of management develops in connection with joint-stock companies, in that, over and above the actual managing director, a number of governing and supervisory boards arise, for which management and supervision are in fact a mere pretext for the robbery of shareholders and their own enrichment. (514)

Today, we are more likely to construe the role of directory boards as ensuring that a sufficient portion of a company's profit is directed to shareholders – an overdetermined motivation when board members and shareholders are one and the same.

However, despite these new and perennial means of swindling portions of social wealth, the tenor of Marx's discussion of the credit system and its twin, the joint-stock company, in chapter 27 ('The Role of Credit in Capitalist Production') is distinctly utopian/dialectical: the credit system, and its derivatives, the joint-stock company and the cooperative firm, are presented as *transitional forms* – as unrealized but objective portals beyond capital itself, that is, as 'the latent abolition of capital ownership' (572).[5] Marx enumerates four primary functions of the credit system in capitalist production; the first two – the equalization of the rate of profit and the reduction of circulation costs – have already been discussed in the previous part and are mentioned merely in

---

5   I've chosen to describe Marx's depiction of capital's internal movement as 'utopian/dialectical' in that it is, simultaneously, a movement of self-reproduction and self-abolition.

summary and passing. The third and fourth functions of the credit system – the formation of joint-stock companies and the credit system as the centralization of command over social labour – occupy the entire remaining chapter. It is clear from the discussion that, for Marx, the credit system represents the socialization of capital itself: a society's members directly combine their individual surplus wealth to form a pool of socialized wealth, administered by a centralized mechanism, to carry out collective projects – infrastructure, enterprise, and so on. This formation, along with socialized production and the cooperation of labour, characterizes the more general social comportment of capitalist production, a movement that still manages to reproduce itself as private property, *but just barely*:

> Capital, which is inherently based on a social mode of production and presupposes a social concentration of means of production and labour-power, now receives the form of social capital (capital of directly associated individuals) in contrast to private capital, and its enterprises appear as social enterprises as opposed to private ones. This is the abolition of capital as private property within the confines of the capitalist mode of production itself. (567)

Sounding like practitioners of cooperative enterprise today, Marx points out that credit will not only be central to associated production in general but will facilitate the redirection of social surplus wealth to newly emerging or experimental enterprises, or to enterprises that are desired but that can only operate in deficit and will never produce a social surplus of their own. The socialization of wealth in credit abolishes the distinction between donating and drawing on surplus resources, and capitalist property is turned back into the property of producers. According to Marx, this utopian/dialectical movement points to nothing less than 'the abolition of the capitalist mode of production within the capitalist mode of production itself, and hence a self-abolishing contradiction, which presents itself prima facie as a mere point of transition to a new form of production' (569):

> The result of capitalist production in its highest development [in the form of the joint-stock company] is a necessary point of transition towards the transformation of capital back into the property of the

producers, though no longer as the private property of individual producers, but rather as their property as associated producers, as directly social property. It is furthermore a point of transition towards the transformation of all functions formerly bound up with capital ownership in the reproduction process into simple functions of the associated producers, into social functions. (568)

However, when capital's self-abolishing potential is unrealized, the credit system and its twin, the joint-stock company, cleave to their capitalist characters and throw off one distorted, predatory, parasitical form after another, generating the configuration of corporate swindling that bears its bottom to the world on a daily basis. The global financial meltdown of 2008 is emblematic of the hyperbolic dysfunction of the capitalist credit system today and makes Marx's litany of corrupted forms seem quaint in comparison:

[Capitalist production in its highest development, i.e., in its transitional forms of the credit system and joint-stock company] presents itself as such a contradiction even in appearance. It gives rise to monopoly in certain spheres and hence provokes state intervention. It reproduces a new financial aristocracy, a new kind of parasite in the guise of company promoters, speculators and merely nominal directors; an entire system of swindling and cheating with respect to the promotion of companies, issues of shares and share dealings. It is private ownership unchecked by private ownership. (569)

'Private ownership unchecked by private ownership' is an apt signature for the quagmire of credit and speculation that culminated in 2008, and which continues to build steam today as the next meltdown of the system looms. The credit system in its capitalist form puts the power of social capital (which, as we know, is actually the power of social labour) in the hands of individual capitalists while releasing them from the social responsibility, and liability, of engaging this power. The role of the credit system in capitalist production is to give the individual capitalist disposal over social wealth, that is, command over social labour. The command over social capital/labour 'becomes simply the basis for a superstructure of credit'. Marx continues, 'What the speculating trader risks is social property, not his own. Equally absurd now is the saying that the origin of capital is saving, since what this speculator demands is precisely that *others* should save for him' (570). Marx returns to this point again in chapter 32, but this time to elaborate the full extent of its perverted dynamic:

> As capitalist production and its division of labour progress, the job of genuine saving and abstinence (by hoarders), in so far as this supplies elements of accumulation, is left to those who receive the minimum of such elements, and often enough lose what they have saved, as workers do when banks collapse. For the industrial capitalist does not 'save' his capital but rather disposes of the savings of others in proportion to the size of this capital; while the money capitalist makes the savings of other people into his capital, and the credit that the reproductive capitalists give one another, and that the public give them, he makes into his own source of private enrichment. The final illusion of the capitalist system, that capital is the offspring of a person's own work and savings, is thereby demolished. Not only does profit consist in the appropriation of other people's labour, but the capital with which this labour of others is set in motion and exploited consists of other people's property, which the money capitalist puts at the disposal of the industrial capitalist and for which he in turn exploits him. (640)

But even the process of expropriation, expanded on an enormous scale through the credit system, and separating not only the immediate producers but eventually small and medium capitalists from the means of production, undergoes its utopian/dialectical reversal in Marx's exposition. Associated production is the outcome not of *arresting* the process of expropriation but, rather, of its fullest development and expression. In the progressive expropriation of virtually *every* individual from the means of production, the dwindling number of holders of private property and means of production prepares the ground for the emergence of its only alternative: social production, or the 'means of production [held] in the hands of the associated producers'. Worker-controlled cooperative firms are examples, for Marx, of the crystallization of *full expropriation*, of the 'emergence of a new form from within the old form':

These [cooperative] factories show how, at a certain stage of development of the material forces of production, and of the social forms of production corresponding to them, a new mode of production develops and is formed naturally out of the old. Without the factory system that arises from the capitalist mode of production, cooperative factories could not develop. Nor could they do so without the credit system that develops from the same mode of production. This credit system, since it forms the principal basis for the gradual transformation of capitalist private enterprises into capitalist joint-stock companies, presents in the same way the means for the gradual extension of cooperative enterprises on a more or less national scale [and, today, global scale]. Capitalist joint-stock companies as much as cooperative factories should be viewed as transition forms from the capitalist mode of production to the associated one, simply that in the one case the opposition is abolished in a negative way, and in the other in a positive way. (571–2)

'The credit system has a dual system immanent in it', which is why representatives of finance capital are both swindlers and profits (572–3)! Marx's method of analysis, here, is utopian (I argue) – a form of speculative materialism, the enunciation of the dialectical reversal.[6] The dynamic of self-abolition, the utopian movement, is immanent to capital's concept itself. What Marx calls the concept of capital is sometimes mistaken for a precondition of a capitalist mode of production; if anything, it is the reverse. The concept of capital is the immaterial, formless, social objectivity *precipitated by* the collective doing that constitutes the historical emergence of a capitalist mode of

---

6   Ernst Bloch's elaboration of a utopian method of analysis has more affinity with Marx's than is conventionally recognized. (On this point, see, in particular, Cat Moir, *Ernst Bloch's Speculative Materialism: Ontology, Epistemology, Politics*, Brill, 2019). So far as I know, Fredric Jameson elaborates a dialectical and utopian method of reading capital's social forms that bears the closest affinity with Marx's method of analysis in *Capital* III. Like Marx, Jameson unfolds the inner logic of forms to the point of their dialectical reversal, exercising the narrative self-abolition of capital's categories by extending through them to their immanent (and, based on the commentary they solicit, often counterintuitive) figurative possibilities. See Fredric Jameson, 'An American Utopia', in *An American Utopia: Dual Power and the Universal Army*, Verso, 2016, 1–96; and Fredric Jameson, 'Utopia as Replication', in *Valences of the Dialectic*, Verso, 2009, 410–34.

production. It is an accidental *outcome* of that historical process, an objectivity that is subsequently posited as the condition for the ongoing reproduction of that same process; it comes to function in capitalist society, in all its formations, like a centre of gravity. It is the invisible social content that expresses itself in new, specifically capitalist social forms, or, which evacuates and occupies older, pre-capitalist forms; Marx cautions us to avoid thinking of these forms as locked into their capitalist demeanours: 'forms developed in the womb of the capitalist mode of production may be separated and liberated from their antithetical capitalist character' (511). What the concept of capital introduces to history is the ineradicable future-orientation of its forms of expression, the latter's innate capacity to shed their capitalist disguises and move towards something else. The utopian function of the value form operates in these terms, and it represents the emergence of the conditions of capital's self-abolition as historical potential.

The Credit System

Continuing to follow the trajectory of Marx's analysis, we now turn away from the objective transitional moment of the *not-yet-become* and return to the 'actually existing' upside-down world of capitalist forms,[7] where 'expropriation takes the antithetical form of the appropriation of social property by the few; and credit gives these few ever more the character of simple adventurers': 'Since ownership [of capitalist property] now exists in the form of shares, its movement and transfer become simply the result of stock-exchange dealings, where little fishes are gobbled up by the sharks, and sheep by the stock-exchange wolves' (571). The absurdity that the potential abundance of social property is negated in order to be put at the disposal of a few adventurers, to be controlled by a handful of sharks and wolves, is as acute today as ever – or, we may *wish* the absurdity sufficiently naked, and the necessity of eradicating its conditions (as opposed to 'restructuring' or 'reforming' them), to be standing common sense. The extent of popular anger directed towards financial industries and their elites after 2008 suggests

---

7   The 'not-yet-become' is, once again, a term borrowed from Ernst Bloch, *The Principle of Hope*, MIT Press, 1986.

that a more adequate analysis continues (if too slowly) to build towards this tipping point.

However, the persistence of the perverted and topsy-turvy situation asks that we examine the distortions generated by interest-bearing capital and the credit system – sustained by their apologists and political representatives, their economists and commentators. Today's explanations – popular, professional, and academic – often reproduce yesterday's mystifications with astonishing consistency, if dressed in a new language of cybernetics and data-driven risk calculation. The continuity of the movement of interest-bearing capital from Marx's time to the present is obfuscated by several extra zeros on the figures representing the malignant growth of new (and old) financial industries and instruments that continue to facilitate the appropriation of socially produced wealth.[8] The ongoing function of a credit system otherwise dramatically altered in its empirical forms consists of two core dynamics: (1) mystifying the process of exploitation by removing it from the narrative of profit-making while amplifying the profit-making capacity of the system (i.e., facilitating growth in the *scale* of production while the overall rate of profit falls); (2) mitigating the risks involved for functioning capitalists in carrying out profit-generating production, and providing a means for money capitalists to expand their wealth without getting involved in the increasingly risky business of production. The credit system, while entirely necessary for the reproduction of capital at all historical stages of development, introduces ever-deepening hazards and vulnerabilities for the process, intensifying volatility and the inflation of asset bubbles (the bigger the bubbles, the greater the shock of their 'corrections' in human terms), particularly in periods (like now) of chronic stagnation (i.e., in periods where the falling rate of profit exerts, and sustains, a greater pressure than its countertendencies).

These two dynamics represent a continuity across the lifespan of capital that operates at a deeper level than its institutional, legal, regulatory, and growth or technology-related transformations. As such, with interest-bearing capital, 'the capital relationship reaches its most superficial and fetishized form', and the story of M–M′ – the automatic fetish, 'money that produces more money, self-valorizing value without

---

8   Wealth that is *always* created elsewhere through the 'old-fashioned' process of producing commodities for the market.

the process [of production] that mediates the two extremes' – captures collective perception, especially among bourgeois economists and their pundits who 'seek to present capital as an independent source of wealth [and] value creation' (515; 517). As Marx argues,

> This form [of capital] is of course a godsend, a form in which the source of profit is no longer recognizable and in which the result of the capitalist production process – separate from the process itself – obtains an autonomous existence. (517)

To this day, more than in any other form, interest-bearing capital appears as unmediated wealth, a 'mysterious and self-creating source of interest', rather than a social relationship (516).

The misrecognition of interest-bearing capital as an unmediated thing, as a substance with the innate capacity to expand, is a function of a more general obscuring of the social content of *all value* as objectified socially necessary labour. This qualitative dimension of value determines its quantitative limits: *as objectified socially necessary labour time*, value has a definite, if incalculable, quantitative ceiling that is determined by the rate of profit – that is, by historical levels of productivity and the development of the forces of production, a finite maximum length of the working day, and the rate of exploitation (which is also historically and regionally determined). In other words, what is concealed in the value form are the 'human determinants' on the length and mode of the working day and hence on capital's social content; what Marx calls the 'identity of surplus-value and surplus labour' puts objective limits on – and the *lie* to – the exponential growth of capital, most deeply concealed and distorted in its interest-bearing form:

> The identity of surplus-value and surplus labour sets a qualitative limit to the accumulation of capital: the *total working day*, the present development of the productive forces and population, which limits the number of working days that can be simultaneously exploited. But if surplus-value is conceived in the irrational form of interest the limit is only quantitative, and beggars all fantasy.
>
> Interest-bearing capital, however, displays the conception of the capital fetish in its consummate form, the idea that ascribes to the accumulated product of labour ... the power of producing

surplus-value in geometric progression by way of an inherent secret quality, as pure automaton, so that this accumulated product of labour, as The Economist believes, has long since discounted the whole world's wealth for all time. (523)[9]

Marx's exemplar of such confusion are the financial models of Richard Price, eighteenth-century philosopher and politician, whose image of the self-generating geometric expansion of wealth through financial activity alone – specifically, through compound interest – captured the economic common sense, dominant political opinion and, consequently, the policy agenda of his day, including that of William Pitt the Younger:

> Price was simply dazzled by the incredible figures that arise from geometric progression ... He viewed capital as a self-acting automaton, without regard to the conditions of reproduction and labour, as a mere number that increases by itself ... Pitt took Dr. Price's mystification quite seriously; Price's conception has unwittingly been taken over by modern economics; [As we can see,] it would be impossible to drivel out a more hair-raising absurdity. (520–1)

> Its content is formed out of everyday prejudices, skimmed from the most superficial appearance of things. This false and trivial content is then supposedly 'elevated' and rendered poetic by a mystifying mode of expression. (522)

Popular and professional narratives concerning the role of finance in the functioning of the economy reflect, in their ambivalence, the ongoing perceptual distortions generated by interest-bearing capital as the automatic fetish. The sharks and wolves of capitalist finance generate

---

9 Further to this point: 'As was shown in Part Three of this volume, the profit rate decreases in proportion to the growing accumulation of capital and the accompanying rise in the productivity of social labour, this being expressed precisely in the relative decrease of variable capital vis-à-vis constant. In order to produce the same rate of profit, therefore, if the constant capital set in motion by a worker increases ten-fold, the surplus labour time would have to increase ten-fold as well, and very soon the total labour-time, or even the full twenty-four hours of the day, would not be sufficient, even if it were entirely appropriated by capital. Price's progression depends on the idea that the rate of profit does not decline, as does every idea of this "all-engrossing capital at compound interest" ' (523).

both enmity and admiration; they are perceived at once as innovators, disruptors, and parasites. The foundation for ideological construction arises from the fact that interest-bearing capital – finance – is a fundamental and necessary component of a system where the generation of new value is disjointed, temporally and spatially, between processes of production and realization (or circulation). And yet, as we have established, the money capitalist does not contribute any value directly to the total social capital but, rather, appropriates a portion of newly generated or already-existing capital. 'Wealth creator', 'parasite' – neither of these perceptions captures the actual movement of interest-bearing, capital even if a partial truth is common to both. Let us examine more precisely what is actually going on.

On a basic functional level, the credit system is an integral component of capitalist production tout court; capitalist production is simply not viable without a system of credit. This is the case in two respects. First, both production and circulation require that money and commodities be available to serve certain functions at various stages of the process, as payment, as means of purchase, or as means of production. This is simply another way of observing the movement that Marx theorizes in chapter 2 of *Capital* I: that the reproduction process is an ongoing, (ideally) uninterrupted metamorphosis of value, C–M and M–C. Credit is largely the means by which this ongoing metamorphosis is carried out: 'The metamorphosis of the commodity . . . is mediated here by way of credit; not only C–M, but also M–C and the actual production process' (613). In fact, 'the entire interconnection of the reproduction process rests on credit' (621). Without the ability, at various stages of the process, to procure money (or commodities) on credit, the functioning capitalist would be required to withhold payment or arrest production until the value produced in the previous cycle was realized, or, alternatively, hoard a portion of the profit from the previous cycle to facilitate the next. Either of these situations would dramatically reduce both the scale of production and the speed of circulation. In the course of capitalist development, expansion of production and expansion of the credit system are mutually implicated. As we observed above, progressive growth in the productivity of labour expands the total social product, which, in turn, expands and 'globalizes' consumer markets (612). Despite today's transportation and communication capacities, the speed and dexterity with which commodities circumnavigate the globe have not made the function of credit any less crucial, nor have revolutionary logistics tamped down the speculative activity encouraged by the process – quite the reverse:

> Large-scale production for distant markets casts the entire product into the arms of commerce; but it is impossible for the nation's capital to double, so that commerce would purchase the entire national product with its own capital before selling it again. Credit is thus indispensable here, a credit that grows in volume with the growing value of production and grows in duration with the increasing distance of the markets. A reciprocal effect takes place here. The development of the production process expands credit, while credit in turn leads to an expansion of industrial and commercial operations. (612)

Further, the credit system collectivizes individual surplus wealth (in the money-form) withheld (for whatever reason) from productive investment and puts it at the disposal of the functioning capitalist class as capital, propelling the expansion of capitalist accumulation (as we explored in chapter 3).[10] For this reason, historically, the credit system emerges simultaneously with capitalist production itself, infusing the earlier feudal relation of usury with the newly emerging social content of capitalist production. (We will return to the question of the historical emergence of interest-bearing capital and its subsumption of the older form of usury at the end of the chapter.) The process also produces banking as a specific capitalist function, and bankers as a specific genre of capitalist, performing the management of interest-bearing capital's necessary collectivization on both sides of the transaction:

> The business of banking consists . . . in concentrating money capital for loan in large masses in the bank's hands, so that, instead of the individual lender of money, it is the bankers as representatives of all

---

10 As we demonstrated in that chapter, the impact of the credit system on accumulation is expressed in the double movement of the tendency of the rate of profit to fall, on the one hand, and its countertendency, on the other. It does this by simultaneously expanding production, propelling productivity, and thereby increasing the organic composition of capital – forces that both push and pull in opposite directions with respect to profit rates.

lenders of money who confront the industrial and commercial capitalists. They become the general managers of money capital. On the other
hand, they concentrate the borrowers vis-à-vis all the lenders, in so far
as they borrow for the entire world of trade. A bank represents on the
one hand the centralization of money capital, of the lenders, and on
the other hand the centralization of the borrowers. (528)

The second way in which the credit system is inherent to capitalist
production more generally is in the movement of capital between
branches of production.[11] Competing capitalists, generally speaking,
invest capital only in branches of industry that are expanding, or at least
provisionally stable; investment in declining branches where the average
profit is falling is, by the system's terms, irrational. When branches of
industry begin to decline, capital that has been concentrated in these
branches is increasingly withdrawn. The function of the credit system is
to take capital from one branch where it cannot be absorbed and turn it
into available credit where it can be deployed in another growing branch,
facilitating the absorption of capital in this new branch until an
overconcentration causes it to flee and once again deposit itself
elsewhere. The credit system circulates capital between branches of
production, a process we know as equalization, and thereby forms the
general rate of profit – again, a movement that makes capitalist
production viable altogether:

> The competition between capitalists – which is itself this movement
> of equalization – consists here in their withdrawing capital bit by bit
> from those spheres where profit is below the average for a long period,
> and similarly injecting it bit by bit into spheres where it is above
> this . . . Equalization takes place by the expansion or contraction of
> production . . . mediated by the immigration or emigration of capital
> with respect to these particular spheres of production. It is the
> equalization brought about in this way, whereby the average market
> prices of commodities are reduced to their prices of production, that
> corrects divergences between the particular rates of profit and the
> general or average profit rate. (488–9)

---

11   This second function is really just the first function from a different standpoint
on the process.

On the one hand, the operation of interest-bearing capital in the formation of a credit system (a system of financing production costs) that, in turn, facilitates the equalization of profit rates between branches of industry is a necessary dimension of capitalist production – and, consequently, of accumulation. On the other hand, financial speculation *also* derives organically from the operating capacity of interest-bearing capital while being *not* a necessary dimension of the system but, rather, an inherent possibility of it, and one taken up all the more aggressively in periods of economic stagnation.[12] In this way, speculation comes to appear as a *causal* factor in economic crisis – as with the profligate financial practices identified as precipitating the 2008 financial crisis, and thereby demanding greater regulation – rather than what it actually is: a *symptom* of capital's crisis tendency and simply a catalyst of the destruction and devaluation that follows in the wake of crisis.[13] This appearance adds a predatory dimension to the popular image of the financier as parasite. However, the mystification at the heart of interest-bearing capital and the formation of 'financialization' lies in its appearance as a substance with the quasi-geometrical and enchanted capacity to multiply its value, as well as the value of the total social capital in circulation.[14] Once again, appearance departs from the actual

12   See Giovanni Arrighi, *The Long Twentieth Century: Money, Power, and the Origins of Our Times*, Verso, 1994.

13   For analyses that articulate the 2008 financial collapse with the deeper movement of capitalist crisis see, David Harvey, 'The Enigma of Capital and the Crisis This Time', paper prepared for the American Sociological Association, August 16, 2010, available at davidharvey.org; John Bellamy Foster and Fred Magdoff, *The Great Financial Crisis: Causes and Consequences*, Monthly Review Press, 2009; David McNally, *Global Slump: The Economics and Politics of Crisis and Resistance*, PM Press, 2011; Paul Mattick, *Business As Usual: The Economic Crisis and the Failure of Capitalism*, Reaktion Books, 2011; Robert Brenner, 'What Is Good for Goldman Sachs Is Good for America', Verso Blog, 13 November 2018, versobooks.com; Wolfgang Streek, *Buying Time: The Delayed Crisis of Democratic Capitalism*, Verso, 2014; Joseph Choonara, 'The Political Economy of a Long Depression', *International Socialism* 158, 2018; Chris Harman, *Zombie Capitalism: Global Crisis and the Relevance of Marx*, Haymarket Books, 2010; Gérard Duménil and Dominique Lévy, *The Crisis of Neoliberalism*, Harvard University Press, 2011; Murray E. G. Smith, *Global Capitalism in Crisis: Karl Marx and the Decay of the Profit System*, Fernwood Publishing, 2010; Michael Roberts, *The Long Depression*, Haymarket Books, 2016.

14   In the remainder of the chapter, we will work with more contemporary terms in order to move the discussion of these dynamics towards their contemporary expressions in current practices around securitization and the buying and selling of financial derivatives, futures, credit default swaps, and other instruments.

movement of interest-bearing capital: a social relation that allows for the redistribution of value generated in the sphere of production into the pockets of the owners of money capital. The role of what Marx calls 'fictitious capital', and its distinction from (and exchange with) money capital, is instrumental in this operation of redistribution, and in the inverted appearance generated by the process.

So-Called Financialization and the Dynamics of Fictitious Capital

Marx uses the term 'fictitious capital' to refer to legal and contractual claims on portions of future surplus-value based on an underlying capital-asset. The capital-asset in question could be commodity capital (that is, a capital that will be mobilized in production to produce surplus-value), or a capital that is poised to attract interest (that is, a capital-property, intellectual or landed, that is situated to attract rent). We can think of fictitious capital as claims to a share of any ongoing or future income stream: all 'accumulated claims, legal titles, to future [revenue from] production' (599). Stocks, shares, bonds, securities, derivatives, and other financial instruments of all kinds are examples of fictitious capital, the formation of which is referred to (by Marx and more generally) as capitalization (597). Debt itself can be construed as a capital-asset (banks hold the debts of borrowers as assets, for example) that represents an ongoing income stream in the form of interest payments. Today, any and all imaginable income streams are financialized, including interest payments on all forms of debt: commercial, consumer, mortgage, credit card, student debt; property rent; copyright fees; monthly payments on electricity, phone, water; even remittance payments.

Contracted claims (legal titles) to shares of the income appropriated through these income streams can be sold by the holders of the debts (again, banks, credit card companies, retailers who provide customers with credit, etc. – any institutional lender) as interest-paying investment products, often referred to today as collateralized debt obligations (a financial product that gained popular familiarity, and infamy, in the wake of the 2008 financial collapse). This creation of investment products for money capital by combining individual debts into one big 'debt pie', then slicing the pie into tranches that are sold as financial products for 'growing' the capital of those who buy them, carries on today undiminished in pace and scale after the 2008 financial crisis, despite the wide criticism the practice received. The staying power of the practice, which, despite opprobrium, will never recede in the context of late capitalism, reflects its double function: first, it is one of the few means of expanding money capital without mobilizing it directly;[15] second, the process of bundling individual debts together and selling them off in pieces mitigates (or eliminates altogether) the risk involved for the original lender in holding the debt – removing the debt but not the profit from the lenders' books. It is a process of collectivizing and socializing risk, referred to as securitization. The creation of fictitious capital as the accumulation of these contract-products in the form of claims to future surplus-value – slices of interest-paying debt – is the modality of securitization:

> Even when the promissory note – the security – does not represent a purely illusory capital, as it does in the case of national debts, the capital value of this security is still pure illusion. We have already seen how the credit system produces joint-stock capital. Securities purport to be ownership titles representing this capital. (597)

> All these securities actually represent nothing but accumulated claims, legal titles, to future revenues from production. Their money or capital value [i.e., their notional or 'face value' (600)] either does not represent capital at all, as in the case of national debts, or is determined independently of the real capital value they represent.
>
> In all countries of capitalist production, there is a tremendous amount of so-called interest-bearing capital or 'moneyed capital' in this form. And an accumulation of money capital means for the most part nothing more than an accumulation of these claims to a portion of the revenue from production, and an accumulation of the market price of these claims, of their illusory capital value. (599)

---

15 We will elaborate how these claims to capital expand money capital by redistributing existing value to their holders rather than through creating new value; as such, the movement of fictitious capital pushes down profit rates and propels the system towards crisis, throwing up barriers to the expansion of money capital down the road.

But let us step back: the redistribution of value in which fictitious capital participates derives immediately from the movement of credit money, an abstraction of commercial and bank credit. This is its most immediate derivation, even as the genealogy of fictitious capital, like all expressions of the movement of value, leads back to simple commodity circulation. For instance, the sale and purchase of commodities requires money as general equivalent, as the medium of circulation, as well as money as means of payment (when the segments of the circulation process are disjointed). The situation where a purchaser lacks the money-equivalent at the point of transaction summons the relationship of creditor and debtor, and a promise to pay, or 'bill of exchange', is substituted for the money-equivalent:

> With the development of trade and the capitalist mode of produc-
> tion, which produces only for circulation, this spontaneous basis for
> the credit system is expanded, generalized and elaborated. By and
> large, money now functions only as means of payment, i.e. commod-
> ities are not sold for money, but for a written promise to pay at a
> certain date . . . we can refer to all these promises to pay as bills of
> exchange. (525)

Bills of exchange represent titles on future surplus-value, and, as Marx explains, 'until they expire and are due for payment . . . [they] circulate as means of payment [and thereby function as] actual commercial money' (525). For instance, instead of settling a one-hundred-pound debt with money as means of payment, I might transfer to my creditor a bill of exchange for that amount – a title to a future value of one hundred pounds – in lieu of money. My creditor might be a debtor as well and owe another creditor a similar sum and transfer the same title to settle this second debt; and on and on this transfer of the bill – the title to future value – might go, settling any number of debts before it expires, and without any money changing hands (610). As Marx states, 'To the extent that [these titles] ultimately cancel each other out, by the balancing of debts and claims, they function absolutely as money, even though there is no final transformation into money proper' (525).

These titles, therefore, in their initial form as bills of exchange, function as commercial money and form the basis of credit money and banknotes (525; 610). As such, they also prefigure forms of fictitious capital, which, as legal claims to future surplus-value, after their initial purchase, can be bought/sold many times over – indefinitely in the case of shares, stocks, and the like (if the capitalized property remains viable), or before the expiration of the contract in the case of derivatives, futures, and so on. Like bills of exchange from which it derives, fictitious capital can function as credit money – that is, circulate *like* money without *being* money – and does so today on a comparatively gigantic and proliferating scale in its contemporary empirical forms – futures, securities, derivatives, etc.[16] Claims to future surplus-value are not money; that is to say, they are not constituted as value in their social substance. This becomes clear when they are removed from the specific contexts in which they are produced and circulate (I cannot buy milk from the corner store with a financial derivative, for example). Fictitious capital, unlike other forms of capital – commodity, money, commercial, merchant, interest-bearing/finance, and so on – only *appears* to be a form of value (and, again, only in certain contexts) while not actually constituting a magnitude of objectified socially necessary labour time. In other words, fictitious capital *is not capital per se*:

> They [interest-bearing securities, government bonds, stocks, financial derivatives, etc.] are not capital in themselves, but simply creditor's claims; if they are in mortgages, they are simply claims on future payments of ground-rent; and if they are stocks of some other kind, they are simply property titles which give the holder a claim to future surplus-value. None of these things are genuine capital, they do not constitute any component of capital and are also in themselves not values. (590)

> The greater part of banker's capital is . . . purely fictitious and consists of claims (bills of exchange) and shares (drafts on future revenues). It should not be forgotten here that this capital's money value, as represented by these papers in the banker's safe, is completely fictitious. (600)

---

16   That is, fictitious capital is not money with respect to the actual social content of value's general equivalent as congealed socially necessary labour (i.e., abstract labour).

That fictitious capital appears as capital, even though it is not, defines the process widely referred to today as financialization. And, while the 'bait and switch' of fictitious capital animates one aspect of capital's perceptual physics more generally, it is especially evident today as the methods and momentum of financialization ratchet up in periods of systemic value-machine stagnation. The accumulation of enormous notional claims to future surplus-value is often characterized as a vast proliferation of 'value' itself in the system, a misconstrual of fictitious capital for actual value (i.e., money and/or commodities) that obfuscates the viability of the value-generating capacity of the system as well as generates the inverted appearance that wealth can be created (and now predominantly *is* created) in circulation as opposed to production.[17] In this distorted surface appearance, there is no need for the category of fictitious capital, because there is no perceived distinction between claims to future surplus-value and surplus-value itself (even though there are contexts where the former can step in for the latter). Making the necessary distinction, however, allows us to theorize and explain current empirical characteristics of global capitalism in evidence since the 1970s: falling profitability, stagnant and falling wages, falling rates of productivity, a growing proletarian reserve army and surplus population, deep economic stagnation and corresponding financial volatility and asset bubbles, capital flight from production to investment in real estate, new categories such as underemployment, precarious labour, feminized labour, informalization – all symptoms of a system whose capacity for producing new value is in long-term decline. We cannot reconcile these symptoms with the analysis that finance is generating historical quantities of value for the capital-machine – a confusion worthy of Dr. Price.

Sitting in the banker's safe, or circulating and functioning like money, claims to future surplus-value represent a 'fictional' doubling (and sometimes tripling) of the underlying capital-asset:[18] my creditor's legal

----

17   Today, several hundred trillion US dollars' worth of fictitious capital routinely circulates – a notional sum that far exceeds global GDP.

18   'With the development of interest-bearing capital and the credit system, all capital seems to be duplicated, and at some points triplicated, by the various ways in which the same capital, or even the same claim, appears in various hands in different guises. The greater part of this "money capital" is purely fictitious' (601). In a footnote to this passage, Engels describes the way in which the duplication and triplication of capital

title to the one hundred pounds in my pocket *is not* the one hundred pounds in my pocket but, rather, a faux doubling of that value that can circulate and settle debts, and/or capitalize the one hundred pounds in my pocket at, say, 10 percent (ten pounds) a month – interest that represents 'real value' appropriated by my creditor in addition to the one hundred pounds when the debt is settled. Perhaps my creditor sells the claim to a second investor, maybe even at a discount. The purchaser of the claim is now entitled to appropriate the interest, which represents, as it did with the original financier, the means of extracting a portion of real value from the system until the time the debt is settled. In this way, the claim (the fictitious capital: stock, bond, security, derivative, etc. – or the bill of exchange, if the one-hundred-pound advance was for commodities not yet sold) is not value but rather value's ghostly double that allows the holder to appropriate actual value from the system (what I will shortly refer to as fictitious capital's exchange with actual value):

> The shares in railway, mining, shipping companies, etc. represent real capital, i.e. capital invested and functioning in these enterprises . . . But the capital does not exist twice over, once as the capital value of the ownership titles, the shares, and then again as the capital actually invested or to be invested in the enterprises in question. It exists only in the latter form, and the share is nothing but an ownership title, *pro rata*, to the surplus-value which this capital is to realize. A may sell this title to B, and B to C. These transactions have no essential effect on the matter. A or B has then transformed his title into capital, but C has transformed his capital into a mere ownership title to the surplus-value expected from this share of capital. (597–8)

That fictitious capital is not capital per se but, rather, a faux doubling of capital is made especially transparent in the case of government bonds and state debt. When creditors lend money to a government by purchasing government bonds, the state pays the bondholder an annual sum of interest (595). As is commonly understood, the 'capital' borrowed by the state is not generally used as capital – that is, not

---

in its fictitious forms had, since Marx's notes on the practice, been 'taken very much further'. Since then, its forms have, of course, become even more convoluted, but the character of the inner movement remains the same.

invested productively – but rather applied to government expenditures. At the same time, the interest paid to the bondholder is simply a portion of the revenues from taxation. In this scenario, it is clear that the capital collected by the state is in no way value that maintains and expands its value; it is value that is put into general circulation and subsequently no longer exists – that is, is entirely 'illusory and fictitious' (595) – long after the bond in question continues to generate interest (i.e., for as long as the state remains viable) and no matter how many times it may pass into the hands of different buyers/owners/money capitalists. As Marx points out,

> No matter how these transactions are multiplied, the capital of the national [or provincial, or municipal, etc.] debt remains purely fictitious, and the moment these promissory notes become unsaleable [in the case of state bankruptcy, for example], the illusion of this capital disappears.

Nonetheless, in the case of debt, held by the state or otherwise, 'a negative quantity appears as capital' – an everyday 'insanity' indeed (596).[19]

These examples may seem too simple to capture the complex dynamics of contemporary financial transactions, globalized derivatives markets, and so on. And yet, despite today's byzantine surface-forms of finance wherein armies of mathematicians and computer scientists build unimaginably complex algorithmic machinery to calculate minute risk differentials, the comparatively simple objective depicted above – to extract portions of surplus-value from the system with as little risk to the owner of money capital as possible – continues to be the underlying movement and rationale for the production, purchase, and sale of financial instruments, the latter commodities in themselves. Marx describes cases where commodities are produced for the purpose of buying and selling titles to a portion of the surplus-value that the sale of the commodities will eventually realize, where a portion of surplus-value is extracted each time the title changes hands.[20] Given that they

---

19 'Moving from the capital of the national debt, where a negative quantity appears as capital – interest-bearing capital always being the mother of every insane form, so that debts, for example, can appear as commodities in the mind of the banker' (596).

20 'It is clear however, that with the development of labour productivity and hence of production on a large scale, (1) markets expand and become further removed from

represent the opportunity for financial extraction of value, these cases illustrate a progressive inversion of the rationale for commodity production itself: instead of finance serving the production and circulation of commodities, the production of commodities facilitates 'financialized profit-making', an inversion that is now commonplace. It thus upends the ideology that scale of production and price are a function of supply and demand (536).[21]

While fictitious capital is not capital per se, it is a mechanism for extracting value, which it does in circulation – in its metamorphosis into money and vice versa in the ongoing shapeshifting of M–C and C–M: first, money (M) trades places with the financial product (C; stocks, bonds, derivatives, etc.). Second, the financial product (C) trades places with money (M) again when it is sold to another buyer – through the sale of one's shares in a company, for example – or when the product expires according to its contracted terms.[22] From the point of view of the owner of the financial product, circumstances determine whether value (interest, or, in its surface-form, financial profit) has been extracted or lost at the expiration of the contract. From the totalized point of view of the system, no value has been created or destroyed; it has simply been redistributed, moved from one pocket to another. Discounting on bills of exchange or futures contracts are simply another example of the routine metamorphosis of C (fictitious capital in the form of a bill of exchange) and M (money) (536), constituting the redistribution of value in the system – its movement from the pocket of one 'stakeholder' to another. Crises are opportunities to exploit, even more deeply, the redistributive mechanism represented by the metamorphosis of financial paper into money and back again:

> In the bad phases of the industrial cycle . . . the prices of government paper and other securities fall. This is the moment when money capitalists buy up this devalued paper on a massive scale, as it will

---

the point of production, (2) credit must consequently be prolonged, and (3) as a result, the speculative element must come more and more to dominate transactions' (612).

21   In a note to Marx's description, Engels points out that the building of the Suez Canal shortened commodities' long journey time from England to the Indian market, curtailing the timeframe for fictitious capital to undertake its extractive activities (537).

22   'Interest-bearing securities, government bonds, stocks, etc. . . . have to be sold if gold or notes are to be obtained' (590).

soon go up again in the later phases, and even rise above its normal level. They will then sell it off, thereby appropriating a part of the public's money capital. Those securities that are not sold off yield a higher interest, since they were bought below their price. But all the profit which the money capitalists make, and which they [may] turn back into capital, they transform first of all into money capital. (634–5)

In non-crisis periods, the relatively stable fluidity of metamorphoses of M into C (financial products) and back again generates the erroneous perception that forms of fictitious capital are indistinguishable from money and, today, have simply become a form of money. If this were the case, the transformation of money into financial instruments would be pointless, a functional tautology. It is the very change of form itself that allows the financial product to function as a mechanism of value redistribution at all. This crucial change of form *is* the mechanism of concealing what is going on under the surface appearances of things: the exercise of power on the part of private property owners (in this case the property of the financial instrument) to extract a portion of socially produced wealth. Without the change of form – the crucial *difference* between money and financial instruments – the power of certain individuals to arrogate the social power of capital (ultimately, a state-enforced coercive power) would be naked, that is, would operate in transparency.

In more banal terms, if financial paper were money, there would be no need to transform it back into money for 'everyday' purposes – activities too extensive to list, including virtually all purchases for the sake of consumption, either as of means of production or subsistence:

> What the industrialist or merchant needs when he wants to have bills discounted or take out a loan is neither shares nor government stock. What he needs is money. That is why he pledges or sells these securities if he cannot obtain money in any other way. (609–10)

In other words, if fictitious capital *were* money, this would undermine the very purpose of the former as a means of growing one's wealth, at the same time as it would eliminate any associated risk involved in their temporary swap in position. The confusion of claims to future value for money is not unique to current perception; Marx observes, 'This is the point where there enters the confused notion that both things are "money", the deposit as a claim to payment from the banker, and the deposited money in the banker's possession' (642n10). An analogous error would be to claim that money has doubled when it is deposited in the bank. My deposited one hundred pounds still exists for me as my money, but it now also exists for the banker to loan and as a claim to money that I make on the banker – that is, a faux doubling, not an actual one: 'Here the deposit has a double effect as money, i.e. first as actual money and subsequently as a claim to money. Mere claims to money can only take the place of money in the balancing of claims' (642n10).

The management of interest-bearing capital, and the production, purchase, and sale of financial products (fictitious capital), proliferates what Marx calls 'middlemen' or 'intermediaries'. These financial mediators facilitate the extraction of value on behalf of those who own money capital for a share of the revenue:

> [The credit system develops] the management of interest-bearing capital or money capital as the special function of the money-dealers. The borrowing and lending of money becomes their special business. They appear as middlemen between the real lender of money capital and its borrower. (528)

The two-part function of financial mediators – 'bankers', still, for the most part – is largely the same today as it ever was: (1) *borrowing* from individual owners of money capital, namely industrial capitalists, other money or finance capitalists, speculators, or those sections of the working class who are in the position of 'saving' surplus revenue from wages or investing collectively (as with pension plans); and (2) *lending* socialized money capital to these same parties. However, one development that has taken place largely (but not exclusively) since the 1970s is the proliferation of types of financial mediator: bankers are joined by hedge fund managers, stock and bond brokers, managers and functionaries of the shadow banking system, and private vendors of generic and over-the-counter financial products of all kinds.

As we established above, the redistribution of value through a system of credit is immanent to generalized commodity exchange that necessarily excretes money as a means of circulation whose constitutional moments of sale and purchase are disjointed. As we have also established, since credit is an autonomized dimension of the production process, the function of the money capitalist represents non-productive labour (i.e., not involved in creating new value) that redistributes value generated in production to the pocket of the money capitalist. If credit is immanent to capitalist production, speculation is immanent to the credit system; the difference is that forms of speculation – hedging, shorting, securitizing, and so on – even as they derive from a structural possibility internal to credit, are *not* necessary to the production process. The instruments of such speculation – derivatives, securities, credit default swaps, collateralized debt obligations, for example – are commodities, financial products in the form of contracts, that are produced for exchange and whose use-value is to serve the need of owners of money to grow their wealth. The exchange-value of the financial commodity takes the even more superficial and irrational form of a fee for the service of preparing and/or issuing the contract. Nonetheless, the contract-product is produced, in categorial terms, as any other commodity.[23]

In analysis, therefore, it is important to make a distinction between the production and initial sale of this financial commodity and its subsequent circulation (however many owners it might attract in the duration), along with the outcome of the 'wager' it represents. To do so is to differentiate between (1) the redistributive movement of fictitious capital and (2) the production and circulation of financial commodities. In the first case, value is redistributed and participates in the tendency for profit rates to fall. In the second case, new value is generated in the production process (in the financial service rendered), accumulated by the system, and distributed as various forms of revenue to members of the capitalist class in the formation of production prices that express the general rate of profit. In other words, it expresses a countertendency to the first. Empirically, service fees for issuing financial instruments represent a substantial portion of the profit that falls to financial industries. This situation turns the financial mediator, at least in some of

---

23   That is to say, like all commodities, financial products are produced (largely) by private firms which bring together means of production (constant capital) and (skilled) living labour (variable capital) to produce a product whose price (service fee) is the phenomenal form of its exchange-value.

their activities, into a functioning capitalist operating – nominally – in the sphere of circulation. Those firms that are involved not in producing financial products but, rather, only in retailing them, step into the role of the merchant capitalist, realizing surplus-value created elsewhere and, consequently, appropriating a portion of it.

'The Mother of Every Insane Form'

The movement of interest-bearing capital constitutes a specific set of perceptual distortions that Marx describes as the 'automatic fetish'. 'The mother of every insane form' (596), interest-bearing capital systematically upends the concept that forms the analytical core of *Capital* III: the viability of 'genuine capital accumulation' (607) – that is, the state of the system's capacity to produce new value – determines, in the last instance, the range of movement available to the system as a whole. In other words, at any given stage of development, the balance between capital's crisis tendencies and its reproductive capacities determines the system's combination of empirical characteristics and expressions. The mathematical formula for this balance is the value composition of the total social capital, $\frac{c}{v}$, at the average rate of surplus-value (where c represents the investment in means of production, and v represents the investment in labour-power). The movement of interest-bearing capital obfuscates what is cause and what is effect in the course of accumulation because it breaks the index between actual accumulation and the magnitude of surplus money excreted by the process – money available to be loaned, that is, money seeking to become interest-bearing capital. The analysis of capital's configuration and viability, at any given historical conjuncture, as a value-producing machine cannot be read directly from the supply of surplus money it generates, which can expand *or* diminish under any set of circumstances: relative stability, growth, stagnation, or crisis. The observation of existing circumstances alone, therefore, cannot capture the composition, relative stability, or volatility of the value-machine; observation must be mediated by theoretical deduction, by what Marx in *Capital* I calls 'the power of abstraction' or, simply, science. The bulk of chapters 30, 31, and 32 (in a section titled 'Money Capital and Real Capital') undertake the theoretical mediation of empirical data with the objective of demonstrating the non-indexical relation between the systemic precipitation of money capital on the one hand, and what Marx calls 'genuine capital accumulation' on the other:

> *Firstly*, the accumulation of money capital as such. How far is it, and how far is it not, an index of genuine capital accumulation, i.e. of reproduction on an expanded scale? Is the phenomenon of a 'plethora' of capital, an expression used only of interest-bearing capital, i.e. money capital, simply a particular expression of industrial overproduction, or does it form a separate phenomenon alongside this? Does such a plethora, an over-supply of money capital, coincide with the presence of stagnant sums of money . . . so that this excess of actual money is an expression and form of appearance of this plethora of loan capital?
>
> And *secondly*, to what extent does monetary scarcity, i.e. a shortage of loan capital, express a lack of real capital (commodity and productive capital)? To what extent, on the other hand, does it coincide with a lack of money as such, a lack of means of circulation? (607)

In answering these questions, Marx begins with the scenario where the identity of loan capital and industrial capital is the most transparent: the case where a growth in the supply of loan capital is indeed an expression of genuine capital accumulation. Here, loan capital (surplus money) necessarily expands as a function of the actual growth of the reproduction process. Industrial capital and loan capital grow proportionately because they are identical: loan capital is the 'M' of M–C–M:

> The capitals loaned are commodity capitals designed either for final individual consumption or to replace constant elements of productive capital. So what appears here as loaned capital is always capital that exists in a certain phase of the reproduction process, but is transferred from one hand to another by purchase and sale while the equivalent for it is paid by the buyer only later, after the stipulated interval. (612)

In the context of stable reproduction (i.e., expanding but always provisional) and capital growth, loan capital is not 'unoccupied capital' but, rather, capital 'at a high level of employment' (613). It is capital in the course of expanding by means of changing form. In some instances, the expansion of fictitious capital can also correspond to a growth of industrial capital (and the expansion of reproduction), just as the nominal value of shares on the stock market *can* (but does not necessarily) indicate a growth in the profitability of certain firms and, indirectly, the productive sphere more generally.

However, as we know, in a capitalist mode of production, a period of stability and growth is a structural prelude to a period of falling profitability, recession or crash (and concomitant devaluation), and post-recession stagnation, often (but not always) followed by a return to stability and growth. This is the built-in dynamic of capital that Marx calls overaccumulation. The second scenario, then, in which to observe the relation between genuine accumulation and the precipitation of money capital is that of contracting reproduction, that is, periods of stagnation and/or crisis. A period of stagnation is characterized by several interconnected movements: the metamorphosis of capital, both M–C and C–M, is delayed and, in some cases, permanently arrested; industrial capital stands idle and cannot be employed; there is a surplus of commodity capital as stocks of goods, both means of production and subsistence, are unsaleable; fixed capital is idle and, in some cases, abandoned permanently. In these circumstances, credit genuinely contracts for several reasons; as capital is now unemployed, it 'congeals in its phases', and its metamorphosis is arrested. As such, without movement and growth, capital contracts in general and, thereby, in both its forms of industrial and loan capital (614). The circulation of money is also arrested as a result of a subsequent 'loss of confidence' in the reproduction process; money capitalists, in periods of stagnation, will either hoard potential loan capital or divert it towards finance, insurance, and real estate industries. Marx describes this loss of confidence as a reversion of the system from its Protestant to its Catholic comportment:

> The monetary system is essentially Catholic, the credit system essentially Protestant. 'The Scotch hate gold.' As paper, the monetary existence of commodities has a purely social existence. It is *faith* that brings salvation. Faith in money value as the immanent spirit of commodities, faith in the mode of production and its predestined disposition, faith in the individual agents of production as mere personifications of self-valorizing capital. But the credit system is no

more emancipated from the monetary system as its basis than
Protestantism is from the foundations of Catholicism. (727)

The tendency for there to be a spike in the price of gold following a
recessionary downturn, as was the case in the wake of 2008, signifies a
collective – so far, temporary – loss of faith in credit, and the need for
the spiritual security of more material forms of wealth. Of course, in a
capitalist mode of production, gold is 'more material' in appearance
only; as a form of wealth, the substance of gold is pure sociality.

Nonetheless, this second scenario also lends greater transparency to
the identity of loan capital and industrial capital. The stagnation and/or
interruption of reproduction represents an actual contraction of capital
in general and therefore of loan capital as a portion of it. Following a
crash, there is a freezing up of credit, and of commercial credit in
particular:

> So if there is a disturbance in this expansion [of capital], or even in the
> normal exertion of the reproduction process, there is also a lack of
> credit; it is more difficult to obtain goods on credit. The demand for
> cash payment and distrust of credit selling is especially characteristic
> of the phase in the industrial cycle that follows the crash. (614)

At the same time, while there is an actual contraction of capital, it is
expressed not in a *lack* of productive capital but rather in the reverse: the
contraction of capital that follows a crash takes the form of a *surplus* of
productive capital:

> Capital already invested is in fact massively unemployed, since the
> reproduction process is stagnant. Factories stand idle, raw materials
> pile up, finished products flood the market as commodities. Nothing
> could be more wrong, therefore, than to ascribe such a situation to a
> lack of productive capital. It is precisely then that there is a surplus of
> productive capital, partly in relation to the normal though temporarily
> contracted scale of reproduction and partly in relation to the crippled
> consumption. (614)

Marx's reference to 'crippled consumption' is noteworthy. The
breakdown of reproduction that is from one standpoint expressed in

massively unemployed productive capital is from another standpoint expressed in the crippled consumption of masses of people. Unemployed productive capital is the equivalent of unemployed workers; the deepening immiseration of those who produce wealth is the human cost of capital's crisis tendency:

> [Workers] are employed only as long as they can be employed at a profit for the capitalist class. The ultimate reason for all real crises always remains the poverty and restricted consumption of the masses, in the face of the drive of capitalist production to develop the productive forces as if only the absolute consumption capacity of society set a limit to them. (615)

A surplus of capital walks hand in hand with human misery. The tourniquet on mass consumption begins to tighten before the collapse, and the reproductive means of the working class diminishes: 'Even if their demand remains nominally the same, it still declines in real terms' (622).

As Marx's discussion sinks more deeply into the dynamics of capitalist crisis, we see corresponding dissociations between money capital (as available credit) and capital in general. Leading up to crisis, in order to compensate for declining returns on invested capital, production may ramp up to utilize, as quickly as possible, stores of raw material and value-rich fixed capital. Commodities may be produced even more frantically for the sole purpose of discounting bills of exchange, speculation grows more frenzied, and 'the appearance of very solid business with brisk returns can merrily persist' (615) right up to last moment: 'This is why business seems almost exaggeratedly healthy immediately before a collapse' (616). Marx refers to this stage as 'the period of overproduction and swindling, [where] the productive forces are stretched to their limit, even beyond the capitalist barriers to the production process' (621). If the run-up to breakdown is disguised as productivity in this way, so is the full extent of its fallout, particularly in the current era of historical government bailouts of failing companies, both financial and productive, in combination with state pressure on central banks to lower interest rates in order to free up debt-spending of all kinds – corporate, government, and consumer. The accumulation of enormous quantities of debt without any means of reversing the downward spiral entails that wealthy national economies can appear to remain vibrant, even post-collapse, by transforming themselves into giant Ponzi schemes relying, with even more feverish tenacity, on Protestant faith alone. Low interest rates and high levels of borrowing have, in late capitalism, become the conventional two-part strategy for absorbing enormous quantities of idle money capital created in the wake of the crisis stage of capital's cycle of prosperity and expansion to crash and contraction.[24]

The redeployment of surplus money towards speculation creates enormous concentrations of wealth – 'more and more the result of gambling' – in the hands of money capitalists and generates the appearance that profit-making no longer relies on productive industry and the need to exploit labour at all. The actual determination of speculative profit-making by the value-generating capacity of productive industry is inverted in the appearance that productive industry answers to those who control the money supply and the distribution of credit:

> Talk about centralization! The credit system, which has its focal point in the allegedly national banks and the big money-lenders and usurers that surround them, is one enormous centralization and gives this class of parasites a fabulous power not only to decimate the industrial capitalists periodically but also to interfere in actual production in the most dangerous manner. (678–9)

Overaccumulation is an overproduction of value that cannot be realized. In its surface-form, overaccumulation presents as the overproduction of commodities that cannot be sold; at its core is insufficient consumer demand, or, more precisely, the restricted reproductive capacity of the working class (including its reserve armies and surplus populations). However, as Marx points out, 'in a system of production where the entire interconnection of the reproduction

---

24 This cycle is capital's business-as-usual. On pages 633–4 (chapter 31), Marx chronicles the cycles of prosperity and expansion to crash and contraction based on the statistics for imports and exports from 1824 to 1863. What the chronicle demonstrates is that in each subsequent cycle, the minimum value of the products exported from Great Britain, the level to which the total exports fell immediately following a crash, was still higher than the maximum value of the products exported in the high point of pervious prosperous cycle. This demonstrates the extent to which each cycle between downturns ramps up the value of the total social product.

process rests on credit', the standpoint of the money capitalist assumes the dominant collective perception of the functioning economy in general (621). In its surface-appearance, overproduction is a paralysis of credit, 'a violent scramble for means of payment', and the '[in] convertibility of bills of exchange into money'. Again, as Marx points out, 'the majority of these [inconvertible] bills represent actual purchases and sales', already an expansion of the total social capital sufficiently beyond social need such that it forms the basis of the crisis. However, add to this over-expansion of claims on produced but unrealized value the financial dregs of burst asset bubbles and fraudulent speculations, and 'the entire crisis presents itself as simply a credit and monetary crisis': 'On top of this . . . a tremendous number of these bills represent purely fraudulent deals, which now come to light and explode; as well as unsuccessful speculations conducted with borrowed capital' (621). When capitalist crisis assumes the more superficial disguise of a credit and monetary crisis, its actual cause – the shedding of labour that produces the only real value in the system, and the devaluation of the commodity capital in which that value is objectified – is nowhere on the radar: 'Everything here appears upside down, since in this paper world the real price and its real elements are nowhere to be seen, but simply bullion, metal coin, notes, bills and securities' (622).

The identity of money capital and industrial capital is obscured by the fact that 'loan capital has a different movement from industrial capital' (720), and this dissociation is exaggerated in the stages of capitalist crisis. The nature of crisis, at the same time, is obscured by the dissociation of money capital and industrial capital. A build-up of money capital (available as loan capital) in the system can indicate one of two entirely different and opposing situations. First, it can be an index of genuine accumulation: the 'accumulation of loan capital simply means that money is precipitated as loanable money' from a reproduction process that undergoes expansion (639). Second, increasing productivity (which both expands the product and cheapens the individual unit) may expand the value congealed in the product faster than the industrial capitalist can expand their reproduction process to absorb it. In this case, 'money capital is ejected from the circuit as superfluous and is transformed into money capital for loan' (638). This scenario, an index of pending overproduction, also presents as an increase in loan capital. Finally, an increase in available loan capital can also be an index of a crisis-initiated interruption of reproduction more generally because money capital will be withheld from productive investment on a wider scale. Marx states,

> In the first case, the accumulation of money capital expresses the repetition of the production process under more favourable conditions, the genuine release of a portion of capital previously tied up, enabling the reproduction process to be expanded with the same monetary means. In the second case, on the other hand, there is simply an interruption in the flow of transactions. But in both cases money is transformed into loanable money capital, representing an accumulation of it, and has the same effect on the money market and the rate of interest, even though in the one case the genuine accumulation process is promoted, while in the other case it is inhibited. (638)

Adding to the 'mental confusion' of vulgar economics,[25] loan capital can be in high demand *either* as means of payment in order to resolve outstanding debts in times of crisis, *or* as means of purchase in order to procure means of production in times of productive expansion. The rate of interest, determined by the supply and demand for loan capital, will therefore rise in the context of high demand of either kind, 'irrespective of whether real capital . . . is abundant or scarce' (647–8). The rate of interest, therefore, as an index of the competitive push and pull over loan capital – of its supply and availability – that is, as an indicator of the overall health of 'the economy', is a datum which generates much sound and fury but which does not indicate anything per se. The fetish of the rate of interest, and the commonplace economic belief in the separate but parallel movement of loan and industrial capital, *does* serve a purpose from the point of view of the money-capitalist: the inference of a 'booming' productive economy from a 'plethora' of available loan capital seeking expansion in finance and real estate elevates the priorities of the money capitalist to a dominant place in the general economy. It is an inference, however, that can be – and in a post-2008 recessionary global economy *is*, in fact – the inversion of the actual state of things.

---

25 Engels uses the term 'mental confusion' in a supplementary insertion to the chapter (688).

Nonetheless, the illusory equation of a high rate of interest with a healthy economy serves the money capitalist, as voiced in the parliamentary testimony of their class representatives – Lord Overstone, Mr. Chapman et al., and their pundits in the *Economist* – who propagate this perception and then benefit from its legal institution.[26] Chapter 34, 'The Currency Principle and the Legislation of 1844', is a collection of Marx's notes on 'the ignominious fiasco . . . suffered both in theory and in practice, after [legislative] experiments on the largest national scale' were undertaken 'by means of . . . Peel's Bank Acts of 1844 and 1845', legislative experiments that reflected precisely the obfuscation Marx elaborates in chapters 30 through 33 (683).[27] The faulty assumption that formed the basis for this legislation was extrapolated from Ricardo's currency theory and the original erroneous idea that commodity prices are tied to the amount of gold (metal money) in circulation at any given time.[28] One possible expression of crisis is a fall in commodity prices; according to the 'currency school' thinkers – Lord Overstone and Co. – a fall in commodity prices is explained by the rise in the relative value of money in circulation. Since the relative value of money to commodities rises with a greater magnitude of money in circulation, the currency school stipulated that crisis could be pre-empted with the direct management of the amount of money in circulation, specifically its *restriction*, and consistently so, even in phases of crisis and stagnation (681–2).

---

26   Marx discusses historical cases that illustrate the perceptual inversions around rate of interest and the wider economy in chapters 34 and 35.

27   In the introduction to chapter 34, which is a long quotation from *A Contribution to the Critique of Political Economy* inserted into the text by Engels, Marx establishes that the erroneous theoretical assumption on which the Banking Act of 1844 rests is an offspring of 'Ricardo's wrong assumption that gold is simply specie and that consequently the whole of the imported gold is used to augment the money in circulation thus causing prices to rise, and that the whole of the gold exported represents a decrease in the amount of specie and thus causes prices to fall' (683). This chapter is one of the few where Engels makes several explanatory glosses on Marx's analysis. Nonetheless, the insertions are clearly indicated and consistent with the analytical thrust of the chapter. With the exception of Engels's unfortunate changing of the title of *Capital* III, the editing he undertook in preparing the text for publication does not detract from the work or distort Marx's analysis. See Fred Moseley's introduction to Marx's recently published unedited material for this volume in Karl Marx, *The Economic Manuscript of 1864–1865: Capital, Book Three: Forms [Gestaltungen] of the Process as a Whole*, ed. Fred Moseley, trans. Ben Fowkes, Brill, 2015.

28   Ricardo's 'currency theory' is refuted directly by Marx in *A Contribution to the Critique of Political Economy*, and step by step in theory across *Capital* III.

But why institute such a law? What motivation underwrites a policy that, when money becomes scarce following a crisis in the context of sclerotic circulation, artificially restricts the movement of money even further, 'thereby accelerating and intensifying the crisis' instead of abolishing it? (689). The answer is revealed in its 'secondary' consequence: the elevation of interest rates to new heights. Less money in circulation entails that loan capital is scarcer, which in turn inflates the price of that capital-commodity (i.e., the rate of interest) to the benefit of the money capitalist. As Marx points out, this is, again, an expression of the perceptual conflation of the movement of loan capital with real capital, which infers that the availability of both is equally reflected in the 'discount rate' – that is, the rate of interest, or price of loan capital. And yet, as we have already determined, the scarcity of loan capital can actually (and in times of crisis *does*) coexist with an abundance of idle productive capital:

> The contention that commodity prices are governed by fluctuations in the total amount of 'currency' is now concealed beneath the phrase that the fluctuations in the discount rate [of interest] express fluctuations in the demand for actual material capital, as distinct from money capital ... This is in actual fact the old humbug that changes in the quantity of gold, since they increase or decrease the amount of means of circulation in a country, must necessarily raise or lower commodity prices there ... In actual fact, a decline in the amount of gold simply raises the rate of interest, while an increase lowers it. (685)

Restriction of the amount of gold in circulation 'simply raises the rate of interest' and, as Marx states, a 'high rate of interest was precisely the aim of the Act' (694). As the testimony before the Bank Acts Committee of 1857 illustrates, it made 'money-lending a most profitable pursuit' and 'afforded a rich harvest to bankers and money-capitalists' (694), even as it intensified and prolonged the duration of the crisis itself. However, as Overstone's testimony demonstrates (worth quoting in full), the rich harvest of the money-capitalist was presented then, as it is today, as the expression of greater wealth and prosperity for all:

> By strict and prompt adherence to the principles of the Act of 1844, everything has passed off with regularity and ease, the monetary

system is safe and unshaken, the prosperity of the country is undisputed, the public confidence in the wisdom of the Act of 1844 is daily gaining strength, and if the Committee wish for further practical illustration of the soundness of the principles on which it rests, or of the beneficial results which it has ensured, the true and sufficient answer to the Committee is, look around you, look at the present state of the trade of this country . . . look at the contentment of the people, look at the wealth and prosperity which pervades every class of the community, and then having done so, the Committee may be fairly called upon to decide whether they will interfere with the continuance of an Act under which those results have been developed. (698)

Four months later, Parliament suspended the act in response to the ensuing crisis, in Engels's words, 'in order to save what could still be saved' (698).

The Beautiful Theoretical Dualism (or, The Material Idealism of Gold Convertibility)

Each part of *Capital* III takes a distinct step in the elaboration of capital as a mode of socialized production truncated by the strictures of private property. Each step examines a different set of formations that emerge when producers, in general, do not produce for themselves but rather 'exchange qualitatively different use-values with one another in order to satisfy their needs' (707).[29] Social production generates what Marx calls a collective 'confidence' or 'faith' in the system – the necessary working assumption that the market will, by in large, deliver what we need (707; 727). But the conditions of private property – formal equality before the law – impose the necessity of exchanging *equivalents*, the necessary appearance that no one party receives more or less than what they have alienated, that is, that no one receives more than that to which they are entitled. Under this imperative, in a mode of generalized exchange, qualitatively different things must be rendered as equal things. Value is the form in which qualitatively different use-values are transformed into

---

29   This sentence was inserted into Marx's text by Engels.

quantitative equivalents; value is the function of abstraction through which all commodities are made exchangeable.

Value performs this function by taking the form of the general equivalent – of money – in one moment of its continuous movement. Generalized exchange sweats money from every pore. From the universe of commodities – that is, from the logical infinity of exchangeable equivalents – one commodity must step forward as universal equivalent. *Which* commodity is not a matter of logic but, rather, a matter of practical and historical rationality; practical reasons made precious metal, if not an inevitable, a historically rational development. Gold (and to a lesser extent silver) takes on the role of equalized mass of social/abstract labour time, the role of universal-equivalent designate, the role of the money commodity (648). We know from *Capital* I (chapters one to three) that money, as a function, is formless. However, in its function as the measure of value, money must take form. Money is coincident with its form as the *embodiment* of value, as the autonomized expression of social wealth. Money, as the body of the value of every commodity, must therefore be a definite and equitable magnitude of socially necessary labour time.[30] For practical reasons, then, the material that serves as money must also be divisible; that is to say, the money's material form must be able to be turned into units of measurement. In the history of global capital, by circumstance, gold becomes money, the body of value:

> In what way are gold and silver distinguished from other forms of wealth? Not by magnitude, for this is determined by the amount of labour embodied in them. But rather as autonomous embodiments and expressions of the *social* character of wealth ... This social existence that it has thus appears as something beyond, as a thing, object or commodity outside and alongside the real elements of social wealth. (707)

However, the coincident body/form of money – its autonomization and 'thingness' in gold – makes money's form finite, subject to the physics of space and time and, consequently, entirely incompatible with

---

30   The symbolization of money's embodied form in fiat money, and the subsequent digitalization of its symbolic form, makes it *falsely appear* as if it *need not* take form, as if it is not a congealed magnitude of value.

a system oriented to logically infinite growth. This is what Marx calls 'the beautiful theoretical dualism' (707); it is a 'beautiful dualism' that Marx also refers to as a 'grotesque form of absurd contradiction' (708): in a capitalist mode of production, social wealth must take the form of something other than its real (immaterial but objective) elements. But that *something other* – gold, the money commodity – in which social wealth is expressed is vastly more limited as a magnitude of value than the social wealth produced by the system, that is, the totality of social wealth as a magnitude of value:

> A certain quantity of metal that is insignificant in comparison with production as a whole is the acknowledged pivot of the system. Hence, on top of the terrifying illustration of this pivotal character in crises, the beautiful theoretical dualism. As long as it claims to treat 'of capital', enlightened economics looks down on gold and silver with the utmost disdain, as the most indifferent and useless form of capital. As soon as it deals with banking, however, this is completely reversed, and gold and silver become capital *par excellence*, for whose preservation every other form of capital and labour have to be sacrificed. (707, first emphasis added)

The finitude of money's embodied form compels the emergence of the credit system. Credit is a means to work around the beautiful dualism of money's value form, a way to delay its material discipline – or avoid it altogether, as when credit functions, in circulation, *like* money. Recall that if A owes one hundred pounds to B, B owes one hundred pounds to C, and C owes one hundred pounds to A, one circulating note of credit can resolve each of these debts and eliminate the need for money to intervene at any stage. Again, as Marx explains, the structural possibility for credit to stand in for the circulation of money is the means by which accumulation expands beyond its inherent limit established by the money-form itself. Capitalist growth is facilitated by credit and faith: 'Credit . . . displaces money and usurps its position. It is confidence in the social character of production that makes the money form of products appear as something merely evanescent and ideal, as a mere notion' (707–8). That the capitalist system pivots on money, a reliance from which it cannot break free, animates the development of both the credit system and, as we will see, fiat money.

However, in crisis, credit as well as forms of fictitious capital (claims to future value) search frantically, once again, for the security of money – they seek their metamorphosis into real value – as they must do, or collapse as unsaleable. As Marx states, 'It must never be forgotten . . . that money in the form of precious metal remains the foundation from which the credit system can *never* break free, by the very nature of the case' (741). In the context of crisis, faith is broken and the credit system's ultimate dependency on real value is reasserted:

> But as soon as credit is shaken, and this is a regular and necessary phase in the cycle of modern industry, all real wealth is supposed to be actually and suddenly transformed into money, into gold and silver – a crazy demand, but one that necessarily grows out of the system itself. And the gold and silver that is supposed to satisfy these immense claims amounts in all to a few millions in the vaults of the bank. A drain of gold, therefore, shows strikingly by its effects that production is not really subjected to social control, as social production, and that the social form of wealth exists alongside wealth itself as a *thing* . . . it is only with [the capitalist] system that the most striking and grotesque form of this absurd contradiction and paradox arises . . . because with the development of the credit system, capitalist production constantly strives to overcome this metallic barrier, which is both a material and an imaginary barrier to wealth and its movement, while time and again breaking its head on it. (708)

If, as Marx asserts, money can never be separated from its commodity form, how is it the case that money routinely functions separated from its commodity form? To state the obvious, we do not carry out our daily market transactions with gold, and neither does industry, nor does the state. This was already the case in Marx's day; by that time, as today, credit operations and fiat money had already displaced gold as the typical means of payment and in domestic circulation; gold continued to be used only as world money in international trade, as it did until 1971. The obsolescence of money that circulates in the body of gold – the anachronism of so-called 'commodity-money' – particularly since the suspension of US dollar-to-gold convertibility, is a matter of fact. It is widely perceived today that so-called 'valueless credit money' and 'valueless fiat money' have entirely usurped the role of gold as 'commodity-money'. The claim has been grounds for concocting theories where the production of surplus-value carries on as before, but now (somehow) with money no longer functioning as the universal equivalent, or where the value form (and value theory) are now redundant.

The term 'commodity-money' is sometimes used to connote the form of gold as world money, again, a form now obsolete. 'Commodity-money', in these theories, signifies a chronology, 'the path of development of the form of money', differentiating a historical period when money took the legal form of gold from the current period characterized by the suspension of convertibility and the dominance of 'other forms of valueless money', such as credit money and fiat money.[31] However, these theories are departures from Marx's analysis: in all stages of capitalist development, money is the function of universal equivalence and expresses, in every instance, a definite magnitude of value, a quantification of pure sociality. Even though, historically, gold is the commodity that steps forward to perform the function of money, the function itself is 'purely imaginary' (649) and takes place in the presence *or absence* of the 'palpable and real bodily form' of gold.[32] Marx articulates the idealism of the money-form most emphatically in *Capital* I: 'The price or money-form of commodities is, like their form of value generally, quite distinct from their palpable and real bodily form; it is therefore a purely ideal or notional form'.[33] Every commodity is equated with gold, but the equation is 'a purely ideal act, [and] we may use purely imaginary or ideal gold to perform this operation':

> Every owner of commodities knows that he is nowhere near turning them into gold when he has given their value the form of a price or of imaginary gold, and that it does not require the tiniest particle of real gold to give a valuation in gold of millions of pounds' worth of commodities. In the function as measure of value, money therefore serves only in an imaginary or ideal capacity. This circumstance has

31   Costas Lapavitsas's terms in 'Money and the Analysis of Capitalism: The Significance of Commodity Money', *Review of Radical Political Economics* 32(4), 2000, 631–56.

32   Karl Marx, *Capital: A Critique of Political Economy*, vol. 1, trans. Ben Fowkes, Penguin, 1990, 189.

33   Ibid.

given rise to the wildest theories. But, although the money that performs the function of a measure of value is only imaginary, the price depends entirely on the actual substance that is money. The value, i.e. the quantity of human labour, which is contained in a ton of iron is expressed by an imaginary quantity of the money commodity [i.e., gold] which contains the same amount of labour as the iron. Therefore, according to whether it is gold, silver or copper which is serving as the measure of value, the value of the ton of iron will be expressed by very different prices, or will be represented by very different [but imaginary!] quantities of those metals.[34]

'Convertibility', in this sense, is an imaginary process, before and after 1971. Much has been made, understandably, of the changes to the legal and institutional forms of money signified by this date, and the speculative pathologies they introduce. However, a transformation in money's superstructure is not necessarily an index of a transformation of money's internal dynamics; the suspension of formal convertibility demands, as much, a theory of continuity as transformation. Forms of credit and fiat money are not money per se but, rather, legally guaranteed representatives of money: 'Credit [and fiat] money is itself only money in so far as it absolutely represents real money to the sum of its nominal value' (648). Credit and fiat money are symbolizations that stand in for money's value form, that is, that represent the absent, palpable body of gold, deferring its presence indefinitely. Gold haunts the circulation of capital after formal convertibility as it did before. In fact, after 1971, we are closer to the truth of money's ideal function in practice. But this situation requires even more confidence in a system that, at the same time, becomes increasingly volatile.

A commodity's price (its money-form) is expressed by the value of the money-commodity (gold). Like all commodities, the value of gold is a historical index of social productivity; its value will decline as social productivity rises. A change in the value of gold, as universal equivalent, is expressed as a change in the price of other commodities. But, at all stages of capitalist development (and, of course, long before the suspension of gold convertibility as formal and legal policy), the total social product, and therefore the total money in circulation as an ideal

---

34   Ibid., 190.

magnitude, exceeds the existing supply of gold in circulation and reserve. The practical impossibility of the conversion of the total notional sums of circulating credit and fiat money into actual gold is therefore a structural dimension of the system at all times. Even so, according to Marx, 'it must never be forgotten . . . that money in the form of precious metal remains the foundation from which the credit system can *never* break free, by the very nature of the case' (741). The system expresses a theoretical dualism: money is the universal equivalent per se, and credit derives from money; the idea that either can 'break free' from the function of equivalence is, in capital's terms, nonsensical. At the same time, the function of universal equivalence is an idealism in essence, and while the entity that steps forward to perform that role *must* – by logical necessity – be a commodity, money can always potentially break free, under given circumstances, from its phenomenal body in the commodity, gold.

Marx's value-theory of money is therefore inherently a theory of crisis by nature of the object. The commodity nominated to perform (ideally) as money can only be 'valueless' in a post-capitalist scenario – that is to say, when value itself is obsolete as a mode of sociality. Before that time, the impossibility of absolute convertibility confers an imperative on the collective faith that upholds the credit system. In times of crisis, faith is shaken, and for capital's reproduction it is more urgent to restore the bonds of debt than it is to avoid the devaluation of existing commodity capital:

> A devaluation of credit money . . . would destroy all the existing relationships. The value of commodities is thus sacrificed in order to ensure the fantastic and autonomous existence of this value in money. In any event, a money value is only guaranteed as long as money itself is guaranteed. This is why many millions' worth of commodities have to be sacrificed for a few millions in money. This is unavoidable in capitalist production, and forms one of its particular charms. In former modes of production, this does not happen, because given the narrow basis on which these move, neither credit nor credit money is able to develop. As long as the *social* character of labour appears as the *monetary existence* of the commodity and hence as a *thing* outside actual production, monetary crises, independent of real crises or as an intensification of them, are unavoidable. (649)

The contradictory nature of the system is such that the only response to crisis deepens the conditions for volatility on a wider scale. In crisis, when 'we get the demand that all bills of exchange, securities and commodities should be simultaneously convertible into bank money all at once, and this bank money again into gold', the only response that can 'alleviate the ensuing panic' is to release more credit money into the system – in fact, to double down on the system's Protestant faith against its Catholic aversion to credit's inherent risk (708). To restrict credit, and thereby increase its price, serves the interests of the money capitalist only and undermines that of the merchant and industrialist. This is what the suspension of the Bank Act of 1844 and the suspension of Bretton Woods in 1971 have in common; the drain of gold and the squeeze of mandatory convertibility serves one faction of the capitalist class while putting the greater system under critical strain. The suspension of the Bank Act of 1844 in response to the crisis of 1847 subordinated the interests of the likes of Lord Overstone to the needs of the system, just as President Nixon's abolition of gold-backed world money in 1971 subordinated the interests of the money capitalist to the merchant and industrial factions of the US capitalist class. A few years later, the so-called Volcker shock of 1979 (the dramatic raising of interest rates in an effort to slow down the US economy) would reverse the balance of power in favour of the money capitalist once again in the battle of competing capitals.

Conclusion: From Usury to a New Sociality

Money's haunting of exchange – simultaneously present and absent in its duty – is determined by its substance as social wealth (a social *relation*), the excrescence of a particular mode of production. We can tell the story of the becoming of capitalist money through the figure of interest-bearing capital emerging from its pre-capitalist ancestral mode of usury. The historical process that subordinates the practice of usury to interest-bearing capital is also the transformation of money into capitalist money per se. Or, we might describe it as the transformation of an immediate and transparent social relation into a mediated one, a practice and social relation that takes the appearance of a thing – one that stands outside of, and apart from, its own social substance. It is the historical process of usury's subordination to an emerging sociality.

Usurer's capital is the archaic form of interest-bearing capital; it 'belongs together with its twin brother, merchant's capital, to the antediluvian forms of capital which long precede the capitalist mode of production' (728). Usurer's capital presupposes and indexes several circumstances: (1) the 'predominance of petty production' (729); (2) a developing system of merchant trade; (3) the production of a surplus that takes the form of commodities – a surplus product that becomes the source of the usurer's profit; and (4) a 'professional hoarder' of wealth who functions as money-lender (728). The characteristic modality of usurer's capital is the appropriation of a portion of the borrower's wealth generated through the latter's enterprise, whether this is petty production or rent on land. By and large, usury involves lending money for a price to landed proprietors, and to small producers (artisans and peasants) who own their means of production. As immediate appropriation, and therefore not yet a modality of accumulation, the growth of usurer's capital is had at the cost of the impoverishment of both landed proprietor and petty producer. Usurer's capital expands into the primitive hoard that prefigures the function of the money capitalist. We recognize this lineage only in retrospect, that is, as an accident of history and not as teleology (729). The hoard of the usurer comes at the ruin of the landed proprietor, the artisan producer and the peasant, as it confronts them all as individual producers who own their means of production. For the artisan and the peasant, the emergence of capitalist production is the inversion of this situation; as Marx describes it in *Capital* I, it is a history of separation:

> Usurer's capital . . . corresponds to the predominance of . . . peasants and small master craftsmen working for themselves. Where, as in the developed capitalist mode of production, the conditions of production and the product of labour confront the worker as capital, he does not have to borrow any money in his capacity as producer. When he does borrow, this is for personal necessity, as at the pawnshop. When the worker is, on the other hand, the proprietor of his conditions of labour and his product, in reality or in name, then it is as a producer that he relates to the money-lender's capital, which confronts him as usurer's capital. (729)

As a pre-capitalist relation, the usurer determines the magnitude of the peasant's (or landed proprietor's or artisan's) surplus-value by being in a position to take some or all of their product. In Marx's words, usury 'has capital's mode of exploitation without its mode of production' (732). By appropriating all surplus-value, or at least more than is required to sustain the reproduction of the borrower and their product, the usurer 'cripples the productive forces instead of developing them', 'undermines and ruins small peasant and petty-bourgeois producers', destroys ancient and feudal property, and thusly prepares the ground for 'a real revolution in the mode of production itself' (731). In this way, usury introduces the conditions for the formation of capital. It becomes a transitional force in the succession of traditional forms of wealth (wealth in kind, such as property or labour) by *socialized* forms of wealth (wealth-as-value, abstract wealth, money and commodities): 'Where the means of production are fragmented, usury centralizes monetary wealth. It does not change the mode of production, but clings on to it like a parasite and impoverishes it' (731). This is not an inevitable course of history but rather one of chance and opportunity:

> It is only when and where the other conditions for the capitalist mode of production are present that usury appears as one of the means of formation of this new mode of production, by ruining the feudal lords and petty production on the one hand, and by centralizing the conditions of labour on the other. (732)

The usurer's expropriation of the worker's conditions of labour does not yet assume the movement of capital, but we can consider it 'the presupposition from which it [capital] proceeds' (730).

In the destruction of the traditional mode of production, capital carries forward the practice of usury as form, empties it of its pre-capitalist social content, and fills it with a *new* social content.[35] Crucially,

---

35 'What distinguishes interest-bearing capital ... from usurer's capital is in no way the nature or character of this capital itself. It is simply the changed conditions under which it functions, and hence also the totally transformed figure of the borrower who confronts the money-lender. Even where a man without means obtains credit as an industrialist or merchant, it is given in the expectation that he will function as a capitalist, will use the capital borrowed to appropriate unpaid labour. He is given credit as a potential capitalist' (735).

usury 'brings about the formation of monetary wealth independent of landed property'; this is the initiation of 'wealth in general' – that is, wealth as social abstraction (732–3). The alchemy of value emerges from the ground of these new circumstances: the development of the product as commodity, money as the (autonomized) body in which every commodity expresses its value, (autonomized) money as means of payment, and credit as payment delayed (733). The usurer's hoard is money that can be lent to producers and merchants, expanding the production process among those emergent capitalists that remain standing in the ruins of the old mode of production.[36] The value form permeates the social ground ever more deeply.

In this historical process that will eventually stand the traditional social relation of usury on its head, the needs of the usurer-cum-money-capitalist are eventually subordinated to the viability of accumulation, that is, to commodity production as value-machine, and to the self-valorizing capacity of abstract wealth: 'The credit system develops as a reaction against usury ... It means neither more nor less than the subordination of interest-bearing capital to the conditions and requirements of the capitalist mode of production' (735). Usury may continue to be practiced 'in the pores' of the new mode of production (733), as it does to this day, but it does so as exception, no longer playing a determining role in reproduction. 'In the modern credit system, interest-bearing capital becomes adapted on the whole to the conditions of capitalist production' (735), and in the capitalist mode, instead of the usurer's 'take' determining the profit of the borrower, the money capitalist's profit is determined by the rate of interest – a legal claim on a portion of the total social surplus and, therefore, determined by the magnitude of that total surplus.

The lending of money for a price to immediate producers presupposes a pre-capitalist relation between lender and borrower (745). Loaning money at the rate of interest to industrial and merchant capitalists, as buyers of labour-power, presupposes the predominance of a capitalist mode of production. In the capitalist mode, every occasion of lending situates the borrower as capitalist and, therefore, as subject to the rate of interest, regardless of whether or not the borrowed money is put in

---

36 Or it is the usurer who becomes the new capitalist in expropriating the wealth of those who do not remain standing.

motion as capital. The peasant or petty producer, in their ruin, are succeeded by the wage-labourer, now a wage-slave but no longer a debt-slave in the earlier guise of immediate producer. The petty producer-cum-wage-labourer now enters the relation of debt-slavery only as a consumer. But, despite transforming the economic landscape by the dramatic increase in borrowing to meet subsistence needs, consumer credit does not recalibrate the internal movement of capital. What it does represent is a means of pushing of the price of commodities above their value, the difference redistributed to the pocket of the money capitalist. The price of the fridge is higher when we buy it on credit, and a university education costs more when we take out student loans to pay for it. Despite appearances, the dynamic of the swindling is consistent: an opportunistic hike in the price of food, tuition, transportation, health care, and so on that Marx calls secondary exploitation – a deeper reach into the pockets of workers, and a redistribution of that social wealth to the capitalist class:

> In this way the internal articulation of the capitalist mode of production is completely misconstrued ... The distinguishing thing here again is whether they are loaned to the immediate producers ... or whether they are loaned to industrial capitalists ... It is ... irrelevant and senseless to drag in the renting of houses, etc. for individual consumption. It is plain enough that the working class is swindled in this form too, and to an enormous extent; but it is equally exploited by the petty trader who supplies the workers with means of subsistence. *This is secondary exploitation, which proceeds alongside the original exploitation that takes place directly within the production process itself. The distinction between selling and lending here is completely immaterial and formal, and ... appears fundamental only for those who are in complete ignorance of the real context.* (744–5, my emphasis)

The immense inflation of consumer credit now required to cover the costs of everyday life for most people alters the surface appearance of capitalist society dramatically and introduces seemingly infinite new opportunities for the appropriation of wealth on the part of the money capitalist. However, as Marx points out, the secondary exploitation of consumer credit is carried out alongside the original exploitation; and the movement of determination, in a capitalist mode of production, is consistently from exploitation in production to expropriation by credit.[37]

More than with capital's other social forms, 'it lies in the very nature of the matter that interest-bearing capital should appear to the popular mind as the form of capital *par excellence*' (744). As we explored in the case of its twin form, merchant's capital, the merchant's involvement in setting capital in motion – buying, selling, supervising, and so on – generates the appearance that the capitalist 'works' for their profits, that ingenuity is the magical source of capital's expansion. In the case of interest-bearing capital, there is no such mitigating activity; the separation between owning capital and setting it in motion is complete, and 'the self-reproducing character of capital, self-valorizing value, the production of surplus-value, appears as a purely occult quality' (744). But the purity of interest-bearing capital's occult quality is an expression of its purely social constitution:

> The social character of capital is mediated and completely realized only by the full development of the credit and banking system . . . It places all available and even potential capital that is not already actively committed at the disposal of the industrial and commercial capitalists, so that neither the lender nor the user of this capital are its owners or producers. It thereby abolishes the private character of capital and thus inherently bears within it, though only inherently, the abolition of capital itself. (742)

Once again, we face a beautiful theoretical dualism: interest-bearing capital is immanent to a capitalist mode of production and, as such, drives 'its development into its highest and last possible form' – a mode of production of associated producers. The social character of interest-bearing capital is purely capitalist in its drive *beyond* capital, towards its dialectical and utopian abolition.

---

37 See Beverley Best, 'Political Economy through the Looking Glass: Imagining Six Impossible Things about Finance before Breakfast', *Historical Materialism* 25 (3), 2017, 76–100.

6

Transformation of Profit III: Ground-Rent

What Ground-Rent Is, and Is Not – Differential Rent and Its Forms – Differential Rent I – Differential Rent II – Three Cases of Differential Rent II: The Cause and (Mediated) Effect of Productivity and Price – Absolute Ground-Rent – Conclusion: Capital's Self-Image in Embryonic, Pre-capitalist Forms of Rent

For several reasons, Marx's chapters on the transformation of surplus profit into ground-rent pose a greater challenge to exposition than the other chapters in *Capital* III. The analysis in part VI is more 'unfinished' than in other parts: Marx's arguments are less synthesized and more in draft form; the order of the sections flows less intuitively; the purpose of the long discussion of differential rent is elusive at first, even though the relatively few commentators on these sections have identified them as the most original aspect of Marx's treatment of ground-rent.[1] One challenge to comprehension presented by the chapters on differential rent is that they are largely driven by a polemical engagement with the economic arguments of David Ricardo.[2] On the one hand, this comportment of debate is typical of the

---

1 See Michael Ball, 'Differential Rent and the Role of Landed Property', *International Journal of Urban and Regional Research* 1(3), 1977, 380-403; Ben Fine, 'On Marx's Theory of Agricultural Rent', *Economy and Society* 8(3), 1979, 241–78; and David Harvey, *Limits to Capital*, Verso, 2018.

2 Marx, in a letter to Engels: 'The only thing I have got to prove theoretically is the possibility of absolute rent, without violating the law of value. This is the point

entire study, which proceeds simultaneously as both an analysis of the movement of capital and a critique of bourgeois political economic thought.[3] On the other hand, polemics take up even more space in part VI in an effort, as Marx suggests, to deal theoretically with the 'mass of facts that contradict the concept and nature of ground-rent and yet appear as its modes of existence' – modes of existence that are reflected in, and rationalized by, the commentaries of the bourgeois economists of Marx's day:

> Important as it is for the scientific analysis of ground-rent – i.e. the autonomous, specific economic form of landed property on the basis of the capitalist mode of production – to consider it in pure form and free from all adulterations and blurring admixtures, it is just as important for understanding the practical effects of landed property and even for theoretical insight into a mass of facts that contradict the concept and nature of ground-rent and yet appear as its modes of existence, to know the elements from which these obscurities in the theory arise. (762)

In differentiating his analysis, Marx submerges into the details of the movement of differential rent, rarely re-emerging to paint a totalizing picture of their significance. The effect for the reader can be to lose sight of the forest for the trees (or to fail to locate the forest in the first place). On top of this, as Engels demonstrates, Marx's numerous mathematical tables are often inaccurate in their calculations (if sound in logic) and require revision, which Engels provides. Rather than give a comprehensive examination of the tables' calculations and their revisions, in this chapter I stick to pointing out the dynamic that Marx illustrates with them, and how this dynamic expresses a certain perceptual inversion – the *same* perceptual physics – that is the through line of Marx's exposition in *Capital* III.

The material that constitutes part VI is distinctive in another respect: its subject matter – the social form of capital as private property in land;

---

around which the theoretical controversy has turned from the days of the Physiocrats up till now. Ricardo denies this possibility. I maintain that it exists.' Quoted in Harvey, *Limits to Capital*, 349.

3   I am not suggesting that Marx's critique is simply a matter of polemics; however, it sometimes takes the immediate form of polemical engagements with other thinkers and commentators.

the appearance and modality of land as 'source' of capitalist wealth – is both timely and untimely. Its timeliness lies in the ongoing development of capital's inherent movement towards overaccumulation, which today redirects surplus capital, searching for profitable investment in the context of chronic and structural stagnation, towards the acquisition of land, and of other forms of rent-seeking property – intellectual, digital, or technological.[4] Capital's desperate appropriation of land and rent-seeking assets – encouraged, facilitated, and sometimes carried out by nation-states – bears out Fredric Jameson's claim that 'today, all politics is about real estate. Postmodern politics is essentially a matter of land grabs, on a local as well as global scale.'[5] Radical critique and activism, responding to this aspect of the historical conjuncture, find in it a means to demonstrate the through line of dispossession that articulates colonialism and the early modern enclosures with the modalities of contemporary global capitalism. At the heart of both the enclosures and the colonial project were two valences of a single process: (1) the appropriation of land and its resources for wealth creation; and (2) the separation of original inhabitants from the land and the resources that constituted their means of subsistence and way of life, creating bonded, enslaved, racialized and subalternized, and eventually waged workforces from among those who survived the process, in addition to those made 'surplus' and forced to survive, where possible, in the interstices of the developing global market. As critics and activists rightly observe, both modalities of dispossession persist to this day, where private property in land – for so-called agri-capitalism, for real estate development and

---

4   Capital's ongoing struggle to reproduce itself on its own narrow conditions of profitability excretes observations of the emergence of 'new kinds' of capitalism such as platform capitalism, circulatory capitalism, or even suggestions of the transition to a new mode of production altogether – for instance, one organized around the control of information. Sometimes these proliferating analyses take capital's own reflection and self-presentation at face value. Other times, theorists of informational capitalism do recognize that capital reinvents itself in the sphere of competition in dramatically altered phenomenal forms and appearances for the very purpose of preserving its exploitative relation with living labour (while jeopardizing its reproductive viability in the process). For a good characterization of how digital platforms have allowed certain large companies to both invent new goods and services to sell *and* redistribute/appropriate significant portions of the total social value by putting digital platforms to work as interest-bearing capital, see Nick Srnicek, *Platform Capitalism*, Polity, 2017.

5   Fredric Jameson, *An American Utopia: Dual Power and the Universal Army*, Verso, 2016, 13.

speculation, for extraction industries such as oil and mining – reproduces capital, from its earliest formations to the present, as an ongoing history of separation. The material in part VI of *Capital* III is foundational for situating at the centre of this narrative of continuity the emergence of capital as private property in land.

However, Marx's analysis of ground-rent also provides the means of theorizing the trajectory from colonialism to globalized capital as a narrative of *inversion*. To draw out this second narrative (the reverse side of the first) requires, as I have been describing throughout this book, that we expose the invisible compulsions that animate the surface appearances of capital, revealing the movement of what Marx calls the automatic fetish. Colonialism and the enclosures ('so-called primitive accumulation'), together with the development of trade and the world market, made possible and compelled the emergence of capitalist production, which is also to say, the emergence of capitalist property and a historically new mode of accumulation that Marx calls exploitation. As historical forms and categories, exploitation derives from dispossession. However, the history and process of capital's emergence – the emergence of exploitation as the demeanour of capitalist production and the *outcome* of dispossession – is also the history and process of the logical *subordination* of dispossession to exploitation, of the reversal of their formal and categorial derivation. In a capitalist mode of production 'full blown', dispossession is now mediated by exploitation, in that the profit that falls to those who own land or rent-seeking assets is *always*, if indirectly and invisibly, a portion of surplus-value that is produced in productive enterprise. In other words, with capital, exploitation becomes the submerged but determining logic of ongoing acts of dispossession that, on the surface, may appear to be carried out as before. In a capitalist mode of production, even violence becomes a social form whose social substance departs from its surface appearances.

In this process of inversion, land and its resources are transformed from forms of wealth in kind – forms of wealth in and of themselves – to forms of capital as means of production, that is, as titles to a portion of future, anticipated profit produced elsewhere. Land and its resources are transformed, quite literally, into means to an heteronomous end. As capital investments, they represent constant capital when their owner mobilizes them directly, or interest-bearing capital when they are leased rather than alienated outright. In both cases, they are value forms that must now confront capital in the form of living labour (variable capital), somewhere in their reproductive cycle, in order to participate in accumulation. The timeliness of Marx's analysis of ground-rent for today lies in its persistent exposure of the hidden capitalist logic of contemporary modes of dispossession as the inverse of their pre- and emerging capitalist expressions. To grasp this historical process of inversion, for instance, is to fathom why there is no capitalist or capitalist-state resolution of indigenous land claims.[6] There is no 'ground' (so to speak) for reconciling land in its pre- or post-capitalist form as wealth in kind and held in common, with land in its (capitalist) form as means of production.[7] As Marx demonstrates, the expropriation of the mass of people from the land – of immediate producers from their means of reproduction – is the 'permanent foundation' of a capitalist mode of production; it is a necessary continuity from capital's first day to its last (754). However, capital, in the process of turning expropriation into a means of creating wealth, compels the *inversion* of what is expropriated. Landed property is transformed into an economic form that corresponds with capital itself and its identical modality, exploitation of living labour.

If Marx's analysis of ground-rent is thus timely, its time is also out of joint. The characteristics of the production processes of industries that involve land (or sea, in some cases) as means of production and hence produce ground-rent – for Marx, agriculture, mining, forestry, fishing and, for us, oil extraction is added to the list – have changed dramatically since Marx's theorization of them.[8] This has not been the case with any of capital's social forms that we have looked at so far. Marx points out that these industries in question are interchangeable at the deep core of abstraction where we situate the analysis of ground-rent; nonetheless, in

---

6   For instance, to use Jasbir K. Puar's words, there can only be a 'no-state solution' to indigenous land claims in the territories occupied by the Canadian state. Jasbir K. Puar, 'A No-State Solution: Palestine and the Question of Queer Theory', lecture at Concordia University, Montreal, January 30, 2020.

7   See Glen Sean Coulthard, *Red Skin, White Masks: Rejecting the Colonial Politics of Recognition*, University of Minnesota Press, 2014; Leanne Betasamosake Simpson, *As We Have Always Done: Indigenous Freedom through Radical Resistance*, University of Minnesota Press, 2017.

8   Marx's definition of land is expansive: 'It should be noted that what we understand here by land also includes water, etc. in so far as this has an owner' (752).

illustrating the latter, Marx focuses on the case of agriculture. Marx's theory of ground-rent is contingent on the capacity of agricultural industry to appropriate a *surplus* profit, a portion of the total social surplus-value over and above that which represents the general rate of profit. This capacity, in Marx's day, was a consequence of agricultural capital's lower organic composition – that is, its higher labour-intensity – than was average for industrial production, in a way particular to agriculture (and/or mining), and whose surplus profit was therefore not absorbed in other spheres of capitalist production by its redistribution through the general rate of profit across the capitalist class. In other words, agricultural profit was not subject to competition across spheres of production in the manner of other forms of industry, which prevented it from participating in the equalization process.

It was historical fact for Marx that agriculture was not yet characterized by mechanization and automation at a scale large enough to allow it to achieve average levels of productivity. Agricultural production always faced obstacles to achieving levels of productivity that characterized manufacture, and this situation persisted up to the time of Marx's study of it:

> The capitalist mode of production takes hold of agriculture only in a slow and uneven manner ... Market price is determined by those producers who work on inferior soil, i.e. producers whose conditions of production are less favourable than the average. A large part of the total capital applied in agriculture, and generally at its disposal, is to be found in their hands ... The peasant, for example, devotes a great deal of labour to his small parcel of land. But this labour is isolated, and deprived of the objective social and material conditions of productivity ... The effect of this factor is that the genuinely capitalist farmers are in a position to appropriate a portion of surplus profit [surplus profit that forms the substance of ground-rent]; *this would disappear ... if the capitalist mode of production were as uniformly developed in agriculture as in manufacture.* (815, my emphasis)

Today, the situation is different: large-scale mechanization/automation is the reality of agricultural production (as well as of mining and oil extraction), as is a high composition of capital investment that tracks the average composition. The question today is, therefore, is farming sufficiently integrated into the wider circuitry of capitalist industry such that capital flows freely between farming enterprises and (potentially) all other capitalist enterprise? Or, put another way: Is agricultural capital an equal player on the battlefield of competing capitals such that the former participates in the formation of the general rate of profit? This question presses an 'updating' of Marx's analysis by observers of contemporary global agricultural, mining, and fossil fuel extraction industries to supply the needed empirical data and to determine the current portion of the total social product represented by the products of these industries. We will return to this question later in the chapter; the more limited objective of this discussion, however, is the exposition of Marx's analysis of the transformation of surplus-value into ground-rent and the attendant fetish of private property in land.

What Ground-Rent Is, and Is Not

Marx's object of analysis in part VI is capital in its social form as private property in land. In working through the material in part VI, it is helpful to keep in mind the specificity of the analysis, the narrowness of the object, and the single-mindedness of Marx's orientation. Here and throughout, Marx's sole intention is to demonstrate that when land becomes capital, the virtually infinite ways in which human beings can be in metabolism with land are subordinated to the exigencies of the capital–labour relation – that is, to the law of value. The transformation of land into capitalist property is established first through direct coercion, then indirectly as economic compulsion, once a capitalist mode of production has subsumed social reproduction more widely, even as traditional and pre-capitalist modalities may continue to exist in the interstices of capital 'full blown': 'The analysis of landed property in its various historical forms lies outside the scope of the present work' (751). As social form, capitalist private property in land presupposes the transformation of landed property from all its pre-capitalist guises; it presupposes land as wealth in kind dissolved by capital as its newly constitutive social substance. Neither the proprietor nor the use of land must necessarily change in order to carry out this historical process, even though, as we have seen, changes in the nature of proprietorship and use of land is almost invariably the case. What transforms land into a capitalist social form is that its proprietor appropriates a portion of the total social surplus-value as a function of that proprietorship. In the exposition of part VI, Marx is concerned with land, as he states, 'only in so far as a portion of the surplus-value that capital produces falls to the share of the landowner' (751). Under such circumstances, presupposing that a capitalist mode of production has taken control of all spheres of production, including agriculture, capital intervenes to transform land into capitalist private property in land, and the landowner into a landowning capitalist.

The circumstances under which land is transformed into a capitalist social form are deeply contradictory: they are narrow and exacting, at the same time as they entail a new social reproductive order of things on a world scale; they are accidental and spontaneous, at the same time as they entail an intentional process of almost-fathomlessly violent separation of immediate producers from the means of their subsistence – the separation of people from land as both preparatory and ongoing condition. As Marx argues, only those bourgeois critics who mistake the narrow and rigorous conditions that constitute capitalist private property in land for eternal, timeless social relations of landed property will object to the narrowness of a study whose objective is the delineation of those rare, violent, and world-ordering conditions:

> If the capitalist mode of production always presupposes the expropriation of the workers from the conditions of labour, in agriculture it presupposes the expropriation of the rural workers [and inhabitants] from the soil and their subjection to [capital personified in] a capitalist who pursues agriculture [or mining, or oil extraction, or real-estate development, etc.] for the sake of profit. It is thus completely immaterial for our presentation if we are reminded that other forms of landed property and agriculture have existed or still exist besides this. This reproach can affect only those economists who treat the capitalist mode of production on the land and the form of landed property corresponding to it not as historical categories but as eternal ones. (751–2)

Moreover, Marx's concern with capitalist landed property in this study is not per se but, rather, as it serves the analysis of the movement of capital more generally – in its concept, before the dimensions of this or that historical conjuncture shape its empirical manifestation. As Marx points out, 'Our analysis of capital would be incomplete' without considering the impact on the movement of capital (i.e., production and exchange) 'from the investment of capital on the land' (752). This latter orientation is to ask, what is the role of landed capital in the formation of a particular form of redistributed portion of surplus-value that Marx calls ground-rent; and, further, what is the impact of ground-rent, if any, on the formation of the general rate of profit? As such, Marx's examination is limited to production at a certain scale – that is, to large-scale agricultural production and large-scale extraction industries – as well as limited to production of a certain kind – that is, to those industries that produce products that have becomes staples among a population's means of subsistence. Only industries that operate on these quantitative and qualitative dimensions intervene on the formation of the general rate of profit and, therefore, have a significant impact on the dynamics established by freely competing capitals, which is to say, on the process of equalization. The question is, to put the matter yet another way: How, in a capitalist mode of production, is land-capital valorized when, as Marx points out, the legal title to land, in itself, explains nothing?

> Landed property presupposes that certain persons enjoy the monopoly of disposing of particular portions of the globe as exclusive spheres of their private will to the exclusion of all others. Once this is given, it is a question of developing the economic value of this monopoly, i.e. valorizing it, on the basis of capitalist production. Nothing is settled with the legal power of these persons to use and misuse certain portions of the globe. The use of this power depends entirely on economic conditions, which are independent of their wills. The legal conception itself means nothing more than that the landowner can behave in relation to the land just as any commodity owner can with his commodities; and this idea – the legal notion of free private landed property – arises in the ancient world only at the time of the dissolution of the organic social order, and arises in the modern world only with the development of capitalist production. (752–3)

This latter process, the dissolution of the organic social order and the development of capitalist production, is both cause and effect, a dialectical process that represents two great unintended services to history and their one tremendous cost: (1) the rationalization of agriculture that enables food security on a social scale (at least as objective possibility, even if unrealized to this day); and (2) the 'reduction of [feudal] landed property [as an expression of divine design] to an absurdity' (755). The tremendous human cost for these services is 'the complete impoverishment of the immediate producers' – if, that is, they survive the process at all. Marx recognizes other ecological costs of capitalist agriculture and extractive industry in the depletion of soil and natural resources such that the pursuit of 'rational agriculture' in its capitalist form becomes an internal contradiction that cancels out the 'service' it potentially provides. Today, in the era of irreversible species extinction, global warming, and the industrial toxification of the global food supply, Marx's ecological warning to future generations resonates as understated:

> The entire spirit of capitalist production, which is oriented towards the most immediate monetary profit, stands in contradiction to agriculture, which has to concern itself with the whole gamut of permanent conditions of life required by the chain of human generations. (754n27)

We will return to examine the historical emergence and dialectical movement of capitalist landed property, and the social form of ground-rent, at the end of the chapter, as we did with merchant's capital and interest-bearing capital. For now, we return to the conditions that stage the question at hand, that constitute capitalist agricultural production, and that generate ground-rent on landed property as the legal form taken by a portion of the total social surplus-value. The presuppositions of capitalist agriculture are the same as those of capitalist production more generally: immediate producers are wage-labourers employed by a farmer-capitalist. If the farmer-capitalist is not also the owner of the land they exploit, they will pay a fixed sum of money at a determined date and interval of time – both contractually fixed – to the landowner-capitalist. Ground-rent is the form taken by the sum of money paid by the farmer to the landowner for the opportunity to exploit the latter's land in the course of productive enterprise. The questions involved in part VI are these: How is ground-rent to be configured with respect to the movement of value? In what ways and by what means does land come to appear and function as capital, and landownership a source of profit, when, within the terms of the law of value, land is valueless? If a theory of ground-rent is coherent with a theory of value, how can value critique reveal that capital investment towards enhancing the fertility of the soil is a matter of increasing not the productivity of land but, rather, the productivity of labour? What sorts of mystifications are generated by the fact that land is the 'reservoir from whose bowels use-values are to be torn', but not a reservoir from which value can be pulled?[9] Finally, if capital is invested in the land for the purpose of increasing its yield, what is the effect of this investment on the production of value and its distribution? Each of these questions is also to ask, what is the *social basis* for the valorization of capitalist landed property?

The dynamics of the mystification of the source of ground-rent and its components as the revenue that falls to the landowner are, of course, Marx's principal concern in part VI. We are not surprised to consider, at this late stage in the analysis, that ground-rent is a mystified portion of the total social surplus-value that finds its way back to the pocket of the landowner in the course of inter-capitalist competition. From *Capital* I, we are already conversant with the idea that rent is a cost of production, and that it constitutes both a means of production and a constant capital investment on the part of the functioning capitalist. Only a slight shift in standpoint is required to see the landowner as sharing in the profit that falls to the functioning capitalist tenant. And, as we know from our discussion in chapter 5, rent is the landowner's 'share of the profit', even if the tenant is not a functioning capitalist at all: the tenant is presupposed as functioning capitalist whether or not they consume the borrowed land-capital productively, in the same way that all those who borrow money step into the structural place of the functioning capitalist whether or not they use that borrowed money capital for consuming means of production or means of subsistence.

While the category of ground-rent, as with each of the economic categories we have looked at so far, was by the early nineteenth century commonplace in both bourgeois political economy and vulgar economic discourse, debate and disagreement circled, then as now, around what constitutes the source and substance of ground-rent. Today, we are more

---

9   Marx, *Theories of Surplus-Value*, part 2; quoted in Harvey, *Limits to Capital*, 335.

familiar with the simplified category of 'rent', using it universally in reference to rent on land as well as other forms of property such as buildings or vehicles (while typically using 'fee' to designate payments for the right to exploit intellectual property). While Marx also uses the category of rent in this more universal way, he distinguishes between rent and ground-rent, the latter designating 'a portion of the surplus product that is both quantitatively and qualitatively specific' to landed property within a capitalist mode of production (770). The more universal category of rent, as distinct from ground-rent, is constituted as that which we established in chapter 5 as the irrational form of interest – irrational in that its rate is derived solely from inter-capitalist competition. Rent is constituted as interest on property – property that is alienated by its owner to the functioning capitalist for a period of time – thereby assuming the form and movement of interest-bearing capital. Just as money (when it is loaned out as capital in the form of a commodity) is valorized as interest (M–M′), other forms of property are valorized as rent, and land, as we will see, is valorized as ground-rent: 'Ground-rent is thus the form in which landed property is economically valorized' (756). One of the invisible 'foreign components' of ground-rent can be the interest that falls to additional capital invested in – incorporated into – the land (in the form of fertilizers, pesticides, genetically modified seed, drainage technology, irrigation systems, etc.) for the purpose of increasing its fertility. In this way, rent, in the form of interest, is both analytically distinct from ground-rent and a possible component of ground-rent. In all cases, however, ground-rent is *not* interest; to confuse ground-rent with interest would be to misconstrue the specific character of ground-rent as one of land-capital's typical mystifying appearances (760).

While ground-rent is always a portion of surplus-value, in its 'pure form' (i.e., in its concept), it is an excess portion of surplus-value *over and above* that congealed in the agricultural product as surplus labour. If, as is the case, the agricultural product is realized (when successfully alienated) by the farmer-capitalist as a commodity-value – a portion of which is surplus-value (surplus labour) expressing the general rate of profit on investment, or production price – ground-rent is a portion of surplus-value in excess of this profit; it is surplus profit, or, a surplus portion of surplus value that is transferred to the landowner in the form of ground-rent. In other words, ground-rent is *surplus* surplus-value that falls to the landowner, and which is a social form specific to production processes in which land is incorporated as a means of production (773). We will look at how this excess portion of surplus-value constituting ground-rent is formed in the discussion of differential rent. For now, we note that its formation leads Marx to argue that 'rent corresponding to the capitalist mode of production' cannot be explained 'simply by explaining the general conditions of existence for surplus-value and profit' (773).

In the distribution of surplus-value between farmer and landowner, ground-rent takes the immediate form of appearance of the lease-price on a piece of earth; lease-price is the payment made 'to the landowner . . . for the use of the soil, whether for productive purposes or those of consumption' (772). In the 'world as it actually is', lease-price appears identical to ground-rent: 'In practice, everything that the farmer pays the landowner in the form of the lease-price for permission to cultivate the soil appears as ground-rent' (762). However, despite appearances, lease-price can comprise other 'foreign components' – other 'adulterations and blurring admixtures' – of additional portions of surplus-value from various mediated sources.[10] It is also possible that the lease-price does not contain any ground-rent whatsoever. If circumstances prevent surplus profit from being realized, the lease-price consists of a portion of the profit that would otherwise fall to the farmer (i.e., a portion of the surplus-value congealed in the product), or, a portion of the wages that would otherwise purchase labour-power. The landowner's 'monopoly to a piece of earth' allows them to extract this lease-price regardless of whether it comprises ground-rent or not (763).

As we know, only products of human labour are values. Land, water, minerals, wind – living labour itself – in capitalist terms are valueless (763; 772). Capital appropriates as 'free gifts' those things that it requires, but which have no value. However, being valueless does not preclude these gifts from having a price. For a thing to have a price, that is, as Marx says, 'for a thing to be sold, it simply has to be capable of being monopolized and alienated' (772). Land is valueless, but it has a price.[11]

---

10   I say 'mediated sources' of surplus-value because, as we know, the ultimate origin of surplus-value, or surplus labour, is always living labour in its productive confrontation with capital (i.e., in its legal form as waged labour).

11   If living labour has a price, it takes the form of slavery.

The price of land is a mystified form derived from its lease-price (and, on a deeper level of abstraction, from ground-rent) as the capitalization of this revenue stream:

> Any particular money income can be capitalized, i.e. can be considered as the interest on an imaginary capital. If the average interest is 5 percent, for example, an annual ground-rent of £200 may be viewed as the interest on a capital of £4,000. It is the ground-rent as capitalized in this way that forms the purchase price or value of the land, a category that is *prima facie* irrational, in the same way that the price of labour is irrational, since the earth is not the product of labour, and thus does not have a value. On the other hand, however, this irrational form conceals a genuine relation of production. (760)

The operative appearance, of course, is the reverse: that rent on land is derived from the 'value' or price of land. Both lease-price and the price of land are empirical forms into which its objective, *social* components disappear; its movement constitutes the objective mystifications of the land-fetish:

> The fact that the capitalized ground-rent presents the appearance of the price or value of land, so that the earth is bought or sold just like any other commodity, provides some apologists with a justification for landed property; the buyer has paid an equivalent for it, as with any other commodity, and the greater part of landed property has changed hands in this way . . . To derive a justification for the existence of ground-rent from its purchase and sale is nothing more than justifying its existence in terms of its existence. (762)

The tendency for the rate of profit to fall, the historical expression of expanding social production capacity that we explored in chapter 3, has an alternative valence in the tendency for the price of land to rise, particularly in periods of deep and protracted economic stagnation.[12]

---

12   This statement is a tautology: deep and protracted economic stagnation *is* the phenomenal form taken by the dynamic of falling profit rates when its inertia has been 'stabilized' over a relatively lengthy period of time – protracted stagnation amounts to relatively stabilized volatility. For a pertinent discussion of the movement of stability, see Michel Serres, *The Birth of Physics*, Rowman & Littlefield, 2018, 82.

The dynamic is in clear evidence today, and especially since 2008: to quote Fredric Jameson's understatement once again, today all politics is about real estate. To illustrate the double valence of this tendency, Marx posits ground-rent as a constant magnitude. With ground-rent constant, 'the price of land will rise or fall in inverse ratio to the rate of interest':

> If the standard rate of interest should fall from 5 percent to 4, an annual ground-rent of £200 would represent the annual valorization of a capital of £5,000 instead of one of £4,000 and so the price of the same piece of land would rise from £4,000 to £5,000. (761)

As we know (from chapter 5), in the context of a surplus of money capital unable to find productive investment, the rate of interest tends to follow the downward trajectory of the rate of profit. A greater magnitude of available money capital puts a downward pressure on the rate of interest. As Marx expounds, 'It follows therefore that the price of land has a tendency to rise, even independently of the movement of ground-rent and the price of the products of the soil' (761).

That the price of landed property is derived from the ground-rent it commands (i.e., that the price of land *is* ground-rent capitalized at the rate of interest) takes a profoundly contradictory expression in the current context of deep and irreversible economic stagnation, low profitability, and crisis-inflected low or negative interest rates. In these conditions, commercial property owners are in a position to secure greater benefits from the financialization of their property – by using property as an asset against which to borrow – than they are from the rents that the property may secure as payment to the property owner from a functioning capitalist, and especially from a small business owner whose profits are often low and precarious. In this instance, the higher the perceived 'value' of the asset (i.e., the higher the price of the landed property), the more advantageous for the purposes of its financialization, and hence the stronger is the motivation to increase the lease-price demanded, even though that lease-price may never materialize as payment. Here, the purpose of high, and often unpayable, commercial rents is to establish a higher 'land-value' against which to borrow. The outcome of this situation is either the eventual (sometimes rapid) destruction of the rent-paying commercial enterprises leasing the property, or the deterrence of viable enterprise altogether, particularly in the case of small and local enterprises. The resulting commercial landscape today is characterized by neighbourhoods with growing numbers of empty shopfronts, and a dearth of viable local business and locally produced goods and services, while property owners redirect ever-larger portions of the total social surplus-value into their own pockets. In part VI (758–9), Marx documents the growing concentration of ownership of landed property as it had developed into the mid-1860s, although he could not have imagined the degree of concentration that presently characterizes the ownership of landed property, where vast majority portions of a city's or country's real estate – commercial and residential – are held in a small number of hands. It is more clearly the case today than ever that 'landed property is distinguished from the other forms of property by the fact that at a certain level of development it appears superfluous and harmful even from the standpoint of the capitalist mode of production' (760).

Capital 'fixed in the earth', or *la terre-capital*, as Marx calls it, is a means of production in agricultural industry that takes the form of fixed capital (756). Further investments of fixed capital (again, in the form of fertilizer, irrigation technology, and so on) can be, and in most cases are, incorporated into the land for the purpose of enhancing, from the farmer's point of view, the fertility of the soil or the facility of the production process, and thereby, from the social standpoint of capital, the productivity of agricultural labour. These 'improvements' can be made either by the landowner (in the case of buildings erected on the land) or the farmer (in the case of fertilizer, designer seed, or drainage technology). As additional fixed-capital investments, they attract interest proportionately; these portions of interest fall to the farmer in the form of increased profits and, eventually, to the landowner in the form of increased ground-rent. From the point of view of capital, the interest on these fixed capitals forms additional, invisible components of ground-rent without actually constituting ground-rent proper.

Before the expiration of the farmer's lease, all interest on these newly incorporated fixed capitals falls back to the farmer. However, after the lease expires, these extra portions of surplus-value fall to the landowner through means of the ownership of an improved piece of earth that now demands a higher ground-rent; the outcome of the fixed-capital investments now becomes the property of the landowner: 'A cultivated field is worth more than an uncultivated one of the same natural quality' (757). As these improvements are now inseparable from the land, and the property of the landowner, they take the form of a now-expanded ground-rent, proper. Eventually, all value generated through the process of improving the soil and its yield – a social process with potentially social benefits – is redistributed away from any socialized advantage and back to the landowner. The topsy-turvy consequence of this historical process of constantly (and logically) expanding rents on land is the increasing enrichment of an otherwise historically redundant class of landowners:

> This is one of the secrets – quite apart from the movement of ground-rent as such – of the increasing enrichment of the landowners, the constant inflation of their rents and the growing money value of their estates as economic development progresses. Thus they put away in their own private purses the result of a social development achieved without their participation . . . But this is equally one of the greatest obstacles to a rational agriculture, since the farmer avoids all improvements and outlays which are not expected to give their full return during the duration of his lease. (757)

There is the possibility, of course, that the farmer-capitalist is also the landowner. Here, ground-rent is still formed, although it becomes an invisible portion of the overall profit that falls to the farmer-capitalist, in the same way that the industrial capitalist pays themselves interest when they own the money capital or the fixed capital that they invest productively. A farmer who is also the landowner stands to absorb a surplus profit over and above the general rate of profit, the *surplus* surplus-value that would otherwise fall to the landowner as ground-rent. When we arrive at the discussion of differential rent, we will see that this (potential) surplus profit is unique to agricultural production (or to industry that incorporates land as a means of production) as a portion of the total social surplus-value that does not enter into the equalization process, whether it falls to the landowner or the farmer-capitalist as landowner.

Despite the possibility that the farmer may also be the landowner, capital's historical drive and necessity – at least in earlier stages of development – is to exploit the internal possibility of splintering its personifications between the farmer-capitalist and the landowner-capi-talist. Capital's ongoing development requires that it take the form of *competing capitals*, even as this competition between capitals animates an irreducible contradiction that continues to throw up obstacles to its own ongoing reproduction (as we explored in chapter 3). Ground-rent, as the economic valorization of land, 'presupposes landed property, the ownership of particular bits of the globe by certain individuals' in all the variety of forms that this 'ownership' has taken in history (772).[13] Capital proceeds to exploit the distinction between the farmer and the proprie-tor of land, which long predates a capitalist mode of production, in order to compel competition between individual capitals and to instil the need to increase productivity on the part of the farmer. The sponta-neous consequence is the crystallization (and subsequent objectification in law) of the transformation of pre-capitalist forms of agriculture into *capitalist* agricultural production, and to contain the potentially wide-spread benefits of social labour in agriculture, not only to the enrich-ment of the landowner but to the reproduction of the capitalist class more generally:

> The level of ground-rent (and with it the value of land) rises in the course of social development, as a result of the overall social labour. Not only does the market and the demand for agricultural products grow, but the demand for land itself also grows directly, since it is a condition of production competed for by all possible branches of business, including non-agricultural ones. (775)

At same time, the splintering off of the landowner and the farmer as the personifications of competing capitals, as agriculture develops in scale and as ground-rent develops in magnitude, exposes the increasing redundancy of the role of the landowner, whose action has no impact whatsoever on this development; indeed, it is entirely the outcome of the 'development of social labour that is independent of him and in which he plays no part' (775). In this way, the socialization of agricultural production that capital makes possible prepares the ground for the real redundancy, and potential elimination, of landownership itself.

---

13 Ground-rent presupposes the 'legal fiction by virtue of which various individuals have exclusive possession of particular parts of the globe' (772).

We have established that ground-rent is not interest – that is, it is not the form of rent that falls to property loaned as fixed, constant, or money capital or, as we might say today, the profits that fall to owners of rent-seeking assets. In other words, the economic valorization of landed property is not constituted as interest-bearing capital. Nor is ground-rent lease-price – which is the empirical form of appearance of ground-rent, as well as the empirical form taken by rent on other forms of property, such as buildings or vehicles. Lease-price on land may contain 'foreign components' of interest, or an extracted portion of wages, or an extracted portion of the surplus product, that would have otherwise constituted the 'full' profit portion of the functioning capitalist. However, at the level of capital's concept, Marx emphasizes that ground-rent is quantitatively and qualitatively distinct from 'surplus labour and hence surplus product in general', if necessarily still consisting of a *mediated* portion of the overall social surplus product (770).

Once again, only a totalized or system-wide standpoint on the movement of capital can bring the observer to the analysis of the substance of any portion of surplus-value that takes the social form of profit or revenue in a capitalist mode of production, including that portion that takes the form of ground-rent. The development that produces this situation reaches back to the organic continuity between agricultural and industrial production characteristic of *all* modes of production: while human reproduction and collectivity presupposes the capacity to produce and procure food, at the same time, the production and procurement of food presupposes and is conditional on the production of tools, instruments, clothing, shelter, and so on. What Marx calls 'indigenous productivity', or the 'indigenous basis of surplus labour in general' (770), refers to the human capacity to produce a quantity of food equivalent to a day's requirement with less than a full day's labour time. In other words, 'indigenous productivity' refers to the human capacity to produce an agricultural surplus product as the basis of the development of human sociality itself.[14]

---

14   Marx returns to this 'natural foundation' for the production of social wealth, including its capitalist form, at the end of part VI: 'The Physiocrats were also correct in seeing all production of surplus-value, and thus also every development of capital, as resting on the productivity of agricultural labour as its natural foundation. If [people] are not even capable of producing more means of subsistence in a working day, and thus in the narrowest sense more agricultural products, than each worker needs for [their]

In chapter 14 of *Capital* I, Marx demonstrates how the emergence of a capitalist mode of production is also the development of a social division of labour, dividing agricultural labour and industrial labour systematically for the first time (logically as well as historically), and founded on the separation of town from country.[15] In this development, the ontological and irreducible reciprocity between agricultural and industrial production becomes the autonomization of both production processes in their social modalities, even as their ongoing growth continues in mutual dependency. An expanding industrial proletariat, which, as we know (from chapter 3), grows in absolute terms, is entirely dependent on the growth in scale of agricultural production – which is also to say, on the productivity of agricultural labour. On the other hand, the number of people who undertake the labour of farming – the developing agricultural proletariat – diminishes in absolute terms, that is, not simply as magnitude of variable capital in relation to the value magnitude of the agricultural product:

> It lies in the nature of the capitalist mode of production that it constantly reduces the agricultural population in relation to the non-agricultural, because in industry (in the narrow sense) the growth of constant capital in relation to variable is linked with an absolute growth in variable capital (even if a relative decline in relation to constant); while in agriculture the variable capital required for the cultivation of a particular piece of land declines absolutely and can therefore grow only in so far as new land is cultivated, which however presupposes in turn a still greater growth in the non-agricultural population. (775)

own reproduction, if the daily expenditure of the worker's entire labour-power is only sufficient to produce the means of subsistence indispensable for [their] individual needs, there can be no question of any surplus product or surplus-value at all. A level of productivity of agricultural labour which goes beyond the individual needs of the worker is the basis of all society, and in particular the basis of capitalist production, which releases an ever growing part of society from the direct production of the means of subsistence . . . and making them available for exploitation in other spheres' – whether, as potential workers or surplus population, they are absorbed by other formal spheres of production or not. (921)

15   'The foundation of every division of labour which has attained a certain degree of development, and has been brought about by the exchange of commodities, is the separation of town from country. One might well say that the whole economic history of society is summed up in the movement of this antithesis.' Karl Marx, *Capital: A Critique of Political Economy*, vol. 1, trans. Ben Fowkes, Penguin, 1990, 472.

The social division of labour characteristic of a capitalist mode of production is embodied in a social product as a whole – which *must* be considered as a whole, as the individual product is an abstraction in a capitalist mode of production – that is a congealed ratio of socially necessary labour time to surplus labour time. All labour carried out in a capitalist mode of production is concrete labour that can only be expressed as socialized labour, in the form of its product – again, one portion of which is objectified necessary labour and another portion of which is surplus labour. Therefore, *all* surplus labour congealed in the social product is the formation of both agricultural and industrial labour. On top of this, we know that the profit that returns to the pocket of the functioning capitalist – industrial or agricultural – is not the surplus-value generated directly by the individual capitalist's enterprise but, rather, a portion of the total social surplus-value that falls to them as the average rate of profit on their total capital investment. The implications that follow are as such: the division of labour (or what we could also call, from a different standpoint, equalization), as two aspects of a singular process, entails that both agricultural and industrial labour are objectified in every individual product, including luxury products; every bearer of the collective worker performs necessary labour and surplus labour regardless of the concrete labour they perform:

> Just as a part of agricultural labour is objectified in products that either serve simply for luxury or form industrial raw materials but in no way go into foodstuffs, at least not foodstuffs for the masses, so on the other hand a part of industrial labour is objectified in products that serve as necessary means of consumption for agricultural and non-agricultural workers alike . . . [Industrial labour is] just as much necessary labour as the necessary portion of agricultural work is. It is also simply the autonomized form of a part of the industrial labour which was formerly linked indigenously with agricultural labour, a necessary reciprocal supplement to the purely agricultural labour that has now become separate from this. (771)

In fact, considered from the internal movement of capital as a function of abstraction – which is also to say, as a particular mode of sociality – no *individual* producer or enterprise actually generates value at all; as Marx expounds, 'No producer considered in isolation produces a value or commodity, neither the industrialist nor the agriculturalist. His product becomes a value and a commodity only in a specific social context' (777).

Marx's point here is that it is a mistake to conceive of ground-rent as simply a portion of the surplus product produced by the farmer. This would be to confuse the dynamic of capitalist ground-rent with a pre-capitalist dynamic, such as the feudal tithe or corvée, where surplus labour/product – a portion of it or its entirety – is handed over directly to the landowner, forming the immediate substance of rent. Rather, in the capitalist dynamic, ground-rent is a portion of the total social surplus labour/product/value. And, as we just considered, this entails that it is as much a portion of industrial surplus product as it is agricultural surplus product. As a portion of surplus-value, ground-rent is a portion of socialized labour, that is, labour abstracted from its concrete embodiment as a certain expenditure of either industrial or agricultural labour. In this way, ground-rent is always carried by each of these concrete processes or flows. Marx's material point in making the distinction between immediate surplus product and mediated/socialized surplus product is that 'rent', as universal category, is ultimately a mystification: the '*common character* of the different forms of rent – as the economic realization of landed property ... leads people to overlook the distinctions' (772).

Having thus established what ground-rent is, and what it is not, we turn, as does Marx at this stage of the analysis, to consider ground-rent's material, and abstract, perceptual physics.

Differential Rent and Its Forms

We begin with the assumption that the sale price of the agricultural commodity, like all commodities, is its production price – that is, its cost price plus a portion of surplus-value reflecting the rate of profit on the total capital investment. This latter portion of surplus-value constitutes the farmer's profit on a particular product yield. The question, then, is, if all the components of the production price are already spoken for – namely cost price and average profit – where does ground-rent come from? Whence comes the portion of surplus-value that falls to the landowner as rent under 'normal' circumstances (i.e., when rent is not a coerced share of the cost price or profit)? As Marx asks, 'How [is it that] a portion of [the farmer's] profit can be transformed into ground-rent, so that a part of the commodity price thus accrues to the landowner', valorizing their landed property (779)? As we have just suggested, it cannot be a portion of the agricultural product's production price, at least not consistently or for long, without jeopardizing the viability of the farmer's enterprise and, eventually, terminating it.

The farmer-capitalist is, first, a capitalist; they must be able to sell their product at its production price – capital investment plus the general rate of profit (884). Production price is the threshold of viability with respect to the return on their productive investment. As we know (from chapters 1 and 2), cost price is the threshold cost of engaging in capitalist enterprise; production price is, therefore, the threshold of market competitiveness. Without meeting the threshold of production price, viability is precarious at best, and the enterprise in question does not participate in the flows of capital that objectify as a capitalist mode of production and its ongoing reproduction. Ground-rent must therefore be *in surplus* of profit, which is exactly what it is: *surplus* surplus-value, or surplus profit.

How is surplus profit generated? The laws of motion of ground-rent pertain to all extractive industry where land takes the form of a direct means of production. As we have established, land is a form of constant capital and does not create value but rather makes the production of value possible. The distinction between the fertility of land and the productivity of labour in capitalist production is crucial:

> The natural force [of fertility] is not the source of the surplus profit, but is simply a natural basis for it, because it is the natural basis of the exceptionally increased productivity of labour ... Thus landed property does not create the portion of value that is transformed into surplus profit [ground-rent]; rather it simply enables the landowner... to entice this surplus profit out of the manufacturer's [or farmer's] pocket and into his own. (786)

Land of high fertility is the natural basis for agricultural labour of higher productivity. The greater the fertility of the piece of land in question, the higher the productivity of labour, or the greater the product yield per hectare. The value of the commodities produced on more fertile land will therefore be lower than the value of the commodities produced on less fertile land; in the case of more fertile land, the farmer requires less labour to produce the same yield, at the same cost price of production, as the farmer who produces with less fertile land. The more fertile land requires a smaller quantity of constant capital to produce the same yield as other pieces of less fertile land, as it requires less living labour to yield the same product. Since the farmer of more fertile soil has a lower cost price, they also have a lower individual production price for the same product than farmers who produce with less fertile land; in other words, they produce below the actual production price and, therefore, below market price. Because the farmer producing on more fertile land continues to sell the product at its value – its market price, that is, its *social* price – they pocket the difference between their lower, individual production price, and the actual (general, social) production price of the product. The difference between individual production price and actual production price is also, as we know, 'the difference between the individual and the general rate of profit' (781).

Therefore, in the case of production processes where land is a direct means of production, in the sense that it is the natural basis *for* production (for Marx, agriculture, mining, forestry, and fishing – and today, we would add fossil fuel extraction to the list of case industries), *the surplus-value that falls to the producer as the realization of the difference between the individual and the actual production price of their product takes the form of surplus profit and thereby constitutes the formation of ground-rent*. Landownership is simply the legal mechanism by which an accidental surplus profit is transformed into ground-rent – an extra portion of surplus-value redirected from the pool of social surplus to the farmer and, ultimately, to the landowner:

> Surplus profit is . . . equal to the difference between the individual price of production of these favoured producers and the general social price of production in the sphere of production as a whole, which is what governs the market. This difference is equal to the excess of the general production prices of the commodity over its individual production price. (780)

The capacity of the farmer who produces with more fertile soil and thereby attracts a surplus profit is similar to the industrial producer who is 'ahead of the curve' in adopting a new technology, or a new division of labour, or a new cooperative form of labour, such that it allows them to increase the number of commodities produced per labour hour, for a certain period of time, before the use of that method or means is generalized across the sphere of production. The industrial capitalist absorbs an extra portion of surplus-value (that is, they are able to corner an extra share of the market) while the window for this advantage on the competition remains open. The difference in the case of the farmer who produces with land of greater-than-average fertility is that, by having a monopoly over this piece of land, the benefits of its natural capacity cannot be generalized (i.e., its effects cannot be equalized) across the sphere of production, and the advantage is sustained. It is an advantage that, as we know, is appropriated, in the long run, by the landowner.

There is a significant difference, therefore, between the farmer who produces with more fertile land and the industrialist who creates an advantage by incorporating new technology into the production process ahead of competitors. New technology represents an investment to the capitalist, a new or additional value magnitude added to the cost price of production. The more fertile soil, in comparison, is a 'free gift', something that does not take the value form and which, therefore, cannot be acquired by competing farmer-capitalists. A new division of labour and a new mode of cooperation are social forces of production that are also free gifts to the capitalist and do not take the form of value magnitudes incorporated into cost price. However, like technology, which takes the form of objectified labour, and which can therefore be purchased by competing capitalists and its use generalized across the sphere of production, these social forces of production can also be taken up by competing capitalist enterprises and generalized across the sphere, lowering the value of the commodity in question. In other words, unlike more fertile soil – a free gift of nature – social and technological forces of production cannot be monopolized. Patents and intellectual property rights are, of course, legal fictions that express the compulsion of individual capitalists to monopolize social and technological forces of production as well.

Some natural forces applied in industry cannot be monopolized: water that expands as steam, light that photosynthesizes, carbon that fossilizes, and so on can affect the general rate of profit by reducing the amount of labour required to produce the necessary means of subsistence. A force of production, regardless of its origin or orientation, can only be the basis of surplus profit if and when its application provides an exceptional advantage for a functioning capitalist. As Marx expounds, the advantage that manifests in surplus profit is cancelled out 'as soon as the exceptional manner of production becomes universal [if that is a possibility], or is overtaken by one still more advanced' (783):

> Nothing inherently prevents all capital in the same sphere of production from being invested in the same way ... Competition between capitals ... cancel[s] out these distinctions more and more; the determination of value by socially necessary labour-time leads to the cheapening of commodities and the compulsion to produce commodities under the same favourable conditions. (783–4)

Things are different in the case of more fertile soil because, as a natural force that *can* be monopolized, it is 'available only to those who have at their disposal particular pieces of the earth's surface and their appurtenances'. Capital cannot call into being this particular advantage. Possession of more fertile land 'forms a monopoly in the hands of its owner, a condition of higher productivity for the capital invested, which cannot be produced by capital's own production process'. Under these conditions, the surplus profit that is generated from farming more fertile soil is transformed into ground-rent and falls to the landowner. Ground-rent 'arises not from capital as such, but rather from disposal over a natural force that is limited in scope ... and monopolizable' (784). For this reason, ground-rent does not have an impact on the value of commodities; therefore, nor does it contribute to determining the general production price or the general rate of profit: 'Ground-rent does not derive from any absolute rise in productivity of the capital applied or of the labour it appropriates, which can only ever reduce the value of the commodities' (785). In other words, the advantage of producing with more fertile soil lies in facilitating labour's ability to produce a greater yield of product, even as the character of the labour process is standard for the agricultural sphere. If the labour process itself were to become more productive, its methods – and the outcome of those methods – would be generalized across the sphere of production, lowering the value of commodities and eradicating the conditions for the formation of ground-rent.

Ground-rent can thus be characterized as *differential rent*: an objectification of inherently differing capacities of land to facilitate a product yield when, (1) those capacities cannot be standardized in the sphere of agricultural production, and, (2) the value-contributions of those capacities to the total social surplus cannot be equalized more widely across spheres of production. The price of more fertile land, derived from ground-rent, is, as we established above, irrational – 'an irrational expression concealing a real economic relationship' (787) – and, therefore, has no impact on production price and the general rate of profit. Ground-rent is therefore a particular mystification, as well as one dimension of the universal fetish-movement of capital more generally: it appears as natural and inevitable that land of high fertility increases both its price and the ground-rent that falls to it. And yet, this thoroughly historical appearance, generated by the perceptual physics of capital, conceals the capital-labour relation – the 'real economic relationship' – that is the condition by means of which otherwise-valueless land-capital is able to confer an accidental portion of the total social surplus on the landowner.

In thinking through the categorial derivation of ground-rent, the next step is to further crystalize the nebulous category of 'differing degrees of land-fertility'.[16] Differences in land fertility, under conditions of competitive production, compel the efforts of farmer-capitalists who produce with less fertile soil to minimize the impact of these differences. As we will see, these efforts inadvertently participate in land-capital's fetish-movement of concealing the actual source of surplus-value in living labour. As we know, ground-rent – or differential rent – is the difference between the production price of a certain product, as the basis of that product's governing market price, and the individual production price of that product when it is produced on land that is more fertile. This situation begs the question: 'More fertile' than what

---

16   It is useful to think of the process of capital becoming, materializing as, various social forms as a physics – that is, as the motion that generates material declination or variation. For instance, for 'material derivation' we could substitute 'material declination'. Although, both terms work. The most advantageous language will be that which best invokes a non-linear sense of capital's movement through its derivations. The process of derivation is not linear; it is not a chronology of forms. The metaphor of the fold, and the image of accordion folds, are useful in capturing an alternative sense of the spatial relation of capital's forms.

average? How is the threshold of land fertility that produces ground-rent established? In the case of production that forms ground-rent, the individual production price will be lower than the general production price, generating a surplus profit. It follows that *no* ground-rent is formed on land with average fertility or below-average fertility. What dynamic, then, constitutes the category of 'average fertility' specific to a capitalist production process that incorporates land as a means of production?

The market price of land is necessarily determined by the parcel with the lowest-possible fertility that can still provide the basis for yielding a product that realizes the price of production. For the sake of following Marx's analysis, we will use his terms and refer to this least fertile, threshold-marking (i.e., still viable) land as the 'worst land'.[17] In the case of the worst land, ground-rent is equal to zero, as it realizes no surplus profit over and above production price while still producing at the threshold of viability. Land that can only facilitate an individual production price that is greater than that of the worst land is not viable for capitalist production and can be discounted. Every piece of land of greater fertility than the worst land facilitates a product yield whose individual production price is lower than that of the worst land. The higher the fertility of the land, the lower will be the individual production price of the product, the greater is the surplus profit that falls to the farmer, and the higher is the ground-rent appropriated by the landowner. Therefore, in the movement of ground-rent, the social average that determines production price, and consequently market price, is derived from the individual production price on the worst land, that is, land that facilitates no ground-rent (or, where ground-rent is zero). It follows that the law of differential rent is independent of the empirical rent that any piece of land attracts. To theorize ground-rent at the level of its concept, therefore, entails the presupposition that no ground-rent is generated on the worst land:

> The price of the product of class A land [the worst land] always represents the limit of the governing general market price, the price at which the total product can be supplied, and to this extent it governs

---

17   In his discussion of differential rent, Marx refers to the 'worst land' and the 'worst soil' interchangeably.

the price of this total product ... whatever the rent [the empirical rent, or lease-price] on the least fertile types of land might be, not only is the law of differential rent independent of it, but the only way to grasp the true character of differential rent itself is to set the rent for the class A land at zero. Whether it really is zero, or something positive, is immaterial as far as the differential rent is concerned, and does not need to be taken into account. (883)

From here, Marx moves from the 'law of differential rent', thus established, to examine the impact, on the formation of differential rent, of the actions of farmer-capitalists in the immediate sphere of competition to increase the productivity of enterprise, which they pursue through opening up new parcels of land to cultivation and increasing the capital investment on land already cultivated. These interventions in agricultural production facilitate two different modes of forming differential rent. Importantly, the distinction between these two forms of differential rent is entirely effaced in the phenomenal form of rent, as is the essential character and source of ground-rent itself. Only the abstraction of analysis reveals the movement and prov- idence of differential rent, itself another mode of abstraction and form of value.

Differential Rent I

Consistent with the thematic through line of *Capital* III, Marx's mathematical illustrations of the two forms of differential rent in chapters 39 through 44 serve the more general argument that capital's immanent movement is mystified in the empirical, social forms that capital necessarily takes in the actual world of capitalist competition. In these chapters, Marx identifies two forms of differential rent, 'differential rent I' and 'differential rent II', the formation of which he illustrates by way of hypothetical case studies laid out in numerous tables of calculations. As we will see, the tables demonstrate that the formation of these two forms of ground-rent, indistinguishable on the surface of things, constitutes one moment of capital's perceptual physics, concealing *la terre-capital* as the bearer of the capital-fetish more generally. What Marx calls differential rent I is the movement that generates the form of ground-rent that we have elaborated up to this point as

> the result of the varying productivity of the equal capital investments on equal land areas of different fertility, so that differential rent [is] determined by the difference between the yield of capital invested on the worst, non-rent-bearing land, and that of capital invested on better land. (812)

We will elaborate this movement further since the formation of differential rent I is the basis for forming differential rent II.

We have established that surplus profit is produced 'if two equal amounts of capital and labour are employed on equal areas of land with unequal results' (788). While industrial production also produces unequal results between enterprises, in the case where land is a means of production, we are talking, more specifically, about unequalizable results – results that cannot be attributed to capital. So far, we have only identified soil fertility in this respect; however, Marx also identifies the location of land as a second such cause of unequal individual production prices (789). Location may be a condition of production that works in opposition to that of soil fertility; land of high fertility may be located disadvantageously with respect to access or proximity to the arteries of circulation. The effects of fertility and location together will result in a balance of conditions, acting with or against each another, and possibly shifting over time. However, the resulting balance between the effects of fertility and location, similar to either condition considered in isolation, does not alter the movement of ground-rent as capital fetish, so we will continue to follow Marx in taking fertility as the example for illustrating this movement.

Before leaving the question of location of land aside, however, it is important to note that, as a condition of capitalist production, location of land is significant for a historical analysis of the geopolitical development of capital and capitalist agriculture. As Marx points out, location of land 'is decisive in the case of colonies, and decisive everywhere for the sequence in which lands can be successively brought into cultivation' (789). The location of land is therefore central to the historical analysis of the conjunctures we refer to as colonialism, imperialism, financialization, and globalization; it is, of course, a decisive category in the unfolding of what we now call the logistics revolution, where developments in communication and transport are compelled, in the era of globalized production chains, to enhance mobility and eradicate the drag of space and time on circulation and profitability. The logistics revolution has virtually eradicated the advantage of proximity of production to consumer markets and facilitates the exploitation of uneven development – both creating geographical distance as the typical spatial configuration of production-circulation and levelling the effect of that distance on the general rate of profit:

> The progress of social production in general has on the one hand a levelling effect on location as a basis for differential rent, since it creates local markets and improves location by producing means of communication and transport; while on the other hand it increases the differences of geographical location, by separating agriculture from manufacture and forming great centres of production, while also relatively isolating the countryside. (789–90)

We leave further reflection on the 'updating' of Marx's analysis for the end of the chapter. Returning to the formation of differential rent I, the scenario where 'equal amounts of capital, labour and land produce unequal results' is, of course, a concrete abstraction; it articulates the gravitational force of capital at the level of its concept. In the actual world, farmer-capitalists do not employ equal amounts of capital and labour on equal areas of land, except in what would be rare and accidental exceptions. Rather, in actual practice, different farming enterprises employ land of various sizes and, consequently, apply different amounts of capital and labour to the production process. The comparison that reveals the formation of ground-rent proceeds therefore from 'equal proportionate parts' – for instance, the rate of profit on each one-hundred-pound investment – and the product of a square hectare of land for each producer. It also requires that we 'assume a given level of agricultural development' – that is, a given historical level of social productive capacity in that sphere of production – and that 'the hierarchy of soil types [from the worst soil to the most fertile] is calculated in relation to this level of development' (791). The reason for this assumption is that the category of fertility, capturing 'actual effective fertility', is always a combination of 'so-called natural fertility' and what Marx calls 'economic fertility'. Technological development – chemical, mechanical, and/or genetic – will change the soil's effective fertility, so 'even though fertility is an objective property of the soil, it thus always involves an economic relation, a relation to the given chemical or mechanical level of agricultural development, and changes with this level of development' (790). Parcels of land demonstrating unequal levels of fertility at one historical stage of development may become equally fertile with the generalized use of certain technical means at another stage. Development may bring into cultivation parcels of land that were not previously viable; or it may reverse the hierarchy of greater and lesser fertility between two parcels of land, and so on. In the calculation of differential rent I, economic fertility is as much a factor in actual effective fertility as is so-called natural fertility (791).

Therefore, in Marx's numerous tables of calculations, comparisons between types of soil of increasing or decreasing fertility (for the sake of comparison, it does not matter which) – A, B, C, and D – capture either a spatial set of distinctions between soils of different climatic regions across one stage of development, or a temporal set of distinctions where the land of one climatic region is compared across progressive stages of development characterized by differing levels of soil fertility. The movement is the same for a spatial/geographical comparison as for a temporal/historical one, and either can be assumed for the purpose of analysis. In seeing what Marx is illustrating with the tables, it is helpful to recall his orienting description of table 1:

> Assume four types of soil, A, B, C, D. Assume further that the price of wheat is £3, or 60 shillings per quarter. Since the rent here is simply differential rent, this price of 60 shillings per quarter is equal to the production costs on the worst soil, i.e. equal to capital plus average profit.
>
> Let A be this worst soil, giving 1 quarter = 60 shillings for an outlay of 50 shillings; i.e. a profit of 10 shillings or 20 per cent.
>
> Let B yield 2 quarters = 120 shillings for the same outlay. There is a profit of 70 shillings or a surplus profit of 60 shillings.
>
> Let C yield 3 quarters = 180 shillings for the same outlay. Total profit = 130 shillings. Surplus profit = 120 shillings.

Let D yield 4 quarters = 240 shillings; 180 shillings surplus profit. (791)

Marx writes, 'We would then have the following sequence:'

Table 1

Type of Soil	Product		Capital Advanced	Profit		Rent	
	Quarters	Shillings		Quarters	Shillings	Quarters	Shillings
A	1	60	50	$\frac{1}{6}$	10	–	–
B	2	120	50	$1\frac{1}{6}$	70	1	60
C	3	180	50	$2\frac{1}{6}$	130	2	120
D	4	240	50	$3\frac{1}{6}$	190	3	180
Total	10 qrs	600s.				6 qrs	360s.

(791)

Table 1 represents a foundational, base-level abstraction from which Marx derives all other comparative series. It is a series of increasing fertility, where A represents the worst soil and D represents the soil of highest fertility, indicated by the growth of product (both in kind and as value magnitude) at a consistent cost price (capital advance) and rate of profit across the series. If D soil yields four times as many tons of wheat per hectare as A soil, then D soil yields a ton of wheat at one-quarter of the individual production price as does A soil. If A soil is the worst soil, surplus profit / differential rent equals zero and increases through the series proportionately. The series in table 1 illustrates a scenario where differential rent I increases proportionately with productivity. This scenario is key to the governing mystification in establishing the working appearance that ground-rent is determined by soil fertility, and that ground-rent (differential rent) will increase with an absolute rise in fertility, as represented by increased productivity – that is, when the land in question yields a greater magnitude of product per hectare. This appearance – the inversion of the actual movement of ground-rent – and the political economists who mistake it for the reality of things, is Marx's orienting and polemical target throughout part VI.

Marx illustrates the mystification at the heart of this appearance by comparing the series in table 1 with two other series (tables 2 and 3), manipulating the conditions in each case.

Table 2

Type of Soil	Product		Capital Invested	Profit		Rent		Price of production per quarter
	Quarters	Shillings		Quarters	Shillings	Quarters	Shillings	
A	1 ⅓	60	50	$\frac{2}{9}$	10	–	–	45s.
A'	1 ⅔	75	50	$\frac{5}{9}$	25	⅓	15	36s.
B	2	90	50	$\frac{8}{9}$	40	⅔	30	30s.
B'	2 ⅓	105	50	1 $\frac{2}{9}$	55	1	45	25 $\frac{5}{7}$ s.
B"	2 ⅔	120	50	1 $\frac{5}{9}$	70	1 ⅓	60	22 ½ s.
C	3	135	50	1 $\frac{8}{9}$	85	1 ⅔	75	20s.
D	4	180	50	2 $\frac{8}{9}$	130	2 ⅔	120	15s.
Total	17					7 ⅔	345	

(794)

Table 3

Type of Soil	Product		Capital Advanced	Price of production per quarter	Profit		Rent	
	Quarters	Shillings			Quarters	Shillings	Quarters	Shillings
A	2	60	50	30	⅓	10	0	0
B	4	120	50	15	2 ⅓	70	2	60
C	7	210	50	8 $\frac{4}{7}$	5 ⅓	160	5	150
D	10	300	50	6	8 ⅓	250	8	240
Total	23						15	450

(795)

The manipulations are hypothetical, and the numerical ratios are arbitrary; however, each series represents a *plausible* historical development (795). To suggest as much, Marx cites historical cases that map onto the scenarios depicted in the three tables throughout his discussion of them (798–9). For instance, in the course of capitalist competition, if demand for wheat falls short of the productive capacity of all four parcels of land, land A, the worst land, drops out of cultivation and land B takes its place as the land of lowest, yet still viable, fertility. If the reverse situation occurs, and demand surpasses the product, more land will be brought into cultivation. Therefore, from a historical point of view, increasing fertility from A to D represents either the spatial comparison of land of different regions at one stage of agricultural development, or the same parcel of land over the course of four progressive stages of development. Decreasing fertility from D to A can represent the progressive introduction of new parcels of less fertile land into cultivation when demand rises and makes less fertile soil viable for use. As we know, if demand cannot absorb the product, then competitive pressure will force the worst land (A) out of production *first* (797). For this reason, Marx explains, even if this scenario – descending order of fertility, D to A – is not the case historically, *logically*, the comparative sequence will always proceed as a descending order, from the most fertile land to the least (796–7).

Examining the series in tables 1, 2, and 3 more closely allows us to discern the way in which the movement of differential rent I departs from its governing appearance. In addition to the reproduction above of the tables as they appear in the text, the following annotation puts the pertinent comparisons in relief. Recall that, for the series in all three tables, Marx posits a consistent cost price (capital advance) of 50 shillings and a consistent rate of profit of 20 percent:

Table 1
- Marx introduces a series of four parcels of land of increasing fertility, A–D.
- Product increases, both in kind and as value magnitude, across parcels of land.
- Rent increases proportionally to increasing product, both in kind and as value magnitude.

Table 2
- Marx introduces a series of seven parcels of land. In this hypothetical scenario, new parcels of land are added to the holdings of the landowners (or farming enterprise, or region) A and B.
- The scenario presupposes that new parcels of the lower- and lowest-fertility land, A and B, are brought into cultivation as a result of technological development (economic fertility), or that once-inaccessible land is now accessible.
- Marx introduces a new series of increasing fertility: A, A´, B, B´, B´´, C, D.
- The worst land, A, also increases fertility; high-fertility lands C and D remain unchanged.

- The scenario presupposes that increased population and/or demand absorbs the larger product.
- Because the worst land now yields more product per hectare at the same cost price, production price falls from 60s. per quarter (as in table 1) to 45s.
- Greater yield on land A, and more parcels of land cultivated in total, entail larger total product, from 10 (as in table 1) to 17 quarters.
- Rent falls on B, C, and D, both in kind and as value magnitude, even though product yield remains the same on each; this is because rent is determined as a differential and not as an absolute – that is, it is formed *in relation to A*, the worst soil, which has increased its yield.
- *Total rent across parcels increases in kind from 6 quarters (as in table 1) to 7 2/3 quarters; total rent falls as value magnitude from 360s. to 345s.*
- Marx points out that in this scenario, it is possible that more relative surplus-value is produced, and possibly even an increase in the rate of profit, following the cheapening of the means of subsistence determining the value of labour-power.

Table 3
- Marx introduces a series of four parcels of land of increasing fertility. All parcels increase yield relative to series in table 1: A and B double yield; C and D more than double yield. (The scenario presupposes technical development that improves differently on different soil types where there is a greater improvement on the higher-fertility soil.)
- Total product is greater. (Increased product will be absorbed if there has been a fall in price that results in increased demand and/or population.)
- *Rent remains the same on A and B, even though product has doubled.* (A is the new worst land, so even at twice the level of fertility, differential rent is zero; B yield is unchanged in relation to A, therefore forming the same differential rent as in table 1.)
- Differential rent increases on C and D because of increased fertility *in relation to A and B.*
- Because fertility increases to a greater extent on high-fertility lands C and D, total rent increases both in kind and as value magnitude.
- If the increase in fertility were greater on A and B than on C and D, then differential rent on C and D would decrease instead of increasing.

The series in tables 1, 2, and 3, taken together, reveal that the formation of differential rent cannot be determined, in positive terms, by the absolute fertility of land. Table 1 serves as the baseline of calculations against which to compare the results of the manipulations depicted in tables 2 and 3. Comparing series 2 with series 1, and series 3 with series 1, we see that changes in differential rent are not proportional to changes in product yield per hectare. With series 1, we have a total rent of 6 quarters/360s. With series 2, we see the introduction of additional rent and product-producing parcels of land to the series, while the yields of the original parcels of land remain consistent, with the exception of that of land A, which increases. If ground-rent were determined by absolute fertility, we would see a proportional rise in ground-rent (both in kind and as a value magnitude) as an expression of the now-greater total product. With this new scenario in series 2, however, we have a differential rent that has risen to 7.66 quarters in kind, while *falling* as a value magnitude to 345s. With series 3, the increase in fertility on all four original parcels of land increases the total product from 10 (in table 1) to 23 quarters – that is, more than doubles. Differential rent in kind also more than doubles, from 6 to 15 quarters. Rent as a value magnitude, however, increases from 360s to 450s – an increase of only 25 percent. Marx's summary of the series in tables 1, 2, and 3 emphasizes this same departure from conventional economic thought:

[Series 3 compared with series 1] gives the result that the price per quarter falls from 60s. to 30s., i.e. by 50 percent, while production grows from 10 qrs to 23, ... i.e. by 130 percent; the rent on soil B remains the same, while on soil C it rises by 25 percent and on D by 33 1/3 percent, the total rental thus rising from £18 to £22 1/2, i.e. by 25 percent. (796)

What these comparisons show is that ground-rent is determined by productivity, however, productivity as a differential relation to a social average that takes the form of market value. Ground-rent, in other words, is a *social* value, a movement that can only be captured from the standpoint of the social totality – that is, from the standpoint of the movement of the value form, and not from the material qualities of any particular, discrete piece of land. The fact that differential rent can be formed regardless of how fertility differentials are expressed – that is, 'with a stationary [spatial/regional differences in fertility], rising [progressive development from better to worse land; D–A] or falling [progressive development to higher fertility land; A–D] price of the agricultural product' (797) – is the ground on which Marx challenges 'the erroneous conception of differential rent which still prevailed with [Edward] West, [Thomas] Malthus and [David] Ricardo and which assumed a necessary progression to ever worse soil, or an ever declining agricultural fertility':

> As we have seen, differential rent can arise with the progression to ever better soil; it can arise if a better soil takes the lowest place instead of that which was formally the worst; it can be linked with the steady advance in agriculture. Its only precondition is the inequality of types of soil. In so far as the development of productivity is involved, it assumes that the rise in absolute fertility of the total acreage does not abolish this inequality, but that it either increases it, leaves it stationary or simply reduces it. (798)

That the formation of differential rent takes place at all indicates that the total social agricultural product is sold at its market value, while its real value – the aggregate of its individual production prices – is always less than this. In series 1, for instance, the market value of the product is 600s, while the real value of the product is only 240s. As we know, the difference between the product's market value (average production price) and its real value (individual production price) forms the social substance of differential rent, and 'it is competition that produces [a product's market value as] a *false social value*' (799, my emphasis):

> The determination of market value of products . . . [by competition] is a social act, even if performed by society unconsciously and unintentionally, and it is based necessarily on the exchange-value of the product and not on the soil and the differences in its fertility. If we imagine that the capitalist form of society has been abolished and that society has been organized as a conscious association working according to a plan, the 10 qrs represent a quantity of autonomous labour-time equal to that contained in 240s. Society would therefore not purchase this product [for 600s, i.e.] at 2 ½ times the actual labour time contained in it; the basis for a class of landowners would

thereby disappear ... [It is] wrong to say that the value of these products would remain the same if capitalist production were replaced by association. The fact that commodities of the same kind have an identical market price is the way in which the social character of value is realized on the basis of the capitalist mode of production, and in general of production depending on commodity exchange between *individuals*. Where society, considered as a consumer, pays too much for agricultural products, this is a minus for the realization of its labour-time in agricultural production, but it forms a plus for one portion of society, the landowners. (799–800)

Marx's point in this passage is that developments in agricultural productivity that cheapen and grow society's agricultural product, when subsumed by capitalist conditions of production, circulation, and distribution, do not materialize as a saving of social labour time, an end to food insecurity, and a common partaking of this greater abundance. Rather, increases in productivity materialize as the enrichment of the most historically and immediately superfluous personification of capital, the landowner.

So far, we have looked at the perceptual physics of differential rent as an absolute magnitude of value, that is, as the total rental for a cultivated area that comprises parcels of land of differing levels of fertility. Marx then offers a second illustration by introducing a new category, rate of rent – rent as a percentage of capital invested per acre. However, Marx observes that it is, rather, the rate of rent for an entire cultivated area that is the statistic typically featured in the work of the political economists, and that this statistic introduces a mystifying appearance of its own (805–6). The rate of rent on a particular cultivated area – a country or region of a country, for example – is the ratio of the total rental to the total capital investment absorbed by the cultivated area. In the hypothetical scenarios represented in the series laid out on pages 800–1 (reproduced below, with descriptions), the cultivated area comprises four parcels of land, A–D. The parcels produce 1, 2, 3, and 4 quarters per acre respectively, where A, the worst land, produces no differential rent. We assume a consistent investment of £2.5 per acre, and a constant rate of profit of 20 percent; the price of production per acre is therefore £3:

Table 4

Type of Soil	Acres	Price of Production	Product	Rent in Grain	Rent in Money
A	1	£3	1 qrs	0	0
B	1	£3	2 qrs	1 qrs	£3
C	1	£3	3 qrs	2 qrs	£6
D	1	£3	4 qrs	3 qrs	£9
Total	4 acres		10 qrs	6 qrs	£18*

* $\frac{£18}{4 \text{ acres}}$ = £4.5 per acre = rate of rent of 180%

(800)

If we now assume that the number of acres under cultivation in each class doubles, we get:

Table 4a

Type of Soil	Acres	Price of Production	Product	Rent in Grain	Rent in Money
A	2	£6	2 qrs	0	0
B	2	£6	4 qrs	2 qrs	£6
C	2	£6	6 qrs	4 qrs	£12
D	2	£6	8 qrs	6 qrs	£18
Total	8 acres		20 qrs	12 qrs	£36*

* $\frac{£36}{8 \text{ acres}}$ = £4.5 per acre = rate of rent 180% (doubling of acreage coincides with a stable rate of rent)

(801)

We shall now take two further cases, the first being one in which production expands on the two inferior soil types, as follows:

Table 4b

Type of Soil	Acres	Price of Production		Product	Rent in Grain	Rent in Money
		Per acre	Total			
A	4	£3	£12	4 qrs	0	0
B	4	£3	£12	8 qrs	4 qrs	£12
C	2	£3	£6	6 qrs	4 qrs	£12
D	2	£3	£6	8 qrs	6 qrs	£18
Total	12 acres		£36	20 qrs	14 qrs	£42*

* $\frac{£42}{12 \text{ acres}}$ = £3.5 per acre = rate of rent 140% (under these conditions, increase in acreage coincides with a falling rate of rent)

(801)

And, finally, an uneven expansion of production and the cultivated area over all four classes of soil:

Table 4c

Type of Soil	Acres	Price of Production		Product	Rent in Grain	Rent in Money
		Per acre	Total			
A	1	£3	£3	1 qr	0	0
B	2	£3	£6	4 qrs	2 qrs	£6
C	5	£3	£15	15 qrs	10 qrs	£30
D	4	£3	£12	16 qrs	12 qrs	£36
Total	12 acres		£36	36 qrs	24 qrs	£72*

* $\frac{£72}{12 \text{ acres}}$ = £6 per acre = rate of rent 240% (under conditions of expanded cultivation on land of greater fertility, otherwise stable acreage coincides with a doubling of rate of rent)

(801)

As illustrated by the series in table 4, rate of rent for each parcel of land will increase in proportion to the magnitude of the product per acre. The rate of rent for the total cultivated area (aggregate of all parcels) will be determined by the number of acres of each type of soil in cultivation:

> The average rent per acre and the average rate of rent on the capital invested in agriculture depend on the proportionate shares that the various classes of soil make up within the total cultivated area; or, what comes to the same thing, they depend on the way in which that total capital applied is distributed over the soil types of different fertility. (805)

As we see in table 4a, if successive acres are introduced to production equally across the types of soil, such that the differential relation between the parcels remains the same, the rate of rent for the cultivated area, now double in size, is unchanged (for example, rate of rent remains 180 percent in series 4 and 4a). However, if a proportionately greater number of acres of lower fertility land – A and B, for example – are introduced to the cultivated area, rate of rent will fall; in series 4b, for example, rate of rent falls to 140 percent. If all new cultivation takes place on the land that produces no rent, the rate of rent will fall even more steeply. On the other hand, if proportionately more acres of higher fertility land – C and D, for example – are introduced, absolute rent will increase in a higher proportion to the number of acres in production, and rate of rent will rise, as represented in series 4c, where rate of rent rises to 240 percent. Meanwhile, the price of production per quarter has remained the same in all series.

Considering the four series together, we can see that the movement of value that forms the rate of rent across the cultivated area as a whole produces a different story than if we were to scale up proportionately from the rate of rent per acre: we arrive at the average rent per acre by dividing the total rental by the total number of acres in production; we arrive at the average rate of rent on capital invested by dividing the total rental by the total capital invested. Both rates will vary substantially under this or that set of circumstances, and the two figures depart in each set of circumstances in ways that reveal an internal *non*-identity between them, contradicting the identity that is otherwise suggested by their surface appearances and narrativizations. Even when the two rates move in the same direction, only accidentally will they move at the same ratio (805).

The dynamic that Marx illustrates in these four series makes reference to the dynamic he elaborates in part I (and which we observed in chapter 1) – the mystification inherent to the rate of profit – except that, now, we observe the mystification inherent to the average rent per acre and the average rate of rent on capital invested. Both phenomena depend on the 'proportionate shares that the various classes of soil make up within the total cultivated area', obscuring that it is the *difference* in fertility between the soil types that forms differential rent, and not 'the fruit of the soil, something that it is only in surface appearance' (807):

> Thus rent appears as determined not by the ratio of differential fertility but rather by the absolute fertility, which would refute the law of differential rent ... Up till now, this factor has been completely overlooked, in a quite striking fashion. It still shows ... that the relative level of average rents per acre, and the average rate of rent ... [on] total capital invested in the soil, may rise or fall even though

prices . . . all remain the same, simply by an expansion of the cultivated area. (806)

Average rent per acre and average rate of rent on capital invested appear to correspond to the absolute fertility of the total cultivated area – an appearance upheld by West, Malthus, Ricardo, Henri Storch, and others.[18] Marx's point, however, is that despite appearances, differential rent is an expression of the law of value, a function of abstraction, an expression of social averages and thresholds – a specific excrescence of capitalist production-exchange. Rather than an expression of soil fertility, differential rent is the expression of the productive capacity of living labour subsumed, inverted, and contorted by the conditions of a capitalist mode of production, and Marx's objective is to illustrate the discordance of social substance and social form with mathematical accuracy.

Differential Rent II

We know that differential rent I (hereafter, DI) is 'simply the result of the varying productivity of equal capitals when invested on the land' (812). Our assumption in this case is that these equal capitals are applied to different parcels of land – parcels that vary in fertility. However, the movement of differential rent would be exactly the same if instead of capital investments on four different parcels of land, A–D, we have four successive capital investments, A–D, on the same parcel of land, where each investment produces a different magnitude of product, reflecting different levels of productivity with each successive investment. This hypothetical, if entirely possible (and even probable), scenario suggests

18   The Penguin edition of *Capital* III glosses Henri Storch as 'a Russian vulgarizer of classical political economy, though he wrote in French'. Marx's commentary on their 'debate', however, is instructive for the general analysis of the perceptual physics of differential rent: 'The controversy between Storch and Ricardo in connection with ground-rent (a controversy only as far as the subject is concerned, as neither party paid any attention to the other), over the question whether market value (in their terms market price or price of production) is governed by commodities produced under the least favourable conditions (Ricardo) or the most favourable (Storch), is thus resolved in this way, that both are right and both are wrong, and also that both have entirely omitted to consider the average case' (284n30).

the rotation of different crops, with different yields, on the same parcel of land, or the development of the land's economic fertility between successive investments, or a fall in yield between investments as a result of depleted soil. The series in 'table 1' on page 800 (herein referenced as series 5 and table 5, for purposes of disambiguation), which we first observed as the formation of DI, we can now observe again as the formation of differential rent II (hereafter DII), without changing the series or calculations in any way (812).

Table 5

Type of Soil	Acres	Price of Production	Product	Rent in Grain	Rent in Money
A	1	£3	1 qrs	0	0
B	1	£3	2 qrs	1 qrs	£3
C	1	£3	3 qrs	2 qrs	£6
D	1	£3	4 qrs	3 qrs	£9
Total	4 acres		10 qrs	6 qrs	£18

(800)

Shifting only perspective and presuppositions for this series, we now have one parcel of land and four successive capital investments (A–D) of £2.5 (with a production price of £3), each investment producing a different yield (1–4 quarters) and, therefore, producing an increasing magnitude of rent for each successive investment/yield.

The logical shift from DI to DII requires no further conceptualization:

> it makes no difference as far as the law of surplus profit formation is concerned whether equal capitals are invested alongside each other on equal-sized tracts of land with unequal results or whether they are invested successively in this way on the same piece of land. (813)

Historically, however, the difference between the formation of DI and DII is highly significant for the struggle between farmer-capitalist and landowner because it will inform the transformation of surplus profit into ground-rent. The transfer of surplus profit to the landowner carries out the transformation of surplus profit into rent. The landowner can only increase rent with a new tenant contract. The farmer-capitalist can better conceal increases in productivity, and any subsequent profits arising therefrom, in a long tenancy contract; the longer the contract, the greater the opportunity for the farmer to benefit from the course of 'economic fertility' or other social developments in agricultural productivity. Hence, 'the assessment of varying fertility between types of land in general' for the purpose of calculating rent becomes increasingly complicated, and the more intensive agricultural production becomes – that is, the more concentrated the application of capital to land – the more intense the struggle over surplus profits. 'In the case of more permanent improvements, the artificially inflated differential fertility of the land is its new natural fertility' (813) – again, what Marx calls economic fertility – and it will have an impact on the increase in rent when tenant contracts expire. In this way, private property in land, personified by the landowner, both accelerates capitalist accumulation in the agricultural sphere by compelling competition and the augmentation of productivity of enterprise, and obstructs accumulation by appropriating the rewards of enhanced productivity and thereby discouraging such enhancements in the first place.

DII is the surplus profit produced when successive investments of capital are made on the same parcel of land. The farmer attempting to increase profit per annum will, for instance, introduce a second or third crop into annual rotation, or invest in a new designer seed that shortens the cycle from planting to harvesting, doubling the yield of one parcel of land. DII therefore *presupposes* DI, in the sense that the conditions that precipitate the formation of DI – varying fertility of parcels of land – also produce the conditions that precipitate the formation of DII, subsequent investments of capital on the same land. With DII,

> its basis and point of departure, not only historically but as far as concerns its movement at any given point in time, is differential rent I, i.e. the simultaneous cultivation alongside one another of lands of different fertility and location, the simultaneous application alongside one another of different components of the total agricultural capital to tracts of land of differing quality. (814)

In order to mitigate the disadvantage of producing with land that is less fertile, or to meet or surpass the yields of competing producers, the farmer-capitalist makes additional capital investments on the same land: 'The variation in fertility is supplemented by differences in the distribution of capital (and creditworthiness) among farmers' (815).

Once again, we encounter the dialectical formulation that recurs throughout the entire study in *Capital* III: DII *is, and is not,* DI. 'It is clear that differential rent II is simply a different expression of differential rent I, and the same thing as far as its nature is concerned' (816). Meanwhile, the distinction between DI and DII, expressing the movement of differential rent *as form*, is as material as is their identity: if differential rent in general is derived from necessarily unequal results of capitalist production when land is applied as a means of production, DI is formed through the differential of equal capitals invested simultaneously on parcels of land *of different types*, while DII is formed through the differential of unequal capitals invested on parcels of land *of the same size* (816). As with DI, in the case of DII – the outcome of successive investments – the worst (lowest-fertility) land will not form rent, and it will function as the land that determines production price so long as its product is required to meet demand. The production of surplus profits takes place in the same way for DI and DII, as represented in series 5 (800), but for one exception: DII *presupposes* DI, and not the reverse (816).[19] It is not just that ground-rent is always a combination of DI and DII; there is a particular (i.e., not random or contingent, but rather necessary) relation of causality between the combined moving parts. Some forces only act on, while others are only acted upon, and it is impossible to discern which is which from the point of view of empirical history alone. It is in this way, as Marx emphasizes, that calculations become complicated, and results difficult to pick apart. In analysis (i.e. in abstraction), we know that DI and DII have different dynamics – a difference that does not have an empirical expression. For instance, it is impossible to discern, empirically, which portion of the resulting profits derives from the formation of DI, and which from the formation of DII. These 'complicated combinations to which differential rent always gives rise', Marx argues, is not adequately considered by Ricardo, who, rather, deals with differential rent as 'something straightforward' (817).

Even though DI and DII are logically identical movements, a whole range of modulations in price, product, absolute rent, rate of rent per

---

19   To use Althusser's articulation, the dynamic that forms DI determines the formation of DII in the last instance, even though that last instance – where the DI-forming dynamic exerts a 'pure' force, uncontaminated by the concrete contingencies of DII – never arrives.

acre, rate of rent on capital invested, and so on are introduced by the differing results of capital investments on land newly cultivated versus successive capital investments on land previously cultivated.[20] In the actual sphere of competition, successive investments are made on parcels of land of differing fertility – parcels that together constitute the totality of agricultural land under cultivation for a given country, region, or market. The ground-rent derived from this process expresses the balance of outcomes between the two movements that form DI and DII. The movement of DII can augment that of DI, and advance it further, or it can be a counterbalancing movement that diminishes or eradicates it. From the point of view of DI in isolation, rate of rent on total capital investment may rise under a certain set of circumstances. These same circumstances, however, when considered from the point of view of the combination of DI and DII, may (1) see a rise in rate of rent on total capital (i.e., produce a result parallel to that of DI taken in isolation), (2) see a fall in rate of rent, or (3) maintain the same rate of rent. The result is in no way random, even though the balance of forces may generate various – even opposing – sets of modulations among the indicators, making it *appear* as though the outcome is random. The illustration of this problematic as a dynamic of appearance and essence is the thrust of Marx's first hypothetical scenario:

> From one point of view – as far as the product and the production prices are concerned – the productivity of labour has risen. From another point of view, it has declined, since this is what happens to the rate of surplus profit and the surplus product per acre for the various capital investments on the same land. (818)

'Here, therefore', Marx points out, 'differential rent I is completely lost sight of in dealing with rent II' (819).

Marx gives another example: higher-fertility land (C and D) may only yield the product, and rate of rent on capital, as the lowest-fertility land (A) on subsequent investments. If this is the case, high-fertility lands, on subsequent investments, will not form surplus profit / rent. The resulting annual yield would express a decline in productivity while the governing production price would remain the same. In this case,

---

20   Marx works through an example of this distinction on pages 817–18.

two investments on D land, with the second yielding no more than A land, amount to the same as two investments, one on D land and one on A land (821). Or, subsequent investments may yield an increased product, and therefore surplus profit/rent would be formed if the price remains the same. Then again, it may not: if the higher yield throws A land out of cultivation, this would make B land the governing production price: 'The profit rate would rise if this was combined with a fall in wages or if the cheaper product was an element of constant capital' (820). And so on: Marx continues to delineate a variety of scenarios and spins out the resulting modulated effects, including their modified appearances.

One final example: returning to the series represented in tables 5 and 5a (originally tables 1 and 1a on 800–1), we recall that when the number of acres under cultivation doubles, so long as the differences between the types of soil remain constant, nothing changes.

Table 5

Type of Soil	Acres	Price of Production	Product	Rent in Grain	Rent in Money
A	1	£3	1 qrs	0	0
B	1	£3	2 qrs	1 qrs	£3
C	1	£3	3 qrs	2 qrs	£6
D	1	£3	4 qrs	3 qrs	£9
Total	4 acres		10 qrs	6 qrs	£18

Table 5a

Type of Soil	Acres	Price of Production	Product	Rent in Grain	Rent in Money
A	2	£6	2 qrs	0	0
B	2	£6	4 qrs	2 qrs	£6
C	2	£6	6 qrs	4 qrs	£12
D	2	£6	8 qrs	6 qrs	£18
Total	8 acres		20 qrs	12 qrs	£36

Here, we see a straightforward doubling of the product, rent in kind, and rent in money. Rate of rent per acre, as well as the rate of rent on the total capital invested for the cultivated area, remains constant. If we were to imagine that the investment on the second acre of each type of soil was instead a second investment of capital on the same acre, nothing would change. As we have already observed, the series in tables 5 and 5a illustrate that the movements of DI and DII are identical. However, their identity is concealed; at the surface level of form, their movements generate different outcomes. The difference between one investment each on two acres versus two investments on one acre is that, in the second case, one acre now produces double the product and rent, and this doubling increases the price of the land because, as we know, the price of land is capitalized rent:

> We can see from this that, with the production price remaining the same, a constant rate of profit and unchanged differences (and hence an unchanged rate of surplus profit or rent measured on capital), the level of both product- and money-rent per acre can rise, and with it the price of land. (822)

In other words, in the actual combination of DI and DII, rent remains constant as a magnitude from one point of view, and increases from another. This dialectical movement is what Marx attempts to capture in the following description, which refers specifically to this example, and which, if removed from the context of the analysis in part VI – or even that of the whole of *Capital* III – would be incomprehensible:

> Given a constant production price and constant differences, the average rent per acre may rise with the total rental in the case of differential rent I, and so may the average rate of rent on capital. But the average is merely an abstraction. The actual level of rent, per acre or reckoned on capital, remains the same here.
>
> On the same assumption, however, the level of rent measured per acre may rise, even though the rate of rent, measured on the capital laid out, remains the same. (821)

The outcome, when capital investment is spread out over more land, is different from when an investment of the same size is concentrated on less land. In this case, Marx illustrates that the movement of capital at the level of its concept, where DI and DII are identical, is refracted – acted upon – by the conditions of capitalist production in the actual sphere of competition, even as the direction of causality (the order of derivation between DI and DII) remains the same. The actual historical development of a capitalist mode of production will tend towards more intensive investment on land, made possible by the concentration of capital. A widening distribution of capital investment on more parcels of land still can, and does, take place. However, the growth of capital goes hand in hand with more intensive investment made possible by the concentration of capital in fewer farmer-capitalist hands, and fewer landowner hands:

> With the result remaining the same, as far as the mass and value of the total production and the surplus product are concerned, the concentration of capital increases the level of rent per acre on a more restricted area, whereas under the same conditions its scattering over greater area, with other factors remaining the same, could not produce this effect. The more the capitalist mode of production develops, however, the more the concentration of capital on the same area increases, so that the rent per acre rises. Hence in two countries where production prices are the same, the differences between land types the same and the same amount of capital is invested, but in one country more in the form of successive investments on a restricted area and in the other more in the form of coordinated investments on a wider area, the rent per acre and therefore the land price would be higher in the first country and lower in the second, even though the total rental in both countries was the same. This difference in the levels of rent could thus be explained neither in terms of a difference in the natural fertility of the land types nor in the amount of labour applied, but exclusively in terms of the different kind of capital investments. (830–1)

With each of these many examples, Marx illustrates that the otherwise-singular movement of value is expressed in a multiplicity of competing, complimentary, or ambivalent effects whose immediate appearances obscure the value abstraction itself. The interaction of immediate conditions – the magnitude of investment, the type of soil on which it is made, comparative differences between the soil types in cultivation, the size and number of successive investments, on which soil, and so on – can potentially generate any combination of outcomes. These scenarios are historically contingent, but they are not random or accidental; intensive cultivation (successive capital investments on the same soil) will predominantly take place on soil of higher fertility, which means that certain results will occur more frequently (818) and, as such, will tend to be perceived as 'the normal case':

This single case in which the declining yield of capitals subsequently added to the types of land already under cultivation can subsequently lead to a rise in the price of production, a fall in the profit rate and the formation of increased differential rent . . . was treated by Ricardo as the only case, the normal case, and he reduced the formation of differential rent II simply to this. (819)

Marx's guiding objective in part VI is to demonstrate that the interacting conditions of production that situate the formation of ground-rent *are not simply relative*; if they were, the very exercise of calculating the potential modulating outcomes would not be possible. Each example scenario is intended to show that one condition – the degree of productivity – is the governing factor while other factors move in response to productivity. From the point of view of the movement of value, Marx asks, in the formation of ground-rent, what is cause and what is effect? What plays a determining role and what is determined? And why is such a consideration significant at all, given that the distinction disappears in the phenomenon – the actual empirical expression – of ground-rent itself? The reason why the critique of value is always also a question of representation and exposition is because the movement of value can only be mapped in abstraction, which is to say, can only be detected in its effects. However, capital cannot be abolished in its immediacy, by mitigating its effects, as crucial as it is to do so wherever possible. Even if it were possible to ameliorate capital's most brutal and immediate effects, the value form remains determinant for as long as social reproduction is subsumed by the capital–labour relation. Value – itself shorthand for a mode of sociality – remains the invisible centre of gravity of the capital formation, and its abolition the cornerstone of its collective disassembly.

In the material constituting chapters 41 through 44, Marx continues to work through numerous examples of modulating conditions in order to 'show the combinations of differential rent II, [a form] which presupposes differential rent I as its basis' (823). The examples elaborate three general scenarios in the formation of DII: (1) the first case, where modulations in productivity are expressed in a production price that remains constant; (2) the second case, where modulations in productivity are expressed in a falling production price; and (3) the third case, where modulations in productivity are expressed in a rising production price.

I will not take up each example here but, rather, briefly identify the thrust of each case as it relates to the perceptual physics involved in the formation of DII.

Three Cases of Differential Rent II: The Cause and (Mediated) Effect of Productivity and Price

The objective of Marx's three case studies of DII is to demonstrate several things, all aspects of the same process: that production price derives from productivity and not the other way around; that productivity is the outward expression of the movement of value; that productivity (and therefore value) ultimately determines price; and that price does not determine the stability of accumulation nor, in actual competition, the viability of enterprise but is, rather, a thermostat of viable profitability and therefore of the formation of surplus profits, and hence of ground-rent. From one point of view, the exercise of demonstrating that the law of value governs the formation of ground-rent – the orientation of the entirety of part VI – is *in the service of* clarifying these other fundamental dynamics, all aspects of capitalist production more generally.

At this point in the discussion, Engels intervenes on Marx's tables of calculations, explaining that the figures representing the differing yields on different parcels of land are 'sharply exaggerated' and 'lead to completely impossible figures when calculations are made on this basis' (851). Nonetheless, he says,

> Marx's original tables had to be given for the sake of understanding the text itself. But in order to give an intuitive basis to the results of the investigation that follow below, I shall now provide a new series of tables in which the yields are given in bushels . . . and shillings. (851)[21]

---

21   Engels warns ahead of time that this intervention is coming. In footnote 34 in the preceding section, Engels writes, 'An error in calculation running through the above tables . . . made it necessary to rework them. This in no way affected the theoretical perspectives developed from the tables, but it did lead in places to quite monstrous [by which Engels means implausible] numerical ratios for production per acre. Even these are not objectionable in principle . . . Anyone who still feels his agrarian feelings have been injured is free to multiply the number of acres by any figure he chooses . . . The result, the relationship between the rise in rent and rise in capital, still comes out just the same' (839n34).

After reproducing Marx's tables to show the logic involved in the formation of DII, Engels revises all the tables with, according to him, more intuitive and empirically plausible calculations. Engels states:

> The subsequent thirteen tables correspond to the three cases of differential rent II dealt with in this chapter and the two previous ones [i.e., chapters 41–43], for an *additional* capital investment on the same land of 50s. per acre, and a price of production that may be constant, falling or rising. Each of these cases is again presented in the shape it assumes (1) with the same productivity for the second capital investment as for the first, (2) with falling productivity and (3) with rising productivity. (851)[22]

In the first case – the formation of DII with constant production price – we see that constant, rising, or falling levels of productivity can, in each of the three scenarios, be expressed in a production price that remains unchanged, disassembling a sense of the specific relation of cause and effect between these two factors. Marx's wider point, with respect to the three cases of DII taken together, is to discern, in the relationships between the factors, *what is cause and what is effect*, and to show that the appearance of causality departs from the deeper governing movement:

> The differences in the rents from the different types of land and their relationship to one another may change in this case; but this change in these differences is here the result of the wider spread of rents and not its cause. (827)

In the first case, a scenario that Marx revisits from the preceding section (and discussed above), the summary is as follows:

---

22 Engels's revised versions of Marx's tables – which provide, according to Engels, rational, or more 'empirically realistic', figures – are given in the text in pages 853–7. We do not need to reproduce these revised tables, or Marx's original series of tables depicting the three cases of DII and their variants, for the discussion that follows, since we will not be referring to the calculations specifically. Instead, we simply summarize what the different cases of DII illustrate with respect to the perceptual mystifications of the source of ground-rent that are introduced with subsequent capital investments on the same parcel of land under differing conditions. The illustration of these perceptual mystifications in question is the entire analytical thrust of chapters 41 to 44 of *Capital* III.

Assuming stable production prices, the extra capital investments can be made with constant, increasing or decreasing productivity on the better lands, i.e. on all land from B upwards. On A itself, this would only be possible, on our assumptions, either with productivity unchanged, in which case the land would continue to bare no rent, or if productivity increases; one part of the capital invested on land A would then bear rent, the other not. But it would be impossible on the assumption that A's productivity declines, for in that case the production price would not remain constant, but would rise. (829–30)

In the second case – the formation of DII with falling production price – we see that constant, rising, or falling levels of productivity can, in each of the three scenarios, be expressed in a falling production price. A fall in production price emerges from circumstances where the production price for A land is no longer the governing price. Multiple sets of circumstances can produce this situation; one scenario might entail the withdrawal of A land from cultivation in response to a smaller demand that can be met by the aggregate product of B, C, and D; or, the product may grow as a result of additional investments on the higher-yielding parcels of land, rendering the product of A land superfluous – in which case B land now becomes that which governs production price (and now produces no rent), with a consequent fall in production price. Marx shows how extra capital invested in C and/or D, in various combinations, produces all possible results, where 'rent per acre may grow, decline, or remain the same' (840). Further, this situation can remain the case when the additional capitals invested in C and/or D have a stable rate of productivity, a falling rate of productivity, or a rising rate of productivity.[23]

Marx did not elaborate the third case – the formation of DII with a rising production price. It is therefore worked out by Engels in the

---

23   Engels offers a brief historical reference for the second case, variant two: falling prices and falling productivity on additional capital investments. This situation, Engels argues, became the rule in Europe after the repeal of the Corn Laws in 1846 and the opening up of grain production to 'global' competition from North and South America and India. Facilitated by transoceanic steamships and railways in these colonial territories, European farmers were put into competition with Indian and Russian peasant farmers, as well as farmers on the North American prairies and the Argentine pampas (859–60).

text: 'A rising price of production presupposes a decline in productivity on the lowest quality of land, which pays no rent . . . or if a still poorer soil than A has to be brought into cultivation' (847). In the first example, productivity falls in the original investment and we see that a rising production price compensates 'for the decline in productivity, both for product and money rent' (848).[24] This scenario can also be considered as a reconfiguration of the formation of DI because it modulates the differences in original fertility between the parcels of land as a basis for DII. For this reason, as Engels stipulates, in order to abstract the movement of the third case, the modification is figured as a fall in productivity on the second investment only, while the productivity on the first investment remains constant. We also see that a fall in productivity will find product and selling price vary in inverse proportion,[25] while money rental and rate of rent remain the same.[26] Here, the rise in selling price makes up for the fall in productivity, even when the number and magnitude of the capital investments remain the same. Engels's observation, upon revising all of Marx's tables and providing the description of the experiments undertaken therein, is to reiterate the formulation that emerged early on as the guiding thread of the analysis in part VI: 'It is not the absolute yields that determine rent, but simply the differences in the yields' (857). Once again, negating the idea that land per se can be the source of any capitalist form of profit, the analysis places the law of value at the abstract core of the formation of ground-rent. Engels also reiterates that even in the event that agricultural productivity should decline, the legal fiction of the landowner bestows the capacity to absorb a certain portion of the total social surplus-value:

> Thus the more capital is applied to the land and the higher the development of agriculture and civilization in general in a country, the higher are the levels of rent per acre and the total sum of rent and the more gigantic therefore the tribute society pays the great landowners in the form of surplus profits. (859)

24 Either Marx's original tables or Engels's revised tables suffice for illustration of the dynamic invoked. Sticking with Marx's original tables, this first example is illustrated by the comparison made in the series in *Table VII* and *Table VIII* on page 848.

25 As illustrated in Marx's *Table X* on page 849.

26 As compared with the series in Marx's *Table VII* and *Table VIII* on page 848.

As DI is the basis for, and presupposed by, DII, the motivation for making additional capital investments in land is to either 'even out the differences [in fertility between different parcels of land] or intensify them' (841). The outcome, however, of the combined formation of DI and DII is that 'their respective effects melt indistinguishably together' (843). The law of value – value itself – is the movement of a particular historical sociality; value is a dynamic of social averages that cannot appear immediately as such. The formation of DII is an expression of this 'social averaging' – forming a material and operational appearance that contains and establishes the limiting thresholds for accumulation. The outcomes of successive investments on the same land (magnitude of product, rent formed, etc.) are aggregated to form the combined outcome that stands as the individual production price (and hence differential rent formed) for that parcel of land. If four successive investments are made on the same parcel, and each investment yields at a different level of productivity, the rent-forming differential will be the aggregate of the four investments. For example, if the first two investments each generate surplus profits and the second two investments generate 'negative surplus profits' (which is to say, generate less than the general rate of profit), and if we suppose that the positive and negative surplus profits are equal magnitudes, they will, in this case, cancel each other out, and the four investments combined have formed no rent (or, more accurately, a rent of zero). If the four successive investments were made on B land, in effect, B land therefore yields at the same production price over the time of the four investments as does A land, the land which governs production price and forms no rent:

> The establishment of equality between the individual average production price on B and the general production price on A, which governs the market, presupposes that the amount by which the individual price of the product of the earlier capital investments stands below the governing price is offset more and more, and finally cancelled out by the amount by which the product of the later capital investments comes to stand above the governing price. What appears as surplus profit, as long as the product of the earlier capital investments is sold by itself, gradually becomes part of the average production price and thereby goes into the formation of the average profit until it is finally absorbed by this entirely. (866)

If the investments that yield at an individual production price above the governing price begin to outweigh the investments that generate surplus profits and continue to the point where B land is producing at a higher production price than A land, then B land takes the place of A as the worst soil. This dynamic represents an upward pressure on the general production price. Nonetheless, the general production price would not actually rise until the better land (as well as the worst land, A) began producing at an individual production price that was higher than the average:

> Even . . . the disappearance of rent on the better types of land would mean only that the individual production price of the product from these better types would coincide with the general price of production; no rise in this general price would yet be required. (868)

Under such conditions of falling productivity on successive investments and a constant governing production price on land of higher fertility than A land (say, B land), differential rent may absorb the positive surplus profits on the first investments such that these surplus profits are unable to balance out the results of the negative surplus profits on the later investments. This event will increase the governing production price from, say, three to four pounds. But this increased production price will in turn cause a rise in the rent on B land for the higher-productivity investments, and rent will now be formed on A land.

This 'moving contradiction' can be described as such: differential rent (as the transfer of surplus profits to the landowner) sets a limit that prevents the balancing out of the yields of the four investments, an aggregate balance that would otherwise keep the governing production price from rising. But as this limit increases production price, it creates the conditions for more surplus-value to be formed into differential rent. Therefore, 'the increase in the capital invested on the same land tends rather to find its limit in this transference [of surplus profit to the landowner] . . . in fact it comes up against a more or less artificial barrier.' The rise in the governing production price is the basis for the rise in differential rent, but differential rent – the very fact of the transfer of the surplus profits that would otherwise balance out the 'negative profits' and cancel out their effects – is the basis for the 'earlier and more rapid rise in the general price of production in order thereby to guarantee the increased supply of the product that has become necessary' (870). And around we go. However, if A land were able to supply the extra product needed for less than the production price, or if new land were brought into competition with a production price that was above the original three pounds but less than four pounds, then the production price would not rise.

Even though DI is the basis and presupposition of DII, and even though this relation of cause and effect is sustained as the process of accumulation proceeds and develops, what we see in this example is that the formation of DII also exerts a reciprocal impact on the vicissitudes of accumulation as the process continues, in setting new thresholds and limits by the social averages that emerge from the movement of competing capitals. The legal fiction of landowning and the absorption of surplus profit erect an 'artificial barrier' to ongoing accumulation to which the farmer-capitalist is compelled to respond in one way or another:

> We thus see how differential rent I and differential rent II, while the first is the basis of the second, at the same time place limits on one another, leading sometimes to successive investments of capital on the same stretch of land and sometimes on adjacent investments of capital on new additional land. (870–1)

Absolute Ground-Rent

Marx devotes a substantial amount of space in part VI to revisiting 'the fundamentals' of the movement of value – value formations that were presented in parts I, II, and III. In particular, we revisit the relation of variable capital to constant capital, that is, the dynamics of capital composition as they take the more concrete forms of productivity, cost price and profit, equalization, production price, general rate of profit, and so on. This summary and rearticulation of the movement of value, undertaken near the end of *Capital* III, is neither a digression nor simply a matter of recalling theoretical formulations that were worked out several hundreds of pages earlier. The analysis of absolute ground-rent once again situates these formations at the forefront of the narrative, demanding that we grasp the full extent of the interconnectedness, consistency, and theoretical coherency of the analysis as presented, step by step, in the material that constitutes *Capital* III. The need to recall earlier formulations in order to present the formation of absolute ground-rent illustrates that the material in *Capital* III is not a collection of formulations from which we can pick and choose but, rather, a systematic *theory* of the capital formation, each moment anticipating and presupposing the totality of the moving configuration, from part I to the final, abandoned chapter of part VII.

The law of differential rent leaves us with a mystery to solve: if the worst land (i.e., the lowest-fertility land made viable for cultivation by demand) forms no differential rent and governs the market price of the product, whence comes the rent paid to the landowner for its use? For the sake of discovering the movement of ground-rent at its concept, we suppose that the personifiers of capital have divided into a landowner and a farmer-capitalist, that the latter is contractually obliged to pay rent to the former regardless of whether the land forms differential rent or not, and that rent – to be consistent with the laws of capitalist production – is not a deduction from wages nor from the farmer's profit as their portion of the total social surplus at the general rate of profit (883). However, in the 'actual world' of capitalist competition, rent must be paid on *all* land, including the worst land; therefore, only land that can form a rent over and above production price will be brought into cultivation, regardless of existing demand. Here, capitalist landed property acts as the first barrier to accumulation:

> It is as an alien power and a barrier of this kind that landed property confronts capital as regards its investment on the land, or that the landowner confronts the capitalist.
>
> Here landed property is the barrier that does not permit any new capital investment on formerly uncultivated or unleased land without levying a toll, i.e. demanding a rent, even if the land newly brought under cultivation is of a kind that does not yield any differential rent, and which save for landed property could have been cultivated already. (896)

Landed property, therefore, must form another kind of rent alongside differential rent but 'conceptually distinct from differential rent'; Marx calls this social form absolute ground-rent (895). The logical formation of absolute ground-rent derives from the organic composition of capital in agricultural production – the ratio of constant to variable capital typical for capital investment in the production of staple crops at a given stage of technological development. The organic composition of capital expresses several factors characterizing a given sphere of production at a given time: the technological composition of production; the value/price of labour-power (value averaged across spheres of production); and the historical and political conditions that have an impact on capitalist producers' *access to*, as well as the value/price of, land, raw material, and other means of production. Access to land is, of course, of crucial significance in the case of land as means of production, and Marx makes reference to the centrality of the process of colonization in the emergence of capitalist landed property early on in the part VI and again in the section on absolute ground-rent with reference to British expansionist politician Edward Gibbon Wakefield's theory of the 'science' of colonial governance as identifying the conditions required for the emergence of capital. For Marx, Wakefield inadvertently makes a crucial discovery: in the emerging capital formation, landownership per se is not the source of wealth but rather represents the power to appropriate a portion of wealth (generated by labour applied to production), as well as the power to block its formation until the conditions for its appropriation are extant:

Our problem [i.e., the formation of absolute ground-rent] is not solved . . . by making reference to colonial conditions. What makes a colony a colony – and here we are referring only to agricultural colonies proper – is not just the amount of fertile land to be found in its natural condition. It is rather the situation that this land is not appropriated, is not subsumed under landed property. It is this that makes for the tremendous distinction between the old countries and the colonies as far as land is concerned: the legal or factual non-existence of landed property, as Wakefield correctly notes . . . Thus if we want to investigate how landed property affects the prices of its products, and rent, in cases where it restricts the land as a field of investment for capital, it is completely absurd to refer to free bourgeois colonies where neither the capitalist mode of production in agriculture nor the form of landed property corresponding to this exists, indeed where landed property does not exist at all. This is what Ricardo does . . .

Legal ownership of land, by itself, does not give the proprietor any ground-rent. It certainly does give him the power, however, to withdraw his land from cultivation until economic conditions permit a valorization of it that yields him a surplus, whether the land is used for agriculture proper or for other productive purposes such as building, etc. (890–1)

The economic conditions for cultivated land, including A land, to yield a surplus profit and consequently form absolute ground-rent are that the value of agricultural products be higher than their production price. This situation exists when the composition of agricultural capital is *lower* than the social average (894); that is, this occurs when agricultural capital expresses a higher ratio of variable to constant capital than is average for production across spheres – a condition that, in more colloquial terms, we might describe as high labour-intensity. At the time of Marx's writing, the composition of agricultural capital was indeed lower than the social average – something that he points out is '*prima facie* an expression of the fact that in countries of developed production, agriculture has not progressed to the same extent as manufacturing industry' and, therefore, that the conditions for the formation of absolute ground-rent could be supposed. Marx anticipates, however, that these economic conditions will cease to exist as capitalist agriculture continues to develop, and he anticipates the obsolescence of absolute ground-rent altogether – a situation that has likely now occurred, but which, as Marx states, 'is a question which can be settled only by statistical investigation and which it would be superfluous *for our purpose* to go into in detail' (894, my emphasis).

Capital is not an investigation of the 'actual' historical development of the capitalist formation – of capital in its institutional and political forms, as a history of marketplace competition or logistics, or as a history of class struggle – even though Marx will use historical examples of each of these formations to illustrate the outward expression of the inner movement in question. Marx's focus on the inner movement of capital, however, does not imply that capital's actual history of development is of lesser significance. If anything, it is the reverse: Marx often betrays an exasperation that seeks to establish the analysis of capital's inner movement *once and for all*, so that the more important and urgent work of mapping capital's historical trajectory, including its 'eventual' abolition, can begin with a new necessary clarity. This latter project is infinitely vaster than that of *Capital*, summoning a division of intellectual labour, and a historical trajectory of its own. The outward expression of capital is constantly transformed – and therefore so is its analysis – by ever-developing productive and technological capacities – a situation reflected in the proliferation of qualifiers associated with 'capital': 'imperial', 'monopoly', 'global', 'postmodern', 'neoliberal', 'financial', 'communicational', 'informational', 'circulatory', 'platform', and so on.

It is consistent, then, that Marx does not explore the historical development of agricultural production yet indicates that such a history is of crucial importance in the wider study of the capitalist formation.[27] For instance, at the end of the chapter on absolute ground-rent, Marx makes a list of factors – exposited briefly but not elaborated – that will have an impact on whether new land will or will not be drawn into cultivation depending on whether those conditions allow or impede the formation of rent: (1) the interaction – that is, the counterbalancing, or outweighing of one by the other – of absolute ground-rent and differential rent, in the sense that fertility and location can bring land into competition that would not be brought otherwise; (2) the development of science and technology; (3) the legal (or political) organization of land as private property versus common lands; (4) the exigencies of market activity and the 'business climate' of a particular country at a particular time (periods of stagnation versus periods of economic growth, credit conditions, and so on).[28]

---

27   Aaron Benanav has provided much of this analysis in *Automation and the Future of Work*, Verso, 2020. Benanav undertakes the kind of updating work on both the technical and value composition of agricultural capital that is required in order to map the path of obsolescence taken by the social form of absolute ground-rent, from Marx's time of writing to the present.

28   The question of the impact of the social formation on the development of capitalist production is, of course, much more involved than this short list suggests; it subsequently moves into the analysis of the capitalist state as the necessary political form of capital, as well as the relationship – always historically specific, today as ever – between the overtly violent and coercive modalities of accumulation and those that proceed by way of the 'silent compulsion' of exploitation as economic necessity: 'It makes a substantial difference whether the national capital is transformed into industrial capital gradually and slowly, or whether this transformation is accelerated in time by the taxes they impose via protective duties, principally on the landowners, small and middle peasants and artisans, by the accelerated expropriation of independent direct producers, by the forcibly accelerated accumulation and concentration of capital, in short, by the accelerated production of the conditions of the capitalist mode of production' (920).

Individual commodities are not sold at their values; except for the occasional accident, commodities are sold at market prices that are the averages derived from individual production prices, both of which sit above or below commodity values. If commodities *were* sold at their values, capital would collapse, or, more accurately, could not have emerged in the first place. Another way of saying this is that capital presupposes the process of equalization. Agricultural commodities are, therefore, not the only commodities sold below their values. The difference, however, is that in the case of non-agricultural commodities, the value magnitude that constitutes the difference between the commodity's value and its production price (surplus profit) is redistributed across the capitalist class through the movement of equalization. In the case of agricultural commodities, surplus profit takes the form of absolute ground-rent and is redistributed to the landowner. In one of the many instances where, in the analysis of absolute ground-rent, Marx rearticulates formulations laid out in much-earlier chapters, he lays down the clearest and most explicit articulation of the movement of equalization in the whole of *Capital* III:

It is the constant tendency of capitals to bring about, by competition, this adjustment in the distribution of the surplus-value that the total capital produces, and to overcome all obstacles towards it. It is therefore their tendency only to tolerate such surplus profits as arise, under whatever circumstances, not from the difference between the values of commodities and their prices of production, but rather from the general price of production governing the market and the individual production prices differing from this; surplus profits which therefore do not arise between two different spheres of production but rather within each sphere of production, so that they do not affect the general production prices of the different spheres, i.e. the general rate of profit, but rather presuppose both the transformation of value into price of production and the general rate of profit. This presupposition, however, depends as already explained on the continuously changing proportionate distribution of the total social capital between the various spheres of production; on a continuous immigration and emigration of capitals; on their transferability from one sphere to another; in short on their free movement between these

various spheres of production as so many available fields of investment
for the independent parts of the total social capital. (895)

Capital can tolerate the virtually nominal competition between
producers within a given sphere of production – competition that may
reward one enterprise one year and remove it from the field the next.
As Marx explains in this passage, this kind of superficial competition
presupposes general production prices and the general rate of profit,
and it does not jeopardize the reproduction of either. Capital *cannot*
tolerate significant, systematic, and consistent discrepancies in profitability at the most concrete expression of the total social capital, that
is, in the levels of profitability across spheres of production. In such a
situation, the conditions of possibility for a non-organized ('free
market') social division of labour disintegrate, and, with them, the
conditions for a capitalist mode of production altogether. In this way,
we see that capitalist landed property functions not only as obstacle to
accumulation, as we established above. It functions, at the same time,
as the facilitator of accumulation by absorbing the surplus profit that
would otherwise make agricultural production more profitable than
other forms of industry, and which would bring the necessary, equal-
izing flow of value across spheres of production to a halt. Like all
aspects of the moving contradiction that constitutes capital in its totality, this moving contradiction of capitalist landed property as both
obstacle and facilitator of accumulation can be described as dialectical, but it may be better understood as the historical substance of the
dialectic itself.

Absolute ground-rent may absorb the entirety of the agricultural
product's surplus profit, or it may absorb only one portion of it, leaving
another portion to enter into general equalization (896). In either case,
market price must be higher than production price (while still being
below the product's value) to form absolute ground-rent, and Marx
refers to this market price as the product's monopoly price (897). This is
not a 'genuine' monopoly price, in the sense of a price detached from the
movement of value and expressing a circumstantial demand backed by
an ability to pay – the dynamics of which Marx consigns to the
hypothetical study of competition, 'where the *actual* movement of
market prices is investigated' (898, my emphasis). The value form of the
agricultural product's market price is, rather, a relative monopoly price

whose logical, quantitative limits are the gap between the product's production price and its value:

> It equally follows that it is only as a result of the monopoly of landed property that the excess value of the agricultural product over their price of production at a particular moment can come to be their general market price. It finally follows that in this case it is not the rise in the product's price that is the cause of the rent but rather the rent that is the cause of the rise in price. (897)

The monopoly of landed property – the 'landowner always ready to draw a rent' – demands the formation of absolute rent. Whether or not the conditions exist for capital 'to fulfil this desire' is another story. If conditions are extant, landed property catalyses the production of absolute rent as a logical component of the surplus-value of every commodity – agricultural commodity or otherwise – whose value composition exceeds the social average, whether or not that value-component manifests as rent or enters equalization:

> Rent then forms a part of the value of commodities, in particular of their surplus-value, which simply accrues to the landowners who extract it from the capitalists, instead of to the capitalist class who have extracted it from the workers. (906)

Absolute rent continues to be a logical component of a commodity's surplus-value so long as agricultural capital sets more labour in motion on average than industrial capital. Once the composition of agricultural capital rises to meet the composition of the average social capital (the average of all large-scale productive capital across spheres) – or surpasses it, as could imaginably be the case today with agriculture's increasing 'technologization' (mechanized harvesting, computerized irrigation, genetically modified seed, etc.) over the past century and a half – the formation of absolute rent is obsolete:

> If the average composition of agricultural capital were the same as that of the average social capital, or even higher than this, the result would be the disappearance of absolute rent in the sense developed above, namely a rent that is different both from differential rent and

from rent depending on an actual monopoly price. The value of the agricultural product would not stand above its price of production, and agricultural capital would not set more labour in motion, and would thus not realize more surplus labour, than did non-agricultural capital. It would be the same thing if the composition of agricultural capital were equalized with that of the average social capital as agriculture advanced. (899)

A prolonged intensification of the exploitation of agricultural labour may also increase the value composition of agricultural capital and thereby push towards the obsolescence of absolute ground-rent. For example, it is now conventional practice – in the imperial core *and* periphery – to import seasonal, non-local agricultural labour at wages below the 'local' value of labour-power. The legal comportment of 'foreign' migrant labour, both formal and informal, excluding workers from the predicates of citizenship – a minimum wage, worker benefits, health care, or the protection and supports of union representation (where these things still exist) – suspends these wages below the value of labour-power. Here, it is not exceptionally low wages that racialize workers but, rather, the process of racialized exclusion that makes it possible to depress these wages below the value of labour-power, as well as to stabilize an economy of remittance payments back to the permanently developing postcolonial periphery. Indeed, the latter flow of value is now so thoroughly established as a permanent feature of the global capital formation that it has been financialized as investment instruments for surplus capital – investments which literally bank on the permanence of global poverty. Permanently 'exceptional' low wages for agricultural labour will also lower the value of labour-power more generally, as they lower the value of staple food commodities that factor into the value of labour-power everywhere.

A higher rate of exploitation of the variable portion of agricultural capital increases its value composition without altering the technical composition, reducing the gap between the value of the agricultural product and its production price – and again propelling the redundancy of absolute ground-rent. Here we see, once again, that the movement of capital is intrinsically contradictory. The development of social production in agriculture is expressed in both force and counterforce, tendency and countertendency: on the one hand, increasing productivity of agricultural labour will tend to increase surplus profits, the fruits of which fall to the landowner as ground-rent by growing the portion of surplus labour that takes the form of differential rent; on the other hand, a growing composition of agricultural capital, as a result of the technological development of production and/or the intensified exploitation of agricultural labour, reduces the gap between the production price of the agricultural product and its value, shrinking, or obsolescing outright, the portion of surplus labour that takes the form of absolute ground-rent. Force and counterforce weigh against each other, and the resulting balance is the outcome expressed at the level of the social formation in the actual sphere of competition, in the strategies of competing capitalists locked in battle for market share. Of course, the outcomes of these capitalist strategies are ultimately expressed in their brutal consequences for agricultural workers – the human cost so apparently unconnected to the capitalist function of abstraction that turns their collective labour into ground-rent.

Both force and counterforce, however, compel the concentration of landownership. The redundancy of absolute ground-rent turns the relative monopoly price of the agricultural product into a genuine monopoly price for those pieces of land that do not produce differential rent. In this event, rent is constituted by a portion of variable capital (wages) and/or a portion of the farmer-capitalist's profit. The first case further intensifies the rate of exploitation of agricultural labour; the second case jeopardizes the competitive viability of enterprise and increases the likelihood of its absorption by larger enterprises that *do* generate differential rent and thus could balance out the impact of producing with some portion of less fertile land.

In chapter 46, Marx returns to the question of the price of land – that most irrational economic form of land, the automatic fetish in land, so to speak, whose substance in socialized living labour is so thoroughly mystified – to think through its relationship to absolute ground-rent. The price of land, formed through the capitalization of rent, appears in its everyday inversion to be the justification for commanding and extracting rent, rather than as derived from rent, and appears unrelated to the surplus-value generated by productive labour in any respect. In a demeanour almost uncannily rational, Marx confronts this mystification by framing the conceptual severance of the price of land from its social substance in value in mathematical terms to show that (1) the price of land may rise as rent stays the same, while (2) the price of land may rise *because* rent rises; a rise in rent always brings with it a rise in the price of land, which may or may not accompany a growing product. These dry calculations are an alternative articulation of the same perceptual fetish with which Marx opens the chapter, so dramatically different in tone, but also a denaturalization of a should-be-impossible world made possible by the institution of capitalist social relations of production and property. Here, the perverse figure of human beings owning property in the earth is only surpassed in horrific absurdity by the figure of the racialized, enslaved person as the property of another human being:

> The fact that it is only the title a number of people have to property in the earth that enables them to appropriate a part of society's surplus labour as tribute, and in an ever growing measure as production develops, is concealed by the fact that the capitalized rent, i.e. precisely this capitalized tribute, appears as the price of land, which can be bought and sold just like any other item of trade. For the buyer, therefore, his claim to rent does not appear as something obtained for nothing, without labour, risk or the entrepreneurial spirit of capital, but rather as the return for his equivalent. Rent seems to him, as we have already noted, simply interest on the capital with which he has purchased the land, and with it the claim to rent. In exactly the same way, it appears to the slaveowner who has bought [an enslaved worker] that his property in the [enslaved person] is created not by the institution of slavery as such but rather by the purchase and sale of this commodity. But the purchase does not produce the title; it simply transfers it. The title must be there before it can be bought, and neither one sale nor a series of such sales, their constant repetition, can create this title. It was entirely created by the relations of production. (911)

Slavery – as institution, as mode of production – is overcome after centuries of violent struggle; at the same time, the institution of wage labour, and a function of abstract wealth creation (exploitation), moves to the core of socialized life-making. It is only apparent in retrospect that slavery must be 'sloughed off', that it must become exceptional as a production relation for this to happen (it need not disappear entirely, as we know it has not). Slavery's corresponding form of wealth, wealth in kind – even when that wealth is property in human chattel – prevents the full development of capital (as much as it is a necessary basis for its emergence), prevents the full subsumption of labour and production, and prevents the emergence of 'the concept of capital', the invisible function of abstraction that subsequently becomes a mediating determinant in social reproduction.[29]

The concept of capital, a force of propulsion, capitalist social movement itself, introduces to history the necessity of constant motion, and Marx takes a moment to rehearse, as he does so many times throughout *Capital* III, capital's real but unrealized trajectory towards the horizon of its own obsolescence:

> Once [capitalist production relations – like slavery before them –] have reached the point where they have to be sloughed off, then the material source, the economically and historically justified source of the title that arises from the process of life's social production, disappears, and with it all transactions based on it. From the standpoint of a higher socioeconomic formation, the private property of particular individuals in the earth will appear just as absurd as the private property of one man in other men. Even an entire society, a nation, or all simultaneously existing societies taken together, are not the owners of the earth. They are simply its possessors, its beneficiaries, and have to bequeath it in an improved state to succeeding generations, as *boni patres familias*. (911)

Conclusion: Capital's Self-Image in Embryonic Forms of Rent

The objective of the final chapter, 'The Genesis of Capitalist Ground-Rent', squares up with the thrust of the whole of part VI: to denaturalize the capitalist form of ground-rent. In the final chapter, however, mathematical illustration relents to other expositional strategies. First, Marx spars with the theories and conceptions of ground-rent advanced by the physiocrats, mercantilists, classical political economists, modern

---

29 'The specific economic form in which unpaid surplus labour is pumped out of the direct producers determines the relationship of domination and servitude, as this grows directly out of production itself and reacts back on it in turn as a determinant. On this is based the entire configuration of the economic community arising from the actual relations of production, and hence also its specific political form' (927).

bourgeois economists, and certain economic historians.[30] The purpose of engaging with past and contemporary economic theory at this stage of the analysis of ground-rent (an engagement that Marx develops more systematically in *Theories of Surplus-Value*) is to show that a particular conception of the economic form of land in rent, representative of both popular and 'expert' understanding, is itself an excrescence – the 'theoretical expression', in Marx's words – of capital's own movement:

> [Ground-rent] has still not been understood even by the large number of more recent writers, as is shown by each new attempt to give ground-rent a 'new' explanation. The novelty ... consists almost invariably in regression to a standpoint long superseded. (917)

Capital's self-narrative is an endless (and origin-less) line of newly dressed-up versions of itself that are, as Marx points out, always already obsolete. It is a perceptual physics that plays out today, as it did then, in calls to attend to this or that 'new capitalism', or to the death of capital altogether and its succession by something meaner (a new feudalism, a new colonialism, a new mode of dispossession), without attending to what is unique to capital that stays the same across these so-called new capitalisms. It is true that capital's surface forms do – indeed *must* – continually transform over time; but for these transformations and hence capital's reproduction to proceed (they are one and the same), capital's 'hidden basis' must persist, a content–form relationship that cannot be read or analysed directly from capital's surface expressions

---

30   In this chapter, Marx spars with the ideas of (in order of appearance): William Petty (regarded by Marx as the founder of classical political economy); Richard Cantillon (English economist and merchant); James Steuart (mercantilist school); Eugène Daire (minor economic writer and editor of a collection of physiocratic writings); H. P. Passy (contemporary economic writer); Jean Herrenschwand (Swiss economist); Adam Smith; Herr Mommsen (economic historian and author of *Römische Geschichte*); Johann Karl Rodbertus (contemporary political economist); and Hermann Maron (journalist and revolutionary). He makes reference to many other economic historians and thinkers for confirmation of his own arguments, such as Pierre-Denis Vinçard, Karl Arnd, Simon-Nicolas-Henri Linguet, Justus Möser, Antoine-Eugène Buret, De Tocqueville, Sismondi, Thomas Tooke and William Newmarch, L. Mounier and M. Rubichon (co-authors of *De L'agriculture en France*, 1846), Joseph Massie, Christophe Mathieu de Dombasle, and Justus von Liebig. The Penguin Classics edition of *Capital* III includes an Index of Authorities Quoted that includes all authors cited by Marx, and the titles and dates of their cited publications.

(forms, appearances) alone. A theoretical approach (Marx's term is 'scientific') is singularly adequate to capture in analysis capital's hidden basis, even as theory/science collaborates with all kinds of thinking, knowing, investigating, and articulating: historical, empirical, statistical, ethnographic, aesthetic, embodied, poetic, affective, and so on. Marx's alternative figure for this dynamic that can only be captured in theory, and which continues to be as relevant as it is consistently misconstrued, is 'base/superstructure', a figure that encompasses the entire thematic material assembled in *Capital* III:

> The specific economic form in which unpaid surplus labour is pumped out of the direct producers [the base or 'hidden basis' – as below] determines the relationship of domination and servitude, as this grows directly out of the production itself and reacts back on it in turn as a determinant. On this is based the entire configuration of the economic community [the superstructure] arising from the actual relations of production, and hence also its specific political form. It is in each case the direct relationship of the owners of the conditions of production to the immediate producers – a relationship whose particular form naturally corresponds always to a certain level of development of the type and manner of labour, and hence to its social productive power – in which we find the innermost secret, the hidden basis of the entire social edifice, and hence also the political form of the relationship of sovereignty and dependence, in short, the specific form of state in each case. This does not prevent the same economic basis – the same in its major conditions – from displaying endless variations and gradations in its appearance, as the result of innumerable different empirical circumstances, natural conditions, racial relations, historical influences acting from outside, etc., and these can only be understood by analyzing these empirically given conditions. (927–8)

If bourgeois (i.e., unscientific, non-dialectical, 'evidence-based', etc.) economic thought is the inverted theoretical surface-form of capital itself and, as such, produces novel figures already superseded, the second beat of Marx's defamiliarizing strategy is to walk through pre-capitalist forms of rent whose superseded standpoints form the trajectory of capital's becoming (a non-teleological trajectory and, as such, only recognizable in retrospect). Marx puts capitalist ground-rent in relief by differentiating it from superseded forms of rent – its genetic material – characterized by perceptual dynamics of immediacy and transparency that are eventually succeeded and inverted by a capitalist mode of mediation and fetish.

1. Labour rent

The case of labour rent, where the producer works part of the week for themselves and part for the landlord, is a special case and particularly strategic in this regard. Labour rent expresses an immediate relation of domination and servitude that renders rent transparent as nothing other than a portion of the immediate producer's surplus labour:

> In all forms where the actual worker . . . remains the 'possessor' of the means of production . . . the property relationship must *appear* at the same time as a direct relationship of domination and servitude, and the direct producer therefore as an unfree person . . . Under these conditions, the surplus labour for the nominal landlord can only be extorted from them by extra-economic compulsion, whatever the form this might assume. (926)

In the case of labour rent such as the corvée, even though surplus labour is extracted by coercive means, the producer is not separated from the means of production and maintains a degree of personal independence. This ambivalent independence, however, is extinguished in the case of slavery:

> This differs from the slave or planation economy in that the [enslaved person] works with conditions of production that do not belong to him, and does not work independently. Relations of personal dependence are therefore necessary, in other words personal unfreedom, to whatever degree, and being chained to the land as its accessory – bondage in the true sense. (927)

Despite this distinction, slavery and the corvée system share a mode of direct extraction and, as relations of domination, are both immediate and transparent. Conditions of immediate and transparent domination are also the case when the state is the nominal landlord. Here, the form of possession may be either private or communal; nonetheless, in the case where landed property is concentrated on a national scale, tax and rent coincide: 'Under these conditions, the relationship of dependence does not need to possess any stronger form, either politically or economically, than that which is common to all subjection to this state' (927).

In all of its possible forms, however, the pre-capitalist relation of labour rent reveals the secret that capital keeps hidden: 'that [all] surplus-value coincides with the unpaid labour of others' (928). With labour rent, surplus-value is extracted 'directly in the brutal form of forced labour for a third party'; here, surplus-value is arrested in its most immediate, 'visible and palpable' form as surplus labour, unlike with capital, where surplus-value undergoes further transformations of form to become profit, interest, dividends, wages, ground-rent, and other forms of capitalist rent on buildings, vehicles, intellectual property, and so on. In other words, it is what labour rent has in common with capitalist rent that reveals the latter's 'secret': that every social form of surplus-value in a capitalist mode of production is constituted by nothing other than surplus labour. While capitalist forms of rent mystify their source, the source of labour rent is immediately clear – 'the labour of the direct producer for himself being still separate both in time and space from his work for the landlord', and no further rent demanded on top of this. Further, with labour rent, there can be no mystification of land as possessing an innate rent-bearing capacity:

> The 'property' the land has of yielding a rent is reduced here to a palpably open secret, for the same nature that delivers rent also includes the human labour-power that is chained to the land, and the property relationship that forces [the owner of labour-power] to exert and activate this labour-power beyond the degree that would be required to satisfy his own indispensable needs. (928)

In other words, labour rent exposes its own conditions and those of capitalist forms of rent alike – namely, that the economic form of land in rent, in all class societies, is a function of the capacity of human labour chained to it.

Labour rent also makes transparent, therefore, the fact that rent can only grow in proportion to the degree of labour's exploitation – another logical limit of capital that is mystified in the transformation of form from labour rent to capitalist rent (934). What is clear with labour rent, and mystified with capitalist rent, is that rent cannot grow to assume a portion of the surplus labour that prohibits the immediate producer from meeting their indispensable reproductive needs. The limit for *all* forms of rent, therefore, is the reproductive needs of labour-power. In the case of labour rent, the social relation between producer and landlord is directly coercive, and the upward limit of labour rent is, therefore, immediately apparent. In the case of capitalist ground-rent, the social relation between producer and landlord is mediated and indirect, and that which establishes the otherwise-identical hard limit on what capitalist rent is able to command recedes from immediate perception. The movement of capitalist rent constitutes a mystification because, unlike labour rent, capitalist rent is a *social* form: the limit of what it can command is no longer the reproductive needs of the individual producer but, rather, the reproductive needs of the producing class, of the collective worker. Capitalist rent generates an absolute limit that is no longer set individually but, rather, is now set system-wide; it is a form of *social* domination rather than the domination of individual producers. As a movement of social domination, capitalist ground-rent is mediated and, as such, involves a perceptual dissolution of the source of collectivized misery.

In a capitalist mode of production, the portion of the working class that can be shed from socialized production is a historical question and is contingent on the development of the production process. As we know, that portion grows with the productivity of capital itself. Today, the scale at which individual bearers of labour-power have been made redundant to the reproduction of global capital, virtually exceeding the imagination as an actual figure, challenges and distorts the perception that surplus labour is the social substance of rent, and that the reproduction of labour-power is the absolute limit of its expression as a magnitude. That so many bearers of the class separated from the means of production are made redundant, or destroyed outright, without appearing to jeopardize the viability of accumulation (the opposite appearance prevails, in fact) hardly serves the understanding that the seemingly independent and legal form, rent, is actually contingent on the reproduction of the collective worker.

2. Rent in kind

Rent in kind, a second embryonic form of capitalist rent, is simply a logical derivative of labour rent, where surplus labour is transferred to the
landlord objectified in the magnitude of some product, or combination
of products. That rent in kind follows labour rent logically has no bearing
on whether it follows, precedes, or is contemporary with labour rent in
any particular historical conjuncture. Nonetheless, rent in kind presupposes certain historical circumstances. As a social form more generally, it
'presupposes the union of rural domestic industry and agriculture . . .
[where] rent is the product of this combined agricultural-industrial
family labour'. In the social formation in question, 'family' refers to any
small, producing collectivity, organized by kinship or any other kind of
social bond. The particular combination of products that constitute rent
in kind also reflects its historical circumstances, whether it 'includes a
greater or lesser amount of industrial products . . . or whether it is paid
simply in the form of agricultural products proper' (931). The only
commonality between 'the endlessly varied combinations in which the
different forms of rent [in kind] may be combined, mixed together and
amalgamated' is precisely their abstraction as expressions of rent in kind,
a social form that meets its obsolescence in the ascendance of a capitalist
mode of production as dominant social modality (932), even as it persists
as an occasional form, as it does to this day. In a capitalist mode of
production, profit ultimately, if indirectly and invisibly, determines rent
because rent is a portion of surplus-value (i.e., a portion of profit itself).

The emergence of a capitalist mode of production is also, therefore,
the process of the inversion of the determining relation between profit
and rent. Whereas in a capitalist mode of production, profit ultimately
determines the magnitude of rent, in pre-capitalist formations – that is,
in transitional formations that only *become* transitional in retrospect,
after capital becomes 'factual' – rent, in the form of rent in kind, or
labour rent (or, as we'll see, money rent) determines profit. Profit in its
pre-capitalist form is, of course, not yet 'profit' in its capitalist guise – it
is also an anticipatory form, transitional, if only detected as such in
retrospect. Nonetheless, it is the portion of labour (or product of labour)
that is held on to by the producer (at this stage, also the owner of the
means of production) that is surplus to their means of subsistence and
which is not appropriated by the landowner:

Profit, if we incorrectly give this name in anticipation to that fraction of the excess of his labour over and above the necessary labour which he appropriates for himself, so little determines rent in-kind that it rather grows up behind its back, meeting a natural limit in the level of rent in kind. (932)

3. Money rent

Money rent, the third station in the emergence of capitalist rent, is, again, simply a logical derivative of rent in kind, where instead of rent in the form of surplus product (and where the bulk of the product constitutes the immediate producers' means of subsistence), rent now takes the form of the price of the surplus product in money (932–3). In the historical parade of forms taken by the surplus product, the empirical form, price, precedes the abstraction of the value form. Capitalist rent as value form emerges from the price of the surplus product as money rent. Money rent is *the* pivotal value formation in the becoming of capital 'full blown'. With money rent, 'the character of the entire mode of production is thus more or less changed. It loses its independence, its separation from any social context' (933). Money rent, like each of Marx's origin stories of capital, is a history of separation. It is also, therefore, the unfurling of a process of abstraction: the abstraction of the product, the abstraction of the labour that produces it, the abstraction of production from any independent, particular context, and its thoroughly socialized outgrowth in the legal form of property (or, wage labour). The abstraction of production from any particular context is in this case – but not inevitably – the socialization of production in its capitalist integument. For the immediate producer, the need to pay rent in money means that production costs become decisive as 'greater or lesser expenditures in money'; the need to pay rent in money forces a concern for productivity in ways that are not extant in contexts of the dominance of labour rent or rent in kind. Unlike the concrete, qualitative specificity of surplus labour (as labour rent) or surplus product (as rent in kind), a certain amount of money (as rent, as the price of the surplus product) is a social form in the process of becoming extant; it is a value form now compelled to arrive. In this way, money rent, as a pre-capitalist form of rent, pivots towards a capitalist mode of production by forcing its own dissolution:

The transformation of rent in kind into money rent that takes place at first sporadically, then on a more or less national scale, presupposes an already more significant development of trade, urban industry, commodity production in general and therefore monetary circulation. It also presupposes that products have a market price and are sold more or less approximately at their values, which in the earlier forms need in no way be the case . . . [This cannot be accomplished] without a certain development of labour's social productive power. (933)

As money rent develops, it compels 'the transformation of the land into free peasant property' – that is, it becomes the 'rent paid by the [proto] *capitalist* [tenant] farmer' (934, my emphasis). Rent now emerges in its abstract form as a legal contract: 'Customary law between landowner and their dependent who possesses the land is transformed into a contractual relationship, a purely monetary relationship.' The now-dependent possessor of land transforms into a tenant farmer-capitalist. This transformation 'anticipates the formation of a class of non-possessing wage labourers' who, eventually, no longer need to be made to work by force but rather assume their exploitation out of economic and reproductive necessity (934). It turns out that Marx's characterization of pre-capitalist forms of rent – a narration from the standpoint of the derivation of rent in kind from labour rent, and money rent from rent in kind – is actually an account of the emergence of the capitalist mode of production tout court (at least at its abstract inner core, if not as a subjective, lived reality). By the time money rent compels the genesis of the farmer-capitalist, the necessary synergy between agricultural and industrial production has begun the process of its historical objectivity. It is clear from the hindsight of capital 'full blown' that the full incorporation of agricultural and industrial production is necessary for the development of a form or mode of production like capital, one defining aspect and possibility of which is a certain *scale* of production. Capital cannot *become capital* without the growth of both agriculture and other forms of industry – a scale of growth that requires socialization – and this requires a synergy between agriculture and other forms of industry, as well as a 'level of development of the world market, trade and manufacture' (935).

Money rent anticipates a constellation of transformations that we can describe as the emergence of capital itself:

Rent has now been transformed from the normal form of surplus-value and surplus labour into an excess over the part of surplus labour that is claimed by capital as a matter of course and normally – an excess particular to one particular sphere of production, the agricultural. Instead of rent, the normal form of surplus-value is now profit, and rent now counts as an independent form only under special conditions, not a form of surplus-value in general but of a particular offshoot of this, surplus profit . . . It is no longer land, but capital, that has now directly subsumed even agricultural labour under itself and its productivity. (936)

In this passage, Marx depicts a process that we could describe in several ways: (1) as land becoming capital, or, the real subsumption of land by capital; (2) as rent becoming profit, or, the real subsumption of surplus labour by capital; or (3) as price becoming value, or, the real subsumption of price by capital. In each case, it is a matter of historical contingency – independent particularity – becoming objective necessity, history generating a universal. As in Marx's famous analogy of human anatomy being the key to the anatomy of the ape, or Walter Benjamin's equally famous figure of the 'angel of history', it is the point of view of development ('progress', so called) in retrospect. The logical trajectory, surplus labour (as labour rent) → surplus product (as rent in kind) → price of surplus product (as money rent), compels the final transformation into *value* of surplus labour (congealed as surplus product) in phenomenal form as *profit*, as a ratio of capital invested in productive enterprise. In this series of mediations that we could otherwise call 'history', rent goes from being labour that is surplus to the immediate producer's reproduction to being an autonomized portion of the surplus-value yielded by capital. The genealogy of all capitalist profit is rent, or surplus labour. As we know (and discussed in chapters 2 and 3), capitalist profit always already takes the phenomenal form of 'average profit'; it is the outcome of the process of socializing production, an average profit that comes to determine prices of production – *all* prices of production, including agricultural prices, which are now 'formed outside the rural situation, in the orbit of urban trade and manufacture' (936). No wonder the architecture of the capital structure is so confounding to conceptualize – it is a house of mirrors!

Only in the form of money rent can rent be capitalized and thereby turned into the operating *price* of land. Money rent, therefore, catalyses the process of the commodification of land itself. The latter is a perceptual dynamic as much as it is anything else, since the generalized perception of land as a commodity that has a price, as something that can be bought and sold, congeals into the associated perception that land is somehow, in itself, the source of its rent-seeking and profit-making capacity, as opposed to being a social production relation that confers on the owner of land the capacity to appropriate a portion of socially produced surplus-value (938). The historical process of the transition to a capitalist mode of production is therefore also, as Marx posits repeatedly in *Capital* III, the transition to a particular capitalist 'mode of conception':

> Where the capitalist conception prevails, as on American plantations, this entire surplus-value is conceived as profit; where the capitalist mode of production does not exist itself, and *the mode of conception corresponding to it* is not transferred from capitalist countries, it appears as rent. (940, my emphasis)

Whether surplus value appears as rent or profit indicates the degree to which capital has congealed as social objectivity, if at all.

In the course of the historical process of capital's formation, embryonic (or transitional) modes of production may sit on one or the other side of the conceptual 'tipping point', as in Marx's example above.[31] For instance, in the case of the corvée, surplus value takes its original form of a surplus of coerced labour – labour rent – a situation that does not at all necessarily 'tip toward' a capitalist mode of production. However, in the case of colonial plantations, the mass enslavement of stolen people as labourers makes possible production on a mass scale. Mass production introduces stability for the production process by way of predictability with respect to the magnitude and availability of the product as means of further production, both conditional factors in capital's becoming.[32] With planation production, a massive magnitude of human

---

31   Identifiable as such only in hindsight.

32   A mass scale of production, and the stability and predictability of production that scale makes possible, are the material conditions for capital's future, and future-perfect, temporal comportment. Over the last two decades of Marxist theorizing, much ink has been spilled on capital's temporalities and future orientation, especially with respect to the dynamics of so-called financialization. See, for instance, Marina Vishmidt, *Speculation as a Mode of Production: Forms of Value Subjectivity in Art and Capital*, Brill,

labour (relatively, for the day) is objectified in the form of products such as cotton. The circulation of a mass product like cotton on the burgeoning world market, and the consequent stabilization of the demand for cotton as a means of production in textile manufacturing, produces cotton *as a commodity in its 'purely' capitalist integument* at the core of its 'actual' bodily form: a *social value* that is a magnitude of objectified social labour (congealed socially necessary labour time), expressed as an internal antagonism between a use-value and an exchange-value, and where a certain portion of the commodity's value is surplus-value that will be expressed in its phenomenal form of profit.

Here, Marx's theory of money rent points to a deeper articulation of capital and modern slavery than is often observed. It is widely recognized that enslaved labour in the colonies was instrumental in allowing plantation owners to amass tremendous fortunes, concentrations of wealth that became the initial productive investments – in labour, raw material, and machinery – required by a burgeoning system of capitalist production. Classical political economists refer to this process as 'primitive accumulation', and Marx's critique of 'so-called primitive accumulation' in the final pages of *Capital* I famously situates modern slavery as preparing the ground for capital's emergence through a bloody campaign of separation – the centuries-long process of separating the bulk of humanity from the land and all other means of reproduction. In this way, enslaved labour in the colonies, along with land enclosures in Europe, are laboratories of proletarianization carried by the wider, ongoing processes of subalternization unfurling in both imperial core and periphery.[33]

To these dimensions of the relationship between slavery and capital, we can add another. In Marx's discussion of money rent, the emergence of capital is a long historical process whose logical (that is, categorial) outgrowth is the transformation of the isolated form of surplus labour into money rent, and the subsequent autonomization of money rent as a portion of surplus labour that now assumes the social form of profit. One condition for the emergence of profit in its social form (that is, for surplus labour to take the general appearance of profit) is the growth in

2018; Christian Lotz, *The Capitalist Schema: Time, Money, and the Culture of Abstraction*, Lexington Books, 2014; Massimiliano Tomba, *Marx's Temporalities*, Brill, 2012.

33   See, Sourayan Mookerjea, 'Accumulated Violence, or, the Wars of Exploitation: Notes Toward a Post-Western Marxism', *Mediations* 31(2), 2018, 95–114.

scale and consequent reproducibility of productive enterprise. Plantation enterprises in the colonies are those rare early examples where that scale of production is realized. In these terms, it is not just that slavery, in this early stage of capitalist development, is profitable; *it is that slavery creates the conditions for profit to emerge as the social form of surplus labour per se*. A mass scale of production feeding a growing world market, an increasingly socialized and international division of labour (comprised of labour 'free' and unfree, formalized and informal) organized around production processes that demand steady and predictable supplies of raw material and labour: these accidental but interlocking developments form the conjuncture from which capital emerges as a social form of value, as a new world system, with the commodity as its cell form and money as its means of motion. It turns out that the exposition of money rent as signalling the historical emergence of profit as percept, and of a capitalist mode of production more widely, is not the *conclusion* of Marx's three-part study of capital but rather, conceptually, the *introduction* to – and the presupposition of – chapter 1 of volume I!

4. Small-scale peasant ownership

Small-scale peasant ownership is the final pre-capitalist relation to land that Marx historicizes in order to distinguish land as *capitalist* social form. The social relation of small-scale peasant ownership (what we might today describe as subsistence farming) corresponds to a historical conjuncture where the 'majority of the population is agricultural and isolated labour predominates over social' (949).[34] The peasant is the free proprietor of the land; therefore, no rent (lease-price) is paid to a land-owner, and the entirety of the product including any surplus profit falls to the farmer (940). Confronted as we are today with the disastrous irrationalities of globalized agri-capitalism, irrationalities that were already evident in the mid-nineteenth century, readers might expect from Marx some nostalgia for pre-capitalist agricultural smallholding. However, this is not the case: with small-scale peasant ownership, 'wealth and the

---

34   Marx identifies instances of these conjunctures in classical antiquity, and in the modern period emerging in the wake of the dissolution of feudal landed property: 'Examples are the yeomanry in England, the peasant estate in Sweden and the peasants of France and western Germany. We are not referring here to the colonies, since there the independent peasant farmer develops under different conditions' (942–3).

development of reproduction . . . both in its material and its intellectual aspects, is ruled out . . . and with this also the conditions for a rational agriculture' (949). The history of agricultural smallholding, Marx argues, is equally as irrational as large-scale capitalist (industrial) farming in one crucial respect: it negates the real potentiality of generalized material abundance that is the power of socialized agricultural production in an associated (cooperative) form: 'The agricultural smallholding, by its nature, rules out the development of the productive powers of social labour, the social concentration of capitals, stock-raising on a large scale or the progressive application of science' (943).

What Marx calls 'rational' development is that which socializes the benefits of growing agricultural productivity and which, by these means, advances the historical movement from the 'realm of necessity to the realm of freedom'. Rational development is ruled out by capitalist agricultural production since the productive power of social labour is negated by its form – the accumulation of privately owned wealth (in actuality a particular form of wealth). However, in these terms, rational development is also ruled out by peasant-owned smallholding. The isolated labour of small landowners cannot achieve the scale of production or magnitude of product that would allow for a sufficient *surplus product* – a product surplus to the needs of immediate producers – that could form the foundation of generalized material security and well-being. More importantly, isolated labour in its pre-capitalist expression arrests expansion of the general intellect, that is to say, it arrests technical innovation in agricultural production – innovation that proceeds by means inherently collective and cooperative in its development and application – that would manifest the capacity to produce a stable agricultural surplus in the first place. If a stable and socialized agricultural surplus is the material foundation of a realm of freedom, the cooperative development of the general intellect is the material foundation of a society built (so to speak) by each according to their abilities, for each according to their needs.

Marx's critique of small-scale peasant ownership is, therefore, a critique of parochialism and of a romantic reverence for it, in reaction to the harsher irrationalities of its capitalist transformation. The immediate comportment of the critique is logical, even mathematical:

> The conflict between the price of land as an element of the cost price
> for the producer and as a non-element of the price of production for

> the product . . . is just one of the forms expressing the contradiction
> between [small-scale] private ownership of land and a rational
> agriculture, the normal social use of the land. (948)

In other words, in the context of private smallholding, the farmer is
burdened with the price of land without that cost factoring into, and
thus being absorbed by, the product's price of production – an
irrationality that jeopardizes the viability of small farming enterprise
without a wider social benefit. From a more totalized standpoint,
however, the comportment of Marx's critique is anti-nostalgic and
revolutionary: the invocation of the power of socialized labour in
agricultural production is a call to push *through* – not against – the
tendencies that the capitalist modality introduces as historical
potentiality. Its standpoint is that of class struggle forcing capital to the
point of its dialectical reversal, where socialized labour is realized in its
rational form as association – where 'a rational [collectivized] agriculture
[is] the normal social use of the land' (948).

The critique resonates today. Pre-capitalist modalities are no longer
available as the stuff of imaginary solutions to capitalist contradictions. However, agricultural production that is 'small-scale and local'
is often invoked as a solution *per se* to the irrationalities of globalized
agri-capitalism. 'Small and local' may very well characterize the
predominant scale and mode of agricultural production in an associated, post-capitalist system. However, small-scale farming cooperatives organized to meet the subsistence and social reproductive needs
of immediate producers and the local community will depend for their
viability on their articulation as nodes in a network of production
cooperatives, agricultural and otherwise, that will extend far beyond
any locality. Planetary interconnectedness, introduced to history by
the ongoing development of the world market and realized by capitalist circulation logistics, mediates every 'local' surplus as a potentially
globally-redistributable surplus, when the need for such redistribution arises (as it will). Pushing through, as opposed to against, the
logic (the 'raw material') of capitalist modality reverses into social
reproduction on a planetary scale of responsibility and accountabili-
ty.[35] Marx's point, as relevant today, is that small and local production,

---

35 It may, or it may not. Potentiality need never be realized, and a new modality

if it takes the form of isolated and atomized production, is insufficient to address the irrationalities of capitalist agriculture. A progressive alternative to capitalist agriculture and private landed property will be 'a conscious and rational treatment of the land as permanent communal property, [a communality that extends beyond the 'local',] as the inalienable condition for the existence and reproduction of the chain of human generations' (949).

The emergence of communal property, as both collective doing and corresponding conceptualization, is arrested by the perceptual physics (also a collective doing) that produce land as private property and inherently rent-bearing, as automatically expanding value – as capital. Despite recent, compelling theories of the generalized transparency of the mechanics of social control (mechanics where modes of oppression are no longer reliant on normalized discursive, performative, or representational conventions), this economic expression of land – in its phenomenal form, at once a discourse, performance, and representation – prevails. Despite persistent challenges to the 'legal fact/fiction' of land as property, it is no less an accepted truism today that landownership entitles the owner to draw rent, tout simplement:

> All [rent-bearing] means in actual fact is that, under the given conditions, the ownership of these square feet of land enables the landowner to seize a certain amount of unpaid labour, which capital has realized by rooting in the soil like a pig in potatoes. *Prima facie*, however, the expression is as if one were to speak of the ratio of a £5 note to the diameter of the earth. But these irrational forms in which certain economic relationships appear and are grasped in practice do not bother the practical bearers of these relationships in their everyday dealings; since they are accustomed to operating within these forms, it does not strike them as anything worth thinking about. A complete contradiction holds nothing at all mysterious for them. In the forms of appearance that are estranged from their inner connection and, taken in isolation, are absurd, they feel as much at home as a fish in water. (914)

---

founded on socialized abundance has no obligation to arrive. However, material conditions of possibility will always be the ground from which any new modality emerges.

In the long part VI on ground-rent, Marx exposits (largely through illustration) the logical movement of rent as the economic expression of land in a capitalist guise, then maps the transition from various forms of rent in kind to rent in its capitalist form – as a portion of the total social surplus labour. This transition, the capitalist formation of rent, is one aspect of the transition to a capitalist mode of production more generally: the supersession of wealth in kind by a social form of wealth – namely, value. The question becomes how to imagine, never mind carry out, the conditions (i.e., the collective doing) that will transform land into a *collective* form of wealth in kind, not as return to a pre-capitalist form of wealth – impossible in any regard – but rather as a movement *through* capital's unrealized historical potentialities for the socialization of agricultural production. What mode of social reproduction would deposit land as permanent communal property, as inalienable means of social subsistence, well-being, and abundance?

Conclusion
The Revenues and Their Sources: The Three Faces of Surplus-Value

The Economic Trinity as the Religion of Everyday Life – Crisis and Utopia

The Economic Trinity as the Religion of Everyday Life

In chapter 11 of *Capital* I – 'The Rate and Mass of Surplus-Value' – Marx makes a certain point, the elaboration of which occupies the entirety of the material assembled as *Capital* III. There, Marx says that the law of value is objectified in the way that 'the masses of value and of surplus-value produced by different capitals . . . vary directly [with] the amounts of the variable components of these capitals, i.e. the parts [of capital] which have been turned into living labour-power.' He continues: 'This law clearly contradicts all experience based on immediate appearances.'[1] To explain why, and illustrate how, the immediate appearances of a capitalist 'economy' contradict the law of value while, at the same time, being determined by it is the singular sustained objective of the analysis in *Capital* III.[2] Contradiction, inversion, mystification, autonomization,

---

1   Karl Marx, *Capital: A Critique of Political Economy*, vol. 1, trans. Ben Fowkes, Penguin, 1990, 421.

2   Marx uses the term 'capitalist economy' here, as he does throughout *Capital*, as the colloquial and inadequate designation for the production and circulation of capital. To contradict the law of value means to invert, in appearance, capital's internal movement, or to mystify its law of motion.

and fetishization are concepts through which Marx theorizes the modalities of capital's law of motion, its perceptual physics. As Marx repeats throughout *Capital* III, this movement becomes a law '*only in a capitalist mode of production*' (970, my emphasis).

In part I of this book (examining parts I through III of *Capital* III), we looked at the movement of surplus-value as it assumes the social form of profit in the course of its circulation and distribution. After its production, surplus-value undergoes a redistribution among the competing interests of the capitalist class – a redistribution that is entirely necessary for capital's viable reproduction from the standpoint of the system, swerving in its course from each immediate, individual standpoint of its agents. This process of redistribution, surplus-value's transformation of form – a process that I have been calling *capital's perceptual physics* – is immanent to a social configuration of generalized exchange, itself both cause and effect of the historical emergence of a system of socialized production among private independent producers. In part II of this book (examining parts IV through VI of *Capital* III), we looked at the movement that generates profit's derivative forms – forms that correspond to capital's competing personifications and redistributional pathways: industrial profit, commercial profit, interest, rent. Part VII of *Capital* III, 'The Revenues and Their Sources', ties all of these threads together. From this most protracted (totalized) stage of the study so far, Marx elaborates the most immediate, surface-oriented appearances of the chaotic whole: surplus-value's transformation into three forms of 'revenue' – profit, ground-rent, and wages.[3] Here, the objective is to put Adam Smith's 'trinity formula' – the 'economic three-in-one' (953) – back on its feet according to the movement of capital as summarized across *Capital*'s three volumes.[4]

In the trinity formula, surplus-value's three outward faces are profit, rent, and wages. These three forms of revenue perform their mystifying enchantment in positing their imaginary sources. As appearances go, the source of profit is capital, the source of ground-rent is land, and the source of wages is labour. In the capitalist phantasmagoria, we could say

---

3 Here, Marx refers to profit of enterprise – industrial, commercial, or financial (i.e., including interest).

4 Marx quotes Adam Smith in *The Wealth of Nations*: 'Wages, profit and rent are the three original sources of all revenue, as well as of all exchangeable value' (965).

capital's economic form is profit, land's economic form is ground-rent, and labour's economic form is wages. For Smith, the trinity formula is a story about the sources of wealth in a modern economy. For Marx, the trinity formula is a story about the faces that capital puts forward to the world, and how the exploitation of living labour in the course of private production for exchange – capital's only genuine source of wealth creation (at least, of wealth in capital's narrow terms, however vast as magnitude) – is hidden in the process: the 'trinity form holds in itself all the mysteries of the social production process' (953). In the case of capital's worldly face, Marx suggests that interest (a profit derivative) is actually the 'purer' representative of capital as a source of wealth given that it is a more deeply mediated social form, a further degree separated from its source in living labour, and therefore more thoroughly mystified – *the automatic fetish*. Even the mystified form of profit of enterprise carries an imaginary link to productive activity of some kind in its guise as the wages of the capitalist.

Nonetheless, the perceived sources of the revenues – capital, land, labour – strengthen the fetish dynamic by having no apparent connection between each other: the 'ostensible sources [of the revenues] . . . belong to completely disparate spheres and have not the slightest analogy with one another. Their mutual relationship is like . . . beetroot and music' (953). Because capital, land, and labour appear as entirely unconnected as sources of revenue (and wealth), their ability to function as such can be construed as the result of their individual qualitative properties, 'one the basis, the other the result; one the cause, the other the effect – and moreover in such a way that each individual source is related to its product as something extruded from it and produced by it' (955). Land produces rent like trees produce fruit, labour produces wages like it produces things of utility, and capital, as money or means of production, produces revenue by virtue of its own innate movement as the automatic subject of circulation. Such appearances, however, are misleading, as the entirety of *Capital* III is dedicated to illustrating. The material forms of the so-called sources of revenue – labour, earth, and the means of production – have nothing to do with their social forms as values:

The earth, for example, is active as an agent of production in the production of a use-value, a material product, say wheat. But it has nothing to do with producing the *value of wheat* . . . it is foolish to counterpose a use-value, the earth, on the one hand, and value on the other. (955–6)

In this way, to speak of the '"price of labour" is just as irrational as a yellow logarithm' (962).

Capital III is therefore a book about physics, a theory of a particular movement that generates new percepts – a movement arising from collective uncoordinated activity that, over a couple of centuries of objectification through repetition, produces a particular appearance of things that launches a specific (but not inevitable) world history. Capital is a social process instigated in the world, not in the mind, which is why we might call it a perceptual physics rather than a mode of conception, even as it generates appearances that are registered in, and mediated by, the embodied consciousness of its bearers. What Marx calls 'science' (and what I have surely oversimplified elsewhere as 'theory') is a work of conception – analysis and imagination, speculative thinking or cognitive mapping – that reveals what is hidden, that links essence and appearance, social content and social form: 'All science would be superfluous if the form of appearance of things directly coincided with their essence'; as it is, without a conception of their dynamic, 'their inner connections remain hidden, *even though they are comprehensible to the popular mind*' (956, my emphasis). Science is therefore popular work – that which may link up with class struggle in its multitude of lived forms, and with the work of surviving by devising (by doing and living differently) what might come next. Science is part of the work of those who produce the world: the work of the commune; the work of protecting land, environment and creatures: the work of students; the work of the party (in some new and not yet existing iteration). It can be the work of philosophers, but it is not their preserve.

From the standpoint of science – that is, from the standpoint of totality – capital's appearances are '*prima facie* absurd, illegitimate, nonsense, contradictory'. As Marx points out, the belief that £100 = £110, an equation expressing the 'occult quality of a value that is unequal to itself', is, to this day, the foundation of the entire edifice of capitalist finance, no matter how convoluted its instruments. Vulgar economics, on the other hand, is quite at home inhabiting capital's 'estranged forms of appearance' and turns them into apologetics (956). *Capital* III is therefore also a book about how capital's 'base' mediation – the capital–labour relation – imperceptible in its legal forms such as market exchange, private property, wage labour, or credit default swaps, becomes sufficiently pervasive as to disappear altogether, like the atmosphere. *Capital* III is therefore a book about what appears and what disappears:

> [The sphere of competition is] where the inner law that prevails through the accidents and governs them is visible only when these accidents are combined in large numbers,[5] so that it remains invisible and incomprehensible to the individual agents of production themselves. Further, however, the actual production process, as the unity of the immediate production process and the process of circulation, produces new configurations in which the threads of the inner connection get more and more lost, the relations of production becoming independent of one another and the components of value ossifying into independent forms . . . All this conceals the true nature of surplus-value more and more, concealing therefore the real mechanism of capital. (967)

Of course, as we know by now, all revenues (profit, interest, rent, wages) generated by a capitalist economy are 'nothing but particular components of the surplus-value' (955). Therefore, despite appearances and apologetics, the entirety of the value magnitude generated by the capital-machine at any given moment, at any stage of development or configuration, is created by labour (labour that must be coincident with the form of waged labour) in the capitalist production process.[6] No value (in its capitalist form) is created outside of this process. Every

---

5 The 'accidents' in question are those of everyday market activity expressed in the transformation of values into prices of production, profit into average profit, market price into averages of prices of production, the push and pull of equalization, and so on. 'Accidents that are visible only when combined in large numbers' is also an adequate definition of Marx's concept of a tendency (discussed in more detail in chapter 3).

6 'Even though the form of labour as wage-labour is decisive for the shape of the entire process and for the specific mode of production itself, it is not wage-labour that is value determining. What matters in the determination of value is the overall social labour-time, the total amount of labour which society has at its disposal and whose relative absorption by the different products determines, as it were, their respective social weight. But the particular form in which social labour-time plays its determinant role in the value of commodities coincides with the form of labour as wage-labour, and the corresponding form of the means of production as capital' (1022).

portion (c, v, s) of the commodity's value originates as the value that workers, and only workers, add to the value of the total social product:

> The total portion of commodity value, therefore, in which the total labour that the worker adds during a day or a year is realized, the total value of the annual product that this labour creates, breaks down into the value of wages, profit and rent. For this total labour breaks down into necessary labour . . . i.e. wages, and unpaid surplus labour, by which he creates the portion of the product's value that represents surplus-value and that subsequently divides into profit and rent. *Besides this labour, the worker performs no other*, and besides the total value of the product, which assumes the forms of wages, profit and rent, *he creates no other value*. (973, my emphasis)

Unpaid surplus labour therefore forms the entirety of the value magnitude that is divided up into the three revenues that, in turn, posit three corresponding classes in the immediate appearance of things: the capitalist class, the landowning class, and the working class (959–60). We can think of these classes as distributional categories corresponding to profit, rent, and wages respectively, each expressing a certain property relation, or legal comportment to social wealth, depending on whether one owns capital (means of production and/or money that one mobilizes, lends, or speculates with), land (and/or other rent-seeking property, including forms of intellectual property), or labour-power. In the 'actual world', the world of capitalist forms, the distributional categories are always already amalgams of other social relations / distributional categories – gender, race, sexuality, citizenship, caste, age, ability, merit – to form complex technologies at work in the sphere of competition for power and resources.[7] In this sphere, for example, the category/ technology of race is inherently 'political economic', in the way that the social relation of modern property is inherently racialized, gendered, imperialized, with or without citizenship, franchise, and so on. Again, a category such as race becomes a technology of 'group-differentiated

---

7   As Sourayan Mookerjea explains, another term for 'distributional category' is 'accumulated violence' and its mediating forms of expression. Once again, see Sourayan Mookerjea, 'Accumulated Violence, or, the Wars of Exploitation: Notes Toward a Post-Western Marxism', *Mediations* 32(1), Fall 2018, 95–114.

vulnerability towards premature death', a means of managing and facilitating accumulation, and a lever for further stratifying the distributional classes[8] – fracturing the working class, for example, into the 'sociological' strata that express a particular historical conjuncture: aristocratic, professional, middle, precarious, floating, migrant, lumpen, informalized, radically surplus, and so on.[9]

The answer to the question 'What makes a class?' therefore depends on whether one is speaking from the point of view of the *actual world* of capitalist social forms or from the point of view of the internal movement of capital (1025). The analysis anticipated by the final, aborted chapter on 'Classes' is, consequently, not a great mystery; if anything, Marx was on the threshold of repeating himself in an already-repetitive set of chapters in part VII. In *Capital* III, the internal movement of capital is the consistently singular (and exceedingly narrow) object of analysis.[10] In the chaotic complexity of capitalist society, classes are social maps crossed, and crossed again, by the tracks of history and struggle: amalgamations that are the sediment of technologies of group differentiation, legal modes of granting and restricting access to social wealth and the means of subsistence, the social scar tissue of those histories of separation, and the combined, deeply stratifying effects of all these modalities in turning over the ground of social experience, material interest, cooperation, and solidarity. On this register, what we call 'classes' are not specific to a capitalist mode of production. They may precede the capitalist formation and always express the historical conjuncture that informs them, capitalist or otherwise – as in, *all history is the history of class struggle*. However, emerging together with the capitalist mode of production is 'class' as objectivity – the capital–labour relation as (social)

---

8   I borrow this definition of racism, so frequently invoked these days, from Ruth Wilson Gilmore, *Golden Gulag: Prisons, Surplus, Crisis, and Opposition in Globalizing California*, University of California, 2007, 28. As she puts it in a subsequent essay, 'Capitalism requires inequality; racism enshrines it.' Ruth Wilson Gilmore, 'Abolition Geography and the Problem of Innocence', in Gaye Theresa Johnson and Alex Lubin, eds, *Futures of Black Radicalism*, Verso, 2017, 225–40, 240.

9   In chapter 14 of *Capital* I, Marx describes the process of fracturing the working class through the hierarchization of labour-power as a function of the division of labour in a capitalist mode of production. He elaborates further in the discussion of the fragmentation of surplus populations that appears in chapter 25 of the same volume.

10   As it is in *Capital* I as well as II.

movement of gravity; as 'logic'; as structural disposition; or as 'the general antagonism'. Whatever we call this 'new' objectivity, it does not precede the emerging capitalist social formation but rather is posited by it as the *presupposition* of every moment of that social formation, in each of its various configurations, as the condition of capital's reproduction going forward. All manifestations of class as lived actuality in existing capitalist society presuppose class in its 'pure form', that is, once capital has risen to its feet and stands its ground as automatic subject. Class, as objectivity, divides its bearers into owners and producers tout simple – a process mystified by capital's three distributional categories – with capital concentrating at one pole and labour at the other (1026):

> It is unnecessary after the argument already developed to demonstrate once again how the relationship of capital and wage-labour determines the whole character of the mode of production. The principle agents of this mode of production itself, the capitalist and the wage-labourer, are as such simply embodiments and personifications of capital and wage-labour – specific social characters that the social production process stamps on individuals, products of these specific social relations of production. (1019–20)

Capital and labour, and their personifications in the (collective) capitalist and the (collective) worker, are the 'two essential agents of production', both functions of abstraction that move to the core of social reproduction in a capitalist society and form the two constitutive classes in the 'great simplification and division' between those who produce surplus-value and those who own it. As such, the social content of class antagonism in the context of the great simplification becomes the 'depersonalized' production of surplus-value:

> The production of surplus-value [is] the direct object and decisive motive of production. Capital essentially produces capital, and it does this only as long as it produces surplus-value. In dealing with relative surplus-value and then with the transformation of surplus-value into profit, we have seen how a mode of production peculiar to the capitalist period is based on this – a particular form of development of the social productive powers of labour, but as powers of capital that

have asserted their autonomy vis-à-vis the worker, thus directly opposing [the worker's] own development. (1020–1)

The function of abstraction – the process of excreting the forms that carry the exploitation of surplus-value – also introduces logical grounds for solidarity across stratification, across all agents of production whether they are engaged by capital directly or not, and across the multitude of hierarchized differentiated identities. The function of abstraction – the means of exploitation that are *potentially separable from it* – introduces to history a logical framework for unifying struggle across actual-world processes of separation, for planetwide struggle, where the possibility for alliances, and emerging social configurations, is infinitely full because it is radically empty.[11] This is the possibility to be exploited by reading the constitution of class, and class struggle, from the movement of the relations of production versus the relations of distribution. It also articulates the dry technicalities of value-accounting with the fleshy, carbon-based politics of alternative world-building. Marx's relentless emphasis throughout *Capital* III is that in the forma-tion of capital, the direction of the movement of social determination *matters* (in all senses), and that the direction of determination in a capi-talist mode of production is from production to distribution – to use that old-fashioned language, from base to superstructure:

The so-called relations of distribution, therefore, correspond to and arise from historically particular and specific social forms of the production process and of the relationships which men enter into among themselves in the process of reproducing their human life. The historical character of these relations of distribution is the historical character of the relations of production, and they simply express one side of these. (1023)

The direction is not reversible, even though distribution feeds back onto production by setting contingent negative limits to valorization

---

11 This may sound like Ernesto Laclau's and Chantal Mouffe's empty signifier, the filling of which in the constitution of group affiliation and identity is politics as such. I would rather think of it as Lukács's proletarian standpoint. It is also the structural dynamic I call utopia. It takes up (if bending it to my own purposes) Jameson's formulation that ideology and utopia are twin expressions in a capitalist mode of production.

(explored further below). So, for example, land appears to be the source of rent when it is not; rather, productivity of labour determines how much labour constitutes the social product, how much labour is added to the reservoir of value system-wide, which in turn determines the possible range for a magnitude of rent that does not jeopardize the viability of agricultural enterprise:

> Distribution ... presupposes this substance [the value reservoir] as already present, i.e. the total value of the annual product, which is nothing more than objectified social labour. But it is not in this form that the matter presents itself to the agents of production, the bearers of the various functions of the production process, but rather in a distorted form. (961)

However, despite the distortions that continue today to place the property owner on top of the world, when rent is emptied of its pre-capitalist social content and replaced with the soul of capital, 'the landowner is reduced from guide and master of the production process and the entire process of social life to a mere leaser of land, usurer in land and simple recipient of rent' – that is, demoted to an anachronism as 'a specific historical result of the capitalist mode of production' itself (1023).

Since, 'added together, [the revenues] form the total social surplus-value' (959–60), we can return, as does Marx in part VII, to speaking simply of value/surplus-value and put aside the categories we have developed and deployed throughout this study of *Capital* III to capture value's convoluted passages through its social forms as price, profit, interest, and rent.[12] We can

---

12 We do not need to put aside the category of wages, the revenue that falls to labour, because in *Capital* III we never take it up; Marx addresses the transformation of surplus-value into wages in *Capital* I. Across that volume, but particularly in parts VI and VII, Marx elaborates the way in which a portion of surplus-value appropriated by the owners of capital is serially exchanged for labour-power in the course of accumulation. Here, too, Marx depicts the process as one of mystification: 'We may therefore understand the decisive importance of the transformation of the value and price of labour-power into the form of wages, or into the value and price of labour itself. All the notions of justice held by both the worker and the capitalist, all the mystifications of the capitalist mode of production, all capitalism's illusions about freedom, all the apologetic tricks of vulgar economics, have as their basis the form of appearance discussed above, which makes the actual relation invisible, and indeed presents to the eye the precise opposite of that relation.' Marx, *Capital* I, 680.

now return to the categories of *Capital* I since, from the totalized point of view of the culmination of *Capital* III, all of value's derivative forms are annulled. The material in part VII illustrates that the three-volume study of *Capital* is, in this sense, the appropriate introduction to *Capital* I. The concept of value as a concrete whole at which we arrive at the end of *Capital* III *elucidates* and finally prepares us to grasp value as a function of social abstraction, as abstract wealth, as the universal inadvertently introduced to history as the outcome of collective doing, as the category with which we set out in *Capital* I.[13] In other words, the standpoint of the whole, of capital's objectified movement, becomes the prerequisite for moving through any one of its narrative entrées.

Thus, part VII reviews the way in which the value magnitude generated by the system as a whole sets the invisible limit for the magnitude of surplus-value that capital is ever able to generate in any given moment. This value horizon is consequently also the invisible determining limit for the magnitude of each of surplus-value's individual transitory forms, even though the situation appears to be the other way around (as it did for rent above), as if the sum of revenues (profit, wages, and rent) forms the aggregate pool of wealth. As Marx iterates, over and over again (993; throughout chapter 50), *commodity value* determines the quantitative limit of wages, profit, and rent, not the other way around, as in the distorted but common perception that wages, profit, and rent are independent constituent cost-elements whose combination forms a commodity's price:

> In actual fact commodity value is the quantitative premise, the sum total value of wages, profit and rent, whatever their relative mutual magnitudes may be. In the false conception considered here, however, wages, profit and rent are three independent value magnitudes, whose total produces, limits and determines the magnitude of commodity value. (1002)

The distinction may appear to be slight and academic, but it is the distinction between two completely different worlds: one capitalist, truncated and deformed by the exigencies of value-creation; the other open, limited only by imagination, ingenuity, and planetary deadlines.

---

13   See ibid., 971

In the mystified appearance of things, a rise or fall in wages, profit, or rent seems to alter a commodity's value (as expressed in its price) when, in fact, a rise or fall in any one of the revenues simply changes the distributional ratio between them without changing the overall amount of value to be distributed (996; 998).[14] Marx unfurls numerous illustrations of these perceptual physics in chapter 50 and folds the analysis from *Capital* II into this bigger picture: the total social capital is reproduced through its division, for part of its circuitry, between two classes of capitalist: department I (producing means of production) and department II (producing means of individual consumption) (975). In *Capital* III, we situate the movement of value between these two departments within the value horizon of the totalized movement:

> In so far as the reproduction process proceeds . . . the sum of wages, profit and rent in department I must be equal in value to the constant portion of capital in department II. Otherwise department II cannot replace its constant capital, nor department I convert its revenue from non-consumable into consumable form. (977)

From the point of view of the end of *Capital* III, the function of the analysis in *Capital* II is simply to show that *the theory of value holds throughout*, and that value, as social function of abstraction, is capital's singular centre of gravity at every moment of its circuitry, for the length of its zombie-span, despite contradicting appearances – that is, despite an increasing fragmentation of the production process; despite the protraction and complexification of logistics; despite the growing prevalence of more immediate and brutal surface-modes of extraction and dispossession; despite the acrobatics of circulation, inter-capitalist competition, distribution, and their financialized opportunities; despite a growing surplus humanity; despite the approaching threshold of planetary extinction; and so on.[15]

---

14 We are speaking here of a change in wages, for example, that does not express a genuine change in the value of labour-power, that is, an increase in generalized productivity that reduces the value of labour-power.

15 If circulation (buying and selling, certain aspects of logistics, marketing, communications, data collection and surveillance, etc.) does not have a positive impact on value formation, it does set a negative limit on it by determining the magnitude of the newly added value that can be realized. This can make it appear as though the activities

The key to the analysis of the moving disaster that is capital – its assembly as well as its potential disassembly, on the level of its internal movement – lies in the dusty-dry technicalities of the value components of the commodity, c-v-s, reproduced at every level of abstraction: that of individual commodity, the product of any particular capital investment, annual national product, and total (global) social product (978). Marx identifies five fundamental perceptual dynamics that generate the inverted appearances that comprise capital's dogma, and which it is the work of science to put back on their feet: (1) the relationship and distinction between constant and variable capital (*Capital* I); (2) the process by which labour both adds new value and preserves old value in a new form (*Capital* I); (3) the interconnections of the reproduction process from the standpoint of the total social capital (*Capital* II and III); (4) revenues as, in essence, forms of value already realized (*Capital* III); and (5) the transformation of surplus-value into separate, mutually independent social forms expressing the various elements of the production process – industrial profit, commercial profit, interest, rent, wages (*Capital* III) (982–4). Marx describes the percepts that arise from these dynamics – percepts that animate the discourses of both vulgar bourgeois economics *and* classical political economy,[16] as well as the 'common

---

of circulation are determining in a way that they are not. Marx's analytical and polemical emphasis is relentless throughout part VII, echoing the point made in *Capital* I with a similar emphasis: do not mistake for an attribute of capital what can only be attributed to labour mobilized in capitalist production: 'This appearance [that wealth can be generated through the activities of circulation] is reinforced by two circumstances in particular: firstly, profit on alienation, which depends on cheating, cunning, expertise, talent and a thousand and one market conjunctures; then the fact that a second determining element intervenes here besides labour-time, i.e. circulation time. Even though this functions simply as a *negative limit* on the formation of value and surplus-value, it gives the appearance of being just as positive a ground as labour itself and of involving a determination independent of labour that arises from the nature of capital' (966, my emphasis).

16   Mind you, this is where the similarity between the insights of classical political economy and the apologetics of vulgar economics ends. According to Marx, 'It is the great merit of classical economics to have dissolved this false appearance and deception, this autonomization and ossification of the different social elements of wealth vis-à-vis one another, this personification of things and reification of the relations of production, this religion of everyday life . . . Yet even its best representatives remained more or less trapped in the world of illusion their criticism had dissolved, and nothing else is possible from the bourgeois standpoint; they all fell therefore more or less into inconsistencies,

sense' that entraps the minds of its agents 'on the immediately visible surface of capitalist production' (1007) – as illusions (985), false ideas (987), distortions (1007),[17] tautologies (1003), inversions (1010), and upside-down appearances (1011) – and as the 'specific shape in which the value components confront one another . . . presupposed because it is constantly reproduced, and . . . constantly reproduced because it is constantly presupposed' (1012).

In light of these descriptions, perhaps we could even say that *Capital* III is a book about ideology, or at least one aspect of what that overburdened concept has come to name. Marx never uses the term 'ideology' for this subject–object dynamic, but he does use, like a refrain, many of its kin – 'mystification', 'naturalization', 'objectification', 'personification', 'autonomization', 'ossification', 'reification' – and, sometimes, several of these concepts jumbled together in one description:

> [Capital] is the means of production monopolized by a particular section of society, the products and conditions of activity of labour-power, which are rendered autonomous vis-à-vis this living labour-power and are personified in capital through this antithesis. It is not only the workers' products which are transformed into independent powers, the products as masters and buyers of their producers, but the social powers and interconnecting form of this labour also confront them as properties of their product. Here we therefore have one factor

---

half-truths and unresolved contradictions . . . It is equally natural, therefore, that vulgar economics, which is nothing more than a didactic and more or less doctrinaire translation of the everyday notions of the actual agents of production, giving them a certain comprehensible arrangement, finds the natural basis of its fatuous self-importance established beyond all doubt precisely in this trinity, in which the entire inner connection is obliterated' (969).

17 Distortions figure prominently in the analysis in part VII: 'We have already shown in connection with the most simple categories of the capitalist mode of production and commodity production in general, in connection with commodities and money, the mystifying character that transforms the social relations for which the material elements of wealth serve as bearers in the course of production into properties of these things themselves (commodities), still more explicitly transforming the relation of production itself into a thing (money). *All forms of society are subject to this distortion, in so far as they involve commodity production and monetary circulation. In the capitalist mode of production, however, where capital is the dominant category and forms the specific relation of production, this bewitched and distorted world develops much further*' (965, my emphasis).

of a historically produced social production process in a definite social form, and at first sight a very mysterious form. (953–4)

Or consider, for example, this well-cited statement:

> This economic trinity as the connection between the components of value . . . and its sources, completes the mystification of the capitalist mode of production, the reification of social relations, and the immediate coalescence of the material relations of production with their historical and social specificity: the bewitched, distorted and upside-down world haunted by Monsieur le Capital and Madame la Terre, who are at the same time social characters and mere things. (969)

Social powers, capacities of cooperative production, that are the source of capitalist wealth (and, of course, the potential source of wealth alternatively constituted, in *other-than*-capitalist terms) appear as the properties of the product of labour, also the means of production, instead of as the capacities of the producers themselves. In other words, the capacity for wealth to expand is attributed to capital, and the fetish character of the product of labour / means of production – the capital fetish – is the effect of the misattribution of social power, of the mystification of the latter's source. *Capital* III is, therefore, also a book about the autonomization of capital's fetish expressions, the reification of the means of labour (those means being dead labour) as they confront living labour as capital:

> The formal autonomy these conditions [i.e., means] of labour acquire vis-à-vis labour, the particular form of autonomy they possess, is then a property inseparable from them as things, as material conditions of production, an immanently ingrown character that necessarily falls to them as elements of production. (964)

Capital's autonomy is the ossification of form against substance, of appearance against essence, a process carried by the devolution of surplus-value into profit, and profit into its various forms of revenue, in the sphere of value's circulation – the sphere of competition – where surplus-value not only 'retains no memory of its origin', nor 'simply obliterates this origin', but is placed 'in a form that is diametrically opposed to this origin':

> The division of profit into profit of enterprise and interest (not to speak of the intervention of commercial profit and money-dealing profit, which are founded in the circulation sphere and seem to derive entirely from this, and not from the production process itself at all) completes the autonomization of the form of surplus-value, the ossification of its form as against its substance, its essence. One portion of profit, in contrast to the other, separates itself completely from the capital-relation as such and presents itself as deriving not from the function of exploiting wage labour; it seems to derive from capital as its own independent source . . . the inner connection [is] definitively torn asunder and its source completely buried, precisely through the assertion of their autonomy [the autonomy of profit's forms]. (968)

In production, where capital functions as the immediate facilitator of the process, or, as Marx calls it, the 'pumper-out of surplus labour', the connection between surplus labour and profit is less mediated than in the sphere of circulation – in a way, closer to the surface appearance of things (966). Consequently, the distortion of the inner connection, the capital fetish, requires less theoretical reconstruction – it more readily relents to cognitive mapping, you could say – in that it suggests at least some kind of relationship between profit and the activity that is carried out in the enterprise. For Marx, it is always *the development of relative surplus-value expressed in the growing productivity of social labour* that propels the mediations of production into the arena of circulation (competition) in more convoluted and protracted ways, their mutating forms expressing the ever-deepening contradiction of a growth imperative in the context of withering conditions for growth. The mediating formations assume, in one way or another, an array of expressions, all instruments for skimming value from a shrinking value-reservoir: the pathological mutations of the credit system and circulating financial instruments, the funhouse of monetary policy, the equally illusory and Godzilla-like power of the rentier or asset-holding segment of the capitalist class, the distorted social weight of real estate and property development – in other words, all the symptomatic formations of today's speculative ecology.[18] Marx's point in part VII is to remind readers that all these formations are historically developing mediations of the production and distribution of surplus-value, and that all serve to obfuscate the original situation – the place, time, and means – of 'pumping-out' surplus labour.

Crisis and Utopia

The development of relative surplus-value expressed in the growing productivity of social labour (as we explored in chapter 3 of this book) also propels a falling rate of profit across the system that erects barriers to ongoing accumulation that, in turn, compels adjustments to the system without actually changing the nature of the system (i.e., without its revolution) – the mutations just mentioned are examples. When these adjustments no longer provide ample 'room to move' for the contradiction between the productive forces (socialized labour) and capitalist production relations, crisis follows.[19] Therefore, crisis, endemic to the movement of capital, precedes a more violent adjustment to the system (1024), whether that is a deep devaluation that resets the value metabolism at a level that resuscitates valorization, or whether that is the obsolescence of the system and its succession by a different one. The latter is a possibility that is as endemic to capital as crisis, structurally and historically (the same thing), even if, as yet, unrealized.

Therefore, throughout *Capital* III, crisis is consistently represented as a double movement, towards recuperation on the one hand, and post-capitalism on the other, with surplus-value as the lever in both cases (1017). In all modes of social reproduction, whatever form they assume, a portion of the social product (that is to say, a portion of social labour) must be reserved for the satisfaction of social needs. In a capitalist mode of production, social needs are limited as much as possible, expanding only as serves the needs of accumulation. However, as Marx says,

---

18   For a mapping of these surface forms, see Lisa Adkins, Melinda Cooper, and Martijn Konings, *The Asset Economy*, Polity, 2020.

19   This is how Marx articulates capital's general antagonism in *Capital* I, chapter 3.

after the abolition of the capitalist mode of production [the production of a social surplus is more important than ever]. In this situation, of course, the part regularly consumed by the direct producers would not remain confined to its present minimum level. (986–7)

In other words, in the theoretical (or, speculative) mode of association that succeeds capital (the real but as-yet-unrealized commune), surplus-value in its capitalist form now becomes the portion of the social product reserved for the satisfaction of social needs: first, for *insurance*, in the widest sense, against all contingency, accident, redundancy of a once-necessary social labour, and so on; second, not only for the satisfaction of existing needs but also for *the expansion of* the repertoire of social needs – of what they consist, and how they are materially articulated and aesthetically embodied.[20] At every turn, *Capital* III is a book about social surplus as a portal to another 'higher form' of society, one that represents the transition, famously, from the realm of necessity to the realm of freedom (958–9):

It is one of the civilizing aspects of capital that it extorts this surplus labour in a manner and in conditions that are more advantageous to social relations and to the creation of elements for a new and higher formation than was the case under the earlier forms of slavery, serfdom, etc. Thus on the one hand it leads towards a stage at which compulsion and the monopolization of social development (with its material and intellectual advantages) by one sector of society at the expense of another disappears; on the other hand it creates the material means and the nucleus for relations that permit this surplus labour to be combined, in a higher form of society, with a greater reduction of the overall time devoted to material labour . . . *The real wealth of society and the possibility of a constant expansion of its reproduction process does not depend on the length of surplus labour but rather on its productivity and on the more or less plentiful conditions of production in which it is performed.* (958, my emphasis)

---

20   I'm thinking of, for example, Kay Gabriel's 'Gender as Accumulation Strategy', *Invert*, May 2020. Also see Jordy Rosenberg and Kay Gabriel, 'Pleasure and Provocation: Kay Gabriel Interview with Jordy Rosenberg', *Salvage*, 18 April 2018, salvage.zone.

If, then, as I have been arguing throughout this book, *Capital* is *not* a study of capitalist society, it is a book about how to think the material conditions of what might come after. The preceding passage asks readers to think of the extortion of surplus labour as one of the 'civilizing aspects of capital' (even if we would choose another word for 'civilizing') that may be turned to our advantage in the creation of a 'new and higher' social formation. This would mean exploiting the power of social labour as the 'raw social material' that capital introduces to history – and which it mistakes for its own power – for the purpose of hoisting that raw material into a new form. The utopian/dialectical movement of capital is to drive straight through its own forms and (potentially) out the other end.[21] The necessary struggle against capital, as much as it seeks to block and resist, for Marx, also takes advantage of capital's need to turn into something else.[22] As modes of production, slavery and serfdom do not introduce similar portals to potentially rational forms or self-subverting drives towards 'higher' social modalities. Unlike capital, neither slavery nor serfdom, as modes of production, can be construed as real but unrealized levers of their own obsolescence – not even potentially (or, dialectically): they are modes of domination to the core. Marx's point is that capital is different from these modes of production in precisely this particular, historical aspect. Capital concentrates and centralizes (monopolizes) wealth in order to command social labour. But the force released by combined labour is potentially too vast and compelling for the legal form of property (capitalist value) to contain.

The exploitable outcome of capital's monopolization of social development, a history of unmitigated brutality, is the force of combined labour, along with the possibility for cooperative labour's self-determination. This is equally to transport, on a global scale, the advantageous potential of interdependency, the fruition of a now-necessary sharing and collective building of ingenuity – a planetary general intellect – to the project of minimizing the burden of social reproduction through both its technological rationalization and its communization – which is, in the end, to say the same thing. Throughout

---

21 Yes, like waste, but also *compost* – as in, the utopian sense of 'shit happens'.

22 This is a long-standing point of Bertell Ollman's: that the intent of Marx's analysis is to demonstrate how capital has an inherent drive to turn into something else. See Bertell Ollman, *The Dance of the Dialectic*, University of Illinois Press, 2003.

Capital III, but concentrated in part VII, are a series of speculative projections where Marx points to capitalist dynamics that serve dual purpose as extant but unrealized conditions for the emergence of a society organized around the logic of association, the generalized partaking of real wealth, and a theoretical – *because historically possible* – infinite expansion of the modalities of social reproduction. Once unbound from the need to claw back a portion of one's (that is, the bulk of humanity's) own objectified surplus labour as the means of survival, each projection becomes a fleeting image of the obsolescence of the value form as the theoretical beginning of history.

Index

Abdelhadi, Eman 113n11
absolute ground-rent 294–305
  formation of 295–7
  and landownership 296–7
  obsolescence 302
  redundancy 302–3
  and surplus profit 303
  and surplus-value 300–1
absolute surplus-value 107, 109–10
abstract labour 11, 55–6, 113
abstraction 6, 57–8, 66, 140, 167–8,
  257, 312
  function of 9, 331
  power of 2–3, 213–14
abundance, negation of 131–3
accounting 145
accumulation 92, 94, 95, 140, 142,
  161–2, 213
  agents of 143
  contradictions of 128
  and the credit system 199n10
  genuine capital 214
  intensification 149
  perceptual physics of 140
  process 47–8, 144–5
  scale of 161
  stability of 288
  wealth 318
accumulation cycles 142–3
Adkins, Lisa 339n18

administrative labour 145
Adorno, Theodor 5n6
agency, collective subjects 89
agri-capitalism 239, 317
agricultural capital 297, 301–2
agricultural commodities 258–9,
  299–300
agricultural labour 252, 255–6n14,
  256–8, 259–60, 302–3, 303
agricultural production 242–3, 245,
  246, 246–7, 252–5, 256, 265,
  274–5, 281, 291–2, 296, 298, 318,
  319
agricultural proletariat 256
agricultural smallholding 317–20
alienated wealth 85–6
anti-capitalist mobilization 132
appearances 53, 63
Arrighi, Giovanni 117, 201n13
asset bubbles 195, 219
associated mode of production 187
austerity 131
automation 117
autonomization 5, 18, 31, 87, 129, 161,
  163, 224, 256, 316, 323–4, 337
  of interest 180–2
  of merchant's capital 141–51
autonomy/dependence contradiction
  161–2

Ball, Michael 237n1
Banaji, Jairus 92n2
Bank Acts Committee, 1857 222
Bank Acts of 1844 and 1845 221–3,
    230
banking and bankers 199–200, 211,
    218
Bannerji, Himani 92n2
barbarism 140
base/superstructure metaphor 1–5
Bellamy Foster, John 201n13
Benanav, Aaron 46n30, 108n6, 298n27
Benjamin, Bret 92n2
Benjamin, Walter 314
Betasamosake Simpson, Leanne
    131n15, 241n7
Bezanson, Kate 112n11
Bhattacharya, Tithi 112n11
big data 115
bills of exchange 204–5, 219
Bloch, Ernst 188, 193n6, 194n7
Bonefeld, Werner 5n6, 30n12, 106n5
borrowing 174–5, 176, 177, 211
Brenner, Robert 201n13
Bretton Woods 230
business shrewdness 49

Canada, Temporary Foreign Workers
    Program 111n10
capital
    autonomy 337–8
    base mediation 326–7
    centralization 121–2
    circulating 26
    civilizing aspects of 341
    as commodity 171–8
    concentration of 70, 128–9, 158–9,
        160
    concept 9, 53–4, 193–4
    conditions of 54
    constant 17, 19–21, 24, 25, 26, 36,
        39, 48, 61, 64, 97, 106, 114–15,
        118, 240–1, 335
    definition 95
    emergence of 138, 313–17
    essential core of 53–64
    fetish-character of 177
    finance 26n6
    first appearance 167–8
    fixed 26–9

forms of appearance 10
forms-in-waiting 4n4
function of abstraction 6
functioning contradictions 121–8
general laws 58
growing organic composition 98–9
hidden basis 306–7
historic mission 130
historical determinacy 3
historical emergence of 54–9
historical mission of 94
historical preconditions 58–9
historical trajectory 297–8
ideology 84–6
internal antagonism 121–2
internal contradictions 91–4
justification 130
level of employment 214–15
as logic 138–9
lowering of composition 106
mobility 69, 75–6
monopolization of social develop-
    ment 341–2
movement of 8–9, 10, 22–3, 41–2,
    45–6, 49–50, 51–2, 56, 60, 88, 91,
    93–4, 122–5, 130, 132–3, 158–9,
    170, 179, 180–1, 200, 257, 306,
    324, 329, 333
mystification 86
objective 122
obsolescence 341
organic composition of 49–50, 61
outward expression of 298
as own obstacle 46
perceptual dynamics 335–6
perceptual physics 8–12, 15, 23, 37,
    47–50, 100, 160–1, 263, 265, 324,
    326
plethora of 125
possession of 25
productive 19
as property 184
radical alterity 7
radical historicity 3
reproduction 140
self-abolishing potential 190–1, 194
self-image 305–21
self-narrative 306
self-representations 10
as social content/essence 7, 170

as social formation 139–40
social forms 137–8, 161
social power of 37, 88, 129, 210
as social process 326
socialization 190
surplus 127–8, 217
trajectory towards obsolescence
   304–5
unoccupied 125, 126–7
use-value 174–5
utopian/dialectical movement
   339–42
valorization process of 25
variable 17, 19, 25, 48, 61, 64, 88, 97,
   103, 156, 241, 335
volatility 130
capital fetish, the 10, 338
capital flight 70, 127–8, 206
capital formation 8, 30
capital growth 103, 196–7, 214–15
Capital I (Marx) 2, 16–17, 19, 20, 21,
   23, 41, 44n26, 48, 51, 53, 56, 59,
   67, 95, 97, 98, 107–9, 111, 113,
   141, 142, 198, 213–14, 224, 227,
   232, 247, 256, 316, 323, 329n9,
   333, 335
Capital II (Marx) 2, 44n26, 48, 51, 141,
   334, 335–6
Capital III (Marx) 2, 3–4, 28–9, 52,
   129–30, 141, 159, 213, 223, 282,
   299–300, 315, 323–4, 325–6,
   326–7, 335–6, 339–42
   arrangement of material 8n8
   central thesis 8–9, 27–8, 33
   chapter 1 17, 30
   chapter 2 30–1, 33
   chapters 3 through 7 34–8
   chapter 5, 'Economy in the Use of
      Constant Capital' 36–8
   chapter 6 139–40
   chapter 8 53
   chapter 27 189–90
   chapter 34 221–3
   chapters 39 through 44 265
   chapters 41 through 44 287–8
   chapter 46 303–4
   'Cost Price and Profit' 15
   and the economic base 6–7
   emphasis 331
   expositional strategies 305–6

part I 35, 47–8, 59, 85
part II 29, 51–2, 53–64, 66, 85
part III 91, 94, 96
part IV 138–40, 237–43, 243, 247,
   252, 269, 285, 287, 288, 291,
   294–5, 296, 321
part V 170–1
part VII 324, 329, 333, 336n17, 339,
   342
preface 3
'The Rate of Profit' 15
'The Genesis of Capitalist Ground-
   Rent' 305–8
theoretical coherency 294–5
capital investment 17
capital ownership 176
   abolition of 185–94
   and wealth creation 187
capital-asset 202
capital-in-general 137, 143, 145, 147,
   166, 170, 173, 178, 179
capitalism, new kinds of 239n4
capitalist, the
   immediate material interests 85
   insignificance 89
   internalization of production price
      86–8
   objective 95–6
capitalist accumulation, development
   of 6
capitalist base, disappearance of 4
capitalist class 28, 49, 328
   agency 89
   freemasonry of 88–9
   motivation 94
capitalist crisis tendency 91–4, 104,
   121–8, 161–3, 201, 213, 215,
   217–23, 230, 339–42
capitalist development 28, 138
capitalist extortion 16
capitalist industry, structural requirements 118
capitalist landed property 244
capitalist mode of conception 315
capitalist mode of production 3, 9, 16,
   93, 95, 170, 193, 215, 257, 285,
   298n29, 300, 310, 321, 324
   abolition of 186, 340
   ascendancy of 169
   capitalist 3

capitalist mode of production
     (*continued*)
   and class 329–30
   and the credit system 198–201
   and division of labour 256
   emergence of 256, 315–17
   historical development 95–105
   and money rent 312
   overcoming 188
   permanent foundation of 241
   replacing 130
   role of finance in 170
   and social needs 339–40
capitalist money 230–5
capitalist rent 310
capitalist sociality 9
capitalist society, disappearance of
     social substance 4
capitalist system, core characteristics
     63
capitalization 202
Carchedi, Guglielmo 64n7
cheap nature 115–16n12
child labour 108–9
China 108, 117, 119
Choonara, Joseph 201n13
Chowdury, Kanishka 92n2, 131n15
circulating capital 26
circulation
   and competition 52
   fetishism of 26n6
   and production 32, 51–2
   of value 17–18
circulation costs 189
circulatory capital 141, 158–9
circulatory capitalism 26n6, 239n4
class struggle 31–2, 32–3, 52, 84–6, 89,
     122, 128–33, 139, 180–1, 184, 319,
     326, 329, 331
classes 328–31
climate crisis 246
Clover, Joshua 46n30, 108n6, 131n15
cognitive mapping 49
collective capitalist, the 29
collective subjects, agency 89
collective will 140
collective worker, the 29
collectivized misery 310
colonial project 239
colonial territories 127–8

colonial trade 119–20
colonialism 240, 266–7
colonization 296
commerce, subordination to produc-
     tion 168
commercial capital 75, 141–2, 145–7,
     150–1, 151–4, 157, 161–2, 163–6,
     166–7, 173n1
commercial profit 137–40, 146
   merchant's capital 138, 141–51
   merchant's profit 151–66
commercial property 251–2
commercial workers 156–8, 159–60
commodities 16–17, 26, 55
   agricultural 258–9, 299–300
   circulation 168–9
   and the concentration of capital
     158–9
   conversion into money 151
   cost 19–20
   excess value 32
   financialization 209
   price 56–7, 68–71, 162, 228, 299,
     333
   profit rate 69–70
   real value 155
   sale price 152–3, 155
commodity capital 202
commodity circulation 141
commodity exchange 56–8
commodity production, ruling idea of 34
commodity value 19, 21–2, 55–6, 67,
     95–6, 316, 328, 334, 333
   agricultural commodities 299–300
   components 335
   composition 69
   magnitude of 299–300
   realization 156
   reduction 109
   and supply and demand 78–81
   transformation into production
     price 74
commodity-money 226, 227
common good, the 49, 122, 128–9
common sense 18, 31, 84, 152, 194,
     197
communal labour 28
communal property 320
community-building activity 114
company directory boards 189

competing capitals 126, 254
competition 21–2, 51–2, 59–60, 76–7,
    89, 94, 96, 139, 303, 338
    basic law of 29
    between capitals 126, 254
    and circulation 52
    and cost price 64
    foreign trade 120
    inter-capitalist 52
    and interest rates 181–2
    labour market 110
    and land-fertility 269–70, 282
    national 118
    rate of profit 69–70
    significance of 52
    superficial 299–300
    and surplus-value 337–8
competitive production 263
competitive struggle 94
consciousness 1, 4, 8, 10, 15, 29n11,
    29, 33, 34, 36, 45, 47, 49, 87, 105,
    145, 185, 326
constant capital 17, 19–21, 24, 25, 26,
    36, 39, 48, 61, 64, 97, 106, 114–15,
    118, 240–1, 335
constant capital investments 146
consumer credit 234–5
consumer demand 158–9
consumer-become-producer 39
consumption
    crippled 216–17
    hierarchy 131
    limits 131–2
    patterns 54
    power of 124
contracted claims 202–3
Contribution to the Critique of Political
    Economy (Marx) 1–2
conventionalization 54
Cooper, Melinda 339n18
cooperative firms 187–8, 189
cooperative labour 11, 341–2
Corn Laws 290
corvée system 308–9, 315
cost price 26, 34, 41–2, 45–6, 73, 95,
    259
    autonomy 18
    and competition 64
    conceptualization 16–26
    dialectical formulation 66–7

independence 18
materiality of 18
and production price 64–7
and profit 20
significance of 20–1
transformation into production
    price 52
and value 65
value composition 17
cost reduction 36–7, 114–15
Coulthard, Glen Sean 241n7
countertendency 107–9, 114–18,
    199n10, 212
tendency and 107–8, 117, 119, 156, 302
credit contraction 215
credit freeze 216
credit money 204, 205, 228
credit restriction 221–3, 230
credit system 75–6, 139, 148, 176,
    194–202, 225, 233, 338
    as abolition of capital ownership
        185–94
    and the accumulation 199n10
    and the capitalist mode of produc-
        tion 198–201
    core dynamics 195
    dependency on real value 226
    and expropriation 192–3
    formation of 201, 226
    functions 189–90, 195
    role of 191–2
    and speculation 212
crippled consumption 216–17
currency conversion 147–8
currency school thinkers 221
customary demand 79
cybernetics 195

Dalla Costa, Mariarosa 112n11
De'Ath, Amy 112n11
dead labour 6, 38, 45, 74, 337
debt 202–5, 208
    democratization of 170
debt-slavery 234
decapitalization 121
defamiliarizing strategy 307–8
deflation 81
deindustrialization 120
demand 77–83, 220
dependency 6–7, 54

depreciation 97
derivatives 189
derivatives markets 208
deskilling 43
determinacy 2
devaluation 126
developing capital 155
dialectical determinism 7
difference representing profit 31
differential rent 238, 249, 253, 258–65
    conceptualization 263
    as expression of the law of value 279
    formation of 265
    and land-fertility 267–74, 295
    law of 264–5, 295
    movement of 279–80, 282
    perceptual physics of 275
differential rent I 265–79
    and capital invested per acre 275, 279
    formation of 267–74, 281, 291
    and land-fertility 267–74, 277–9
    and market value 274–5
    movement of 270
    per acre 275–9
    relation to DII 282–5, 292, 294
    shift to DII 279–80
differential rent II 265, 266, 279–94
    and capital invested per acre 285–6,
        292–4
    formation of 280–8, 281, 288–94
    and land-fertility 281–2, 291–3
    movement of 280–7
    perceptual physics of 288
    relation to DI 282–5, 292, 294
    shift from DI 279–80
    three case studies 287–8, 288–94
digital labour, unpaid 39–43
digital traces 42, 115
dispossession 239–41
distribution, relations of 331–2
distributional categories 328n7
distributional classes 328–9
division of labour 120, 143–4, 146,
        148–50, 153–4, 159, 186, 188, 192,
        256, 257, 261, 300, 317, 329n9
domination 308–9, 310
Duménil, Gérard 65n7, 201n13

ecological costs 246
ecological crisis 115–16n12

economic base 5n6, 6–7
economic community 6–7
economic determinism 2, 4–6
economic fertility 268, 281
economic form 6–7
economic objectivities 9
economic relations 60
    inner connections of 53
    movement of 52
economic stagnation 45, 94, 127, 201,
        206, 215, 250
Economic Trinity, the 323–39
economics, science of 170
economics, vulgar 77, 79, 87, 220, 247,
        326, 332n12, 335, 335n16, 336n16
economizing strategies 36–8
economy, the 9
empire 127–8
Endnotes 45n28, 112n11
Engels, Friedrich 2n1, 8n8, 209n21,
        221n27, 223, 238, 288–9, 290–1
enslaved labour 58, 169, 304–5, 316
equality 132
equalization 52, 59–60, 64, 68–9, 70–3,
        76, 77–8, 140, 182, 189, 200–1,
        257, 299–300
essence-appearance dynamic, the 9,
        53, 59
excess value 32, 33
exchange, systematization of 54–6
exchange value 99
exchange-equivalence 56, 224
exchange-value 56, 116n12, 168–9
exclusion 131
exibilizing 110
exploitable labour 46
exploitation 32, 88, 92–3, 103, 157,
        184, 309–10, 325, 341
    agricultural labour 303
    emergence of 240
    intensification of 43, 107–9
    rate of 40, 302–3
exports 118–20
expropriation 192–3, 194, 241
externalization 18–19, 87, 100–1, 145
extraction industries 245

family 311
farmer-capitalist, the 253–4, 259, 265,
        267, 280–1, 303, 313

farmers 252–5, 260
Federici, Silvia 112n11
female labour 108–9
Ferguson, Susan 112n11
fetish, the 29, 48
fetish character, deepening 52
fetishization 10, 29, 323–4
feudalism 168, 169
fiat money 225, 226–7, 228
fictitious capital 189, 202, 202–13, 215,
    226
finance 176
    role of 197–8
finance capital 26n6, 75, 76, 165–6,
    170, 192–3
financial commodities, exchange-value
    212
financial industries 176, 195
financial instruments 189, 210, 212–13
financial mediators 211, 212–13
financial speculation 201
financialization 26n6, 185n4, 201–2,
    206–13, 251–2, 266–7
Fine, Ben 65n7
fixed capital 26–9, 105, 107
Floyd, Kevin 112n11
Foley, Duncan 65n7
foreign trade 118–20
Fortunati, Leopoldina 112n11
free labour 38–46
free trade 75
free trade agreements 110, 118, 119
freedom 340–2
Fuchs, Christian 39–41
functioning capitalist, the 174, 177,
    182, 185, 186–7, 213, 247, 255

Gabriel, Kay 113n11, 340n20
gendered labour 108–9
general intellect, the 42–4, 159, 341
general laws, capital 58
general rate of profit 52, 64–77,
    97–100, 113, 126, 153, 154, 155,
    161, 165, 182, 259, 295, 300
    conceptualization 67–8
    determining factors 75
    equalization process 70–3
    and foreign trade 119–20
    formation of 67, 69
    measurement 74

and production price 67–9
genuine capital accumulation 214
Gilbart, James 175
Gilmore, Ruth Wilson 131n15, 329n8
Gimenez, Martha E. 112n11
global financial crisis of 2008 26n6, 94,
    191, 194–5, 201, 203, 216, 220
global poverty 302
global warming 246
globalization 60n6, 107–9, 119, 120,
    266–7
globalized capital 240
gold
    convertibility 228–9
    prices 215–16, 222, 223–30
    as universal-equivalent designate
        224
    value 228–9
    as world money 227
Gonzalez, Maya 112n11
goods, equivalence between 54–5
government bonds 207–8
Grossman, Henryk 106n5
ground-rent 137
    absolute 294–305
    and agricultural production 242
    conceptualization 243–58
    and differential rent 258–65
    and differential rent I 265–79
    and differential rent II 265, 266,
        279–94
    embryonic forms of 305–21
    foreign components 248, 249
    formation of 267, 287
    and land-fertility 259–65, 266,
        267–74, 277–9, 281–2, 291–3,
        295
    laws of motion of 259
    lease-price 249
    limit of 310
    Marx's treatment of 237–43
    movement of 264, 295
    per acre 275–9
    perceptual physics of 238
    and productivity 267–74
    as social value 273–4
    sources of 246–8, 262, 324
    and surplus-value 245, 247–9, 255,
        258–9, 260–1
    and value 246–7

growing organic composition of capital
    98–9
Grundrisse (Marx) 28, 42–3, 132n17,
    159

Harman, Chris 201n13
Harvey, David 201n18, 237n1, 238n2,
    247n9
historical conditions 3
historical determinacy 3
Holloway, John 30n12, 131n15
human need, proliferation of 50
human suffering 93
Huws, Ursula 42n24

ideology 84, 336–7
immaterial goods 97n4
immiseration 217
imperialism 266–7
impoverishment 246
independence 18
India 119
indigenous land claims 241
indigenous productivity 255
individualization 5n7
industrial capital 144–5, 149–51,
    152, 161, 165, 214–15, 216,
    219–20
industrial capitalist, the 144, 253, 261
industrial production 169, 242, 255–6,
    266, 313
industrial profit 137
inequality 55
inflation 81
informalization 206
informalized labour 109
informational capitalism 239n4
insurance 340
intellectual labour, division of 298
intellectual property rights 261
inter-capitalist trade 63
interest 137, 172–3, 177, 325
    contracted terms 180
    sources of 174–5, 179
interest rates 173, 181–2, 217, 220–3,
    233–4, 251
interest-bearing capital 148, 170–1,
    240–1, 255
    abolition of capital ownership
        185–94

as the automatic fetish 178–85,
    197–8, 213–23
autonomization 180–1
capital as commodity 171–8
and capitalist crisis tendency 201,
    213, 215
capitalist crisis tendency 217–23,
    230
circulation 177–8, 179–80
conceptualization 172–3
and the credit system 185–94,
    194–202
dialectical movement 180
and fictitious capital 202–13, 215
and financialization 201–2, 206–13
loan capital 214–18, 219–20
material idealism 223–30
mediating movement 177–8
movement of 195, 213–23
perceptual distortions 197–8
perceptual physics of 184
pre-capitalist form 138, 231–4
as pure capital 183–4
social constitution 235
social form 186
socialization 188–9
use-value 174–5
value as 173
intermediaries 211
investment 69, 70, 75, 97, 107, 149,
    200, 285–6
investment strikes 122

James, Selma 112n11
Jameson, Fredric 46, 49n36, 84n10,
    193n6, 239, 331n11
joint-stock companies 187, 189, 190,
    191

knowledge, accumulated 28–9
Konings, Martijn 339n18

la terre-capital 252, 265
labour force 92
labour hierarchy 43
labour investment 44, 70
labour market competition 110
labour mobilization 139
labour rent 308–10, 312, 313, 315
labour-power 27, 323

commodified form 34
depression of wages below the value
    of 110–14
devaluation 126
distinctiveness of 34
growth in 101–5
hierarchization 329n9
local value 302
minimum price 163
as productive capital 19
reproduction of 310
role 24–5
value 42–4, 108–9, 110–14, 116, 118,
    120, 156–8, 160, 302
value creation 38–46
Laclau, Ernesto 331n11
land 275, 332
    access to 296
    automatic fetish in 303–4
    commodification 314–15
    definition 241n8
    economic expression of 320
    fertility 259–65, 266, 267–74, 277–9,
        281–2, 291–3
    fixed-capital investments 252–5
    legal title to 245
    location 266–7
    as means of production 260
    price 249–52, 264, 303–4, 314,
        318–19
    private property in 238–40, 242,
        243–6
    and rate of profit 267
    transformation into a contractual
        relationship 313
    transformation into capitalist prop-
        erty 243–6
    valorization of 254, 255
    value 249–50, 303–4
land appropriation 239–40, 244
land enclosures 239, 240, 316
landed capital 245
landed property 295–6, 300, 301, 309,
    320
land-fetish 250
landownership 238–9, 260, 320, 332
    concentration of 252, 303
    pre-capitalist form 138
    as wealth 240–1
    and wealth 296–7

landowning class 328
Lapavitsas, Costas 65n7, 227n31
Larsen, Neil 112n11
late capitalism 203
lease-price 249, 250, 255
lending 174–5, 176, 179, 211
levelling out 67–9, 70
Lévy, Dominique 201n13
Lewis, Sophie 113n11
life-making 114, 131, 133, 304
Linebaugh, Peter 59n5
living labour 36, 38, 130, 161, 171, 177,
    241, 325
loan capital 182–3, 214–18, 219–20
logistics 198–9, 267, 319
Lord Overstone 221, 230
Lotz, Christian 316n32
low-wage production zones 108–9
Lukács, Georg 133n19, 331n11
Luxton, Meg 112n11
luxury goods 138
Lye, Colleen 112n11

machinery 26, 28–9, 105
Malthus, Thomas 26n6, 27, 274, 279
Mandel, Ernest 139n3
market circumstances 56–7
market demand 77–83
market dynamism 82–3
market price 77–83, 260, 299, 300–1
market saturation 70
market value 77–83, 274–5
market-exchange transparency 55
marketplace 123
mass production 315–16, 317
material, social production of 2–3
material idealism 223–30
materialist analysis 31
Mattick, Paul 106n5, 201n13
Maynard, Robyn 131n15
McNally, David 112n11, 166n8,
    201n13
means of production 34, 101, 171, 337,
    210, 215, 247
    cost reduction 37–8, 114–15
    and foreign trade 118
    proletariat separation from 132–3
means of subsistence 17, 23, 52, 54, 74,
    80, 104, 109, 111, 116, 118, 121,
    128, 137–8, 177, 210, 215, 234,

means of subsistence (*continued*)
    239, 245, 247, 255n14, 261–2, 272,
    311–12, 319, 329
mediating movement 177–8
mercantilism 142, 168
merchant capitalist, the 143
merchants 149
merchant's capital 178, 180, 235
    autonomization of 141–51
    and commercial capital 141–2, 145,
        151–2, 157
    decomposition into commercial
        capital 145
    decomposition into money-dealing
        capital 145
    fetish character 170
    formation of 143–4
    function of 156
    and industrial capital 144–5,
        149–51, 152
    money-dealing capital 141–2
    movement of 142–3
    perceptual physics of 151–66
    pre-capitalist form 138
    and productive capital 149–50
    profit 146
    terminology 141–2
    turn over 150–1
merchant's profit 149, 161
    calculation 153–6
    and capitalist crisis 161–3
    and the concentration of capital
        158–9
    and labour-power 156–8
    magnitude of 163
    perceptual physics of 151–66
    and turnover time 163–5
middlemen 211
Mies, Maria 112n11
migrant labour 111, 302
Mill, John Stuart 43, 106n5
Milios, John 178n3
monetary policy 338
money 15, 56, 171–8
    alienated as capital 177
    autonomized 233
    breeds money 180, 183, 195–6
    circulation 167, 169, 176, 215, 225
    currency conversion 147–8
    as embodiment of value 224–5

faith in value 215–16
finitude 225
form of value 69
internal dynamics 228
metamorphosis of fictitious capital
    into 209–11
as potential capital 171–2, 176
proprietorship of 176
specialized functions 148
surplus 213–18
transformation into capitalist money
    230–5
and universal equivalence 227, 229
use-value 171, 174–5
as value 224–5
value as capital 177
value-theory of 229
money capital 206n18, 217, 219–20, 251
money capitalist, the 172, 173, 174–5,
    177, 179, 180, 185, 212, 219
money market 182–3
money rent 312–17
money reserve 150
money-dealing 148–9
money-dealing capital 141–2, 145, 147–9
money-lending 183, 231–2, 233–4
money-related services 148
monopoly price 300–1, 303
Mookerjea, Sourayan 132n16, 316n33,
    328n7
Moore, Jason 115–16n12
Moseley, Fred 64n7, 221n27
Mouffe, Chantal 331n11
multiplication 96
Murakawa, Naomi 131n15
mystification 10–11, 25–6, 84–6, 269,
    323–4, 336

national economy 60
natural forces 261–2
natural rate of interest 181
Nealon, Chris 112n11
negative universality 132–3
Nesbitt, Nick 59n5
Neton, Jeanne 112n11
new capitalism 306
non-value generating activity 44–5

objectified labour 99, 130, 171
O'Brien, M.E. 113n11, 131n15

O'Kane, Chris 5n6, 106n5
Ollman, Bertell 341n22
overaccumulation 125–6, 128, 162, 215, 218–19, 239
overproduction 125–8, 217, 218, 219–20

parochialism, critique of 318–19
patents 261
perceptual distortions 213–23
perceptual physics
    of accumulation 140
    of capital 8–12, 15, 23, 37, 47–50, 100, 160–1, 263, 265, 324, 326
    conceptualization 9–10
    of merchant's capital 151–66
    merchant's profit 151–66
performative boundaries, dissolution of 6
plantation production 169, 315–16, 317
platform capitalism 239n4
political economy, critique of 3, 140n4
political subtext 16
Ponzi schemes 218
population growth 103–5
postcolonial periphery, remittance payments 302
post-industrialism 127–8
postmodern politics 239
potential capital 176
    borrowing 174
    money as 171–2
power, technologies of 131, 132
price 56–7, 68–71
    commodities 56–7, 68–71, 162, 228, 299, 333
    fluctuations 57, 82–3
    labour 163
    monopoly price 3001, 303
    state regulation 163
    and supply and demand 77–83
    and turnover time 163–5
    and value 53, 56–7
    See also cost price; land; market price; production price
Price, Richard 197
primitive accumulation 240, 316
private ownership 191
private property 128–9, 175, 184, 210, 223

financialization 251–2
    in land 238–40, 242, 243–6
production
    abstraction of 312
    and circulation 32, 51–2
    dependence on trade 169
    emergence of capitalist 232
    forces of 261–2
    hidden abode of 17
    increase in 107–10
    relations of 6–7
    scale of 6
    and surplus labour 338
    of surplus-value 10
    technological composition 296
production chains, globalized 267
production costs 17, 44, 114–15, 146
production cycle 17
production decisions 18
production price 52, 64–9, 71, 74, 82, 85–8, 153, 154–5, 163, 258–9
    capitalist internalization of 86–8
    commodity value transformation into 74
    externalization 87
    falling 290
    and productivity 288–94
    rising 290–1
    stable 290
    unequal 266
production processes 60–2
production-circulation cycle 11, 20
production-for-exchange 167
production-for-subsistence 167
productive capacity, growth in 101–5
productive capital 149–50, 161
    labour-power as 19
    unemployed 216–17
productive consumption 65
productive forces, non-humanized representation of 93–4
productive labour 39–43, 44–5
productivity 36, 50, 123, 219, 259, 310, 332
    falling 291–3
    and falling rate of profit 96–100
    and ground-rent 267–74
    growth of 198
    historical development 95–105
    increasing 44–5, 96–100, 275, 339

productivity (*continued*)
  and production price 288–94
  rate of 67
  value as 6
  value of 35
profit 324
  autonomization 129
  calculating 38–9
  capitalist share 87–8
  and cost price 20
  decomposition 100–1
  delinking from surplus-value 10–11,
    18–19, 48
  derivatives 137
  difference representing 31
  disappearance of 4
  division 100–1, 338
  increasing 95–6
  interest-portion 179
  justification 185
  legal right to appropriate 188
  limit of 333
  loss of 126
  magnitude of 20–1, 41n19, 59, 85,
    88, 101, 103, 179
  mass rise 101–2, 106
  pre-capitalist form 311–12
  pursuit of 52
  rate of 24, 41n19
  and rent 311–12
  returning 22
  social form 316–17
  sources of 36, 324
  subcategories 100
  surplus 120, 253, 266, 280–1
  and surplus-value 15–16, 20–4,
    27–8, 30
  transformation of surplus-value into
    30–8, 47, 66, 85
  true rate 70–1
  as wage 185–6, 186–7
  See also rate of profit
profit margins 49, 77
profit-in-general 101
proletariat, the 129–30, 130–1, 132–3, 256
property development 338
property law 175–6
prosumption 39–40
Puar, Jasbir K. 241n6
publicly traded companies 187, 188–9

race 328–9
rate of profit 24, 29, 30–8, 46, 49–50,
  52, 59–64, 94, 95, 181
  average 64
  and capital flight 70
  changes to 34–7
  commercial capital 164–5
  commodities 69–70
  competition 69–70
  and depression of wages below the
    value of labour-power 110–14
  determination of 31–4
  equalization 59–60, 64, 70–3, 77–8,
    182, 189, 201
  falling 96–100, 101–5
  fetish character of 48–9
  and foreign trade 118–19
  and increase in production 107–10
  and land 267
  law of the progressive fall 101–5
  laws of 16
  magnitude of 59, 62
  and market saturation 70
  mystification 84, 278
  price fluctuations 83
  restoration 105–6, 105–20
  transformation into general rate of
    profit 52
rate of profit, law of falling 96–105,
  212
  and capitalist crisis 121–8
  and cost reduction 114–15
  countertendencies 105–20
  and foreign trade 118–20
  and population growth 103–5
  and productive capacity 101–5
  and productivity 96–100
  and surplus populations 103–5, 111,
    116–17
rational development 318
raw materials 42, 70, 105, 114–15
real abstraction 9n10
real estate development 239
reappearing value 20
regulation 201
relative surplus-value 107–9
remittance payments 302
rent 174, 247, 248, 303
  abstract form 313
  embryonic forms of 305–21

growth of 309–10
limit of 310, 333
and profit 311–12
sources of 309, 332
and surplus-value 311
see also ground-rent
rent in kind 311–12, 313
reproduction cycle 151
reproduction process 51
reproductive labour 111–12
retail capital 141
returning profit 22
revenue 335
fetish dynamic 325
forms 324–5
sources of 325–6
and surplus-value 327–8
revolutionary 33, 319
counter- 130
envisioning 132n16
force 169
logistics 199
text 140
tipping point 130
transformation 166
Ricardo, David 93–4, 221, 237–8, 274, 279, 282
risk calculation 195
Roberts, Michael 201n13
Rosenberg, Jordy 113n11, 340n20

Saad-Filho, Alfred 65n7
sales effort 21, 25–6
scale, economies of 149
Scholz, Roswitha 112n11
Schor, Juliet 110n8
science 326
secondary exploitation 234–5
securitization 203
serfdom 341
Serres, Michel 9n9, 250n12
service fees 212–13
servitude 308
Shaikh, Anwar 65n7
shareholders 187
shares 194
skills 42–4, 160
slavery 58, 59n5, 169, 304–5, 308–9, 316, 317, 341
small capitalists 121

small-scale peasant ownership 317–20
Smith, Murray E.G. 201n13
Smith, Adam 324
social averages 43
regime of 5–6
social capital 33, 75, 85, 99, 101–5, 125–6, 150, 151, 300, 335
social consciousness 4
social content, capital as 7
social development, capital's monopolization of 341–2
social domination 310
social formation, historical character of 45
social forms 4, 9, 10, 29, 161, 186, 329
capital 137–8
externalization 145
fetish character of 10
value 18
social labour 55–6, 119, 130, 341
command over 190
growth in 101–5, 339
social labour time 6
social needs 80, 339–40
social physics 5
social power 88
of capital 37, 129, 210
social product 6, 123, 339, 340
social production 2–3, 125, 223
social relations 54, 57–8
social reproduction 55, 92, 111–12, 133, 339
denial of 131–2
modes of 2–3, 138
social reproduction theory 111–12, 113–14
social substance, disappearance of in capitalist society 4
social value 316
social vulnerability 131
sociality 2–3, 9
socialized (abstract) labour 41, 257, 319, 339
Sohn-Rethel, Alfred 9n10
soil fertility 259–65, 266, 267–74, 277–9, 281–2, 291–3, 295
solvent effect, of trade 168
sovereignty 6–7
species extinction 246
speculation, and credit system 212

speculative ecology 338
speculative materialism 193
Srnicek, Nick 239n4
stagnation 45, 94, 127, 201, 206, 215, 250
stasis 82–3
state, the 139
stock-exchange dealings 194
storage industry 146
Storch, Henri 279
stratification 132
Streek, Wolfgang 201n13
structural requirements, capitalist industry 118
subalternization 131, 132
subjugation, technologies of 131
subsistence farming 117, 317, 319
Suez Canal 209n21
supervisory work 186–8
supply and demand 77–83, 220
surplus capital 127–8
surplus labour 15, 255, 257, 312, 328
    civilizing aspect of 341
    decline in 101
    and production 338
    and surplus-value 11, 27
surplus money 213–18
surplus populations 91–2, 103–5, 111, 116–17, 127, 128, 329n9
surplus product 138, 318
    circulation 167
surplus profit 120, 253, 266, 280–1, 303
surplus wealth 128, 199–200
surplus-value 19, 340
    absolute 107, 109–10
    and absolute ground-rent 300–1
    agricultural production 242
    and class 330–1
    and competition 337–8
    delinking from profit 10–11, 18, 48
    disappearance of 4, 15
    distortions of 81
    distribution 10, 60–1, 151, 338–9
    extraction of 32
    and foreign trade 118
    functioning contradictions 124–5
    generation of 23, 259–60
    and ground-rent 245, 247–9, 255, 260–1

increase in 107–10
    intensification of exploitation 107–10
    laws of 16
    magnitude of 20–1, 24, 35, 36, 59, 62, 151, 333
    mediated sources 249
    movement of 22–3, 137, 324
    mystification 11, 84
    original form 315
    production of 10, 38–46, 122–3, 142–4, 330–1
    and profit 15–16, 20–4, 27–8, 30
    rate of 24, 33–4, 35–6, 42, 49–50, 59–64, 85, 99, 107, 118
    redistribution 73, 146, 324
    relative 107–9, 339
    and rent 311
    and revenue 327–8
    in social product 123
    sources of 26–9
    and surplus labour 11, 27
    transformation into profit 30–8, 47, 66, 85
    transformation into revenue 324
    transformations of 335
    and unpaid labour 309
    and wages 332n12
swindling 52
system adjustment 339–42
systemic vulnerability 123

technical means 70
technological development 261, 268, 296
technologization 301–2
Temporary Foreign Workers Program, Canada 111n10
theoretical coherency 294–5
Theories of Surplus-Value (Marx) 44n26, 306
tithes 258
Toffler, Alvin 39n17
Tomba, Massimiliano 316n32
Torrens, Robert 26n6
trade
    expansion of 169
    foreign trade 118–20
    free trade 75
    solvent effect of 168

trading capital 142
transformation and the transforma-
    tion problem 30–8, 47, 52, 64–7,
    73–4
transportation 61
transportation industry 146

under-consumption 128
underemployment 206
underproduction 128
unemployment 110
unequalizable results 266
universal equivalence 227, 229
universal labour 28
universal-equivalent designate 224
unoccupied capital 214–15
unpaid labour 156–8, 309, 328
unproductive labour 41–2, 44–5
unskilled labour 43
unwaged labour 111–12
use-value 99, 223–4
usurer's capital 231–2
usury 183, 231–2, 233
utopia 331n11, 340–2
utopian method of analysis 193
utopian/dialectical movement
    339–42

valorization 24–5, 331–2, 339
    of capital 25
    of land 254, 255
    of value 113, 177
value 223–4, 332–3
    circulation of 17–18
    commodities 19, 21–2, 55–6, 67,
        78–9, 109, 316, 328, 334
    content 44
    and cost price 65
    critique of 95, 287
    dissimulation 5n7
    distribution 334
    distortions of 80–1
    embodiment of 224–5
    as essential core of capital 53–64
    financial extraction 209
    formation of 38–46, 142, 157
    functioning contradictions 124–5
    general law of 58, 62–3
    gravitational force of 11
    and ground-rent 246–7

historical emergence of 54–9
as interest-bearing capital 173
labour power 108–9, 110–14, 116,
    118, 120, 156–8, 160, 302
land 249–50, 303–4
law of 78, 279, 323
magnitude of 99, 261, 333
money as 224–5
money form 69
movement of 6, 10, 49, 141, 286,
    288, 334
as an objective condition 56
and price 53, 56–7
and production price 71
as productivity 6
quantitative limits 196
redistribution 166
resetting 339
self-cannibalization 45
self-valorization 177
social content of 196
social forms 18
that returns 17–18, 31, 34
unit of measurement 6
valorization 113
see also surplus value
value, theory of 5, 9
value composition 17, 69
value creation 152–3, 181, 196, 198,
    212, 213, 257–8, 333, 335
value critique 115–16n12
value determinism 5–6
value form
    abolition of 140
    historical production of 166–70
    utopian function 194
value horizon 333
value realization 156
value transfer 34, 121
value-generating activity 44–5, 46
value-in-motion 7
valueless credit money 226
value-producing capacity 45
value-producing labour 38–46
value-theory of money 229
variable capital 17, 19, 25, 48, 61, 64,
    88, 97, 103, 156, 241, 335
Virno, Paolo 10n11
Vishmidt, Marina 113n11, 315n32
Vogel, Lise 112n11

358

Index

volatility 195
Volcker shock, 1979 230

wage contract 171
wage labour 15–16, 41, 44n26, 46,
    180–1, 304
wage obligation 103, 107
wage relation 113
wage-labour 246
wages 43, 61, 80, 97, 103, 116, 302,
    332n12
  depression below the value of
    labour-power 110–14
  downward pressure 159
  limit of 333
  profit as 185–7
  sources of 324
Wakefield, Edward Gibbon 296
Walmart 158–9
wealth 167, 225
  access to 131
  accumulation 318
  collective form 321
  concentration of 128–9, 168, 341
  entitlement to 185
  expansion of 95, 197
  in general 233
  land as 240–1

and landownership 296–7
location of production 25–6
and slavery 304–5
socialization 190
sources 15–16, 30, 337
surplus 128, 199–200
traditional forms 232
wealth creation 51–2, 187, 195n8, 206,
    304
Weeks, Kathi 112n11
West, Edward 274, 279
workers
  competition between 92
  growth in 103–5
  health 38
  immediate material interests 85–6
  reproduction of 310
  in reserve 116
  training and disciplining 36, 43
working class 328
  agency 89
  conceptualization 91–2
  hierarchy 92–3
working conditions 36–8
working hours 110, 196
world market 36, 50, 139, 319
world money 169